SO-AKF-079

CHAIN of
MIRACLES

By Tricia Kell

PEACOCK
ENTERPRISES

Book Design by TATE PUBLISHING, LLC.

Printed in Canada by Printcrafters Inc.

Kell, Tricia

Chain of Miracles / Tricia Kell

Originally published in Mustang,OK:TATE PUBLISHING:2004

1. Inspirational 2. Autobiography

ISBN 0-9759124-3-7 $19.95(US$) $25.00(CDN$)

Copyright 2004

First Printing: September 2004

Second Printing: November 2005

"Some days are easy, some days are tougher, some days I find totally ridiculous, but then there are the days I experience the miracles . . ."

ACKNOWLEDGEMENTS

To my loving mother I want to express how grateful I am for always standing by me through the heartache you endured from my situations over the years. I love you Mom! Thanks to all the people in this book that helped me through the all the tough times particularly Janet and Henry Scholz for always knowing the role of "Friends" with no exceptions for so many years.

I also want to acknowledge and express my appreciation to my friend, Linda Pauls who knew the answer to whatever was bothering me and when she didn't know the answer, she knew what to pray for and to Betty Baergen for being such an inspiration in my life.

Very special thanks to Pastor Ron Wuerch, his wife Donna and their daughter, Staci Wallace who didn't hesitate to take so much time from their busy schedules to encourage me when I was down, to help me say what I was trying to say when I couldn't find the words and for walking the second mile with me to finish this book.

My lawyer, Richard Beamish, I want to thank for not only accepting to read my book to make sure I stayed within the legal guidelines but also for being only a phone call away the many times I called for information or just for someone to talk to. Your valued consideration has not gone by unnoticed.

To Word Alive Inc, I thank you for always making me feel important. Your kindness was appreciated from start to finish.

To my editor, Julie Kelley, I so much value all the hours we spent together turning my manuscript into a book and for your kind words and letters of encouragement when I got discouraged. You brought so much joy into the process.

Last but definitely not least to my loving husband, Gord, whose passionate support, faithful companionship, and tremendous patience never wavered through the whole course of writing this book and to my three children who had to be very tolerant, sharing my attention with my writing.

TABLE OF CONTENTS

INTRODUCTION

How many times over the past several years has Trish been asked, "How did you get through all the hurts and tragedies you have encountered?" or "How did you ever stay sane?"

Her reply was more often than not very vague. "I have faith," or "God pulled me through." Depending on who she was talking to and considering at times, she has been known to have a sick sense of humour, her answer could have been, "Do you see me as a person who is sane?"

Any more than this has generally stayed her secret. Then there were the many times people would say "Tricia, one of these days you're going to have to write a book so that others can be encouraged by your story."

She finally did start to write some of the story down and as she wrote, the words seem to flow. It was as if each word written was from God's heart to hers, helping her recount the details of her very extraordinary life.

Chain of Miracles was written to unmask Tricia Kell . . . a lady who has experienced many challenges. Through her book she reveals her many trials and tests, but more importantly you will read about the remarkable and miraculous victories and triumphs that would always follow.

Especially after all I've been through with Trish, I can personally say this book is about miracles. . . . no, not the instantaneous kind where you see a leg appear where there has been none, but the kind of miracle when you see a dead man brought back to life. That dead man was me. I was born on the day I met Trish. As you read this incredible story, I'm sure you, too, will experience the miracle of a brand new life.

Gord Kell

How Did It Come to This?

The car swerved and came to a halt. We both knew we had a flat tire. I got out to help change it and when Jeffrey opened the hatchback, right there in the front was a gun. I was petrified of guns. I was raised with them, but I think I was more petrified of Jeffrey having a gun. I panicked and immediately questioned him, wanting to know what he needed it for. He told me to be quiet, and by the tone of his voice, I knew I had better not push my luck. I helped change the tire and then we got into the car to leave. As we were driving, my mind was going crazy with terrible thoughts. My insecurity had me visualizing myself being found dead in our apartment. I would never speak out of place again, I thought. But that wouldn't work, and I knew it. Fear would overtake me eventually. He would probably threaten me with the gun but would never really use it. I was so afraid just thinking about it that I started to cry, one of those silent cries where the tears were rolling down my face. I just kept looking out the window so he wouldn't see.

But he knew and asked, "What's your problem?"

I took a deep breath before I quietly answered, "Nothing," but that answer wasn't good enough.

The harsh tone in his voice got a little louder when he stated, "I asked you, what is your problem?"

I knew I had to answer, so quietly replied, "The gun is my problem."

His hand quickly left the steering wheel and with such force, hit me in the nose, which promptly started to bleed. He looked at me and said, "Bitch," then stopped the car and told me to get out.

I said that I was sorry, but he got out of the car and came around to my door. He already had a hold of my arm before he got the door fully opened, and within a second I was laying in the ditch.

He quickly drove off. I panicked because J.J. was still in the back of the car. He was only three months old! I chased the car down the gravel road and ran as fast as I could, tripping on the stones, but he drove so fast that it was only a matter of a minute before I couldn't see the car anymore.

I looked around and remembered I was half way between Ponton and Thompson. I was forty miles either way of nothing but woods and bears. The sun was already starting to go down. I didn't worry too much about J.J. because I knew Jeffrey wouldn't hurt him. He really did love him. I started to walk and found a Kleenex in my pocket to try to stop my nose from bleeding. For a moment I thought, "Oh no, can bears smell blood?" but quickly came to my senses and remembered it was sharks that could smell blood.

Being raised a Roman Catholic, I was always a strong believer in prayer, even though I pictured God as really far away. I started to say the Lord's Prayer and Hail Mary. Anything else I had learned, I couldn't remember. As I was praying, it was like reciting from memory, and I really didn't think about the words. Finally, I asked God outright to send a police car, so they would pick me up. Could he please do it fast as it was starting to get quite dark and I didn't think anyone would see me on the road after dark. I didn't want to admit to God that I was always afraid of the dark–as if He didn't know.

I was walking for about ten minutes when I heard a car coming behind me. When I turned, I could see the headlights but couldn't tell if it was a police car or not. By the time it got to me, I was waving as hard as I could, so they would see me. The car stopped, and the interior light went on. My heart dropped when I saw an old rusted car with four Aboriginal men inside. I was raised to not be prejudiced at all, but my "knight in shining armor" who was coming to rescue me was a little different than what I had expected. They told me to get in, and in a split second I thought of what my mother always told me about never talking to strangers. I had to wonder how she would feel if she knew I was about to get into a car with four of them. My choice was to take a chance of getting in the car and possibly getting raped or staying on the road and being eaten by the bears. I can't understand how I got to this point and how my life had become so out of control.

Chapter 1

FOR BETTER OR FOR WORSE

From the time I was born in Halifax, Nova Scotia, our family was stationed at bases from Germany and France to North Bay, Ontario. Not having my feet on the ground–sometimes for more than two years at a time–made me grow to become quite a flexible person. I had a very easy life, raised as an air-force brat. I think people got the term "brat" because being a child of someone in the military at that time meant they were very spoiled. Everything was handed to us on a platter. I think the reason for that was to always keep us occupied with no time to get into trouble.

My father retired when I was in my early teens and was offered a job with Air Canada in Winnipeg. Civilian life was really hard on everyone in the family. My dad became an alcoholic, my mother did everything she possibly could to persuade him to get help with this problem, and I didn't have a clue what to do with all the time I had on my hands. Not knowing too much about Winnipeg, my dad bought a house for us in the west end of the city. It was a big two-story house, which was quite different from the houses we were used to on the Air Force Bases.

We arrived on June 13, 1969, and I didn't have to go to school for the rest of the term, but this left me with not much opportunity to meet new people that summer. I spent most of the summer sitting on our front veranda reading books.

Every day I would see the boy from across the street riding around on his bike. He had very curly blonde hair and was always in blue jeans with a white T-shirt and black leather jacket. He looked like someone out of the fifties. It appeared as if he was the youngest of four boys and must have had a summer job with his family, because he and his brothers always came home with their clothes full of paint. Finally, after a month of seeing each other daily, he came over and introduced himself. Rudi was ten months younger than I and came from a very German family. He was in fact the youngest of four boys and his dad (who had only one arm due to an accident) did own a paint company where all the boys worked. Rudi and I became good friends and through him, I met the girl two doors down whose family were friends with Rudi's family. She was introduced to me as Siglinde, but I called her Linda. During the next couple of years, the three of us were best of friends–riding bikes and watching movies together.

Linda really liked Rudi, so I thought it would be better if Rudi and I just stayed friends to save the trio. But it wasn't long before Linda saw that Rudi and I wanted to be more than friends and stepped aside. Not much changed for the next three years, until I turned sixteen. I guess girls mature faster than boys do, and I seemed to outgrow Rudi.

It was around then that my father had taken responsibility for his drinking problem and started going to Alcoholics Anonymous. I went with my mother to Al-anon, and from there, I was sent to Alateen. There, I learned how to deal with having a father that was an Alcoholic and what affect it had on me.

My favorite pastime–when I wasn't at school or with Rudi–was going to Brooklyn Speedway. It started to suit my stage of life–life in the fast lane where I was in the driver's seat and started to make my own decisions. I met a guy named Jeffrey, who at the time was pit crew for his cousin's racecar. Jeffrey was a few years older than I was, drove a car and at that time, was a heavy drinker. This also seems to be the time when I started to do nothing but get myself into trouble. I didn't do drugs, though I did take up smoking. I didn't get arrested for anything, but only because I didn't get caught. I managed to squeak my way through high school, but only because my father still had somewhat of an upper hand over me.

Jeffrey lived in a house with two of his cousins in the North End. That became the place for drinking parties every weekend, in which I started to get involved. Rudi's parents separated around that time and his mother moved to the North End of the city with Rudi. Their house was only two blocks from where Jeffrey was living.

After about six months of bouncing between the wild life with Jeffrey and still seeing a lot of Rudi, one night it all came to a halt. I was at Rudi's house and we were drinking coffee with his mother. I said I had to leave. He had already figured out that I was going to meet Jeffrey. He offered to walk with me. It didn't matter how much I was against the idea; he insisted.

We weren't walking very long before I could see Jeffrey coming to meet us. We all stopped, and I was actually in the middle of the two of them when Rudi declared, "It is time to make a choice. You can't keep playing both ends to the middle."

I was very torn. One part of me, the more responsible part, wanted to stay with Rudi, but the wild side of me won and chose Jeffrey. I stood for a long time looking at the ground before I turned to Rudi and whispered, "I am sorry," and walked away. I felt so sorry for him. We were good friends for a long time but if I was forced to choose, then who knew?

I was naive and didn't really fit into the crowd that Jeffrey came with. I didn't have much confidence in myself, so I did whatever it took to fit in. One of those things landed me pregnant at seventeen. My parents seemed to know before I did. They were the ones who approached me when my morning sickness lasted until the time I went to bed at night. It was a real eye-opener when they came to me and suggested that maybe it wasn't the flu I had for the past two weeks after all. They didn't want to give me consent to get married, so I ran away with Jeffrey to Edmonton. Between being homesick and morning sickness, I lasted two weeks and insisted I go back home. Jeffrey wasn't too happy about it, but he did agree. My parents were so glad to see me when we returned that they finally gave consent for me to get married.

The wedding was planned very quickly so I could still wear a wedding dress and not show that I was pregnant. Although I didn't have too much family here, Jeffrey came from a nearby farm community and had a very large family. There were two full bridal showers, two huge socials, and four hundred people were invited to the wedding.

The night before the wedding, we had a rehearsal and dinner at my parent's house. I was so exhausted and there were so many people in the house that I thought I could just slip away to my bedroom for a few minutes to get a break. I felt that everything was happening so fast, and it was hard to believe I was getting married the next day. All of my dreams when I was growing up of my Cinderella Wedding were never pictured like this. I sure didn't feel too excited about the situation, but I felt guilty–guilty that I was pregnant, and guilty that my parents had to plan this wedding in such a short time. My dad had just had surgery for his gall bladder and could hardly stand up, and now he had to try to make that long walk down the aisle with his pregnant daughter. It shouldn't have been like this.

I quietly slipped away from everyone and went up to my room. When I opened my bedroom door, I stood there–not believing what I was seeing. I found Jeffrey, my fiancé, in my bed with my maid of honor, Gwen. I was very quiet; I think it was the shock. I didn't scream or run for a gun. I think part of me was–in that split second–relieved that I didn't have to get married now. I remember, with my sick sense of humor, saying something like "Is this part of the tradition I haven't heard about yet?" What I really wanted to do was scream at the two of them. I wanted to let everyone at the party know what was going on. But I had already become Jeffrey's enabler and felt it was my duty to cover for any wrongdoing he had committed.

This seemed to have become a common practice with me. I had been to Alanon and Alateen because of my dad's addiction. I had thought the Twelve Step Program had already taught me to be responsible for my own actions and not cover or be responsible for anyone else's. Somehow, I had fallen away from it; maybe it was because I was pregnant. I wasn't raised in a house where my parents didn't look after us. Even when my dad was in his drinking years, my parents were both financially responsible and took very good care of us.

I walked quietly out of the house so as not to cause a scene. I didn't think it would be very good if my parents found out what was going on. I thought to myself they would say, "I told you so." I ran to a friend whose house was two blocks away and cried to her.

Merle was really a friend of my older brother. She was divorced from her husband and had two boys, whom I babysat while she worked. She was an excellent seamstress and when she heard I was getting married, offered to make my wedding dress for me. I told her that I wasn't getting married now. I sat for the next two hours listening to how much money my mother and father put out for this wedding and about all the money and gifts we had received from the socials and the showers. By the time we finished talking, I felt guilty that Jeff was in bed with my maid of honor!

The next day I was married. The one brave decision I did make was that Gwen was, quite literally not in the picture. I may have been expected to smile at my fiancé as I said my vows, but that was where I drew the line. I made an excuse to my family that Gwen had a family emergency and my sister-in-law, Louise (my older brother's wife), agreed to step in at the last minute. What a joyous occasion it was.

The weather was 90 degrees and neither the church nor the reception hall had air-conditioning. Of course with that kind of heat, morning sickness was inevitable. My dad did walk me down the aisle and did dance with me, but he was not well. He could barely stand up. After a couple of hours, he just couldn't handle any more and went home early.

After the wedding, things did change with Jeffrey and me, but it wasn't an improvement. Everything got worse. Yet, I was still sure that after the baby was born, our lives would change for the better. Five months later, I was the proud mother of a seven pound, six ounce baby boy. We named him "J.J."–short for Jeffrey James. J.J. was so much fun to have around–maybe because since my wedding day, I had been so alone.

Jeffrey started spending more time with Gwen than with me and I was afraid to say anything about it. From experience, I was sure if I did, I would be beaten up, and it was getting harder to hide the bruises from people, especially my family. Since J.J. had been born, my family was coming around to visit more often.

It had become very obvious to others that I was physically abused, and I had to listen to everyone from doctors, to family and friends try to talk me into leaving Jeffrey. "I have a son," was my excuse. How could I raise him on my own without his father?

I had become a bit more independent–doing different things with J.J. We started to get out more until I got a shocking report from my doctor. When J.J. was just 6 weeks old, I found out that I was again pregnant. That really threw me out of control. I had gotten pretty good at keeping my mouth shut, but the news was too much. I had a huge fight with Jeffrey. All of my bottled hurts and fears seemed to come out at once. I told him I couldn't have two kids when my husband was sleeping around with another woman. I threatened that I would leave him. He started to get rough and I picked up the phone to call the police. I was at the point of desperation, and I think he realized I wasn't kidding. For the first time, he backed off. I hung up the phone and sat very still, afraid of what would happen next.

He sat quietly for about an hour having a drink, and then he suggested we should move away from Winnipeg. We would be away from Gwen and both families, and get a fresh start. It seemed like our only hope, and he seemed so sincere for the first time since I started to date him. Things stayed pretty quiet and I said that I would think about it. I had a hard time thinking about moving away from my family, but maybe it was the answer.

The next morning I was reading the newspaper and saw an article that a mining town up north was looking for workers. The pay was excellent, and it was the kind of work Jeffrey liked to do. I showed it to him and he was very interested. A week later he was hired to work with a mining company called Inco, in Thompson, Manitoba, a nine-hour drive straight north of Winnipeg.

Within two months, we sold the house and moved right away. I was really hoping things would change and that there would be hope for us. It was really hard living so far away from the family. We had gotten a suite at a brand new apartment. The town was small, and I knew no one. I always thought it was easy for me to make new friends, but there just weren't many families living there–just a lot of men that worked in the mines.

I became so lonely in Thompson that I started to drive home at least once a month to visit my family. One time, when I was coming home to visit, Jeffrey had the weekend off and wanted to come home with me. He went to his family's for the weekend, and I went to mine. He picked me up to go back to Thompson on Sunday at noon. It was a very quiet ride back. I had just enjoyed a great weekend and didn't want my bubble to burst, so I thought it was best to just be quiet. We got to the eighty-mile stretch between Ponton and Thompson where at that time it seemed the road was made out of big jagged stones. There was nothing for that whole eighty miles except thick woods and wild animals. The car we had was a Pinto Hatchback. I had folded down the backseat and made a space amongst all the care packages that my mother and mother-in-law had sent back with us for J.J. to sleep. Being only three months old at the time, he usually slept all the way back to Thompson. It was a quiet ride and probably would have stayed that way if the tire hadn't gone flat and I wouldn't have found the gun.

Now, here I was, standing in the dark and trying to decide whether to get in the rusty car with the four Aboriginal men or risk saying no and getting eaten by the bears. Weighing the two choices, I was very quick to choose going with the guys. I felt I had more of a chance to live. I was told to get into the back seat between two of the men. I guess I was a sight. My eyes were already turning black and my nose had become quite a bit larger than it was originally. I had blood on my shirt and I was freezing. The guy in the passenger seat introduced everyone and handed me a jacket. I didn't hesitate to put it on. I think in some way, I thought if they were going to rape me, I could bide my time with more clothing on. They asked me why I was out there, and I told them the story very slowly through lots of tears. That way, the longer I took, the closer I was getting to Thompson. I told them about J.J., the gun, and pretty well all the gory details I could think of from the past year of being married. I was also quick to let them know that I was pregnant.

Boy, did I learn a big lesson that night. They were four of the nicest, most considerate people I have ever met in my life. They drove me all the way to Thompson, right up to my apartment building. Then, as I got out and thanked them, they all got out of the car and said they weren't going to let me go in alone. They followed me to the apartment and I was surprised to find the door unlocked. It was quiet, and on the fridge was a note from Jeffrey telling me he was flying back to Winnipeg with J.J. I wasn't that far behind them. He couldn't have gotten a plane that fast, not from Thompson. The guys told me to quickly get in the car, and they would take me to the airport. It was only ten minutes from the apartment, and I wasn't afraid to go. With these four guys at my side, Jeffrey wouldn't have any choice but to hand J.J. back to me. We got to the airport in just enough time to see the plane taking off. I felt so alone. The guys drove me back home where I thanked them and told them I would never forget what they did for me. It wasn't until years later that I realized God had sent them. He sent them because I had asked for help. I can't remember any of their names, but that doesn't matter. I will never forget what they did for me.

I tried to get some sleep but I never liked being alone. Suddenly, our small two-bedroom apartment seemed to be very large. I kept hearing sounds. I wasn't afraid of Jeffrey coming in. I was afraid of the space around me. I dozed off a couple of times but kept waking up. I finally gave up on sleep and started to try to find the extra set of car keys so that I could go back to Winnipeg to get J.J. I finally found them on top of the fridge. I packed a few things and left at five in the morning. I didn't want to be driving in the dark since my first eighty miles were on the road built out of rocks. I didn't want to chance getting a flat tire and get stranded again on the road with the bears. "Been there, done that, didn't like it."

It was a really long ride back. I spent the whole nine hours stopping the car because of morning sickness and thinking of how I would tell my parents that Jeffrey took J.J. I was used to lying to people and defending Jeffrey, so it was really hard for me to go back and tell the truth. I kept looking in the rear view mirror at my eyes and nose. I was so black and blue that no amount of make-up or sunglasses would hide it from my parents. It really didn't matter anymore. What was important was to get J.J. back. I have to confess it was bittersweet; it was good to know I was away from Jeffrey, but still I really missed J.J.

I was so tired by the time I reached my parent's house, that I just told them the whole truth through a flood of tears. My dad told me to get some sleep, and he called his lawyer at home. We had an appointment in the morning. In my naive mind, I thought I just had to get the police to go and pick J.J. up for me and bring him home. Did I ever find out quickly what people's rights were!

We sat at the lawyer's desk and listened to details of how Jeffrey had rights too. The best chance we had was to press charges against him for abuse. I thought about the gun Jeffrey had, but to my surprise, it didn't matter so much anymore. I just had to get my son back. We pressed charges immediately but found out Jeffrey had taken J.J. to his parents' farm outside of Beausejour and placed him in his mother's care. This changed things. It was a unique situation I was told, because even though Jeffrey was charged with abuse, he wasn't looking after J.J. directly. He had the right as a father to place him somewhere else. I was only the mother. I would have to take the family to court to get J.J. back. "No problem," the lawyer told me. "Just know that it will take some time."

The lawyer hired an investigator to check out the family to see if we could claim them to be "Unfit." That would be a shortcut instead of waiting for court. We had to go to court in Beausejour because that is where J.J. was placed. Every time we went, the other lawyer would have the case remanded. Four months went by and I didn't see my son. I was six months pregnant and felt huge. How could life be so unfair?

The investigator found out that Jeffrey's mother was institutionalized before Jeffrey was born. Everyone thought he was the oldest, but we found out that she had had a baby before him. The baby had died. I didn't ever find out why. I was told she had taken the baby out of the coffin and wouldn't let anyone take him from her. She was then taken to an institution for six months. I couldn't imagine the devastation she went through, but still we had something on her, which we could use. The lawyer demanded to be in court immediately and was granted a court date the next day because of the new information.

I drove out with the lawyer in the morning, and my dad followed. It was short and sweet. The judge didn't grant me custody because of my mother-in-law's past issues, but because I was a "fit" mother. Jeffrey was charged with abuse so I was granted custody. The court ordered a police escort so that J.J. would be picked up without delay.

As we drove out to the farm with the RCMP (Royal Canadian Mounted Police) car in front of us, I was thinking: What if J.J. doesn't remember me? What if he starts to cry when I pick him up? I quickly put that out of my head as we drove down the road to the farmhouse. I was so excited. Six months had gone by since the time I had last seen my son. The police officer carried him out to me; he looked so big. I wrapped my arms around him, and it felt so good. He looked at me and smiled, and I burst into tears. I was relieved that he didn't forget me. When he smiled, I noticed that he now had two teeth. It broke my heart that I had missed my son getting his first teeth. I had missed so much. We went back to my parent's house and thoroughly enjoyed having J.J. back in our lives.

About a week later, reality started to hit. I couldn't get a job because I was too pregnant. I was about to have my second child and was a single parent. I kept the car but couldn't afford to make the payments. Jeffrey was ordered to pay me maintenance but never made the payments. My parents had paid all my legal bills, so I didn't have the heart to ask them for money. I felt I had made this mess, and I would have to fix it. I was never very good at accepting help. I felt very insecure if I couldn't do it myself.

The following week I went into the Pan Am car dealership and explained my situation. The gentleman I dealt with was very helpful and understanding. After an hour of tossing around numbers and looking at what was available, he made me an offer I couldn't refuse. He told me he would down-trade my Pinto to a 1969 Volkswagen Beetle and give me two thousand dollars. He suggested I make arrangements with the finance company to put the two thousand dollars in a separate account and use it to make my payments on the Pinto. That would take me through the next year and give me time to have the baby and get back on my feet. By then I could find a job, and I wouldn't be without a vehicle. Besides, the new one would be cheaper on gas. He told me I would have to get approval from the finance company to do it. I phoned right away, and they agreed it was alright, so I made the deal right then and there.

As I was driving the Volkswagen Beetle to my parent's house, I, for the first time, felt independent. I felt like there was hope and I had just made the first step to surviving on my own. When I got home, my parents came out to see the car, and I could see by the look in their eyes that what they were saying and what they were thinking, were two different things. They both drove brand new vehicles, so I could understand how they felt. But they were both so nice about it, as they didn't want to burst my bubble.

One afternoon I was sitting in the back yard at my mom and dad's house when my mom yelled that I was wanted at the front door. I was shocked when I went and saw Rudi standing there. He stated that he had heard some of what was happening and wanted to know if there was anything he could help with. I started to laugh. I was so pregnant, I could sit my dinner plate on my stomach. He asked if I wanted to take a break and go out to the Lake with him. He was still dating Linda, and her parents were out at the trailer for the weekend. I hadn't seen any of them for so long. It seemed quite innocent, so I replied "Yes," thinking it would be fun. I asked if Linda knew he was asking me. He answered no, but he would let her know before the weekend. He made arrangements to pick me up at my mom and dad's at ten o'clock on

Saturday morning. He had a slight tone of seriousness in his voice as he made me promise not to go into labor while we were there.

My parents offered to keep J.J. for the weekend to give me a break. Rudi was right on time to pick me up, but Linda wasn't with him. I asked where she was, and he told me that she had driven out with her parents the night before. When he informed them that I was coming out for the weekend, they were really looking forward to it. It was such a nice drive out, and we talked mainly about what had happened and what my plans were. It seemed like no time had passed and we were there.

After he parked the car, we walked down the road to the trailer where I could see Linda sitting outside with her parents, along with one other guy. I asked Rudi if he knew who it was, and he replied, "No." We were still too far away to see his face. As we got closer to the trailer, I could see more clearly; I froze on the spot. It was Jeffrey; it immediately hit me what was going on. Linda was threatened by Rudi inviting me, so she thought the best way to fix this was to try to get Jeffrey's and my marriage back together. By the look on Rudi's face and the German that poured out of his mouth at Linda and her parents, it was quite obvious that he knew nothing about their little matchmaking scheme. I had turned around just wanting to run, but Jeffrey turned and handed me a large bouquet of flowers. He said he was so very sorry. He looked sincere, but still, I backed away. I think if I wasn't so pregnant, I would have run for sure.

Linda's mom made me a cup of coffee and suggested that Jeffrey and I go into the trailer to talk just between ourselves. Rudi and Linda promised they would stay right outside the door, so I agreed. Jeffrey seemed so convincing and knew all the right words to say. He missed J.J. and me so much and was sorry for what had happened. He assured me that he had gotten rid of the gun. He stated that he would quit drinking. He promised to never ever lay a hand on me again. He also said that he had rented a two-bedroom apartment in Winnipeg. I inquired about all the furniture and belongings back in Thompson. He replied that he had sold everything, but that my personal belongings were in boxes at the apartment. He got a new job in the city and had really straightened out. I told him I really didn't want to talk anymore because he was so convincing that it was taking away my fear of him. He said that he had pitched a tent at the campsite for the weekend and suggested that we just hang around with Linda and Rudi and see how it goes. I agreed. I felt pretty safe with all of them around.

As the day went on, he started to convince me that it was too hard to raise two kids on my own. With this new job, we could buy a house and a new car. I wouldn't have to work or worry about money because he would support me. He even threw in that I deserved so much good in life and all he wanted was the chance to make it up to me.

That night there was a huge campfire down by the water that all the campers went to. Jeffrey suggested we party that night. That would be his last drinking party; then he would quit. Both Rudi and Jeffrey started to drink. After a couple of hours, the two of them were sitting on a log with their arms on each other's shoulders, singing in German (a different song than what they were playing over the loud speakers).

I looked at the two of them and thought, "What a joke." I kicked the log and surprised myself when it started to roll, and they both fell over on the ground laughing.

As Jeffrey was lying on the ground, he looked up and yelled, "When I die, I want to be buried in my Stomper boots (which he wore all the time), and I want to be buried with a bottle of rye beside me, and I want my wife to wear the shortest dress she can find."

It wasn't the first time I had heard him say that. I usually heard him say it when he had a lot to drink.

Linda and I got the two of them into the tent at the campsite and went back to the trailer to sleep. That was the arrangement I had made when I agreed to stay. I didn't get much sleep. I was thinking that maybe I should give him another chance. He was very convincing when he told me that he had changed. Raising two children, eleven months apart, would be very hard to do on my own. How could I go to work? Then I thought about what the lawyer said, "If I didn't stay away from Jeffrey, either Jeffrey or I would be dead in a year." But then he didn't know that Jeffrey could change like this. The thought of telling my parents put a pit in my stomach. After all I put them through, they only wanted me to be happy, and Jeffrey wanted another chance. It is only right that we all have second chances in life. I didn't want to think anymore, and I eventually dozed off.

The next day, I was so tired and confused. I kept bouncing back and forth. Rudi could see I didn't know what to do, so he suggested that he drive me back to my parents and that Jeffrey should go back to the apartment. I could make my decision. If I were going to give it another try, I would go to the apartment with J.J. the next day. That would give me a chance to talk to my parents. Jeffrey wanted me to just come with him and started to pressure me for an answer. I started to back off so he agreed with Rudi. He really didn't have a choice.

All the way back to my parents, I talked. I told Rudi I wanted to give it another try, but I was a bit afraid. Jeffrey did seem sincere, and he seemed to have changed. I was due to have the baby in ten weeks. I was angry with him for selling all the furniture, but he promised we could buy new pieces with his next paycheque. I told Rudi I was going to give Jeffrey another chance, so he dropped me off at my parents. As he drove away, he said to call him if I needed anything and wished me good luck. I thought for a moment about how I made the wrong choice that day on the street when I chose between Rudi and Jeffrey. Then I looked down at my stomach and at my mom coming out of the house carrying J.J. and thought to myself, "Don't even go there, it is way too late for that kind of thinking."

That evening, I paced the floor wanting to tell my parents about my choice, but not knowing how to do it. I thought I should just leave the next day while they were at work and tell them in a letter, but they deserved more than that from me. I waited a bit too long; then the phone rang. I heard my dad say, "Don't ever call here again," and I knew it was Jeffrey. I had to tell them. They were in shock and at first, speechless. Then my dad said, "We only want you to be happy, but we don't agree that this is the way." He reminded me of what the lawyer had said about one of us being dead in a year. He wanted to know where we would live and where Jeffrey got a job. They were very angry with Linda's parents for having manipulated this. My dad, already faithful to his AA group for some years, had suggested that if Jeffrey really did want to quit drinking, he could phone him. My dad would sponsor him at AA. I said I would talk to him about it.

I started to pack, and found I was having second thoughts. I gave my parents the new address and phone number for the apartment. My parents were very emotional about the situation. I knew they were really going to miss having J.J. around. They had grown very attached to him while we were living there. Even more, I knew J.J. was really going to miss my parents and my sisters.

My sisters, Estella and Thelma, were only seven and nine years old at that time. My parents had them later in life, and they were like a second family. My younger brother Jimmy was still living at home, but was sixteen years old and wasn't around much. My older brother Grant was four years older than me and had joined the Police department in Calgary and was there living with his wife.

I was always called Patti when I was growing up. When I was younger, my dad always had the same line at night when he tucked us in and turned off the light, "Call if you need anything, I am right here." It always gave me a comforting feeling when I closed my eyes.

I didn't pack everything. I took half of J.J.'s clothes and a couple outfits of mine. I guess I had a reason to come back sooner if I did it that way, but it showed my insecurity in the situation–not sure if I really wanted to leave the security of my parent's home, but part of me wanting to give Jeffrey another chance.

Tears flowed as I put J.J. in the car. I said I would be back for the rest of my things in a couple of days. As I pulled out of their driveway, my dad said those so familiar words, "Call if you need anything, I am right here."

I got to the address on Sargent Avenue, that Jeffrey had given me and sat in the car staring in disbelief. All I could think was, "What a dump." There was a store on the main floor called the Hadassah Bazaar; whatever that meant. There was a door on the side displaying the number of the address given to me. I was supposed to go to the second floor, and it was the front apartment. I could see all the windows of the apartment from the street, and coming out from one of those windows was a wrought iron fire escape–the kind that you step out of the window onto a platform, then the stairs lowered down to street level. I wondered which window that was. It must have been the master bedroom, and that was the balcony. It was like something you would see in the movies where the car goes down the back lane; it's always raining and someone is usually being chased, raped or murdered.

I sat for over half an hour. Part of me wanted to turn back to my parents and part of me felt guilty because I said I would give this a second chance. Finally J.J. started to fuss, so I had to take him inside. As I was climbing the steep stairs, I chuckled when I thought how much exercise I would get carrying groceries or J.J. up them. J.J. was almost eleven months old but couldn't walk yet. I don't think it was that he couldn't walk; he just had no interest. With all the bouncing around he did with different people, I think he just enjoyed being spoiled. I really hoped that would change soon because if he didn't walk by the time I had the baby, how would I carry two kids?

I got to the door and stood there. Fear was setting in. I couldn't do this. Suddenly, I was having flashbacks about the gun. He had promised he'd gotten rid of it, but could I really trust him? Then the door opened. Jeffrey was standing there looking at me with a big smile on his face. He took J.J. from me right away and swung the door open wide. As I followed him inside, I was staring down a long hallway with hardwood floors. I looked to the first room on the left, and there was a dresser in the corner and a double mattress lying on the floor, all made up. That, I took it, was my new bedroom. The ceilings were so high and everything echoed when we walked because the place was so empty. Every step on the hardwood floor echoed. The second door was another bedroom with a crib and a chair. It was the crib Jeffrey's mom had at her house for J.J. when he came over to visit. There were no curtains on any of the windows. The next room was the bathroom, and then, the kitchen. The kitchen had a hotplate and a small fridge that must have been older than I was. There was a small table with two chairs and a high chair. The living room was huge but completely empty.

I stood in shock and was on the verge of tears, but I caught myself very quickly. Those old fears were still close. If he saw me cry, he would feel guilty, and it would be another beating for sure. Suddenly I felt the old feelings of being locked in, stuck in a situation I couldn't get out of. I should just make the best of it. He said he'd gotten groceries that afternoon, so I made J.J. some soup, bathed him and got him settled in the crib. I had missed seeing the TV in the master bedroom, previously. We didn't have cable, but it had very poor reception anyway. I tried to think positive and thought about how I loved to read. The next day I would pick up some books and do a lot of reading.

For a week, it was very quiet. My dad picked J.J. up to go for ice cream a couple of times, but I never let him in the apartment. He couldn't see how I was living. I just kept telling him everything was wonderful. I knew I had fallen into the same old trend of living a lie. Jeffrey never laid a hand on me though. There was really no reason to. He was at work all day, then slept all evening or had an excuse to go out. If I let my mind wander, I was pretty sure he was drinking again.

I brought up my dad's offer one night to sponsor Jeffrey to AA. He laughed and said, "I am not an alcoholic, and I can stop drinking on my own." I tried very hard not to let my mind wander.

I was once again very alone and due to have the baby any day. "That isn't a problem," Jeffrey said, "The Woman's Pavilion (where I was having the baby) is only two blocks away." Being the beginning of November it was already really cold. We had lots of snow, and it was very slippery, so I didn't go out much. It was too hard to walk; I was so pregnant and carrying J.J. was almost impossible.

On the evening of November 13th, I was sitting on the mattress in my room watching the news. Jeffrey asked if we had any ice cream. I said I would get him some and give J.J. some for a snack. J.J. was playing in his crib and after his ice cream it would be time for him to go to sleep. He still wasn't walking and his first birthday was coming up in less than two weeks. There wasn't much opportunity for him to try in that apartment because there wasn't enough furniture around–to try walking from one piece to the other. I didn't like putting him on the floor because he crawled so fast and I was afraid he would get slivers from the old wood in the hardwood floor. I sat in the chair beside his crib and started to give him his ice cream. We were playing "The Airplane Game," and he really started to giggle. His blonde hair had grown quite long and was very curly.

Someone knocked at the door and I yelled for Jeffrey to get it because I was already in my nightgown. It was strange because in the couple of weeks that we had lived in the apartment, no one was ever at the door. I thought it was probably someone who had the wrong address. Jeffrey was suddenly standing at the bedroom door. I was just putting a spoon of ice cream in J.J.'s mouth, and he said quietly that it was for me. I asked who it was, as I was in my pajamas. Before he could answer, there were two men making their way into the bedroom. I jumped up and grabbed J.J. from the crib.

One of the men showed me a badge and said, "Winnipeg Police," and asked if I was Patricia Zieske. I really looked hard at the badge because both men were in suits and not uniforms.

I answered, "Yes," thinking for a split second, "Oh no, has something happened to someone in my family?"

He then said, "You are under arrest for fraud."

I laughed nervously and told him he must have the wrong person. I had never been in trouble with the law in my whole life. Fraud? I didn't even know what fraud was. He then proceeded to tell me I had committed fraud against the car dealership when I sold my Pinto because it had a lean on it. I told him the finance company gave me permission to down trade the Pinto for a Volkswagen and two thousand dollars cash. The money was in an account, and I had made every payment.

He then said I should get a coat on because it was cold. I started to cry and told him I was due to have a baby any day.

They didn't seem to care. He told Jeffrey to take the baby from me.

I asked him if I could get dressed.

He said, "Yes," but he would have to stand outside the bedroom door. I was horrified. I quickly threw on some clothes, and when I opened the door to come out, one of the officers was standing there holding handcuffs, waiting to put them on me. I was in shock.

Jeffrey asked if that was really necessary.

They said, "Yes it is." An officer told me to put my hands behind my back and cuffed me.

I really thought this was a bad dream. They were leading me out the door when I said to Jeffrey, "Take J.J. out to my mom and dad's, and tell my dad what is going on."

He just nodded his head.

They put me in the back of the police car. I couldn't even think or cry anymore. Was this really happening to me? When we got to the Public Safety Building, they took me out of the car and guided me into the building. I was so embarrassed. They asked me if I wanted to make a statement. I couldn't speak. If I opened my mouth, no words could come out. A female officer came and undid the handcuffs. She led me into a room and said I had to be searched. She told me to strip off all of my clothes. I won't even say what happened then. After I got dressed, I was fingerprinted and had my mug shot taken. I thought, "Can I go home now?"

The two officers came back and took me up the elevator. When the doors opened we had to wait for a guard to open the locked bars. As we went through, I realized what was next on the agenda. We came up to a very large cell with five smaller cells inside. The large cell was locked, as were all the smaller cells. There was a girl in each cell staring at me as they opened the large doors. All except one cell was occupied, but not for long. I realized that one had my name on it. I was guided into the empty cell and the door slid closed behind me.

I looked at the officers and asked if Jeffrey had come back with my dad yet. Could I phone them?

They both smiled and shook their heads no. One said, "You can plan on being here for the night, and you will go to court tomorrow."

I sat on the bed and stared around the cell. A toilet, a sink and a bed, that's it. Suddenly, reality hit and I burst into tears. I was in jail!

I lay on the bed for a while in panic, wondering what to do. I thought, I will pretend I'm in labor, and then they will take me to the hospital. Better to spend the night in the hospital than in jail.

I was trying to muster up enough courage to call the guard when suddenly there was a lady standing in front of my cell. She had such a nice smile and asked how many months pregnant I was. I told her pregnant enough to have the baby right here. She told me not to worry, if I had any problems during the night, to let the guard know because they had a great nursing staff there.

Have the baby in jail? Suddenly I did a complete about face. I kept thinking to myself, "Please don't go into labor, I don't want my baby to be born in jail." I lay on the bed, very still, so as to not to cause any turmoil. I kept taking deep breaths, thinking, relax and don't get stressed. I did not want to do anything that might put me into labor.

I did doze off but was then awakened by all the cell doors opening. When I opened my eyes, I couldn't believe this was really happening and not just a bad dream. The other girls had come out of their cells and were wandering around in the larger area of the big cell. They kept staring at me. I really had to go to the bathroom, but I wasn't about to, with these girls and the guard staring at me.

One of the girls came over to my cell and told me breakfast was being served in about five minutes, so I should really get out of the cell.

I asked her why she was there.

She said, "Fraud under $10,000 from stolen credit cards." She didn't ask me what I was in for.

Breakfast was now being served. The trays were passed through little slots in the bars. On the trays were toothbrushes (a sucker stick with a sponge on the end). When my tray came, it was different from the rest.

The elderly man smiled and said, "The nurse told me you were pregnant so I will give you a glass of milk instead of coffee."

I said, "Thank you," and smiled back. Little did he know that I really needed a cup of coffee.

He said, "If you want some more, just tell the guard, I mixed up a whole container for you and put it in the fridge."

Instant powdered milk? Yuck, I hated milk as it was, but instant? I tried to drink it because the man made it for me, but I was gagging with every little sip. I thought that I could maybe pretend to drink it and then dump it in the toilet. But, since we had our toilet on display, everyone would know it. On the tray with the milk was a sad looking bran muffin with a glob of margarine on the top. It was the bright yellow margarine that looks like someone has put food coloring in lard. It really didn't matter anyway because I wasn't hungry.

After breakfast everyone went into their cells and got cleaned up. The guard told me that we would all be taken to the living room at ten o'clock to wait for our turn in court. I thought, "Oh good, the living room, did that mean we would be able to be more civilized to wait for court?"

The girl in the next cell leaned over and whispered to me that the living room was a very large cell closer to the courtroom where they had benches and magazines for us while we waited.

I seemed to have gotten a reputation with the girls as the new girl on the block, and they all kept filling me in on procedure. We went to the "Living Room" and waited for our names to be called. I tried to think positively, but it was getting harder as time went on. Finally, my name was called, and the guard let me out. He led me through a door to a large courtroom.

The room was full of people, but I immediately saw my dad and Jeffrey sitting together. My dad nodded to me with a look that said, "It is okay, I am here." It was a good thing my mom didn't come. She was probably at home with J.J. When the man started reading the charges to the judge, I suddenly had this terrible pain in my stomach.

The judge asked me how I pleaded.

I sat down and said, "I think I am in labor."

He told two police officers to get me out of there. I was in too much pain to realize I had been taken out and put in a police car.

When we arrived at the Woman's Pavilion, they had a hard time getting me into the building. As I got out of the car, everything was a sheet of ice, and they were both trying to hold me up. Finally, one of the officers brought me a wheelchair. By the time I was admitted and taken to a room, my dad and Jeffrey were there with my lawyer. My doctor showed up a couple of minutes later. There was quite a bit of commotion outside my door, and I found out afterwards that the police officers insisted that one should stay. The doctor insisted that there was no way and forced them to leave. The lawyer left word with my dad that we would get together and discuss this after the baby was born.

It was after midnight when Patrick Jay was born–named after my dad. He was instantly called P.J. He was eight pounds, two ounces and was so bald that his head was shiny. I decided to breastfeed so he wouldn't have the same problems that J.J. had with milk and formula. Jeffrey disappeared a short time after I was admitted, and I didn't see him until the next morning. I thought that maybe he had gone to see J.J. or was going to the lawyer to get this all straightened out. I was so exhausted; I slept most of the time until they brought P.J. for his feeding. I had so many stitches inside and out that I could barely sit up. I had called my mother a couple of times to see how J.J. was doing. She said he was great and not to worry about him; it was such a treat to have him there. She said they hadn't seen or heard from Jeffrey since Dad left the hospital to go home.

Finally at eight o'clock that evening, Jeffrey showed up. He was all dressed up and smelled of an expensive aftershave.

I asked him if he had straightened out the mess.

He said that he hadn't even talked to the lawyer or to anyone else about the situation.

I asked if he was at work.

He replied that they had given him a few days off because the baby was born. He was only there for ten minutes when I could see he was getting restless.

I told him they were going to be bringing P.J. soon for his evening feeding.

He said that he was going to meet some friends to celebrate and went to give me a kiss on the cheek.

I could smell liquor on his breath and even though I knew better, I asked if he had been drinking.

He got so angry and said, "Can I not even celebrate my son being born?"

He had that look that I had seen so many times before, and I immediately backed off. He went storming out the door and I felt guilty right away.

I started to worry that they were going to come and arrest me again since no one had straightened things out. I was so paranoid; every time I saw a police car outside the window, I would leave my room in case they were coming for me.

Early the next morning, my doctor came to see me and said P.J. was a little jaundiced. He wanted to keep us both at the hospital for at least five days. He added that I could use the rest too.

I asked him if I could leave right away.

He said, "Absolutely not." P.J. was only born less that twenty-four hours before, and there was no way he could release us. He also said I had too many stitches to leave yet.

I asked him, "If I leave, could I come back and feed P.J. and bring him home in the five days?"

He said that he would not agree to that.

I told him I had to get everything straightened out.

He understood but said he still would not sign me out. If I insisted on leaving, I would have to sign a waiver saying that I was responsible for myself. He told me they would keep P.J. there, and I wouldn't have to worry about him. I could pick him up in the five days, and if I needed more time than that, he would arrange for P.J. to stay longer. He assured me that I didn't have to worry about P.J. being apprehended because I was leaving early, and he really did understand. I fed P.J. then signed myself out. The doctor gave me his home phone number and told me to call anytime if I was having any problems.

It was so cold when I walked out of the Woman's Pavilion. The apartment was only two blocks away, but I really wasn't dressed for this kind of weather. I put my hands in my pockets and started across Notre Dame Avenue. I walked down a couple of short blocks and headed up the back lane. The wind was hitting me in the face, and I was so cold that I tried to run. It was really icy, and when my feet went out from under me, I landed square on my butt! I was too cold to tell if I had broken any stitches, so I just sat there crying, thinking the ice under me would freeze my stitched area and it wouldn't hurt any more.

Through my tears, I asked God what I ever did that was so wrong to deserve all of this. I wasn't a bad person. I tried to be good to people. It had been a long time since I had been in church. I tried to get up, but the ice was too slippery. I started to sob and cried out loud, "God Help Me!"

A car was coming so I started to crawl over the ice to get off the middle of the back lane. The car stopped and someone got out. He came up to me and said, "What are you doing here? You just had a baby!" I couldn't believe my ears. I looked up and it was Rudi. He helped me up and got me into the car. He turned the heat on high and gave me his mitts. They were so warm from being on his hands.

I asked him to take me home.

He asked where the baby was, and I told him. He wanted to take me back to the hospital.

I told him, "No, just take me home." I told him the whole story and he took me home.

He walked up to the apartment with me and came in. I didn't care anymore if he saw the apartment. The place was a mess and Jeffrey was passed out on the mattress. The kitchen had empty rye and beer bottles all over the table. Rudi told me to grab some things I would need and that he was getting me out of there. I agreed and was quick and quiet because I didn't want Jeffrey to wake up. When I was packing up some of my clothes, I found a piece of woman's clothing that didn't belong to me on top of the dresser. We left. Rudi took me back to his place to shower and change. We grabbed a bite to eat and then went to my lawyer's office. The lawyer said to go back to the hospital and not to worry; he had already gone to court and had the case remanded. They would not be picking me up again.

My breasts were so sore. I had used the pump before I left the hospital so P.J. would still have my breast milk. I felt like I was getting a fever–probably from being out in the cold. I asked Rudi to take me to my car; I wanted to go and see J.J.

He said, "No, I will drive you."

We were on our way to my parents' when it seemed so hot in the car, I went to take off my jacket. I was feeling terrible. When I got my jacket off, I was so embarrassed. The whole front of my blouse was soaking wet with breast milk. Rudi turned the car around and headed back to the hospital. I didn't argue or fight it anymore. I was feeling too bad.

When I got back to the hospital, they said my problem was that I had developed what they referred to as milk fever. I stayed at the hospital. Rudi left his phone number and told me to call when I was getting out. He would pick up me and P.J. and take us to my parents. I relaxed for the rest of the day and enjoyed P.J. I had called my parents and J.J. was doing fine. I wasn't going to be thrown in jail again. Nothing else mattered. I was too tired.

Two days went by and I was feeling normal again–whatever normal meant. The doctor said I could go home the next day with P.J. if I had a place to go. My parents had been in to see me but I never told them what was happening. I needed to make a plan before I told them anything. Here I was going home the next day with my new baby and didn't know where home was. I just couldn't go back to the apartment. I didn't have the heart to ask my parents if I could move back home, even though I knew they wouldn't hesitate to take all three of us in. I was out of options. The only other thing I could do was find a place to live, go on welfare, grow up, and be responsible for myself. "Oh no," that sounded way too tough. The truth is, they would probably take my car away if they found out that, according to Pan Am Motors, I was a criminal. They would more than likely reject me. I didn't want to think about it anymore. I just wanted it all to go away and for someone else to make the decision for me on what was best. I lay in bed and started to go on a real good pity trip. How did I end up in this mess? I had been married to Jeffrey for less than a year and a half, had two kids, and I couldn't even look after myself properly.

It was about eight o'clock in the evening, and I was sitting looking out the window at the view. On Notre Dame Avenue, everything looked so cold. Someone said, "Hi," and when I turned around, Jeffrey was standing there. He never did know that I had left the hospital and come back to the apartment that day. I didn't let on that I knew he drank so much he had passed out. I didn't mention the other woman's clothes in the apartment or that there was even a problem. He started with the news that he had a big surprise for me.

I asked, "What's the surprise?"

He replied that he hadn't come in to see P.J. or me for a couple of days because he was out looking for a new apartment. He found a great place for us to live, in a complex on the corner of Portage and Cavalier. He said it was a two-story apartment with a balcony. His parents scraped up enough furniture to furnish it fairly well. He explained how the living room, kitchen and dining room were on the main floor and the patio door was off the dining room. The one part of the surprise that won me over was that he had gotten a hold of Family Services, and they were going to provide us with a social worker to do counseling with us. That was my option. The apartment was much closer to my parents' house. I needed an answer, and this was my answer. He said he would pick me up the next morning at around ten o'clock. Everything was already moved into the new apartment. He added that he had already picked up groceries. My mom offered to keep J.J. an extra week so that I could get settled into the new apartment with P.J.

Jeffrey was a bit early picking me up, but P.J. and I were ready to go. I felt good; I felt like there was hope. I was surprised that the apartment was pretty well exactly as he had described. The furniture was even quite nice but, after living with none for the last couple of months, anything would be better. Upstairs, there was a crib in the master bedroom, and in J.J's room was a brand new bedroom set. He said his parents bought it for J.J's birthday. J.J's birthday?! I forgot.

His first birthday was only five days away. I phoned my mom telling her that I was at home now and asked if they had any plans for J.J.'s birthday.

Mom said, "Yes," she was going to have a party, and maybe I should come out that day with P.J. Then, I could take J.J. home after the party.

I said I was planning on taking him home before that because I really missed him. But maybe it would be good to just be at home with P.J. for a few days before J.J. came home. I had two boys in diapers, and on bottles.

The birthday went really well. Jeffrey didn't come with us. He had some kind of excuse. I packed up both kids to head home at about seven o'clock that night. My dad carried J.J. out to the car and while he was putting him in the seat belt, said to me, "Your mother and I will stand by you in whatever decision you make, even if it means you staying with Jeffrey. You now have two kids to think about. Don't ever let me hear that they are doing without anything they need. If you are having trouble, don't be too proud to ask us for help." I always knew that, but it was really nice to be reassured that I wasn't alone.

Because the kids were so young, Diane, the new social worker was willing to come to our apartment once a week to see us. The first time she came in the door, she brought so much hope, not necessarily for our marriage, but for me as a person. We talked for a long time at the first meeting. She had been completely blind since birth. When she came in the door, she left her boots in place by the door. J.J. must have been playing with her boots while we were talking, and they ended up switched. When she was leaving, she put her first boot on the wrong foot and I mentioned it to her. She started to laugh and said, "I can't see for looking." I really liked her and looked forward to her coming every week.

It was pretty quiet around our place. I was really busy with the kids. P.J. was very colicky, so there wasn't much opportunity for to sleep. He was four weeks old when I heard they were building a new Holiday Inn, downtown. I went and applied for a job in the kitchen–making hors d'oeuvres. I started right away. Jeffrey worked during the day while I looked after the kids. I worked in the evening while Jeffrey looked after the kids. We never had too much of a problem. I think it was because there wasn't money left for Jeffrey to drink after the bills were paid.

I had to get my mom to baby-sit a few times during the day because I had to go to court for the fraud. It kept getting remanded. Just as well because I didn't have time to deal with it.

I really enjoyed my job; I had gotten to know quite a few people there. One evening they asked me to work on Saturday night for their dinner restaurant. Everyone in the kitchen was in a real frenzy because some big shot from the city (I didn't really know who he was, just that he was really important) had come in with some of the city's politicians for supper. I made up all of their hors d'oeuvres, one of which used artichoke hearts. I hadn't had that order before, but it wasn't a problem. I was known to be quite creative in these things, so I did up a small plate–very fancy–and put two artichoke hearts on it. The waiter took out the order and commented on how nice it looked.

A few minutes later, the waiter brought the plate back to me with the very angry "Important Customer" following him. I was told that when he cut into the artichoke heart, he found this ugly red worm inside. I could see the chef standing back in a distance, waving to me to handle this very lightly. I took the plate, looked at it and sure enough there was a big ugly red worm right in the Centre of this artichoke. I smiled at the customer and apologized for this happening. Maybe in the future we should cut the hearts in half so we could see if they have a problem on the inside. The Chef smiled at me, but then I couldn't leave well enough alone and added, "Sir, we will make sure that there is no extra charge for the worm." The Chef fired me on the spot. I worked at the Holiday Inn until February.

I couldn't even think of being without a job, not now. Things were finally starting to fall into place, but a one-income household would really set us a few steps back. Out of desperation, I applied for a job at the Assiniboine Hotel as a waitress. It really wasn't my style. The fact that I had to wear very short shorts with high heels and a halter-top didn't impress me at all. But it was a job, and it would pay the bills and feed my kids. The tips were great.

I had worked for about a month when one afternoon, I was ready to go to work and Jeffrey didn't come home. I had to phone in sick, which didn't make a good impression on my boss. Jeffrey arrived home at about eleven o'clock and had had a lot to drink. The kids were in bed sleeping. I was very angry with him because I really didn't want to lose the job.

I asked him why he would do that.

"Shut up" he told me.

I asked him why he was drinking again when he promised not to.

He yelled, "I said, shut up."

Normally, in the past, I learned to be quiet at that point or Jeffrey would cross the line and get abusive. This time I was just tired of things being so unfair, so I lost it and nagged him.

He picked up a heavy glass ashtray and threw it like a Frisbee. It spun toward me and hit me in the knee. My legs gave out from under me.

I landed on the floor. I swore at him and he came after me. I had forgotten what it was like to be hit by him, but I had had enough. I think it was the first time that I really fought back. We got into a struggle and ended up out on the balcony. He picked me up and threw me off. I landed on a snow bank, but it still knocked the wind out of me.

A police car was driving down the back lane at the time. One of the police officers saw what happened and jumped out of the car to see if I was all right.

I said, "Yes."

Then they asked who was upstairs.

I told them that it was my husband and that my two kids were in the apartment with him.

The officers got me up and we then went to the apartment. Jeffrey was arrested on the spot.

Chapter 2

Till Death Do Us Part

Jeffrey was locked up in jail until his court hearing. I was relieved, but I didn't have a sitter to look after the kids while I went to work. I could have asked my parents, but then I would have to tell them Jeffrey was in jail for beating me again. I went to court because I had to press charges against Jeffrey. It wasn't too bad because Diane had offered to come with me. The judge gave him a fifty-dollar fine, and he was put on probation.

I made the decision that we were finished and I wanted a legal separation. I still had the same problem of needing a babysitter to watch the kids while I worked. Welfare said that they would subsidize my rent and utilities. They would also pay a portion of the babysitting expenses, but not all. It helped, and I started to feel pretty good about myself again. I was too stubborn to ask my parents to help with the babysitting. It didn't seem fair because the two kids could be a handful. J.J. had finally decided to start walking at about fourteen months old, so that was a really big help.

All was going pretty well for the first week until Jeffrey got a lawyer and demanded visiting rights. It turned out he could have visiting rights, but only when I wasn't home–and I agreed. I didn't want anything to do with him. We came to a very good solution. He could come and spend all evening with the boys, for two evenings a week, while I worked. That solved my babysitting problem. It worked out well for a week. I even made him agree to leave as soon as I got home from work because I didn't want to talk to him.

Then, one night, he asked if he could talk to me. I said, "No." I really didn't want to, so I walked out the door and went to work. I never worried about the kids being harmed by Jeffrey because he had never been rough with them or abusive in anyway. He really loved the boys. I knew Jeffrey would be really angry when I got home, as I had refused to talk to him before I left. My shift ended after last call at one o'clock, and I usually got home between one thirty and two in the morning. It wasn't any different that night except that I was so tired when I opened the door to go in the block. (It had security doors, so I let myself in with the key.)

As I was walking up the stairs, I could hear voices in the hall seemingly close to my apartment. I was wondering who it could be at this time of the morning. Usually, when I got back, Jeffrey was asleep on the couch. As I got to the top of the stairs, I opened the hall door and standing outside of my apartment were two police officers and Diane, my social worker. My heart fell into my stomach. I was afraid to ask what was going on.

Diane said right away that the boys were fine and asked, "Why did I leave them alone?"

Apparently, Jeffrey had left the boys by themselves. A neighbor had heard them crying for a long time and knocked on the door. When no one answered, she called the police. I was so thankful for that, but was sick at the thought of them being alone. When the police called The Children's Aid Society, the computer reported that Diane was the social worker, and she was sent right away.

Diane had said that she believed that I would never leave the boys on their own while I went anywhere. This situation was really out of control, and it was time she stepped in to help me get it straightened out. She said she wanted to send the boys to a foster home until she could help me get organized again. The police and Family Services were very concerned for my safety.

I cried and begged them not to take the boys. I told them I would call my parents and we could go there. I said I would never talk to Jeffrey again. I would do whatever they wanted but not to take the boys.

She promised me it was only temporary and said there was a really nice family willing to take both boys together. She then mentioned that she had some friends from her church that would take me until the mess could be straightened out. She said I could know the address and phone number of where the boys were, and that the people told her that I could see them anytime.

I didn't have much choice but to agree. The police drove the boys down to the foster home a few miles away. I helped to get them settled, and the people seemed really nice. Then the police drove me over to where I was to stay.

The people I was staying with were Margaret and Michael. Margaret was a nurse, and they lived in one of those large Victorian houses. I was hurting so much but couldn't really do anything about what was happening until the following Tuesday, considering it was Easter weekend. They asked if I wanted to come to church Easter Sunday. I hadn't been to church in so long and didn't have anything to wear. Margaret said she could help me with that, went into her closet and started to pull out clothes. She gave me about five different suits to choose from. I tried them all on and felt so good in them that I told her to choose because I loved them all. She picked out a green blazer and slacks and then handed me the rest and said this is for another time. They were *all* mine. They even had chocolate eggs hidden for me in the morning when I got up.

We went to church. I don't remember much about the service except praying to God to please give me back my boys. Margaret said she was praying for God to create the best circumstances for the boys and me to live in and for guidance to get there. At that time, I didn't realize just how God was preparing me and answering prayer.

A lady had come to me after the service and said she had a bunch of clothes that didn't fit her anymore. She was sure they would fit me. She asked if I would like them. I thought, "Wow, sure!" I felt like I had just spent the last fifteen months in maternity clothes. I was only a size six or eight, and my wardrobe–to that point–consisted of one pair of jeans, a couple of tops and a dress that was so outdated, I didn't dare put it on.

They took me to see the boys after church, and then we went back to their place for Easter Dinner. When her husband said grace, he included thanking God for providing the guidance and whatever I needed to put my family back together. They never mentioned Jeffrey. Always, the family consisted of the boys and me. We had just finished eating when there was a knock at the door. It was the lady that had offered me the clothes. She and her husband walked in with three big boxes of clothes. She said they weren't all from her, that a couple of other ladies from the church had put in some shoes and clothes that were my size. It was just like Christmas. Everything I could possibly need was there.

On the Tuesday, Diane and I went to court. I really liked Diane. She was so easy to talk to and to be with. I learned from her, after a few trips off of curbs and stairs, how to walk with a blind person. I always figured she and I had the same sick sense of humor.

We were walking once, and she tripped off the curb, turned to me and said, "Lady you tripped me, I saw you," in front of a bunch of strangers. It didn't take long before I had some good "come backs" for comments like that.

When we got into the court, I was surprised to see Jeffrey there. Apparently he was picked up for "desertion"–leaving the boys. The judge so understood my situation that he granted a restraining order against Jeffrey.

Jeffrey couldn't see the boys and couldn't even know where they were staying. He wasn't allowed within fifty feet of wherever I was. When I asked if I could have the boys back, the judge said, "Find a job, a decent job." He said that I was capable of doing much more than slinging beer in a pub. I was to get myself a decent place to live too, then come back and tell him all about it. Then the boys would be mine. Until then, I could see them anytime that I wanted. From there, my only focus in life was to get my boys back, but I didn't know where to start.

Diane and I went out for lunch, then back to her office. As we were sitting at her office, I realized for the first time that I wasn't leaning on my parents for help. I must be growing up. My mom and dad had just sold the house outside of the city and rented a side-by-side at the end of Portage Avenue in Winnipeg. It was right behind a Bonanza Restaurant. My dad was a steak lover, and I teased him about the move. He wouldn't have so far to go for Saturday supper, which was usually with the family to Bonanza, for a couple of years past.

Diane and I went to see the boys and to tell their foster parents what happened in court, and then I went back to Margaret and Michael's. When we sat down to eat that night, Michael said "grace" as usual. This time his grace was: thanking God for the hope I received from court, for guidance, a job, and a place to live, so I could have my boys back. To me, God still seemed far away when we prayed–you know, up in the sky. But since I had been staying with these people, he seemed a little closer than he had been in years.

I was raised to go to church when I lived at home. I was part of the youth group and the choir. I can remember very clearly that when I was ten years old, my mother was pregnant. Up to that point, there were only my two brothers and myself. On the Air Force Base in Marville, France, where we were stationed at the time, I would stop every day after school at the church to pray for my mother to have a girl. I really wanted a sister. Sometimes though, you have to watch what you pray for. I did get my first sister and two years later my mom was pregnant again with my second sister. I guess I prayed twice as much as I needed to. Being ten and twelve years older than the girls respectively, I really didn't get to know them as well as I would have liked before I moved out.

We were only half way through the main course of supper, when there was a knock at the door. Margaret answered it and said it was for me. I was shocked to see Merle standing in the back hall. (Merle was the friend of my brother's I ran into the night before my wedding–when I caught Jeffrey in bed with Gwen.) How did she know? She said that she had heard about what was happening and that her house was big enough–with only her and her two kids there–that the boys and I were welcome to come and board with her. I would only have to pay one hundred dollars a month. I stood in shock for a moment staring at her, thinking about Michael's prayer just a half-hour before. God was already providing a place for us to live, and it was a decent place.

She lived in a townhouse in Westdale, which was a newer community. The house had three bedrooms upstairs with a bathroom. On the main floor, there was the kitchen and living room. The kitchen had a large eating area, which was used as the dining room. Downstairs, she had built a rec room, which would serve as living space for the boys and myself. We could sleep there and share the kitchen. If we planned it right, we could share meals and save money. Now, I just had to find a job to pay for it. I told her, "Yes," and said I would pack my bags the next day and call her. She said she could pick me up on the way back from work. I wouldn't have to start paying rent until I found a job. I didn't have a vehicle. The Volkswagen was lost in the shuffle, but I didn't sell it. I really don't remember where it ended up. I finished supper and didn't say anything, but I am sure the smile on my face told Margaret and Michael exactly how I was feeling. I had a place to live and was much closer to getting the boys back. I didn't worry that night about a job. I just went upstairs and started to pack all my clothes–all those new clothes. Wow, what an awesome day!

The next day, I went to see the boys and bought a newspaper to check out jobs. I met Diane for lunch, and she asked me what job experience I had and what I really wanted to do. I told her if there was anything I did well in high school, it was typing. I remembered my final exam; I had scored 99%. I asked the teacher why I didn't receive 100%, and she said it was because no one was perfect. I told Diane I would love to be a secretary, but I had no experience.

It was such a beautiful day, so I walked back to Margaret and Michael's. Spring! It felt like the air was full of freedom and peace for me. Life was getting good for the first time in years. I was actually standing on my own two feet. I was only nineteen years old, but had the responsibility of a much older person.

I received a call from Merle as soon as I walked in the door. She was picking me up at four-thirty, and I told her I was more than ready. I really did enjoy staying with Margaret and Michael but was anxious to move on. I made sure everything was packed, said my thank-yous, and left with Merle.

I had just put all of our things away downstairs when the phone rang. Merle laughed when she called me to the phone and said, "That didn't take long; it's for you."

It was Diane asking how I was doing. I talked for a while, and then she asked if I would be interested in a job as a secretary of a government project called Project Insight. It was a six-month project set up to find statistics on how many legally blind people there were in Manitoba and to what degree they were blind. I would be working in an office with six other people–three of them blind, with the statistician and two others out on the road gathering the information. I would have to answer phones, use the Dictaphone, type, do the payroll, and keep the ledger. The job paid four hundred dollars per month.

I said, "Yes," without hesitating.

She replied, "But you have to go and apply. I took a chance that you would be interested and set up an interview for you with Frank, the manager, on Monday morning at ten o'clock."

I thanked her, and when I got off the phone, I danced around the kitchen for a few minutes as I told Merle about it. Then, I went into a panic. I hadn't typed anything for a few years, so my speed would probably be atrocious. I've never even seen a Dictaphone, and as for payroll and ledgers, I didn't have a clue. I didn't let any of this burst my bubble, though; I could handle answering the phone. I danced over to the phone, picked it up, and said, "Good afternoon, Project Insight."

Merle was laughing and said, "Don't worry; you have four days before the interview to figure it all out."

She could help me with some of it, and my dad could help me with the rest. I thought of my dad's favorite line, "Fake it till you make it." I quickly phoned my parents and told them the news. My dad said to come over on the weekend and he would help me get ready. I was thinking about all the clothes I had been given and realized why I had them all. They were perfect for the job I was going to be doing. Once again, I wondered if God was guiding me and providing everything I needed to get a job and get my boys back.

I was a little restless after supper, so I decided to go out and jog around the block. I always had a problem jogging. My knees would get tired, but I decided I would master that, starting a little at a time. Besides, one of the ladies had given me a jogging suit and a pair of track shoes. I assumed that I was supposed to run or at least go out and look like I was fitness-minded. I trotted out the door and started to run. It was only half a block when I became winded and my knees hurt, so I decided that was enough and did a power walk the rest of the way. I was almost around the block when I saw a lady standing over a little boy tying his shoes. She stood up as I passed and said, "Hi Pat." I turned around to find Rudi's sister-in-law, Mary and his nephew Paul. We talked for a few minutes and then she asked if I wanted to come for a coffee. Rudi's brother, Heinz, had divorced her a number of years before, so I hadn't seen her in about four years. She lived just two blocks away from Merle's house. I told her that I would shower, then I would be over.

I dug through my closet to see what exciting new clothes I could put on. I pulled out a pair of jeans and a matching jean jacket, which had roses embroidered on the front pocket and on the side leg of the jeans. When I was ready, Merle asked if she could give me some tips on make-up, as I had never worn too much up to that point. The truth is, I never really had time for it. She gave me a make-up bag, which was kicking around doing nothing. By the time she was through, I was really pleased with the way I looked and the makeup bag was full of everything I could possibly need. When I walked out the door to go for coffee, Merle was laughing and said if I look this good when I am going for coffee, she wants to be around when I go on my first date. That got me thinking all the way to Mary's. I was still married. First date? Forget it. I am finally free, and I am going to enjoy this thoroughly.

Starting over gave me such a clean feeling. Mary and I talked for more than an hour about how hard she found being a single mother with two children. She told me she was having a problem with drinking and Heinz rarely ever sees the kids.

Just then there was a knock at the door, and she said, "Just a minute, that's probably Rudi dropping off a cheque from Heinz." Sure enough, I recognized the voice at the door. I heard Mary say to him, "Do you remember Pat?"

Rudi said, "Of course, why?" She must have motioned him to come in because I never heard them speak after that. Suddenly, Rudi was standing in the kitchen looking at me with a shocked expression. All he said was, "You look great, what are you doing here?"

I touched lightly on what happened since I saw him last. He realized I didn't want to talk too much about it with Mary there and asked if I wanted a ride back home. I said it was all right as I only lived a couple of blocks away. Then he stated that he wanted me to see the car he had just bought. I said goodbye to Mary, thanked her for the coffee and went outside to see the car.

I barely got a chance to look at the car when Rudi said, "Get in." It was a 1968 Cougar RX7, two doors, mint green with a black interior, and quite obviously, it was his pride and joy. I did get in, and we drove over by the river where he parked. Then he said, "Now tell me what is really going on in your life."

For an hour, I filled him in on every detail and his only comments were, "Good, great, glad to hear it, it's about time." Later, he drove me back to Merle's house and asked me for my phone number.

Rudi phoned me the next morning and asked if he could take me for breakfast before the interview. I said that would be great. I had spent most of the weekend visiting with the boys, but when I wasn't there, I was at my mom and dad's practicing "ledgers and payroll." By Sunday I was losing my confidence and feeling like I would never be ready to pull off this interview.

Monday morning, Rudi picked me up early and took me to a small restaurant for breakfast. I could only handle coffee because I was too nervous to eat. Then, he dropped me off downtown in front of the office building, where the interview was. He said, "Good luck," and drove away.

It was an old building with just an ancient freight elevator. I decided to take the stairs up to the fourth floor where the office was. When I went in, there was a gentleman sitting in a wheelchair, and when he started to talk to me, it became obvious that he was blind. After I introduced myself, I found out that he was Frank, the office manager doing the interview. He took me into a large office where there was a big desk with a typewriter. In the corner was a recliner, and beside it was a big filing cabinet. I looked at the phone on the desk and saw that it had about eight buttons; one was lit. It was the same one my dad had shown me at his office previously. I figured that at least I would be able to handle answering the phone. I took it for granted this was Frank's office and was looking around to see where I would be if I got the job.

Frank told me to sit at the desk where I spotted a letter on the Dictaphone. He told me to type the letter. I figured out quite quickly how to work the Dictaphone. I started to type but was so nervous that I ended up spelling half of the words wrong. I just kept going. The speed was there, but the accuracy was obviously gone. I was so angry with myself; I just started to type anything stupid. I wasn't even listening to the Dictaphone. All of a sudden, Frank reached for the paper in the typewriter and said, "That is enough," as he pulled the paper out. My heart fell. I thought for sure he would know how stupid I was being and that I wasn't listening to the Dictaphone. Then he surprised me as he held the paper up to his eyes and said, "Looks fine to me; you have the job." Then he ripped the paper up and threw it at the garbage can beside him, which he missed.

He asked if I could start the following Thursday as they were still trying to set up for a secretary. At that point I asked him where my desk was. He started to laugh and said, "This is your office, and so if you want plants, little trinkets or pictures all over the place, bring them with you on Thursday."

I took the stairs again when I was leaving. All the way down the four floors, all I could think about was: My desk! My office! My job! The bottom line was, I did it! I could now have my boys back! Tears were rolling down my face as I went through the exit, and to my surprise, Rudi was standing there.

He said that he'd decided to wait around for either a celebration or to give me moral support. I told him, "We are celebrating!" But first I had to go and tell Diane about the job so she could make the arrangements for court.

When we arrived at Diane's office, Rudi waited in the car while I went in to give her the news. She wasn't surprised and said she was so sure that she had already made arrangements for us to appear before the judge the next morning. I suddenly realized that I probably already had the job before I went for the interview. It didn't matter though because I was determined enough to show that I was the best person for the job, and they would all realize that.

Rudi then drove me to my parent's house to break the news to them. They were thrilled.

The next morning, I wasn't nervous at all. When I woke up, I thought, "Wow, this isn't a dream."

I met Diane at the courthouse, and we were called first. I told the judge all that I had to tell, and Diane confirmed that it was true. The judge asked if I had anyone to look after the boys while I worked. I just looked at him and had to say no. Diane stood up and told the judge the foster parents were willing to do daycare with the boys while I was at work. I would only have to take one bus to the daycare from my house and could use the transfer to get downtown to work and do the reverse for the way home. She had it all figured out. The judge said I could definitely have the boys back, but he would like to see the changeover done slowly. He said for the first month, I could take the boys home on weekends and during the week, they could stay at the foster parents. After a month, they could come home for good. He said he was suggesting this just to give me the time to get into my new job, and I agreed.

The job went well. I had to do the payroll every Monday. The first week, I took home all the cheques, ledgers and everything else I needed, and my dad showed me how to do it. After that first time, I was able to do it all on my own. The project was only for six months, but in that time I could get enough experience to get another similar job.

For the first month, I could hardly wait until Fridays came so I could take the boys home. Weekends were busy, but so much fun! P.J. was now six months old, and J.J. was seventeen months. J.J. always followed Merle's boys into the bathroom and was toilet trained in no time. Usually, Monday mornings and Thursday evenings, Rudi offered to pick us all up and take the boys both back and forth, or, to and from the foster family's house. It was a good thing because they always had a lot of things to take with them for the week, and it would have been almost impossible by bus.

Finally July arrived, and the boys came home permanently. I slept on a large bench made into a bed in the rec room; J.J. had his crib, while P.J. slept in a playpen. I didn't see too much of Rudi because I was always so busy, but we talked a lot on the phone after the boys went to bed. It was quite clear to both of us that we could only be friends as I had a very full life and couldn't possibly think about becoming committed to anyone for the time being. I still had in my mind that in my vows I had said, "For better or worse." After all, my parents had been married for over twenty years already. The more I saw of Rudi, the more I felt like vows didn't really have to stand if a person is being abused. I hadn't figured out at that time that there was a time to draw the line. Besides, I was still in and out of court for the fraud charge, which kept getting remanded.

Work was great. I was able to wear all my new clothes. As I got paid, I started to bank money so I could eventually buy a car. One of the guys in the office, Doug, who was also blind, was around most of the time. When the phone rang, before I could answer it, he would yell, "Good Morning, Eyes for the Blind." I always had to think when I answered so as not to say it after him. They were a great bunch and treated me very well.

My boss, Frank, came and sat in my office one day to tell me how he ended up blind and disabled in the wheelchair. He said he was eighteen years old and was sitting on the top of the seat in the back of a convertible; much like the Queen does in parades. Anyway, he said the car took off and he fell out. I asked him if he was such a nice guy before the accident, and he said, "I told you I was eighteen." I still don't really know what that meant, but he was laughing when he said it. I was really bothered by that most of the day. It was hard to believe a fall like that could leave a person blind and disabled all their life.

I got so good at doing the job that sometimes I finished at lunchtime.

When that happened, Frank told me I could leave. The odd time on Fridays, Rudi would phone me at work to see if I would be finished early. If I was, he usually picked me up to go for lunch. Then we would kick around for the afternoon, and he would take me to pick up the boys and go home. All the people I worked with knew Rudi's voice on the phone, so if they answered, they would say; "Just come and get her, she has the rest of the day off," which he would do whether I was finished or not. Rudi had become my best friend and I really didn't want it to go further than that for a while. So much had happened and I didn't want to jump into another relationship but sometimes I found it too hard to fight. He was always so gentle and so helpful. There were times that gentleness was too close to making me melt.

I received a phone call saying that I was booked for trial regarding the fraud charge the following week. I asked for the day off–which was given–but I didn't say what the real reason was. Rudi offered to take me. He was painting for his brothers' company so was very flexible when it came to taking time off. He picked the boys and I up at home and drove them to the daycare. Then we arrived at the courthouse half an hour early.

We sat outside the door talking, and he asked if I was nervous. I was sick because the outcome of this case could ruin everything I had worked for. I was not guilty of what they were accusing me, and the lawyer insisted not to worry. But what if they put me in jail? Up to ten years was the potential sentence for fraud. If there was big bail money needed, I sure didn't have it. Rudi said not to worry about that and reached in his pocket and said, "I brought the big chequebook with me," as he pulled it out. I told him about the money still sitting in the bank account for the payments on the car. I never touched it and kept it very quiet from Jeffrey because I knew he would convince me physically to give it to him if he knew. Funny, I never even thought about that money for so long. I was advised by my lawyer to forget it was in the bank until this was all resolved. I guess I really did.

The charges were read to the judge. Apparently, it all came about because I "Down traded" the Pinto with Pan Am Motors. Pan Am Motors sold the car to Dominion Ford who in turn sold it to a customer. The finance company, with which I dealt, towed the car away from the customer's house. The customer got his money back from Dominion Ford. Dominion Ford got their money back from Pan Am Motors, and then Pan Am Motors charged me with fraud.

My lawyer got up and told my side of the story – about how I had permission over the phone from the finance company and we had made a deal to pay for the car in payments. I was then arrested and thrown in jail the night before I went into labor. He concluded with how life has been since. The judge asked what I was driving now, and the lawyer told him I didn't have a vehicle anymore. The judge then asked how many times we have been to court and my lawyer answered, "Twelve, but they were always remanded." The judge just shook his head and asked me to stand up. I did, thinking that by his questions to the lawyer, I was dead meat.

I don't remember the exact words he said to me but I do remember it came across quite clear that he was surprisingly unimpressed with the conduct of the complainants. Everything was over very quickly and my head was spinning when I left the courtroom. I wasn't sure if all I had heard was right. I didn't have to go back to court anymore. I didn't have to pay back any money. I was free to leave and told Rudi to put his chequebook away; this lunch celebration was on me.

My parents really liked Rudi now, although they didn't feel that way when we were growing up together. I think the problem was with his family and with the way he was brought up. (He was the youngest of four boys in the family, three of whom were born in Germany along with one sister. His parents came to Winnipeg with the three boys and left the daughter with their grandmother in Germany. From what I understood, they couldn't get her back after that. After Rudi's dad lost his arm in the logging accident, he started to gamble. There were no big gambling casinos around then, just rooms where guys got together and played cards. Sometimes the places ran for twenty-four hours a day. Most of the money made in painting was lost in playing cards. It definitely seemed to be an addiction. There were many times Rudi and I had to go and haul his dad out of the card games.

To survive and put food on the table, Rudi's mom cleaned at the Health Sciences Centre. She found out Rudi's dad wasn't always out gambling like she had thought. In reality he had another lady on the side, and they had a son. Soon thereafter, his parents separated, and his dad moved in with this lady.

The wives told me that his three older brothers seemed to have drinking problems and having already had experience with Alanon, I was surprised that Rudi had escaped it. He just wasn't a drinker. He seemed like a very responsible person. Rudi told me it was because his brothers set an example of how not to be.

Since his early teens, Rudi had always been responsible, reliable, and looked after his mother. My parents really didn't see this until he started to come around with me now. They were always amazed by the way he handled the boys. After all, he was only eighteen.

I didn't see Jeffrey. He abided by the court's restraining order, but when he did get a hold of my phone number, he called daily. We talked a bit, mostly about how the boys were doing. He said that if they needed anything that I couldn't buy, then to let him know. He wasn't paying me any child support. He complained a lot about Rudi, but it didn't work because I told him it was none of his business. Later, if Rudi's name was brought up, I would hang up the phone on him. I stood my ground on this and after hanging up twice, he realized I wasn't kidding and stopped. He was very good at reminding me that a legal separation didn't mean I wasn't still married. He tried to persuade me every time he called to let him see the boys, but I never gave in.

Jeffrey was working in the city, and on weekends, he was going to the farm to help his dad do the planting and baling, etc. He also said he was trying to build a car to race at the speedway. He was putting a Chevy engine into a Dodge. Whatever. I didn't mind talking to him, but I had no ambition or desire to see him. I knew I didn't hate him, but I really didn't like him either. I still wished he would get some help with his problems and get himself a good life. I told him that and made it clear; I was no longer part of his life whether he got the help or not. If he did, it would be for himself and not me.

Starting over for me felt so new. I had started to develop some self-confidence, and I really liked living without the fear of doing something wrong and being beaten. There were so many times I sat and thought about how my life was changing for the good and was very curious about the power of Margaret and Michael's prayers. They told me they were Christians, but I was sure that I was too. I knew in my heart that all the good things happening together like they did, were not just coincidences.

It was Rudi's birthday on July nineteenth, and my parents suggested I take him out and do something fun. They said they would watch the boys at their place if needed. Merle was going away for the weekend and said I could use her babysitter to watch the boys. That way, they could just be put to bed in their own beds, instead of waking them up when I returned. Normally, my parents would just keep them overnight, but this time I didn't want to intrude that much. My sister-in-law, Louise, was visiting them from Calgary, but the house they were in wasn't that big.

I took Rudi out for supper. I told him to dress up a few notches better than normal, as I wanted to treat him to a nice evening. He had done so much for me and I found it hard to do for him in return, as he was old fashioned in his ways and didn't believe in a woman paying the bill. Afterwards, we just drove and talked. He really wanted to get serious and reminded me he had waited a long time for me to come to my senses and leave Jeffrey. I thought for a moment before I answered that we would, but to take it slowly. I really did care a lot for Rudi. I didn't think jumping into a new relationship right away would be a good idea, but if I did, it would definitely be with Rudi. He dropped me off at the house where I paid the sitter and went to bed.

In the morning, I woke up and went up to the kitchen to put coffee on, my usual morning ritual. I turned the radio on as I went by. The news was on, and I heard that some one named Zieske had been killed in a highway accident the night before. I thought that Jeffrey's dad had died.

The phone rang at the same time, and when I picked it up, it was my sister-in-law from Calgary calling from my parent's house. She said, "I have been phoning you all night."

I told her that I sleep downstairs with the boys and can't hear the phone from there.

She said she had bad news.

I told her that I knew, I had just heard it on the radio and was shocked. I asked her if she thought I should phone Jeffrey and tell him how sorry I was.

She was very quiet for a moment; then asked me to repeat what I had said. When I repeated my question, she said, "Pat, he is dead!"

"That isn't even funny," I answered somewhat annoyed.

She sounded so serious when she declared, "I may have a warped sense of humor, but do you really think I would make a joke about that?"

"Jeffrey is dead?" I replied, in shock.

She answered, "Yes."

I told her I would call her back, and I called the farmhouse right away. Jeffrey's mother answered the phone

All she said was, "He's gone!"

I asked her where he was. I don't know why, I just wanted to know where he was.

She again repeated, "He's gone!"

I then tried to be more specific. I asked where they had taken him.

Once again, all I got was, "He's gone!"

My doorbell rang, so I told her I would call her back.

Rudi was standing at the door and just said to me, "I heard about Jeffrey on the radio and I am here to do whatever you want me to do."

With my tears out of control, I told him, "Even with all that happened between Jeffrey and me, I never wanted him to die."

He said that he knew that and so did every one else who knew me.

The phone started to ring, and as Rudi went to answer it, he asked where the boys were. I told him that they were still sleeping. It was my mom on the phone. She was *so* glad Rudi was there. She asked Rudi to bring the boys over to their house along with a suitcase of clothes and some of their toys and bottles, etc. They could stay as long as was required for me to get through whatever I needed to do. Rudi got off the phone and suggested I get in the shower and get dressed. He said that he would get the boys up and get them packed and ready to go. I did just that, knowing that Rudi could handle the boys. So many times already he had helped me get them ready. It was already second nature to him.

My parents lived only ten minutes away from where I was living. My dad met us at the door, and I told him quietly that I hadn't told J.J. yet. Both boys were so young. They hadn't seen Jeffrey for the past couple of months. I didn't think they would understand. I got a big hug from my sister-in-law who I hadn't seen since the wedding. I said that I was really looking forward to visiting and spending time with her. My parents called me into the kitchen and closed the door. They said that even with all the trouble Jeffrey and I had, that he was still the father of their grandchildren and they were sorry this happened. That really meant a lot because I knew how much my parents hated Jeffrey for the way he treated me. He still shouldn't have died; he was way too young. My dad suggested Rudi start by driving me to the RCMP in Beausejour and getting any information I wanted from them. I agreed. My mom said that she would call Diane and let her know where the boys were.

The drive to Beausejour was about an hour from my parent's house. All Rudi had said was that it should never have been on the radio. After all, I was still the next of kin. I told him that I felt so strange with him driving me and listening to me cry about my husband. He told me not to even think twice about it.

I thought about the lawyer stating, the year before, that one of us would be dead in a year. But that was supposed to be if we stayed together. I thought about the boys growing up without a father. All I really knew was that I had not wanted him to die.

When we arrived at the RCMP Station, we both went in, and I told the officer on duty that I wanted to know what had happened to Jeffrey. (It was a small town and everyone knew everyone else in town and in the outskirts.

Jeffrey's family farm was about a fifteen-minute drive away.) The officer asked me who I was, and I told him that I was Jeffrey's wife but that we were separated. I told him that we had driven out from Winnipeg. I added that I had heard about the accident on the radio when I got up. He stood with his mouth opened and was speechless for a moment. Later, he told us to come into the office and sit down. Then he called another officer on the radio and suggested that he come back to the station, stating that he had Jeffrey's wife sitting there. He still appeared shocked, but when I told him that Jeffrey had two sons, he was really blown away. This officer never stopped apologizing and when the other officer came in, they both made coffee and sat with us talking.

They explained he was in the car with two other people when the accident happened. I didn't know them, but I think they were cousins of his. He had a really large family. Apparently, Jeffrey had just finished a car that he was building. When they ran out of beer, they had decided to drive to another town to get some more. The officer said that the car wasn't registered, Jeffrey didn't have a license and that they had been drinking. None of this surprised me. This particular road was gravel–being built up in order to be paved. The officer said that there were sand piles on the sides of the road, which the construction crew was using for building it up. Jeffrey had hit one of the sand piles, and the car had rolled over on its side. He stated that Jeffrey flew out the window and broke his neck when he landed. They found him in the ditch. The officer went on to say that he died instantly. I asked about the other two in the car, and he said they just walked away.

Then one officer told Rudi to take me to the funeral home and talk to them about any arrangements. Apparently, they would need a signature from me in order to do anything. As we were leaving, the officer handed me Jeffrey's wallet. He explained that when he got called back to the station to talk to me, he was just on his way to the farm to give it to Jeffrey's mother.

As we were driving away, I noticed at the gas station down the street the Dodge that Jeffrey had been working on. I asked Rudi to stop. We went to look at the car, and realized by the way it was smashed up on the side, that this was the car that killed him. A guy came out of the gas station and not knowing me, said, "A guy got killed in this accident during the night–hard to believe with such little damage. His funeral won't even be paid by insurance, because he didn't have any." We didn't say anything. Rudi just put his arm around me and took me back to the car.

We parked in the Funeral Home parking lot, but I found that I just couldn't go in. I couldn't imagine that Jeffrey was lying in there dead. I knew

I had to do this, but I couldn't do it alone. I really thought it was so unfair to ask Rudi to go in with me. He had already done so much. I finally got up enough courage to get out of the car, but when I did, Rudi got out of his door. I didn't even have to ask. He said that he wasn't going to let me do it alone.

It was such a strange atmosphere as soon as we walked in the door. It was so quiet and had a weird smell. A gentleman in a black suit met us and asked if he could help us. Rudi told him who I was. Good thing because I couldn't speak. I just wanted to turn around, walk out the door, and run away. I didn't want to deal with this anymore. Being in that building made it all too real.

The man told us to follow him into his office and sit down. He sat at the other side of the desk and started by giving his condolences. He then asked me if I had any ideas for the funeral. What ideas would I have for a funeral? I wasn't even old enough to be married, never mind plan a funeral. Rudi suggested to him that we leave any planning to the next day so we could have some time to just let this all sink in. I felt like I was going to throw up and wanted to leave. The man was very nice about it. He gave me a card with his name and number and told me to give him a call before lunch the next day when he would set up a time to meet to discuss the arrangements. He then asked to be excused for a minute and left the office. When he came back with his hands full, I almost passed out. He handed me all the clothes that Jeffrey had been wearing along with his Stomper boots. I looked at Rudi, and as he took the clothes from me, I said, "Jeffrey said he wanted to be buried in those boots." It all became way too much for me and I got up to leave.

The man then said, "Do you want to go in and see him now?"

That was it. I burst into tears and yelled, "NO!" Then I walked out the door very quickly. Rudi followed and I heard him say thank you to the man, and that I would call tomorrow. I cried so hard for the next fifteen minutes, I couldn't even talk. I felt so sorry for Rudi because I knew that he didn't really know what to do, where to take me or what to say. There was really nothing to say.

On the way back, I remembered what Jeffrey had said, if he died, he wanted to be buried with his Stomper boots on, a bottle of rye beside him and for his wife to wear the shortest dress she could find.

We went back to Merle's house. She was back home from her trip. She had already heard the news and talked to my parents. She suggested I call out to the country to Jeffrey's parents and discuss this with them. I called, and Jeffrey's mom came to the phone sounding so distraught. I told her that I had gone to the RCMP and that they told me what happened. I then told her that I went to the funeral home. She asked if I had seen him, and I told her that they had asked if I wanted to, but I just couldn't. She understood and said they were planning on going the next morning. I didn't even have to ask for anything. She just came right out and said, "Harvey and I will pay for the whole funeral, but we are just asking that you sign the papers, so we can make the arrangements."

I said, "Sure, that seems only right." I would call the funeral director in the morning.

She queried, "You will be coming to the funeral?"

I said, "Yes, I was coming."

Then she asked if I would bring the boys.

I told her that I just couldn't, they were much too young and wouldn't understand. We left the conversation at that, and I told her I would call the next day. I got off of the phone and told Rudi and Merle what was said. It was a relief that they had offered to pay for the funeral.

We sat back and tried to relax. I fell asleep. There was a note from Rudi when I woke up. He was going to drop pajamas off at my parents for the boys, as he had forgotten to pack them earlier. Then, he was going home. The note said that if I woke up in the night and couldn't get back to sleep, to phone him. Otherwise, he would see me in the morning. I lay staring at the ceiling thinking of how every girl would like a "Knight in Shining Armour" to come to their rescue like Rudi did for me time and time again. I tried to think of how I really felt about him. Was it love or was it because he rescued me? He was so comfortable to have around. I couldn't think about it anymore because my emotions were so taken over by Jeffrey dying and so I went back to sleep. I really didn't want to think anymore.

Rudi phoned at seven and said that he was just checking to see if I was up yet. He went on to say that he was just walking out the door. He still lived with his mother in the north-end, which was almost a half hour drive to Merle's. I asked if he had seen the boys when he dropped off the pajamas. He replied that J.J. was awake for about five minutes while he was there, but that P.J. was sound asleep the whole time. He had stayed for over an hour and visited with my parents. My mom had made him something to eat. I then told him that I would see him when he got here and that fresh coffee was perking.

Merle and her boys left before Rudi arrived. She had to go to work and drop off the boys before, so her day started early. Rudi walked in five minutes later. I found out that even five minutes was too long to be alone. I was almost starting to panic when he walked in.

I started thinking that Jeffrey was so mad at me for not letting him see the boys; what could he do now? It was like I was being haunted.

I called my parents, and they said that the boys were awake. We stopped there first to see them. They had already been bounced around so much for their young age. I guess it didn't harm them, but made them more flexible. My parents already had them bathed and dressed. They were both so cute. J.J. had such curly blonde hair and the biggest smile. He was tall and slim for his age. P.J. was a little Rolly-Polly with no hair yet (J.J. was bald until a year old also), and got his cheeks from my side of the family. When he smiled, he would light up the room. We stayed for quite a while and talked. Rudi was on the floor playing with the boys. He was a real kid at heart, and I think he really liked the toys more so than the boys.

We went out to the funeral home and signed the papers, and I said to the funeral director that he should write out one request that Jeffrey's parents needed to know. That was for Jeffrey to wear his boots and that he wanted a bottle of rye beside him. He looked at me kind of strangely but I didn't care. I saw him write it down.

I phoned out to Jeffrey's parents to get the details of the funeral. They said the viewing was Wednesday evening and the funeral itself was on Thursday at noon. He was being buried in the graveyard by the church, just up the street from the farm. I asked if she had gotten Jeffrey's request about being buried in his boots. She said that they had bought him a new suit and shoes and that was really a stupid request. I wasn't going to argue. The agreement was they did what they wanted. I would definitely find the shortest dress though. I said if we left the city at ten on Thursday morning that would be good. I didn't want to go to the viewing. It was a closed family viewing, and I didn't think I should be there.

The dress I chose was a black jersey knit with little pink and yellow flowers and green leaves. It was very feminine, but short. I felt I could wear this and feel good in it. I didn't want to make a spectacle of myself; I just wanted to do something for Jeffrey.

We went to a flower shop and ordered a bouquet of flowers, which said, "DAD" and had them sent to the funeral from the boys. When I proceeded to pay for them, I reached in my purse to get my wallet and pulled out Jeffrey's wallet. I had put it in there at the funeral home and then completely forgotten about it. I opened it and there was some cash and his last paycheque from the company which he worked for. I wrote a cheque for the flowers and put Jeffrey's wallet back in my purse. I thought I would buy something for the boys with that money. Whenever I talked to Jeffrey on the phone, he always asked if the boys had decent shoes. Maybe I would take them to buy them a really good pair of shoes.

Rudi came over after work. He was, once again, full of paint. He asked me to come with him to his place while he showered and changed. I was leery because I knew his mother wouldn't like to see us together. She always wanted a nice German girl for Rudi, like Linda. Linda could speak German, cook German food, and be the typical German wife. Still, I went along with Rudi.

His mother was nice enough. She kept talking in German to Rudi, but I knew she was complaining about him being with me. It really didn't matter. She was really good at doing that–complaining to him in German and turning around and smiling at me while speaking English. I knew enough German from hanging around with Linda, Rudi, and Jeffrey that I could make out enough words in a sentence to figure out what was being said. Rudi just kept answering with, what sounded like, "Siroy." I knew it meant to be quiet.

On Wednesday, I went over to my parents' house and spent the day with them and the boys. I helped my mom clean the house for a while–anything to stay busy.

I got home about two o'clock and the phone rang. It was Rick Schwark, Jeffrey's cousin. He called to tell me that he had a problem that he was hoping I could help him with. He was one of the pallbearers for Jeffrey's funeral and was supposed to pick up his tuxedo from the rental shop. He had to work all day and couldn't make it before the shop closed. Apparently, his boss wouldn't let him go early because he was taking the next day off for the funeral. He figured that I would probably be off of work and maybe would have the time to pick up his suit for him and take it to his grandmother's house who lived in the city.

I got up early on the morning of the funeral because I couldn't sleep and went over to my parent's house so that they could tell me if I was appropriately dressed for a funeral. My dad just rolled his eyes and said, "Well if Jeffrey wanted short, he definitely got it." To my dad, "above the knee" would be too short. Generation gap, I suppose. If he had his way, he would probably make me change into a floor length black dress.

On the way out of town to the funeral, I was very nervous, scared, maybe even terrified, and driving Rudi's car didn't help because I knew it was his pride and joy. I kept thinking of what my dad had always said; "There is nothing to fear but fear itself." It helped to the point that I didn't turn the car around and go back, but I was still petrified.

The pastor was waiting outside. He told me to wait until the funeral car came, as I would be walking in behind the coffin. The church parking lot was full, and there were cars lining the sides of the highway. I just couldn't do it and wanted to leave. I couldn't deal with all the people.

The pastor noticed I was having a problem and then asked me to come and talk to him for a minute. He told me that he knew all about what had happened in the past couple of years and that he felt, for my own good, I should stay and say goodbye. I agreed. He told me that I had nothing to fear, as he and God were watching over me. I said, "Alright" and waited.

It seemed like forever before the black car was finally driving slowly down the highway toward the church, pulling up in front of the doors. The pallbearers came and opened the back doors. There was Jeffrey's lilac suede coffin. As the pallbearers pulled it out, my knees started to give out from under me. Why did I come? I couldn't do this. I wanted to go home. The pastor took one of my arms. As the coffin was proceeding through the big double doors of the church, he led me to follow behind. As we moved along, I could hear crying behind me, and when I looked back, it was Jeffrey's mother and father. My tears were out of control as we walked down the centre aisle of the church. I had never been to a funeral in my life, and I felt that this was not the place to start. There were so many people. I couldn't see any faces, just people. I was shaking so badly, I didn't think I could make it all the way down the aisle.

The coffin was taken to the front, and I was then guided to the front pew with the rest of the family. I didn't feel that I should be in the front, and I definitely didn't want to be there. The pastor started to talk, but I couldn't hear the words. Suddenly he did something that I had never prepared myself for or ever expected. He opened the coffin and there was Jeffrey. All the people started to line up to see him. They were waiting for me to start. I couldn't. No way could I even stand up, let alone walk up and look at his face. I just couldn't. His parents went up. They sobbed so uncontrollably while saying their goodbyes. All the people filed by. I can't remember how long it took. All I wanted to do was go home. The aisles were lined with people. I couldn't possibly have gotten out.

When all the people were finally sitting down again, someone got up and took my arm. I knew I would have to, but I kept crying, "Oh, no" and shaking my head. Finally, I thought to myself, I married this man and we have two children together. I really have to say goodbye. I got up and walked to the coffin. It didn't look at all like Jeffrey. His neck was so swollen because it had been broken. I couldn't say "Goodbye." I just looked at him and through an uncontrollable sob, I whispered, "I am so sorry, I didn't want you to die." At that point my knees did give out.

I don't remember any of the service or anything that was said. When it was over, I don't even remember leaving the church.

Chapter 3

ONCE BURNT; FOREVER CAUTIOUS

Rudi and I kept seeing each other pretty well daily. By the middle of August, we were considered committed to each other. We started taking the boys to his church every Sunday. The pastor had known Rudi's family for many years.

One day, Rudi suggested that we go and visit my brother Grant in Calgary for the weekend. We would drive out on Friday and come back on Sunday. My parents offered to look after the boys. They thought that it would be nice for us to take a break. Merle decided she would come with us. That way there would be three of us to drive. Of course, we would take Rudi's Cougar. It was the most comfortable, and he never left home without it. I was looking for a new job at the time and had sent in applications for different secretary positions. I was waiting for answers, so I was quite free to go.

Rudi had suggested Merle and I take the Cougar on Friday morning because he had to finish a job he was painting. That way we could gas it up, load it and be ready to go as soon as he got off work. I really didn't want to and fought him on it. I asked, "What if something happened to the car? You would hate me." He said that it was only a car and not to be silly.

Rudi did pick me up on Friday morning, and then I drove him to the office. The brothers had a paint company and their office was on Elgin Avenue. I went back, packed up the kids for the weekend, and then Merle and I dropped them off at my parents.

We decided to do a bit of shopping, wash and gas up the car, then load it up. It was so hot by eleven o'clock and I was getting quite comfortable driving the car. The car had a metallic mint green paint job that shined almost silver and had big Tornado tires in the back with chrome rims all around. The interior was all black leather. There were bucket seats with a stick on the floor. It was an automatic transmission and had much more power than it needed.

It was so hot that we had both front windows rolled down. Merle and I were talking and laughing when we saw a little MG convertible driving beside us. The guy was trying to get Merle's attention. She was talking out the window while I was driving and at one point, I had looked over at them. When I looked back, I noticed a big Dodge driving in front of me, which had stopped at a crosswalk. There was lots of room for me to come to a stop behind him. When I applied my brakes, the Tornado tires in the back of the car were so hot, they didn't grab and we started to slide. I applied the brakes harder, and the situation got worse. In that split second, I warned Merle to hang on, and we hit. We hit the car so hard that his trunk was almost sitting in his back seat. The front hood had popped up on the front of the Cougar, and I couldn't see anymore. When we came to a full stop, the Cougar was revving really loud, and the stick shift was sitting in the back seat. It was still in drive. I attempted to shut the car off, but it wouldn't stop running.

I asked Merle if she was all right, and she replied that yes she was okay. I tried to get out to make sure the driver of the other car wasn't hurt, but my door wouldn't open. It didn't matter. The driver of the other car was standing at my window, and he was mad. I told him I was so sorry, but the car wouldn't stop.

Someone had called a tow truck, and it seemed like only a matter of minutes before it arrived. He told us we had better get out of the car and asked if there was someone he could call to pick us up. All I could say was, "This is my boyfriend's car."

He laughed and said, "You mean this WAS your boyfriends car; you can't drive it like this." I told him that he just couldn't take it. He replied that it was impossible to drive it as bad as it was, and that I should shut it off. It wouldn't shut off. He mumbled, "Fine" and walked away. He towed the other car as I started to drive away.

We stopped at the nearest payphone, and I tried to call Rudi at his office. His brother, Heinz, answered the phone. He told me that Rudi was on a job and then asked me what the problem was. So I told him.

He asked, "Do you at least have a driver's license?"

I said that of course I did.

Then he suggested I drive the car to the office. By then, Rudi would probably be back.

We found a rope to tie down the front hood because it was really smashed up and the motor was still revving. I climbed back in the car through the passenger door and started to drive when I noticed the oil light had come on. I knew that Jeffrey's cousin Rick worked at the gas station down the street and I could get him to check it.

When we pulled in, Rick was standing outside in the front. He appeared shocked when he saw the car but was even more so when he saw who was driving it. Merle and I both climbed out of the passenger door and Rick asked what happened. I told him and he said, "You can't drive this car, I can't let you drive this car."

I replied that I had to; it was Rudi's car.

He said, "I hope Rudi REALLY likes you a lot." Then he untied the front hood and looked inside. He just kept shaking his head and then said, "Both motor mounts are broken, and the engine has fallen back into the fire-wall. The transmission is shot. You can't drive this. It isn't safe."

As usual, the tears started and I told him that I just had to. He could see that I was really upset and said, "I will fill it up with oil, but you have to go straight to the office. You can't stop for anything."

I said, "Awe gee, and we wanted to go shopping before we go to the office," with a very sarcastic tone. He just smiled and filled it with oil while asking me lots of questions about what I am doing with my life.

I told him that I was finished working at the project and was looking for another job. He started to laugh and said that he was living at his grand-mother's and Motor Coach Industries was right around the corner. They were looking to train welders. Still laughing, he said, "It pays really well and if you learn how to weld, you can come and work on my pit crew." Rick was still racing. Brooklyn Speedway had shut down but another track opened outside the city. It was a clay oval track and Rick was driving a Late Model Racecar.

I said, "Right," thanked him and attempted to pay him for the oil. He wouldn't accept the money and wished me good luck. He yelled for me to call him for coffee some time as we left.

When Rudi had gotten back to the office, his brother Heinz must have made an announcement to all the painters about how stupid women can be because when we pulled up in front of the office, every guy in the company poured out the door, and I could see he was very upset. He pulled open the door so fast, I thought he was going to hit me. I cowered back and put my hands over my face to defend myself. He grabbed me and asked calmly, "Are you alright?"

Shocked, I took my hands away from my face and said, "Look what I did to your car."

His reply, "I can replace the car, but I can't replace you." I didn't think it was possible, but I felt even guiltier.

Merle and I got out of the car and as I walked around it with Rudi, he kept saying that it wasn't too bad. I knew that he was only trying to make me feel better. When I looked to see what Merle was doing, Rudi said, "See, good can come out of this yet." Merle and Heinz were staring at each other so deeply, while talking, that you couldn't cut between them with a knife. Heinz offered to drive Merle home.

Rudi took the company truck after a tow truck had picked up the Cougar and towed it away. Quite obviously, we phoned my brother in Calgary and told him that we weren't coming.

By the following Wednesday, I was getting quite apprehensive because I hadn't gotten any calls for jobs. I was starting to feel down on myself and knew I had to do something. Out of desperation one day, I thought about what Rick had told me. I went down to Motor Coach Industries and applied. My dad used to be supervisor there, so I used his name as a reference. One of the men gave me a tour of the training Centre where they actually taught an eight-week course on welding. He asked if I was interested, and I replied that yes I was VERY interested.

The pay for the training period was great and got even better when the actual job started. He told me to start at eight the following Monday morning. I was pretty excited about the whole thing and told Rudi that night. He didn't share the excitement and said that I was way above being a welder. I really didn't know what that meant at the time, but found out later it meant this wasn't a job for a woman. It fed my kids and paid the rent, and that's what is important.

Heinz had started to sleep over at Merle's, and Rudi convinced me that this house wasn't the greatest situation for the boys. They needed their own bedroom and should not be sleeping in a rec room. I replied that I would think about it after I finished the course on welding and had started actually working.

When I got halfway through the course, my instructor came to me and said that there was a job open at nights for a spot welder. The pay was fantastic and I could start right away. The training would be finished on the job.

I talked to Rudi about it and told him that it wasn't possible. Who could I get to watch the boys during the night? He saw it as an opportunity and suggested we get an apartment together. He would watch the boys during the night while I worked, and I would watch them during the day. I could take the car to work at night and would be back in time for him to take it to work the following day. It all seemed perfect, so I agreed. We started to look at apartments that weekend.

We found a two-bedroom apartment, which was fairly reasonable. To me, it was great. We stood in the empty apartment looking around and figured out where we could put the boys and what furniture was needed. We moved in right away.

I didn't accompany Rudi when he told his mother he was moving out and living with me. I knew she would be so upset, which she was, and hated me even more. In her mind, I was a terrible person stealing her son away.

Rudi asked me to go with him to buy some furniture. We picked up a nice three-room group for a fairly good price. We moved in and got settled.

That first evening, I made supper, bathed the boys and got them settled in bed while Rudi hung some pictures. After the boys were asleep, he said that he was going out to the car to get something. When he came back in he had a bottle of wine and two wine glasses. He poured the wine and as we curled up together on the couch, I said, "This is so perfect."

Rudi then said, "Not yet." He got down on one knee in front of me.

I just wanted to run. It was too soon. I couldn't marry him. I didn't want him to ask because I didn't want to have to say no and it was too soon to say yes. I guess he recognized the petrified look on my face and knew I didn't want this to be happening.

He just said to me, "I have loved you since I met you, when we were only twelve years old. I have always dreamed of marrying you when we got older. The age we are now is the age I always imagined we would be when I asked you. So we took a bit of a different route than the straight road to get here, but without doing that, we wouldn't have J.J. and P.J. You know I love J.J. and P.J. as if they were my own." I already knew all of this and knew he was being very sincere. Then he rescued me by saying, "I do want to marry you, but I also know, 'once burned, forever cautious." And you have definitely been burned. I am asking you to marry me with no pressure for an answer. I would rather you say, sometime in the future, than to say not at all." Then he pulled out a ring and asked me to marry him.

I looked at the ring and it was so beautiful, so delicate. I really wanted to take it out of the case and put it on my finger. This still wasn't enough to take away the memory of the bad experience I had, already having been married. I just smiled and said, "Sometime in the future."

He smiled, but through it, I could see it was not the answer he was hoping for. He closed the ring case and put it back in his pocket, then said, "I am not giving up."

I was on my way to work one night, when a half-ton truck pulled up beside me just as I was parking at Motor Coach. It was Rick. He couldn't believe that I had actually applied for, and gotten the welding job.

He informed me that Jeffrey's mother had recently died. She apparently went into the hospital for some kind of minor surgery and died on the table. What a blow to that family.

One morning, I came out of work and there was a note under the wipers on the windshield. It was from Rick asking me if we could get together for lunch or a coffee. I rolled it up and stuck it in my pocket. He knew that Rudi and I were living together. I never made anything out of this development, but it got to be a morning ritual to come out to a note on the windshield from Rick. He would ask me to call him or just tell me to have a nice day. I never did call him. I usually stuck the notes in my pocket and threw them away when I got home.

I guess that morning I was so tired, I totally forgot about the note and threw it on the dashboard of the car. As usual, I came home, Rudi would have coffee ready for me, and he would ask me the same question. Would I marry him? I always answered the same, "Not yet." He would then leave for work. Well, that one morning, he came back a few minutes after he had left and was so angry.

I had never seen him that angry with me before. He threw the note on the kitchen table and asked how long this had been going on.

I told him that there had been a few notes, but that I never responded.

He asked how Rick knew that I was working at Motor Coach.

I told Rudi, "It was Rick who told me about the job."

Well, that was the wrong answer. Rudi was so upset, then asked when I could have seen Rick for him to tell me about the job.

I replied, "When I smashed up the car, I drove by and asked him to look and see if I could drive it to the office like it was. I then told him that Rick had put oil in it. Rudi was then even more upset, and I felt so bad. I didn't think that telling him all of this was necessary, at the time. He slammed the door so hard when he left; I thought it had come right off its hinges.

I couldn't sleep at all that day. Usually I would lie down for a nap when the boys did, but I felt so bad that I just sat and stared at the walls.

Later in the afternoon, the phone rang. It was my mother. First she said to me, "Happy Birthday." I hadn't even remembered it was my birthday. She went on to say that she had to tell me some news, and I wasn't going to like it. I thought, "Oh what the heck, it was already a lousy day, why not add more fuel to the fire." She informed me that my dad and her were moving back to Halifax, Nova Scotia with the girls and Jimmy. (Why? What would I do without them? Didn't they love me anymore? The boys would have to grow up without their grandparents around. That seemed so unfair.) She said that they had wanted to do it for a long time but could never leave with my situation the way it was. Dad was offered a job with the oil company in Dartmouth. This was a really good opportunity for them. They were quite satisfied that I was happy with Rudi, and he would look after us. So they felt that they could make the move with a peace of mind.

By the time Rudi got back from work, I was so tired that I could hardly keep my eyes open. He wasn't angry anymore. I told him that I was so sorry, and I would give him any notes that were put on the car in the future to let him handle it in any way he chooses. He said that it didn't matter; he was stupid enough to let me go for a member of that family before and had now decided to smarten up and not let it happen again. I told him about my parents moving to Nova Scotia, and he said he already knew.

He said he met my dad at lunchtime to look at a house. He said that he had this great idea to buy me a house for my birthday and come home with the keys wrapped. Apparently, it was on a movie he watched once. It wasn't so easy to do it like the movie, so he could only tell me about it. He said that it was a lot closer to my work and that the boys could each have their own bedroom. He referred to it as, "Our little Sugar Shack," and said it needed painting, but he had the technology to fix that. He had put in a really low offer on the condition that I like the house. It was accepted. He said that we could live in it long enough to fix it up, then sell it for a good profit and buy a better place. I was so surprised that he would do that after he went out the door so angry that morning. He suggested I should get a couple of hours' sleep and he would make arrangements so I could stop on the way to work, to see the house. He would drive me there and then pick me up in the morning from work. He said he would just get up earlier to get the boys ready.

I did get to sleep right away. I didn't really want to think about all of this. It was really too much. Rudi had a problem waking me up later. When we got to the house, there was still a half an hour left before I had to go to work.

It definitely was a Sugar Shack. So small, but it was a really cute house, medium blue on the outside with white trim.

I said to Rudi as we pulled up in front, "That colour definitely has got to be changed."

He laughed and said, "You ain't seen nothin' yet."

When we got in the front door, I could see what he meant. He informed me that an old Ukrainian lady lived there before. She must have gotten a deal on paint. The front foyer and living room had the same blue walls as the outside of the house, and the ceilings were pink. Rudi's specialty at work was texturing ceilings and he said, "We can paint or wallpaper the living room whatever colour you like, and I will texture all the ceilings." The floor had carpet now, but he said that there was perfectly good hardwood underneath, which could be refinished without any trouble. There were two small bedrooms off of the living room and another bedroom and bathroom off of the kitchen. I loved it.

We could move in any time if we took it, but Rudi said that he would really like to do the floors and ceiling before we moved in.

I asked him, "How much?"

He said that my dad, who was into real estate at that time, had found it. He had put an offer in for $11,000. She was asking for $15,000.

I said, "Okay, Let's do it," and Rudi drove me to work.

I was all right for the first two hours of work, but then really started to fade after that. I had to "spot weld" aluminum frames. When aluminum is welded, if the edge is hit, it causes a small explosion of sparks. I was so tired; I kept hitting the edge. I had on a black turtleneck shirt, and by the time I finished the shift, I had burn holes all over it. I was so glad when it was time to go home. Rudi was waiting with the boys. All three of them were so full of energy, and all I wanted to do was sleep.

Rudi and I took the boys up to the apartment. When I took off my coat, he looked at my top and said that the burn holes were ridiculous. I told him it was just the top that was burnt, and it didn't burn through to the skin.

He suggested I apply for a secretary's job again. I agreed because trying to work nights and look after the boys during the day was really getting to me. But I had already put in so many applications for typing jobs and the welding job paid so well. Rudi said that the pay didn't matter and that I didn't even have to work if I didn't want to. That I couldn't agree with. He was not responsible for the boys. I felt I really did have to work. I had to pull my own weight in our relationship.

The boys and I started to get regular pension cheques every month. It was called orphans' allowance and widows' allowance. It wasn't very much, but it did top up the income. The boys would receive their cheques until they were either eighteen, or as long as they were in school or some kind of training program, until they were twenty-five. If I were to marry again, mine would stop.

Possession date was the first of November. Rudi gave notice to the apartment renters that we would move out on the fifteenth of November, P.J's birthday. He would be two years old.

The boys were both very cute guys with curly blonde hair and though P.J. was a bit shorter than J.J, they were quite often mistaken for twins. P.J. could talk a mile a minute for his age. He was just a ball of energy. J.J. was the quieter one, the older brother, but had twice as much energy. J.J. was the instigator and P.J. followed whatever his big brother did. Rudi was very good looking–the real European look–with soft blonde curls all over his head.

One Saturday, we went grocery shopping and Rudi and J.J. were pushing the cart with P.J. in the seat of the cart. A lady came to him and said," Those boys sure look like you."

Rudi just smiled and said, "Thank-you." The way he was with the boys, no one could ever know–without being told–that he was not their birth father. The boys didn't even know. They called Rudi, "Dad" from day one, and he loved it.

Finally, the weekend came. I worked my nights just waiting for the weekend to come so I could at least catch up a bit on my sleep. As a rule, Rudi would never work on a weekend. Now, he was anxiously waiting for the first of November to come so he could get into the house and get the ceilings and floors done before we moved in. We had no snow yet, as it was a bit early for snow, but it was definitely getting a lot colder.

On the Saturday afternoon, we had just returned from getting groceries and had put the boys down for their nap. Rudi and I were sitting and having coffee. He started to try and convince me to marry him again. He always did it in a joking manner, coming up with points on why it would be such a good idea. This time he came up with a couple of valid points. It would be a shame if we waited because my parents would move to Nova Scotia; then, they would have to come all the way back for our wedding. And, maybe after the move, it would be too expensive and they couldn't come. Then he said that it would surely be nice if we moved into the house as a married couple. I just looked at him blankly and got up to start making supper. I didn't want to answer him because I was starting to cave in. Married when we moved into the house? We were getting possession in just over six weeks.

Chapter 4

I Do

On my way home, I started to really think seriously how I really felt about Rudi. I knew I definitely was in love with him. How can any girl not be after being treated so well in my situation? I wanted to know if I was in love with him because of the situation or if things were different, would I feel the same way? I was reminiscing about when we were younger and drove our bikes together and he would steal my shoe and take off so I would chase him. I reflected on how much fun we had together before Jeffrey and life in the fast lane became part of my life. I finally decided that when Rudi asked me, this morning, to marry him, I would say, "Yes." I knew it was too soon after Jeffrey's funeral but we were moving into our own home together and I didn't want to play house. I looked in the rearview mirror at myself and thought, "Do I really want him to ask me when I look like this?" I tried to fix my hair and my makeup a bit, but it was hopeless. I thought that maybe I would wait until the weekend. By the time I got home, I thought that I should just play it by ear.

He held onto my two arms and gave me a kiss as he walked out the door. This wasn't anything new. His touch was always so gentle and his kiss was never in a hurry, and as usual, he hesitated and asked, "Will you marry me?"

I smiled and said, "Yes."

Well, he closed the door and stared at me. He stammered, "Don't joke about this, I won't think it is funny."

I felt very sure of myself at that moment and reassured him that I was very serious.

He asked if we could get married before we move into the house.

I said, "It's okay, if that is what you really want." He took off his coat and poured himself another coffee. I asked what he was doing, and he answered that he was taking the day off; we had a wedding to plan. We sat and discussed it. I said that we could just elope. He laughed and replied that no, he wanted a real wedding–in a church with tuxedos and dresses and flowers. He didn't just want a wedding; he wanted a miracle.

The phone rang around eight in the morning. It was Merle saying that someone from Standard Aero Engine had just called for me to come for an interview as a secretary. I had dropped my application off a month before. She gave me the number of the guy and I phoned right away. He wanted to see me at three o'clock that afternoon. I was thrilled, but Rudi was even more excited. He said that if I could get that job, it was almost walking distance from the Sugar Shack. In a way this was all confirming to me that I was right to accept Rudi's proposal.

I got a couple of hours sleep and then got ready for my job interview. I had to meet with the boss of the engineering department whose office was located upstairs at the plant.

Outside of his office there were three desks set up at the front of a very large area. In this space there were three rows of seven desks each. If I were to get the job, I would be one of three girls typing for the twenty-one engineers who sat at the other desks. I sat for half an hour talking to the boss who was very interested in hearing my story. I don't think I had the experience he was looking for, but he was willing to give me a chance at the job. I told him that I would have to give notice on my other job, and he was okay with that. I also told him that I was getting married. (Rudi and I had set the date for November sixteenth, which was only six weeks away.)

I phoned in sick that evening at Motor Coach. Rudi and I took the boys to my parents' house to tell them about the new job and the wedding. My parents offered to have the wedding reception in their rec room, which could easily hold about thirty-five people for dinner. They offered to cook all the food–turkey, roast and ham. They could do it smorgasbord style with different kinds of salads, cheese, pickles and the like. This sounded really good to us. I asked my two younger sisters to be Junior Bridesmaids, and they were both thrilled.

Rudi wanted to get married in the family's church, in the North End of the city. I had no problems with that. We wanted to start the boys in Sunday School there, so that would be our church anyway. The Pastor knew his whole family very well.

It was still early when we left my parents, so we drove down to Rudi's oldest brothers (his name was Horst) house. He wanted to ask him to be the Best Man. Horst's wife Elaine and I had gotten to be good friends over the past few months so I asked her to be my Maid of Honour. They both were quite thrilled about the wedding and accepted standing up for us. Elaine was a seamstress and had offered to make the dresses. We became so lost in the wedding plans that we neglected the fact we had a house to get ready to move into.

On the way home, we were laughing so hard at P.J. His favourite person was Uncle Horst. While we were there, they were trying to teach P.J. to say, "Uncle Horst." He could say "Uncle" without any trouble, but he was having a real problem with the "s" in Horst. Not only was it coming out, "Uncle Hortht," but he was saying it with so much emphasis that he sprayed every time he said it. J.J. would keep correcting him and saying, "Uncle Horst." Then P.J. would try again.

Over the next couple of weeks, Elaine and I looked at material and different styles of dresses. I decided to wear a fairly simple dress. I didn't feel comfortable wearing white, so I went with pale yellow satin with an overlay of cream lace. The girls would all wear satin.

Rudi was getting a tuxedo with Horst, and he asked my younger brother Jimmy and his friend Ed to also be a part of the wedding.

After getting to know Ed, I could understand why Rudi wanted to ask him. He turned out to be a really good friend to both of us.

While Elaine and I were doing the dress thing, Rudi was getting the house ready to move into. It didn't take him very long. In the first week, he had the ceilings all textured and the floors finished. Since he had finished those rooms so fast, he decided to get the rest of the house painted right away. He said that he really wanted it ready to move into the day after our wedding. Meanwhile, my mom and dad were planning the food and their house. They said that it was all under control so I should just let them handle it and work on whatever else had to be done.

The next six weeks flew by, but we were totally organized. The house was finished and sitting, ready to move in. The dresses were well on the way to being finished. Tuxedos were ordered. We found a reasonable price on a florist. My new job was great. All was well.

Elaine and I got to know each other so much more while we were making the dresses. She could talk to me about her problems and after being married to Jeffrey, I could really relate to them. I kept hearing about the problems she had with Horst's drinking. I was told how it seemed to run in the family but somehow Rudi was spared from the problems. I could just listen and not really give an opinion. All I knew is I was glad Rudi was different.

Horst pulled a "Horst" the week before the wedding. Rudi

said he had gotten drunk at the German Club, fell and broke his leg. Apparently, he then climbed into his car, managed to drive back to the house, then crawled to the door. At the time, they lived in a two-storey duplex on St. Johns Avenue. They had to go up a long staircase to get to their apartment. Elaine said she heard banging and when she went to the door, Horst was laying on the doorstep. The pain must have been devastating because his leg was so badly broken. The cast was from the bottom of his foot to the top of his leg. This was the Best Man at our wedding.

The night before the wedding, we had dress rehearsal at the church. The flowers were sitting at my mom's; Rudi had picked them up and taken them there in the afternoon. The food was all ready.

Rudi's mom wasn't pleased and didn't hesitate to show it. She said repeatedly that she wouldn't come to the wedding. Rudi just kept saying for us to ignore it.

Everything was already moved into the house, and the apartment keys were given back. The boys and I didn't stay at the house yet. The idea was, we would stay at my parents' house the night before the wedding. Rudi would stay at the house. I would get ready for the wedding at Elaine's house with the rest of the girls and Rudi would get ready with the guys at the Sugar Shack.

We came close to the plan but not quite. Rudi, Jimmy and Ed were supposed to decorate the car at my mom's. Then, they went to get showered and dressed and to pick up Horst. He couldn't get the tuxedo pants over his cast so ended up wearing a brown suit with a split all the way up the seam. The cast was quite obvious but then he wore a green slipper–one of those which all of our mothers knit and made us wear.

I was in my dress, putting on my make-up in Elaine's kitchen. All of a sudden Rudi yelled up the stairs, "Where are the flowers?" My mom said that they were on the car. "No," he yelled, "the other flowers." Elaine could hear him coming up the stairs as he was yelling and made me hide in the bedroom. He asked, "The bouquet of flowers?"

She said, "Oh, they are on the top of the freezer in the basement at our house." OUR HOUSE? That was a half hour drive, one way. The wedding was in one hour. He could make it. Then I heard Elaine ask, "Why aren't you in your tuxedo?"

I thought, "Oh no, he will never make it."

Rudi yelled to me as he was running down the stairs, "I may be a couple of minutes late, but don't start without me."

I sat down and started to laugh. This organized man, Mr. Totally

Responsible, whom I was marrying, was falling apart. But that wasn't the end of it, Rudi didn't have the key to get into my mom's house, and now he had to get changed too.

Ed and Jimmy changed in the car as Rudi drove. They told us later, that he was going so fast they thought it would take their mind off of his driving. They arrived at my mom's house in eighteen minutes. I would have imagined that this was impossible without a plane. He broke in through the kitchen window, and as he was climbing in, he was already taking off his clothes. Then he ran and unlocked the door for Jimmy and Ed, still shedding his clothes along with his underwear. Keep in mind; this was the door, which all the guests would be coming in for the reception. Jimmy and Ed grabbed all the flowers, as Rudi got dressed. They left and drove to the church. I was there five minutes early, and as I walked in the door, my dad handed me the bouquet of flowers. I asked him where he had gotten them, and he replied, "From the box which Rudi brought." I was really impressed.

Rudi's mom did show up after all. She and my mom sat in the front seats with the boys. My parents had them all dressed up with vests, dress pants, white shirts and ties. They were adorable.

We started the Wedding March and I could see by the look on Rudi's face that he was calm. My dad walked me down the aisle. But as we were coming in, he made a comment about the fact that he loved me and would always stand beside me. He added that this was the last time he wanted to walk me down the aisle. Twice for one daughter was enough. Then he went on to say that this time Mom and he agreed with my choice. Rudi was a good guy.

As we were saying our vows, the pastor told me to put the ring on Rudi's finger. I tried, but it wouldn't go on. Rudi looked at me with a shocked look on his face. I had pushed the ring up to the knuckle on his finger when he pulled it back from me. I was so surprised when he pulled it off and put it on the other hand. I had the wrong hand and since he was a painter, his right fingers were a lot larger than his left. He smiled and put it on the proper finger. It slid on without any problem. I started to laugh and cry at the same time, one of those "out of control" emotions that take over. Rudi joked for years that we were never legally married because he had to put the ring on his own finger. I found out later that Diane was sitting close to the front of the church and of course being blind, couldn't see exactly what was happening. When she heard me start to cry, she asked her husband if I was changing my mind.

I got my sanity back when I heard P.J. behind me say, "Uncle Gunther, I have to pee." We had been trying to toilet train P.J. for so long, already. He was really good at following J.J. to the bathroom, but he hadn't yet caught on to doing it by himself. Both Rudi and I started to laugh when he said it, because it was something we were waiting to hear, but the timing was really bad. Soon, everyone started to laugh. Gunther got up and sheepishly walked him to the bathroom. Those are the kind of things that can happen when you take your kids to your wedding.

Soon enough, we finished the ceremony and went quickly out to the wedding car. We led while everyone was to follow to my parents' house for the reception. Elaine was driving because Horst couldn't drive with his cast on. We got just a block away when Rudi remembered he left all his clothes thrown in my mom and dads front doorway. I said to him, "if we don't get there first then you are telling me everyone is going to see your socks and underwear when they come in the door?" He then informed me his long underwear was there too.

So Elaine drove like a maniac, but that was normal for her. She was really good at getting stopped by the police and smiling her way out of it. She was a good-looking lady and quiet spoken, even quieter when she got agitated. She spoke a "Low German," which was different than what the Hardt family spoke, but they all seemed to understand each other. Elaine was driving so fast, we had forgotten that everyone else was supposed to follow the wedding car.

We got to my mom's house when I asked, "How we were supposed to get in?" Rudi said that it was okay; he was good at breaking into my parents' house. He had it mastered already. He headed for the kitchen window when my dad yelled out from inside that he could use the door this time if he wanted to. How did they ever beat us there? The way my dad drove, I was sure we would be eating already by the time they arrived. When we got to the back door, all the other cars were just pulling up and parking. My mom was standing in the doorway holding up Rudi's underwear and said, "Do these belong to any of you?" Rudi was so embarrassed as he grabbed them from her. Then he opened the closet door beside him and threw them in. My mom said, "So now, where do you want them to hang their coats?" Rudi grabbed them again and ran downstairs. For all I know he could have hid them in the deep freeze.

The rec room looked so nice; all decorated to match the colour scheme of the wedding. My mom did a great job. The wedding cake was on a round table in the corner. It was three layers with small wine glasses used as pillars. It was decorated with creamy yellow flowers, and on the top there was a bride and groom. Along one wall was a long table with all the food. As people came in, my dad had the bar set up with all the glasses in rows. People could help themselves if they wanted a drink. They had put so much work into this. My dad made a potato salad in the shape of a cruise ship. It was the Centre attraction on the table, being so big. The smoke stacks were made out of dill pickles and the portholes along the side were sliced olives. Out of the front of the ship, there was a chain hanging to hold the anchor. The chain was bread and butter pickles hollowed out and linked together. It was sitting on a tray with lettuce leaves all around it representing waves in the water. In between some of the leaves there were sardines representing fish in the water.

When all was done, the boys were supposed to stay at my parents' house for the night while Rudi and I went to a hotel. But, I really wanted to go to the house because I hadn't seen what Rudi had done yet. So, Rudi gave the room to my brother, and we took the boys and left. As we were driving down Portage Avenue heading for the Sugar Shack, there were cars blowing their horns at us. The car was still decorated. I was in my wedding dress and Rudi was still in his tuxedo. It was funny to see the looks on people's faces as they smiled and waved with J.J. and P.J. waving out the window back at them. A ready-made family.

Life was pretty peaceful and settled. The girls I worked with were really nice and we became good friends. Usually we ended up chumming with them on weekends. Either we would have them and their husbands over for supper, or they would have us over. We really did like our quiet life.

Christmas was great. The boys were just at the age when they could appreciate it and they would get so excited waiting for Santa to come. We just stayed home for New Year's. We opened a bottle of wine at midnight while the boys slept. We filled their stockings and went to bed. It was a tradition, which my parents picked up when we were living in France. On New Years Eve, they would put their shoes out. If they were good, St. Nick would put goodies in their shoes. But, if they were bad, they got a potato.

Right after New Year's, I got a terrible bout of the stomach flu. I couldn't stay home from work because I hadn't been there long enough. I just toughed it out. After a week of having the flu, Rudi suggested that we take the day off and go to the doctor.

Rudi's mom came to watch the boys for us. She had now accepted the fact that Rudi and I were married. She really didn't have a choice, and she was usually quite available when we needed her. Anytime she was coming over to the house to look after the boys, I usually got up really early, or stayed up really late the night before to clean the house. She was a perfectionist, and it didn't matter how much I cleaned my house, she would get it cleaner. The boys called her Oma, and she would give them a good cleaning too. Whenever they would see her coming in the door, P.J. would yell at J.J. to "Run and hide; Oma is here." They really did love her though. When she washed their faces, it would take off a couple of layers. She was a big strong lady and had so much energy.

I was called in the examining room while Rudi waited in the waiting room. He had to drive me to the doctor because I seemed to be throwing up after five or ten minutes of driving anywhere. Too many times in the past week, we had to stop for me to be sick. I was losing weight. I couldn't keep anything down.

Dr. Goldberg was in his mid thirties and had a very pleasant manner. He gave me a very thorough examination and called the nurse in to take some blood. After a few questions, he came to this conclusion; I didn't have the flu but a good bout of pregnancy. He figured about six weeks. That would mean that I got pregnant during the first two weeks of marriage.

I knew Rudi would be thrilled. He kept saying, "Let's have a baby right away so that all three kids grow up together," and "Because we are so young, we can pretty well grow up with them." He sure had that right. (J.J. was just over two years and P.J. was just over a year.)

The Doctor said that the blood test would be back the next day and that he would call to confirm his diagnosis. I decided not to tell Rudi until I knew for sure, and when I got into the waiting room, I just said to Rudi, "It's the flu, take me home."

He took me home and I went right to bed. I didn't really want to think, and I was so tired. I just wanted to sleep.

The next morning, I was nauseous but not sick. Rudi went to work, and I said that I was fine to stay home and look after the boys. Mr. Dress-up, The Friendly Giant, and Sesame Street were my saving grace. The boys always played The Cookie Monster. In the afternoon, they went down for a nap and so did I.

I woke up to the phone ringing, and when I answered it, my doctor was on the other end. He told me that, "Yes," I was pregnant, "About five or six weeks." He told me to put up with the morning sickness and that it wouldn't last forever, as if I didn't know the routine by now. Rudi came back early and helped me put together a decent supper. I had a bowl of soup, not that I wanted it.

After the boys were bathed and in bed, I didn't waste any time. Rudi was drinking coffee and watching a movie. I walked in the living room and said, "My doctor phoned this afternoon and said we are five or six weeks pregnant." He was so thrilled, as I knew he would be. I told him that they had booked me for an ultrasound in March.

We spent the weekend telling the family. My parents were very happy because Rudi was so happy. Oma had more to say, but in the end she too, was happy. Elaine and Horst were thrilled. Heinz and Gunther were so tied up in their own lives; they really didn't seem to care. The joke was this baby came with a guarantee. It was definitely a girl, and if for any reason we were wrong, it could go back. If we were right and it was a girl, I could get my tubes cut and tied in two knots and three bows.

My parents moved, and I was miserable. By the end of April, I was well on my way to not being able to hide the fact that I was very pregnant. I had put on twenty pounds by then, and the people at my work definitely knew. I thought I would work as long as I could. We did as much work on the Sugar Shack as we had wanted to do, but the house would be too small for the family when the baby came, so Rudi suggested we put it up for sale. He thought that we could sell it for a fair profit and move to Nova Scotia before the baby was born. I was ecstatic and took him up on the offer without hesitating. I knew it would be hard on him to be away from his family, but he said that it didn't matter. It was harder seeing me miss my family so much.

Chapter 5

By the Sea

The house sold so fast; the same day we put up the For Sale sign. We were to move out by June 1st. We had made a good profit considering how long we had lived in the house. By the time everything was paid, we had a profit of $6,000. Rudi had suggested we move all the furniture down East with a moving van. There would still be lots left over to put down on a house when we got there.

We had a hard time telling everyone we were leaving. It was really bittersweet.

Oma was beyond upset when she found out and Elaine was devastated. We agreed to keep in touch all the time but we both knew it wouldn't be the same. We had planned for her and the girls to visit us right after the baby was born but the chances of that were very slim and we both knew it. Going to the Maritimes from Winnipeg was a very expensive trip.

My parents were still living in an apartment in Dartmouth. There was an apartment down the hall from them that would be empty on the first of June. Rudi sent the money to put down for the first month's rent and damage deposit. We thought we would stay there for one month–long enough to find a house to buy.

After all the tearful goodbyes, we left on June 7th, early in the morning. It was so hot and humid. I was really "toughing it out" and didn't like the curved roads and rocks in Ontario. We drove about seven hours the first day, but the boys were so hot in the backseat, we pulled over at a campsite a bit early. It took Rudi a good hour to set up the trailer, but it was sure worth it when it was up. The boys slept on the double bed on one side, and Rudi and I on the other. We carried their toys and tricycles in the trailer so they could play while we put up the tent. The plan worked well, but it was still just too hot and I was just too pregnant.

The next morning, Rudi brought the tent down. It was a lot faster bringing it down than putting it up. I felt so sorry for him, driving all those hours and then having to put the tent up. He seemed to be really enjoying it. Up to that point he had never been east of Manitoba.

The second morning, after we had been on the road for about two hours, I turned to see what was happening in the back seat. It seemed way too quiet back there. The boys were sound asleep, which was very unusual for them that early in the day. The temperature was already about eighty degrees, and it wasn't even noon yet. The sun was shining in the window directly on them and it looked like there were red blotches all over their faces. I was worried because we were still a couple of hours before North Bay, Ontario, the next closest city with a hospital. I had lived in North Bay for four years on the Air Force Base when I was younger so had a peace of mind that I at least knew how to find my way around.

When we got to the emergency entrance of the hospital, Rudi didn't even wait to park the car. He just pulled up to the doors and we took them in. The boys didn't wake up. We were so afraid it was heat stroke.

The doctor examined the two of them right away and his diagnosis was they had the measles. I had visualized us sitting at the hospital for the next ten days while the boys were recovering when the doctor came to talk to us. He had said they were over the worst part and we could continue on our trip if we covered the back windows with towels to keep the sun from shining directly on them. We did exactly that and left the front windows rolled all the way down so they would have a breeze blowing on them.

By day three, we were getting exhausted. I could see that Rudi was having a problem putting up the trailer that night. I suggested it was such a nice campground, that we just stay for a whole day there and take a breather from the highway. He just wanted to keep going. I was having a problem sitting for so many hours in the car, and the heat was really playing hard on me.

On day 4 the boys were still very blotchy, but at least they were staying awake a little longer in the daytime. The temperature was still really high, and it became more humid the further east we went.

We figured we would arrive in Dartmouth the next day in time for supper. We stopped driving at four that afternoon and pulled into a really nice campsite. It was so hilly, unlike Manitoba. Rudi loved it. I kept joking that I could smell the salt ocean air, and I could hear it chewing away at the Cougar. That car would be a showpiece in Dartmouth. With the salt air in the Maritimes, vehicles can't live to be the age of the Cougar because they would have dissolved already.

The next morning we started off early, knowing it was our last day of driving. We left early enough that we should have hit Dartmouth about three in the afternoon. We were on the road for about two hours when we hit a really thick fog. We were in a city, but from the map I couldn't figure out which city. The fog was so thick; we could only see the back of the vehicle driving in front of us. We came to an intersection, and I was going to ask the people beside us what city we were in but thought that would sound stupid. I saw a sign on the side of the street but couldn't make out what it said. Rudi stopped for a red light, so I got out and went to read the sign. I was blown away by what it said. I got back in the car and told him to make a left turn. He asked what the sign said, so I told him, "The Angus L. MacDonald Bridge."

He said, "Okay, whatever that is," and laughed. He turned left like I had said and then asked if I knew where we were.

I told him, "We are here."

He asked, "Where is here?"

I replied, "We are in Dartmouth."

He laughed and said, "Yeah right, so you don't know where we are in other words."

I thought, fine, I would show him. We went down a couple of blocks and I told him to make a left turn. After a couple of more blocks, I said to turn right. That led him right into the parking lot of my parent's apartment block. He was astonished and so was I.

He asked, "How did we end up here?"

I told him that I had no idea, but I really didn't care. We had now finished the trip.

The boys were so thrilled when we knocked on the door of my parents' apartment and their Grandpa answered. My mom and dad were so happy to see us. Apparently the moving van had arrived before we did, so our apartment was already set up and the beds had even been made. My mom said that she didn't unpack all the dishes because she didn't think we would be living there that long.

The girls were up and watching television. They were already eight and ten years old. Thelma, the older of the two, was always very warm and close to me, but Estella was a distant sort of girl who never allowed herself to become too close to anyone. I never did know why. The same parents raised us.

Whenever I think of Estella growing up, I always think of her second birthday. We lived in a house in Winnipeg, where the kitchen was added on years after the house was built. We had to keep an electric heater plugged in during the winter because the floor was always so cold. Estella was standing in the kitchen with me. She was wearing a long red flannelette nightgown. She had really long dark brown hair and was as cute as could be. My other sister, Thelma, had long very blonde hair and was adorable.

This one night, Estella asked me if she could have a piece of her birthday cake. While I was cutting it, she started to scream. I thought she was just being spoiled because I wasn't cutting it fast enough. I was fourteen years old at the time. When I turned around to tell her to wait a minute, she was a standing ball of flame. Her nightgown had gotten drawn in by the heater and started on fire. In a split second, I started to scream for my parents. I picked her up and threw her across the dining room rug. As she rolled, the flames went out. My parents rushed her to the hospital. She was really lucky; she had a burn on her stomach and lost some of her long hair, but that was all.

We unloaded the car and trailer while the boys definitely made up for lost time. They were over the worst of the measles and were being their energetic selves again. Rudi and I just relaxed for the day and thought we would start looking at houses in a couple of days.

McFarlane Construction hired Rudi right away for painting. I think they were the only Construction Company in Dartmouth, certainly the biggest anyway. Mr. McFarlane always flew in his helicopter to check out the jobs.

The second day there, we went to visit my Aunt Joan, Uncle Denny, and my cousins Steven and Wanda. They were living right around the corner from us, but then Dartmouth was so small that everything was right around the corner. We had lots of relatives living in Dartmouth.

My mother was originally from Halifax. She was an only child and was raised in Dartmouth. My grandfather was a house builder and still today, in Dartmouth, there are a lot of houses around that he built. My grandmother died when we were living in North Bay, Ontario. Since we traveled so much when I was younger, I never really got to know her well.

I found a doctor as soon as we moved to Dartmouth. I was so pregnant that I thought it better I shouldn't wait. I had a standing appointment every Thursday at nine-thirty. I had gained almost forty pounds. How could that be? I felt like I was always in a sauna sweating. It wasn't only the hot weather that was bad, but the humidity, which I found to be so brutal.

We found a house. It was supposed to be torn down, not because there was anything wrong with it, but all the houses on the street were being torn down unless their owners were willing to fix them up. It was the property that was wanted. Across the street from the house, there was a huge duck pond and park. What a great view from the front. It was a huge two story Victorian house with a separate suite upstairs and a full house downstairs with formal living room, dining room, three regular sized bedrooms and a master bedroom with a full bath. The master bedroom had a full sized fireplace. It was just like you see in the movies. The upstairs had its own entrance, and was another full sized three-bedroom suite. The set-up was fantastic. It really needed a lot of painting and new floors.

Rudi suggested we put in a low offer. If we got it, he could fix up the downstairs before the baby was born, and we could move in. My parents said that they would rent the upstairs from us. We really low-balled the offer and it was accepted on condition we had a certain amount of time to fix it up.

Possession date was right away, so Rudi started to paint. In the master bedroom where the fireplace was, he stuccoed the feature wall. All the ceilings had Victorian moldings. It must have been quite the house when it was built. He replaced all the carpet in the house and put a new kitchen floor in both upstairs and down. He was more concerned with getting our place done first, before the baby was born, than anything else. We were running out of time. Considering the baby was due any day, the pressure was on. He didn't have to replace the floor in the bathroom because it was the old style hexagonal ceramic tile and I loved it just the way it was. It had a huge bathtub with the big tiger feet on the bottom.

Rudi was working all day at work, coming back and eating supper, then going right to the house to work–sometimes until midnight. He was so glad when the weekend came and I still wasn't in labour because he knew he could get it done by Sunday. Then he decided to apply texture to all of the ceilings in the house. He got his brother Heinz to send some texture along with the hopper and gun. The compressor he could rent. Then we found out that no houses in Halifax or Dartmouth had textured ceilings. Since that was his specialty, he decided after the baby was born, he could start to do side jobs texturing ceilings. He could use ours as a sample for people to see.

We moved in on August 15th, and Rudi started to renovate the upstairs after work in the evenings. He seemed much more content when he could keep coming downstairs for coffee breaks and was close by–in case I ever decided to go into labour.

I kept going to the doctor every Thursday. They seemed so primitive in Halifax, I don't think they believed in inducing labour. I was two hundred and ten pounds and decided I was just fat and wasn't having a baby after all. My Thursday, August 28th appointment was a real eye opener. The doctor was feeling my stomach and said, "Oh my, this could be the reason you are so late and so big. There are two heads here. You are having twins!" He told me I was almost ready to deliver and to just be a bit more patient.

I left and cried all the way back. As I was driving over the bridge to Dartmouth, I could see the McFarlane Helicopter taking off a couple of blocks away. I knew Rudi would be just starting his lunch hour, so I thought I would go and break the news to him.

We had already done the baby's room. Rudi pacified me and did it in pink. We had bought the matching dresser and crib, change table and all the bedding, which I had not opened. It would be easy for Rudi to change the colour of the room, and if need be, I would take back the bedding. I was quite confident that I was having a girl, but then I realized I now had two shots at it. It didn't make me feel any better. J.J. was just going on three years old in a couple of months. P.J. was just turning two a couple weeks before J.J. turned three, and now they were telling me that we would have two babies. Thank God J.J. and P.J. were off the bottle and out of diapers. I was told you were not given more than you could handle in life.

When I turned the corner to the construction site, Rudi was just sitting down on a board opening his lunch pail. He jumped up and dropped his lunch pail on the ground when he saw the car. He thought I was in labour. I was still crying and told him I just came from the doctor and what he had said about twins. He burst out laughing. I didn't think it was very funny. He continued laughing nervously when I told him we would have four kids. He didn't care though. He said, "So we will just get a bigger house."

I told him, "Now we have to get another crib."

By Thursday morning (September 4, 1975), I was completely fed up. I had to go to my usual Doctor's appointment. He said that they wanted to run some tests to find out why these babies weren't making an appearance. He said that he had to be sure there was enough room for them to come out. Maybe the birth canal was too small. My thought was, "Sure, and they were just going to grow up inside of me." That was how it felt. I knew I was big when the Maternity clothes didn't fit anymore. I had the tests done and grabbed a bite to eat while I was waiting for the results.

The doctor came back at two o'clock and said to me that it was all figured out. I was not having twins. For a moment, I was disappointed, then frustrated. Where did the second baby go? He said that he wasn't feeling two heads like he had thought. The tests showed it was the head and the bum, but wrong side up. That is why he made the mistake.

I didn't understand. He explained the baby was breech, coming feet first. There was enough room for me to have natural childbirth. He told me to go run around the block a few times, as I was so close. It was sure to get the ball rolling.

Rudi arrived home from work, and I let him know we were only having one baby, one BIG baby. I couldn't tell if he was disappointed. I think he was already at the stage I was; it didn't matter what it was, or how many there were. Just let it be born.

Mom and dad lived upstairs now so life had gotten easier. We didn't have very far to go to take the boys when I went into labour. Mom could just come downstairs. Rudi wanted to finish the front landing and up the stairs that night. That was all he had left to do except both kitchens. He figured maybe the baby was waiting for him to finish.

Mom asked me if I felt like going shopping. She said that we could buy more wool. I had already crocheted a couple of bunting bags and she had done blankets, but I knew she was just trying to keep me busy. I said, "Sure," and we went to Woolworth's.

I was pushing the cart and Mom was showing me different coloured wool, asking what I thought. We chose some shades of pink and started over to the donut counter to get some donuts to bring home. All of a sudden I felt like I couldn't stand anymore, like I was suddenly bottom heavy. I was leaning on the cart and said to my mom that I thought we should go home after we got the donuts. She asked if I was having pains, but I wasn't feeling anything.

After having the two boys, I knew what being in labour was like, but this wasn't it. After we got home the feeling didn't change but of course Rudi panicked and phoned the hospital. They strongly suggested he get me there immediately because with this being the third birth for me, it could come fast. He was insisting I get in the car but I really didn't want to sit in the hospital for a long time waiting and I still wasn't having pains. Besides, I wanted to have tea and a donut. My mom handed me a cup of tea. Rudi grabbed a donut, and my hand. He said, "We are leaving NOW!" I had never seen him this determined so I didn't argue.

He was driving fine but turned down a one-way street going the wrong way. I was surprised and started to laugh because I knew he had done this drive many times trying to figure out how much time he needed to get to the hospital and to make sure he knew the way. We finally got there and I related that I was still having no pain. They put me in a room and examined me and told me that I was not ready yet. They told Rudi that they were going to keep me and he should go home, get some sleep, and then come back in the morning. There was no way he was going anywhere and sat in a big Lazy-Boy chair, which was beside the bed. I fell asleep right away and woke up at two in the morning. I quietly went into the bathroom so I wouldn't wake Rudi up. All hell broke loose! I could barely stand up; the pain was so bad. I thought to myself, "Now this is labour!" I woke Rudi up and he went running to get the nurse. The doctor came and stated that I was definitely in labour. He had the nurse hook me up to a machine, which was giving the baby's heart rate and mine, and to a scale that was telling how hard the contractions were. I told the doctor I didn't need a machine to tell how hard the contractions were, I could without doubt tell them myself. The contractions were coming hard and fast. Every time I had one, Rudi would say, "Wow, look at that needle climbing." I didn't have to, I had my own gauge of pain.

Suddenly, I had this urge to push. When I told the nurse, she laughed and said, "No, you are just feeling that way, it is not time yet." So I showed her how wrong she was and on the next contraction, I pushed. She told me to stop, and I told her there was something hitting the top of my leg.

She exclaimed, "It is the baby's foot!" The baby was actually kicking me! She then informed me that she didn't think I would make it to the delivery room and ran to get the doctor. The nurse reappeared a minute later with the stretcher to move me. Rudi was just staring and was as white as a sheet. I was sure he was going to pass out.

I got on the stretcher and she started to run with me. The stretcher kept hitting the side of the door and the walls. I was yelling, "My husband is coming in with me!"

"This is 'breech' and they won't let him in." She exclaimed.

I told her I wasn't having the baby unless he was there. She started to laugh.

We got in the delivery room and the doctor was standing and waiting for us. He looked at the baby's foot and laughed as he said, "The kid is in a hurry and decided to run out." A nurse came and stood beside my head and another Doctor came in–all green with the facemask on–and took my hand on the other side. He was rubbing my hand, and I pulled it away.

He said, "It's okay."

It was Rudi. I didn't even recognize him.

"The foot is out of the birth canal," the doctor said, "but the other leg is braced inside, and it is stopping the baby from coming out." He said that he had to reach up inside and pull the other leg into the birth canal. I still can't understand how that is possible. It's enough to push a baby out of that small opening, but when a doctor is going in with his hand and arm; that is inhuman. He did it, and I screamed my head off. After that it was easy. The baby slid out with one push. I hurt so much and was sure I would die, but when that Doctor said to me, "Congratulations it's a girl," all was forgiven and forgotten. The baby was a girl.

She was already named before she was born. At least ten years before she was born, when I was still quite young, I watched the movie, *Tammy and the Millionaire* and said that when I grow up and have a girl, her name will be Tammy. I never forgot that and never changed my mind.

We were able to phone home from the delivery room, and my parents were thrilled they had their first granddaughter. We called Rudi's mother, but there was no answer. We decided to name Tammy, Tammy Jean. The second name of Jean ran through my family in girls. My mother was Thelma Jean, and I was Patti Jean. So I decided to keep it going. Rudi's mother really wanted us to name the baby after her, but her name was Frieda. I just couldn't bring myself to doing that.

My parents came in and my dad said, "Tammy Jean, T.J."

I said, "No way, never." It was enough to keep J.J. and P.J. straight when I was mad at them. Add T.J., and it would have been hopeless.

As promised, three days after Tammy was born, I had my tubes cut and tied. The doctors really fought me on it right into the room before they put me out. I was only twenty years old, and the rule was twenty-five and three kids.

They kept saying to me, "What if your kids died in a fire? What if you divorced and remarried and that husband wanted to have kids?"

I told that guy he was warped, "I could never replace my kids if anything happened, and I definitely would not change my mind because of any '-what-ifs.'" I had three kids and that was enough. (Obviously, I could become pregnant just looking at 'IT.' The joke was to turn the light off before you get undressed, or I would get pregnant.) The Doctors finally figured out that I was determined and tied my tubes.

Five days later, we took Tammy home. It was pretty cold already for September, but it was due mostly to the damp air. It seemed to blow right through.

We started to plan a baptism right away, and with Rudi being Lutheran, we went to the Lutheran Church. I asked if the boys could be re-baptized too, because they had been baptized in the United Church previously. The pastor was really good about it and said that would be okay.

My brother, Grant, and his wife, Louise were flying down for a visit, so I phoned and asked if they would be Tammy's Godparents. They said absolutely. They didn't have any kids yet. We phoned Elaine and Horst and asked them to be P.J.'s Godparents. They were very pleased. Uncle Denny and Aunt Joan said that they would love to be J.J.'s Godparents. Elaine and Horst couldn't come for the christening, so we asked my brother Jimmy and his girl-friend Janet to stand in for them. We planned to have it all on a Saturday morning and then lunch back at our house. During the next few days, I started to bake pies, cakes and cookies to get ready for the lunch.

One morning I was baking and the pastor showed up to visit just when I was in the middle of it. I left everything as it was and took him into the living room to talk. The boys were drawing at the kitchen table, so I just left them while Tammy slept. We talked for about five minutes, and I offered him a coffee. I really wanted to check on the boys. When I walked into the kitchen, I couldn't believe what I was seeing. Both J.J. and P.J. were sitting on the floor, pure white along with the rest of the kitchen. They had gotten into my flour canister and were throwing it up in the air. I went back to the living room and told the pastor that I would have to take back my offer for coffee and cut our meeting short. When he came through the kitchen to leave, he started laughing and offered to help. I didn't think it was very funny. I was very embarrassed. Of course, at that moment, Tammy started to cry. I looked at the pastor and said, "Just one minute." I ran and got Tammy, brought her back out and handed her to the pastor. I said, "You can tend to her while I handle these two." He was great. He played with her. I cleaned up the boys and the kitchen, and we chatted the whole time.

October came and so did Grant (my older brother) and Louise. My sister-in-law, Louise, was a little harsh at times, but I loved her very dearly. She was a great person, a real person who told it like it was, even though sometimes we didn't want to hear it. Grant was four years older than me and was definitely my big brother. My other brother, Jimmy, was two years younger than me. When we were growing up as Air Force brats, we were transferred around a lot and had to leave friends, but we always had each other. This all happened before my sisters were born–chocolates in Germany, tulips in Holland, seeing the Bobbies in England and the cafes in France. That was all part of our life that my two sisters had only seen in movies or read in books.

Rudi had been working side jobs, texturing ceilings in Dartmouth. He did about three ceilings a week. Eventually, when it got really busy, he would quit with McFarlane and go on his own. That was the plan anyway.

The Saturday finally came for the kids to be baptized. Tammy had a gorgeous christening gown, and the boys were dressed in dress pants and vests. Were they ever handsome! I bought them new black leather dress shoes. It was so nice to have so many of my family there.

The front of the church had a table with all kinds of ornament peppers, squash etc. because it was so close to Thanksgiving. P.J and J.J. went running to the front of the church to play with the ornaments. They were getting to be a real handful. J.J. would lead and P.J. would follow. I wasn't too worried though; the pastor had already seen them at their worst. We managed to get control over them, and I was glad it was done. It gave me a sense of peace for some reason to know God was in their lives. We had planned on the boys getting into Sunday School at that church and we were going to attend the mass.

We all went back to our house and had lunch. When I went into the bedroom to change Tammy out of her gown, I noticed the ceiling looked like it had sprung a leak. It was now yellow in some spots. When I showed Rudi, he looked at the other ceilings. A couple of them looked the same. He was surprised but said he would paint them with oil paint the next day.

On Sunday, we got up and went to church. When we came home, the boys went over to the Lake with Grandpa again to feed the ducks. I was surprised to see Rudi in his paint clothes. He was actually going to paint the ceilings right away. He said that it was really bothering him as to why this was happening. When he was painting, the comparison was shocking. They were far worse than we originally thought. One of the ceilings he redid was in the master bedroom and after he had finished, the difference in the ceiling and the stucco wall was frightening. He now had to redo that too.

The next day at work, he had asked his boss, very nonchalantly, why is it no one in Dartmouth or Halifax has stucco or textured ceilings? With the answer he got, he wished he didn't wait so long to ask the question. His boss explained, "The texture turns yellow after a short time because of the salty ocean air. After it turns yellow, it can actually break down and make a heck of a mess. There is a new one being tested right now but it comes from the States and is very expensive." Rudi was ill. When he came home and told me, he didn't know what to do—our own house and so many others. I could see he was in a real state.

I suggested we go home. He was surprised and said, "Home?"

I said, "Winnipeg is really my home and I have been quite homesick since I got here. I have no problem if you want to go home." I told him that I would feel a real loss without my parents around, but maybe it was just time for me to grow up.

At first he said, "No," but then he wanted to go and talk to my parents about it.

When he told them, my dad's reply was, "Ouch, what a shame." He was talking about the ceilings only.

When I said that I wanted to go back to Winnipeg, my parents were obviously upset but stood by us and said it probably was the best thing considering the circumstances.

The time spent out there was pretty short but not so sweet. We all decided Tammy was too young to make a five-day drive. Grant and Louise were flying back to Calgary and had a stopover in Winnipeg on October 31st, which was only two weeks away. If I could get on the same plane as them, they could take P.J., and I could take Tammy. That way, it wouldn't cost anything for those two to fly. Rudi would drive back with J.J, pulling a U-haul with all of our furniture.

When we phoned Elaine and Horst and told them we were coming home, they were so excited. They said I could stay at their house with the kids when I got back until Rudi got there, then we could find a place to live. Horst offered to fly out to Dartmouth to help Rudi drive with J.J. and the furniture. We had some money saved. It would be enough to do it.

We got a phone call from Rudi's mom, saying the duplex next door to her had a small suite available. It was too small for us, but she said it would be big enough for her alone. If she moved into that suite, we could take hers, as it was a three-bedroom unit. Neither of us wanted to live in the north-end of the city. The houses were really old and it wasn't a good area for the kids, but we said, "Yes," for now. It would be a place to move to right away until we could get back on our feet and find a decent place.

Everything was going according to plan. There were a lot of tears at the airport. P.J. didn't want to leave J.J. behind, and J.J. wanted to keep P.J. with him. It became so bad, that Rudi suggested he take both boys with him. I insisted we do it as planned, and the tears would eventually dry up. I think I was really talking to myself. I was so emotional when I said good-bye to my mother. She was such a big help with the kids. My dad was so close to the boys. He found it hard but was kept occupied, controlling J.J. while we walked away. My sisters were more upset that the kids were leaving, as they still really didn't know me that well. Jimmy was out with his girlfriend Janet, being the age where, for a guy, we all know what led the priorities.

When I arrived in Winnipeg, Elaine met us at the airport. It was so good to see her, but then I had to say good-bye to Grant and Louise. At least with them, it was only a one-day drive to go to see them. There was more hope in that, than thinking of a five-day drive to visit my parents. Elaine said that she was just at the airport an hour before, dropping off Horst to fly to meet Rudi. It really was good to be home. When we arrived back at Elaine's house, we met a pizza delivery guy at the door. I laughed because every time I talked to her on the phone, I said that I really missed the Gondola Pizza the most. They didn't have pizza delivery in Dartmouth. She had arranged for them to deliver at the time she figured we would be home. I sat and indulged in the pizza, and Elaine sat playing with P.J. and admiring Tammy. Tammy was really a beautiful baby. My favourite line lately was, "I got my girl."

Early the next morning, Elaine came and woke me up. She said that Rudi was on the phone. There was a problem. When I took the phone, Rudi said that they blew the motor on the car. They were in North Bay, Ontario. He said that they had it towed in and were waiting for the place to open to find out what the damage would be. I asked how J.J. was. He said the only thing that hasn't been a problem was having J.J. with them. He assured me that he would phone me back as soon as he knew anything. I waited for three hours before he finally called again. He explained that a rod went through the block. For all I knew about cars at that time, I could have answered, "Well take it out and continue on." I thought it better if I didn't. Rudi was tired and had no sense of humour left. It was going to take three days and $1800 to fix it. His suggestion was for them to take a bus home, then we would go back to get the car and furniture and I could help him do the driving. I could tell by the way he said it that he really had enough of his brother's company.

After a thirty-two hour bus ride (I couldn't imagine Rudi on a Greyhound Bus, but with Horst, I never thought it was possible.), Rudi and Horst were like bears. They both showered and went to bed. J.J. was full of energy and was so happy to see P.J.

We went back by train to North Bay to get the car. The trip was over thirty hours of sitting up in the coach. When I got up to go to the washroom, I found a book that was supposed to be a good story. It was called *The Catcher in the Rye*. To alleviate the boredom of traveling on a train, I figured we could read this book. Rudi wasn't a reader. I think because he was raised to be very German, he had a problem with the confusion of reading English. It was either that or he just didn't like to read. So, I read the book to him. We got to be completely hooked on it. We read it all the way to North Bay, picked up the car and trailer and read it most of the way back until it was finished. All I really remember about the book now, is the question, "Where did the ducks go when the water freezes?" I wasn't in Dartmouth long enough to find out what happened to the ducks.

Chapter 6

HOME AGAIN

We finally arrived back in Winnipeg and unloaded all the furniture in the duplex. The kids came back home and I got them settled in bed. I really didn't feel too comfortable with the setup as our bedroom was on the main level while the boys had to sleep in a bedroom that had been built in the basement. We both agreed that it wouldn't be this way for very long. Rudi was going back to work for the family painting company right away, and I was going to look for work. Rudi still insisted he wanted me to stay home, but I got him to agree that at least I get a job to pay off the loan and put a down payment on a house. Then we could talk about me staying home. He agreed only because he wanted to get another place to live as soon as possible.

I got a job almost right away at Safeway Grocery Store as a cashier. The pay was great because I took the evening shift and Saturdays so Rudi could be home to look after the kids while I worked.

The boys seemed to be getting more and more hyper. One morning, it was still dark outside; P.J. came running into our bedroom, yelling something about a fire. I could smell something burning. It was my biggest fear in that house, as it was so old and the boys slept downstairs. We jumped out of bed and went into the kitchen. There was smoke pouring out of the oven. J.J. was just standing there. P.J. said, "J.J. turned on the oven." When he saw the fire inside (the coil turning red), he ran and got his Fisher Price Fire-Engine with all the men on it and threw them in the oven to put the fire out. Rudi turned the oven off and when he opened the door, there was five blobs melted on the bottom—what used to be firemen and one very warped fire truck.

Rudi started his own painting company. I was told it was because there was more drinking with his brothers than working. He picked up a few contracts out of town—lots of apartments in Flin Flon and The Pas. He would have to go for four or five days at a time. I hated it, but it was still work. When he would go, I would let the boys sleep upstairs in the living room. I didn't like staying home alone as it was, and I was afraid of not being able to hear them during the night.

Later that year, Rudi had to go back to Flin Flon. It was the usual five-day trip. He was already gone for three days, and I was getting pretty tired. His mother came over and looked after the kids while I went to work. I got home around nine. She had put the boys to bed downstairs in the basement. When I came in, the people upstairs had just gotten home with their new baby. They had lived there for a long time, and we got to know them quite well. I talked to them for a while; then went to bed. The boys came upstairs as soon as I got into bed and asked if they could sleep on the couch. I made a bed for them on the couch, and I don't think my head hit the pillow when I fell asleep.

At about four in the morning, I woke up and smelled smoke. I thought maybe Rudi had come back early and was in the kitchen, smoking. I got out of bed and went to the kitchen; then I saw smoke pouring out from under the basement door. Not thinking straight, I quickly opened the door and was thrown back by smoke and flames. I couldn't even see down the stairs, and I couldn't get the door closed again because it was too hot. I ran in the bedroom to get Tammy out of the crib, then to the living room to get the boys. They both got up crying and in their pajamas; we ran out the door to the front veranda.

I went back in to grab blankets for the kids and to phone the fire department, but when I got to the front door, I couldn't see anything because of the smoke. I looked at the stairs, which led to the neighbours and knew it was their only way out unless they went out a window. There were flames coming up through the staircase, and I started to scream and pound on the wall to wake them up. All three kids were crying on the veranda, but I had to keep trying to wake up the neighbours. Finally John opened the door, looked down the staircase, and said, "Oh my God." I yelled to him that I didn't think the stairs were safe to come down and to go out the back kitchen window. Someone must have phoned the fire department because at that moment I heard sirens. A couple of minutes later, six firemen were trashing the house with axes and putting out the fire. (All I could think about was, "What if the boys were still asleep in the basement?")

Apparently, it didn't take long to put the fire out or to figure out what caused the fire. There were paint rags left on the landing going down the stairs. They started on fire and quickly went to the paint cans, which were stored close by.

The neighbours did get out the kitchen window. The fire department had arrived just in time to help them out. They took the baby and went to their parents' house.

Someone had gotten hold of Rudi, so he phoned his mom and said he was leaving right away and for us to stay there until he got back.

When the firemen walked away, there was burnt furniture, rags and boxes all over the front lawn and in the veranda. They told me that we wouldn't be able to move back in and that we should find a place to live. I just sat at my mother-in-law's with the kids and didn't go back to the house until Rudi came. The fire department told us we could go in and get clothes, but they warned me that although not much actually burned, there was major smoke damage. They came back with some large fans to blow out some of the smoke.

By the time Rudi got back, I had already gotten the newspaper and marked out different places for rent.

Out of all the phone calls, there was only one decent place for rent. It was a side-by-side. The rent was reasonable enough, and we could move in the next day if we wanted.

Rudi got back just after supper. He was sick to find out that the fire was caused by paint and rags. He said he was sure he threw away all the rags. I was too. It wasn't like him to leave things like that lying around.

The side by side was a split-level. When you walk in the front door, you could go upstairs or downstairs. Going upstairs was the living room, dining room, kitchen, master bedroom, bathroom, and another small bedroom, which would be Tammy's room. Downstairs was a large rec room and bedroom. That would be the boys' room. The rec room had built in benches all the way around with tables built in between. It would make a great playroom for the kids. The house was really nothing special but far better than the one we had just left.

We received a call from my parents, saying that they had decided to move back out west. I really think that they realized the same as we did, Nova Scotia was a beautiful place to visit, but the economy just wasn't growing. It was hard to make a living, unless you already lived there all your life. I think too, that my parents were so used to moving around every couple of years in the Air Force that they just got itchy feet again. They found it hard to settle in one place. Also, the girls were getting older, Thelma was already thirteen and Estella was eleven. Grant and Jimmy were living in Calgary already. They had lots of good reasons to move west. They found an apartment on Portage Avenue when they moved here. It was great to have them back - family dinners every Sunday–and the kids loved having them around. The best thing was having them here for Christmas again.

My dad had suggested at Christmastime that since he still had some benefits with the Air Force, there was a gymnastics program every Saturday morning at the Rec Centre. He said that J.J, being so full of energy, should sign up for the program. He was so flexible; he could fold himself up into a little ball. We agreed, and so every Saturday, we met my parents at the Rec Centre. The coach said that J.J. was "a natural." P.J. just sat and watched. It was now time for the boys to start to have their own personalities, and P.J. was not the gymnastic type.

Rudi got P.J. started in skating lessons. He was going to be the little "star hockey player."

My parents sold the house in Dartmouth for us before they left. It was really hard to sell, so when a lawyer in Halifax offered a really low amount, we grabbed it. We didn't make any money on it, but at least it was one less payment we would have to make and one less responsibility for us to think about. It also gave us more flexibility to buy a house in Winnipeg.

Rudi really wasn't the "fix-it" type of person. He could work miracles with houses, but not so much with cars. That is why, at Christmastime that year, I was so surprised when I opened my big gift from Rudi. Everyone had finished opening their gifts when Rudi said, "There is one more," and pointed into the Christmas tree. There sat one of those velvet boxes, which every woman wants to find in her Christmas tree. I slowly opened it waiting to find a shiny ring or bracelet, but to my surprise, it wasn't gold. It was silver, two shiny silver keys. It was quite obvious to me that they were a car ignition and a door key. I couldn't believe it. He bought me my own car. I was so excited.

He said, "Now wait, it is in the garage, but it comes with a letter." Oh no, I thought, not conditions on my new car. The note was folded under the keys.

It was a promissory note, which read, "Dear Pat, this car comes with the promise that it will be drivable and look presentable by May 14th, Mother's Day next year. Love, Rudi."

After I finished reading it, he said, "Okay, now you can go in the garage and look at your car." I was afraid to with a note like that.

I threw my coat on over my housecoat and went outside. It was brutally cold. Rudi opened the overhead door of the garage and, yes, there sat a car. I was shocked. It was a 1969 Oldsmobile Cutlass CONVERTIBLE, my dream car. But, the top was shredded, the interior was a disaster, and the body had holes all over it. It had a motor, but it was lying on the ground beside the car. The first thing I thought was, "There was no hope." Rudi had never let me down up to that point, so I took the promissory note back in the house and while laughing, said, "This note is signed, and on Monday, I am going to put it in the safety deposit box at the bank. Less than six months to keep your promise? You had better put on your long underwear; it is really cold in that garage." I could see the fear in his face. His good intentions now had to be reality.

When I went back to work after Christmas, I told my boss, Butch about my car. He was in awe and said that he and his brother, Murray, could rebuild the motor for a good price. I relayed this to Rudi, and we drove over to Butch's to meet with the two of them to discuss what a "good price" would be. Butch lived on the outskirts of the city. Murray, his wife Jan and two children lived in one house, and Butch and his wife lived in another house close by. Butch and his wife had just put an addition on their house and were in the starting stages of drywall and painting. Both brothers shared a huge shop in the back where they could work on cars. It was a hobby for both of them. Murray was a police officer and his wife was a nurse at Health Sciences Centre.

We had spent most of the evening visiting with them. They were really nice people. The outcome was to put a brand new engine in the convertible. The biggest motor the car could take would cost close to $2,600; I choked. It would come down to a choice of the motor or a new house. I could see it coming.

Murray just laughed and said, "Hang on, I'm not finished, I've got an offer you can't refuse. If Rudi were to paint my house inside and Butch's house inside, you would only have to pay for the materials and parts."

For the next couple of months, we spent a lot of time with Butch and Murray while they worked on the car. Rudi started to price new convertible tops, and I had to decide what colour I wanted the car and the new top to be. The original colour of the car was a deep gold, and I wanted to stay close to the original, so I picked a bronzy brown. The interior was done for a decent price at an upholsterer whom Rudi's family knew. We ordered a white top. With all the wheeling and dealing, we managed to get the cost of finishing the car to its finest for a total of $2,800.

We agreed that we wouldn't touch our house savings, so Rudi had to take on side jobs to pay the bill. He had to work a couple of evenings a week and sometimes on weekends. He picked up a side job in Steinbach, painting a dental clinic for Ron and Carol's nephew. Ron and Carol were friends of my family for years and years. I used to babysit their kids when I was in my teens. From that job, he found another one in Steinbach, painting a house for a new doctor who had just moved out there. Rudi said that when those jobs were done, it would be enough to pay for the car.

Mother's Day was coming soon and the weather was getting warmer. Rudi was determined to have the car done on time. I told him not to push it. It was well on its way to being completed, and I was so excited. But, he didn't have to have it finished by exactly Mother's Day. By the time he finished the dental clinic, the car was completely done except for the new top. The new top was put on, but we had to pay the bill before we could take the car home. Painting the doctor's house would finish paying the bill. There was one week left to Mother's Day, and Rudi was going to Steinbach every evening after work to try to finish.

Chapter 7

A Life-Shattering Blow

On the Saturday, Rudi went to try to finish the house. He got back at seven o'clock in the evening and said that he tried, but he was just too tired. He only had about three hours of work left, so he would drop us off at my mother's for Mother's Day, just after lunch, then go and finish. He would be back in time to have supper with us. Steinbach was about a forty-five minute drive from the city.

On Sunday Morning, May 14th, we went to church. That was our routine on Sundays. The kids had all gotten into the nursery program at the church. Being Mother's Day, the church was packed. Rudi drove us to my parents' house and changed into his paint clothes. My dad handed him a couple of sandwiches as he walked out the door, and Rudi reminded us that he would be back for supper. He asked for us to decide what we wanted from Kentucky Fried Chicken and he would pick it up when he got back.

The kids spent the afternoon occupying my sisters' time. They both loved having the kids around. Tammy was playing her usual game with my dad. Whenever he got up out of his recliner, she would run and jump up on the chair. She would be grinning from ear to ear when he came back because she "stole" his chair. She was almost three years old, and her hair was so blonde it was almost white, a mass of soft curls down to her shoulders.

Dad would say the same old thing to her, "Tummy, get out of my chair." (Tummy was his nickname for her).

Tammy would giggle until she was in hysterics and move over, pointing for him to sit on her lap. That's when dad would pick her up and put her on his lap. This game was played every time she saw her Grandpa.

The kids woke up and were getting pretty restless. It was a big apartment, but they wanted to go outside. I couldn't let them go out when we were at my parents' because they lived in a really big block on Portage Avenue, Winnipeg's busiest street.

Rudi phoned and said that he was just leaving and would be back in an hour.

I told the boys, "If you can play for another forty-five minutes, I will let you sit on the back steps with my sister to watch for Rudi." The back steps were right next to my parents' suite by the parking lot, so they could see when he pulled in. Every five minutes, they asked if it was time yet. So, a little while later, I got their jackets on. They were both dressed in blue jeans and runners with plaid shirts and brown spring jackets. The weather was starting to cool down as it was close to five o'clock.

I told them they could go and stand by the door to wait for my sisters to get their shoes on. Tammy started to cry because she wanted to go with the boys, but she got the usual line that she was just too young. My dad called from the living room to her that he needed help to get all the dishes out for supper. She went into a screaming tantrum, so I picked her up and took her in to see my dad. She was wiggling around so much; he was having a hard time holding her. He was also trying to talk to her over her screaming.

All of a sudden, Estella started yelling at the door that the boys weren't in the back where they were supposed to be. I grabbed Tammy from my dad and went running. She said that Thelma had gone to the front of the block, looking for them. I didn't stop. All I could think of was the front of the block, Portage Avenue. I ran down the halls, trying to get to the front door, still carrying Tammy. I finally got to the front door and pulled it open just as Thelma was running in.

She was crying and screaming, "J.J. got hit by a car." She was holding P.J.'s hand, and he was crying too.

I remember screaming, "Noooo!" and running out the door. There was a crowd of people on the sidewalk, and I just ran through them. Two people grabbed me and wouldn't let me go. I yelled that I was his mother. They told me that I should stay with them and wouldn't let go of me. I could see J.J. lying on the side of the road. On one side of him, there was a man kneeling, and on the other side, a lady. I couldn't see J.J's face. I yelled to him and struggled to get away from the people.

"Mommy is here J.J; it is going to be alright." The man turned around, and I saw that he was a priest. He then got up and came over, while another lady came and took my hand. The priest said that there was an ambulance on the way and that I should just stay with him. I told him to tell me that J.J. was alive.

The priest said, "He is breathing."

I don't remember too much of what was going on, but I do remember looking into the priest's eyes and saying, "Please ask God to not let J.J. die."

I thought that at the time, the priest had more pull with God than I did. I remember thinking, "Where there is breath, there is hope." The lady put her coat on me and started to take my pulse. I told her that I wasn't hurt, and she replied that she was a nurse.

I remember shivering and thinking it was so cold. Then I said, "Oh my God, I don't know where P.J. and Tammy are." My dad came over and said that the kids were in the house with my mom and not to worry about them; they were safe. Someone put his or her coat over J.J, but his feet were sticking out. There was only one shoe on his feet. Where was the ambulance? I looked up to see if the ambulance was coming. There were so many people and the cars were lined up so far away that I couldn't see. My dad was directing traffic out of the way so the ambulance would have room to get through.

I looked in the other direction and saw Rudi turning to park behind the block. I pulled away from the priest and the nurse and said, "That is my husband."

I went running to him, and when he looked at me, he said, "A little boy was hit, tell me the kids are in the house."

I told him that it was J.J.

He went running so fast, I couldn't keep up with him. The same priest and nurse again got a hold of me; I guess they came after me when I ran. A bunch of people tried to stop Rudi, but he was wild and pushed them off as he yelled, "I am his father." Rudi got to J.J. and knelt down. I could see his face. He started to cry. I screamed to him to tell me he is alive. Rudi took his hand and looked at me and shook his head, "Yes." Rudi then came to me and quietly said, "Stay here with them. You don't want to see him like this. He still has a pulse." He then went back, and I could see he was talking to J.J. through his tears. I listened and didn't fight to go anymore. I could hear the ambulance siren coming. My dad was still trying to make room for them to get through. I could see he was so frustrated with the people. I am sure at that point he could have picked up the cars and moved them himself.

The ambulance attendants put J.J. on the stretcher. I was let go and walked behind them as they were loading him into the ambulance. My dad came and said that the other kids were fine and could stay as long as they had to. I remember telling him to not to let them out. Rudi was holding my hand when one of the ambulance attendants said to the other, "This little guy isn't even going to make it to the Grace Hospital." I started to scream and sat on the road. When they turned around, someone said, "That is the mother." I don't remember what response the guy had, but I would bet from that day on he watched what he was saying on the job. The other attendant called for me to be put in the front of the ambulance. Rudi and my dad put me in the front and Rudi said that he was going to follow with the truck.

The sirens started and we were rolling. I kept looking back through the little opening.

The guy was doing a bunch of things, then yelled, "Turn off the siren, I can't hear him breathe." The driver didn't hear him. I started pushing buttons in the front, trying to find the siren. The driver asked what I was doing and started to panic.

I screamed, "Turn off the siren." He did and looked back to see what was going on. The attendant in the back told him what he had said. I asked if J.J. was breathing. I begged them, "Please don't let him die." I screamed at J.J,, "Mommy is so sorry; please don't die."

The attendant put a plastic thing in his mouth and down his throat, and then said, "Okay, he is breathing."

The Grace Hospital was only a few blocks from my parents' apartment. We were probably there in a matter of minutes, but everything seemed to be taking so long. I don't remember getting there or unloading the stretcher. I do remember standing in the emergency room with Rudi and my mother. The nurse said something to Rudi causing him to nod his head. Then another nurse came to give me a needle, which I really fought. Rudi held me, saying, "It's alright." I told him that they couldn't put me to sleep, J.J. needed me. Rudi said to me that I was in shock and they had to give me a sedative. He promised it wouldn't put me to sleep. I don't think the needle did anything for me except stop me from shivering.

The next thing I remember was that the same attendants were wheeling J.J. back out and the nurse was telling us that he had to be taken to the Children's Hospital, downtown. The attendant turned to a police officer standing there and said that he should take me with him. Apparently, they didn't think it was a good idea for me to go with the ambulance. The officer put me in the back of the police car, and my mother got in with me. Rudi said that he would follow.

I can't remember too much about the ride down, except that it was a long drive. I remember talking to the police officer and him handing me a package of DuMaurier cigarettes. I also remember talking to God and asking him to please don't let him die. I remember trying to make a deal with God. I promised to do different things if He would let J.J. live, but I can't remember what I promised. I remember standing in front of the Children's Hospital and refusing to go in because I was so afraid they would tell me J.J. was dead. I told Rudi, "As long as I stand outside, he's still alive."

One of the police officers went in and soon returned with a nurse. I put my hands over my ears and wouldn't look at them. I was so afraid. Rudi then pulled my hands off my ears and said, "He is alive." I then went in. They told us they had J.J. over at another building, doing CT Scans. He would be about a half an hour.

I told Rudi to take me to the chapel. He did, and my mom went to get us coffee. I talked so much to God. I felt He was listening to me from a great distance. I told Him I needed Him to come and show the doctors how to fix J.J. I told Him I was so sorry. I was so guilty that J.J. got hit. I was so sorry I wasn't there to stop him. I begged Him to forgive me and not to take J.J. away as punishment for what I had done. I was so afraid.

We went back to the emergency room where they put us in a room for families to wait. We were told that J.J. was taken to the Intensive Care Unit, and it would be a while before we could see him. There were a lot of doctors examining him. We were directed to the third floor family room for intensive care patients.

A police officer came in with a doctor while we were there and asked us some questions. I didn't even know what had happened. The police officer told us that it was a twenty-two year old girl who hit J.J. with her Datsun. All the traffic had stopped, but she had no brakes, so she had the choice, "To hit a metro bus or swerve and hit J.J." She swerved and hit J.J. J.J. flew about thirty feet, and since she still couldn't stop, she ran over him. I guess it was a good thing they had sedated me. I couldn't handle what was being told to me with a sedative, never mind if they hadn't given me one. He went on to say that J.J. saw her coming and put his hand out for her to stop. The doctor then said that is probably what broke his arm, but then she hit him in the head.

"Broken arm, I didn't even know he had a broken arm."

He said, "The head always bleeds so much, that is why there was so much blood around him."

They were wrong and I stopped them. I didn't want to hear anymore, I just couldn't. I was so guilty and so scared. I said to Rudi that there was no blood. I didn't see any blood. I told Rudi to tell them, "They have it wrong, tell them there was no blood." He was quiet and put his arm around me.

The doctor then said that J.J. was in a coma; there was a respirator breathing for him. He said that we could go in to see J.J., but he also wanted to prepare us for all the machines that were hooked up to him. I asked how long he would be unconscious.

Their reply was, "With a head injury, no one knows. We can't see into the brain, and when it is injured like this, sometimes it can heal with time, and sometimes it never heals." He went on to say, "The part of the brain that was damaged looks after the breathing, memory, speech and mobility. In other words, your son is in a deep coma. Whether or not he ever comes out, time will tell."

There was still hope so we went in to see J.J. His head was taped up and there was, what they called, a floating cast on his arm. They didn't need to put a full cast on because he wasn't moving around. There were many machines hooked up to him along with a coiled tube, which breathed for him. He looked like he was asleep, and I would be able to just shake him and he would wake up. It wasn't that way though. The nurse told me to talk to him a lot, as they believed that people could still hear while in a coma. We could only stay with him for five minutes out of every fifteen because they had so many things to do in the intensive care unit. Someone was constantly checking his machines and the respirator. There were so many doctors still coming and going.

A neurologist, Dr. Fewer, stopped in. "Apparently," the nurses told me, "he is one of the best." Dr. Hay, Dr. West, and Dr. Weidman, J.J.'s own doctor, all came in. They told me the same thing, "It will take time before we have an answer."

The nurses were great. They must have been specially trained to deal with all they had to in the intensive care unit. There was a baby in a crib next to J.J., along with two other beds. Being Sunday night, there weren't very many people around.

Rudi and I went in for five minutes and went back to the family room for the following fifteen, back for five minutes and so on, hoping each time J.J. would open his eyes and look at us smiling.

One time when we came out of the room, Elaine and Horst were standing by the elevator. They looked at us, and Elaine started to cry while giving me a big hug. She asked, "How is he? Is there anything we can do?" I asked how they had found out. She said that my mom had called them and that she had gone home to help with the kids. Elaine said that Rudi's mom was at her house when my mother called. She said that if we wanted, she would go to our house and look after the kids. She could stay as long as we needed her. I told Rudi that I thought it was probably a good idea.

All night we were in and out of intensive care. The nurses turned down a bed for us in the family room, but I could only sit up in the bed and look out the window. Every once in a while, I would doze off but only for a few minutes, then I would wake up and realize this was not a nightmare, but reality. Morning came quickly. Rudi suggested that he should pick up his mom and the kids and take them home. He would bring me clean clothes and my overnight bag so I could shower when he came back. They had supplied us with whatever we needed up to that point.

Rudi left and I called my mom. She said that she would have the kids ready to go. She said that P.J. was pretty upset and missed J.J., but they were trying to comfort him. They had told him J.J. broke his arm, and he started to scream and cry. My dad tried to calm him down and talk to him when finally P.J. said, "Now, he only has one arm, like Opa (Rudi's father who had lost his arm in a logging accident)?" What little kids think.

My dad explained, "No, he still had both arms but the bone in one of his arms was broken." He settled down but still wanted to come to the hospital to play with J.J. This was so hard. How could we ever explain to P.J. that it was possible J.J. wouldn't wake up. They were so close. It wouldn't sink in my head–and I was a grown-up, never mind trying to make a four-year-old understand.

Every chance I got, I went in and talked to J.J. I told him to wake up. I told him his favourite stories. I sang "The ABC Song" and "I'm a Little Teapot," two of his favourites. I did this through the next day for the five minutes they gave me, then would go back to the family room and cry and pull myself back together for the next five minutes they would allow me.

The accident was in the newspapers, so throughout the day, different people we knew either stopped in to see us or sent messages. Carol came by to talk to me and said that she would be by quite often as she was working as a nurse at the hospital. By suppertime, I was already short of sleep to the point where I was having a problem staying positive. I wanted J.J. to wake up and questioned, "Why wasn't he waking up?" I felt so guilty and so helpless because I couldn't turn back time and change it. I would go in the room and start to cry, telling J.J. how sorry I was that I wasn't there to stop the car from hitting him. I was his mother after all; I should have been there. No five year old should be anywhere near Portage Avenue without an adult with them. What was my son doing there? Where was his mother? Where was I? I was trying to piece it all together, but it hurt too much. I felt like the whole world hated me. I couldn't bear to look at Rudi. I told him that I was so sorry; it was all my fault. He tried to tell me it wasn't, but I was still J.J's mother and it wasn't anyone else's job to keep him safe. This was just so hard.

Rudi stayed the second night with me, and I did sleep. In the morning, I went to get us coffee, and when I came back, I told him that we needed some kind of plan or the other kids were going to suffer too much. He said that he would go to work and then home to have supper with the kids. Then he would come in here with me. He said that I should try to go home to let the kids know I was still all right. We decided I would stay another day. Hopefully, J.J. would wake up, and I could give P.J. and Tammy some good news.

Rudi went to work, and I spent the day going in and out, seeing J.J. My parents came in to sit with me for a while, and the nurses said that they could come in to see J.J. for a few minutes if they wanted. I could see it was so hard on them. My mom started to cry as soon as she saw him. My dad held it together as he leaned over J.J. and said, "Come on Butch, it's Grandpa. Wake up and we'll go for an ice cream."

I felt so bad. What had I done to everyone? Everyone I loved was hurting, and my son wasn't waking up. When my parents left, I sat in the family room and cried. I felt so alone.

I remember talking to God and crying to him, "Why are you doing this to me? Please help me. I am so sorry I wasn't there for J.J. Please get him to wake up. Please help him. He is only a little boy and doesn't deserve this." At that moment, a man came in the room and asked if he could talk to me. He said that he was the pastor "on call" for the hospital. I told him that, yes; I wanted to talk to him too. I said to him, "It was my fault; I wasn't there to stop J.J." I went on, "Why did that girl drive with no brakes? Why did this have to happen? What did I do that was so bad for this to happen?"

He then asked me, "What if God's plan was that J.J. die?" I didn't want to listen to this. How can this be God's plan? J.J. was only five years old. I didn't want to talk anymore. He stopped and asked, "Then can I pray with you?"

I said, "Yes, but only if it is for J.J. to get better."

He said, "Alright."

When he finished, we both said, "Amen," and he gave me his card and said for me to call him if I needed to talk anymore.

I was so tired. I wanted to go home and see P.J. and Tammy, but I felt too bad. How could I go home without good news? I knew P.J. must have really been missing J.J. I knew they were well looked after by Rudi's mom, but it wasn't the same and their lives had been thrown into such turmoil.

I was so glad when Rudi came in after supper. We kept going in and talking to J.J. all evening, but there was no change at all. The respirator was still breathing for him. Rudi tried to talk me into coming home for the night. He said, "You can come back every morning when I go to work, I will drop you off. I will go to work and home to have supper with the kids, and then come in with you. We can go home to tuck in the other kids. We will do this as long as we have to."

I felt guilty that I wasn't home with P.J. and Tammy, and then I felt guilty if I left J.J. at the hospital. I felt guilty that Rudi's life had become so chaotic, and I felt guilty that my mother-in-law had to stay at our place to look after the kids. I felt guilty that my parents were hurting so much. I didn't think anything would ever feel good again, so I went home with Rudi. The nurses said that it was a good idea. They promised to phone at the least little change and told me I could call ten times a night if I wanted to see how he was doing. With that, I felt a bit better about going home. I did call several times during the night and then again as soon as I opened my eyes in the morning.

We had breakfast with P.J. and Tammy before we left. I was so determined to smile and be happy, giving them hope that no matter what, it was under control and everything would be all right. We explained to P.J. that sometimes when kids are hit by a car, like J.J was, they sleep for a long time so their bodies heal.

Margaret, my new neighbour, caught me as I was leaving and gave me a big hug. She asked how J.J. was, so I gave her the update. She said, "If there's anything my husband Brian or I can do, let me know." I knew she would be there if I needed her. She was just that kind of person raised in a big family with lots of brothers and sisters. One of her sisters, Monica, was a couple of years younger than Margaret and was born with Cerebral Palsy. Her parents were really strong Christians. I didn't really know them, but I had heard a lot about them.

When I walked away, I stopped and said to her, "You could ask your parents to pray for J.J." She said that they have had half of the city praying since they heard the news.

I had taken some of J.J.'s favourite toys and books in with me. Sometimes, if they weren't busy in the intensive care unit, they would let me stay longer. Days went by and we were still doing the same routine. I could see that my one step at a time teaching in Al-A-Teen was paying off. I did get stronger with each day that passed. But then I would fall again and see no hope. I would cry for a few hours, then pick myself up and start again. J.J. was not responding at all. Three weeks went by. I was looking for anything; a movement, a finger wiggle, a flicker of the eyes, but there was nothing. The doctors then started to set me up for J.J. not waking up. Apparently, if he did wake up now, it would mean there would be damage. Maybe he wouldn't walk or talk. I didn't want to hear this; I just wanted J.J. to wake up.

It was getting harder to go home and face P.J. and Tammy. I could see when my parents came in, they were getting progressively more upset. I found it hard to talk to people.

After three weeks, the neurologist came to talk to Rudi and me. He said that they wanted to disconnect the respirator, but they didn't know if J.J. would keep breathing on his own or not. They felt it was time. I couldn't handle this. I kept asking God to please keep him breathing.

It was almost a month after the accident before the day came. At eleven in the morning, they were taking him off the respirator. Rudi and I were in the intensive care. I held J.J.'s hand and told him to just breathe. The doctor turned off the machine as I held my breath. J.J. kept breathing! They said that they would watch him very closely for the next five minutes. Then the doctor told me that I could breathe again myself. They monitored him while he kept breathing. I thanked God. Finally after a month, there was a glimmer of hope. He wasn't being kept alive by the machine anymore; he was on his own. They told me that as long as he kept breathing well for the weekend, they would move J.J. into a semi private room with another boy who was also in a coma from an accident. They observed that I would have his mother as company, since we were in the same boat.

We went home and tried to explain to P.J. that J.J. was breathing on his own. All he wanted to hear was that J.J. was awake and coming home. We told him that after J.J. got moved to the room, maybe they would let him come and see his brother. He was sure excited about that. Rudi's mom was wonderful. She stayed the whole time and never complained. My mom and dad came to visit with the other kids sometimes, in order to give Rudi's mom a break.

On Monday morning, after I arrived, we packed up all the machines and J.J. was moved to the room. There was a little boy in the other bed, but no one else was around. It was so much more comfortable. I read J.J. his books for a while, and then watched as nurses came in to put a tube down his throat, through his nose. They explained to me that he would be fed with a tube, to start. The tube would stay in his nose and be taped out of his way when it wasn't needed. At feeding time, they would bring in mashed food in a large syringe and plunger it thru the tube. Apparently, the food would go directly to his stomach and be digested. Okay, I thought to myself, he was now going to be eating. I didn't think much of the way this was done, but I chalked it up to be another step forward to J.J. recovering and coming home.

Later in the morning, a very tall, slim lady walked in the room. She gave me a big smile when she saw me. She introduced herself as Bonnie. She told me that the boy lying in the bed was her son, Brent. She told me all about his accident. They lived just out of the city in a town called Grosse Isle. Brent had been hit by a half-ton truck. He was only three years old. Like J.J, he was also in a coma. Bonnie and I got to be really good friends over the next few weeks. We could pick each other up when one fell and keep each other going. We could give each other hope. Brent's brain had swollen so badly, that they had to burrow several holes in this head to allow the pressure to be released.

We were allowed to stay all day and I learned to do the tube feeding, so I could feed J.J. myself. The therapists came in every day to do therapy. They said that they had to keep everything mobile or he would get "foot drop" and his hands could curl up. J.J. was in diapers which made for a very busy day. Always something to do, getting him in the wheelchair and taking him into the shower, or changing him and feeding him. I was going home a lot more often to see the kids and on the weekends, I would stay home with them for part of the day. The hospital social worker suggested Rudi and I go to grief classes across the street at SMD (Society for Manitobans with Disabilities). They said it would help with the grieving process. We did go on Wednesday evenings for an hour, and it did help us to understand what we were feeling–the anger I felt toward the driver of the car, the denial of what doctors were saying, etc.

I was leaving the hospital one afternoon with Rudi when I ran into one of J.J's doctors. He told me that J.J. was not healing well and that we should consider putting him in a place like St. Amant Centre, a permanent care facility for severely handicapped people. I was devastated. I cried all the way home and didn't stop at all that night. All my hope was gone. I gave up.

I stayed home and cried for two days. Margaret tried to talk to me. She phoned her mom and said that I really needed prayers. I didn't want anything other than to be left alone. Rudi tried to talk to me. He kept going to see J.J.

Then I woke up in the morning of the third day and something changed in me. No one had the right to tell me my son wouldn't walk or talk again. I was his mother and I knew he could do more than what they were saying. Who gave any of us the right to give up on my son? I could never give up. I told Rudi and he sighed in relief. He said, "Welcome back, did you have to take so long?" I packed up some of J.J's clothes and more of his books. P.J. helped me. I told P.J. to get all of J.J's favourite things and that now we were going to make him better and bring him home.

Bonnie was really glad to see me when I came back. The nurses were glad to see me back too. When the therapists came into the room, I told them that I wanted to learn the therapy. They said for me to be in the room every morning at ten. and they would show me what to do as therapy for the day. We let P.J. in to see J.J., but it didn't go very well. P.J. just cried and held J.J's hand, telling him he had to wake up and come home. It was very emotional.

There was a television in the room, and I always turned on Sesame Street, telling J.J. what his favourite characters were doing. I constantly read him books and talked to him. I played with his favourite racing cars and made the sounds he made with the cars. P.J. taught me how. I didn't give up. When I started to feel down, I would get J.J. up and dress him in his own clothes, put him in the wheelchair, and go for a long walk outside with him.

Chapter 8

BEATING THE ODDS

One beautiful hot sunny day, we stopped on the courtyard of the Health Sciences Centre. J.J. opened his eyes. I was so excited. He wasn't looking at anything in particular, but he opened his eyes. I started to take him back to the Children's Hospital to show the nurses, but every time I took a few steps, J.J. would hit the tube in his nose. It was bothering him, I am sure. Finally, he grabbed the tube and kept on pulling it until it was out. I went very quickly back into the hospital and started to tell the nurses. They called the doctor.

When the doctor came in, he said, "Yes, his eyes are definitely open but he isn't focusing on anything. He probably was having arm spasms and that is what hit the tube out of his nose." They never wanted to give too much hope, which was understandable. I began to understand that the specialists were at the top of their field and dealt with worse case scenarios, so they were very cautious on where they gave hope. But I knew J.J., and I knew he was getting very frustrated with the tube in his nose. The sad part was it was the only way we could get him fed because he couldn't swallow. So, they had to put the tube back in.

After J.J. pulled the tube out of his nose for the third time, the doctors agreed; he knew what he was doing. From that point on, every little thing that came back was going to be a bonus and that much more of J.J. When you start with nothing, every little thing, you learn to appreciate.

One Sunday, Rudi and I were with him at suppertime. We did the tube feeding. It really did look like gross food. The good thing was, if the food doesn't go past his taste buds, then he couldn't taste it. It just went straight to his stomach and made him feel full, giving him the nutrition he needed. After we finished, I got him into his pajamas, and then Rudi sat him on his lap in the big chair beside his bed. They turned on the television and started to watch the Disney Show. Rudi was telling J.J. to look at the characters and also to look at this or that, and he would tell him what was happening. Over the past while, J.J.'s eyes would be open, but he never focused on anything. Two months had already passed but we refused to get discouraged. Rudi then started to laugh at something that happened in the show and said, "J.J, did you see that?" J.J. turned his head, looked at Rudi, and smiled with a half face smile. Bonnie was in the room and yelled for the nurses. J.J. just looked and smiled. Well, there wasn't a dry eye in the place. J.J. was back.

The doctor came in to check him and said, "He can feel when he is happy and he can feel when he is frustrated. Is that enough for you?"

"Yes," we both agreed, we have only just begun.

The doctors then reminded us that it had been two months since the accident and that meant there was a lot of damage.

It didn't matter what the doctor said; J.J. was smiling at us. No one could burst that bubble. We let P.J. and Tammy come to see him more often. They could see the hope in J.J. looking and smiling at them. On Saturday, we would spend the day together outside with all of the kids. J.J. loved having the other two around.

The next day, Rudi went to work and I went to the hospital. J.J. was such a joy to spend the day with. He smiled a lot, ripped out the tube constantly, and he started to fight with the nurses when they tried to do therapy. The therapist decided that J.J. was alert enough to do more intense therapy. We started to go down in the mornings, to put J.J. on the standing frame. It would force him to stand straight. After a few tries, the nurses showed Rudi and I how to do it, so it could be used more during the day. J.J's legs and feet had become quite crooked over the time in the coma, so we needed to start to get them straight. Rudi and I would put him in the frame after supper. They built a tray on the frame so J.J. could lean on it. To start, he just laid on it. After about a week on the frame, he began to get used to it.

One evening, we had J.J. on the frame and his head was lying on the tray as usual. My parents came for a visit. J.J. was facing away from the door. My mom came in first and said, "Hey, how is our big boy today?" J.J. slowly lifted his head about three inches off the tray and turned to my mom and smiled.

Margaret checked in with us every morning to get an update. She always ended the conversation with, "My mother is still praying for you."

I would always end with, "Tell her not to stop." I would then thank God every day for every little thing we got back. I promised we wouldn't miss church when J.J. came home. I promised I would never swear. I promised I would never leave the kids out of my sight again. I bargained and made commitments, thinking this would please God.

On Wednesdays, Rudi would pick me up and take me home for supper, and then I would get ready for the grief classes. I didn't want to go that night, but it was the last one. I felt that at the rate things were going, the classes weren't for us anymore. J.J. was getting better. While I was waiting for Rudi, I began talking to J.J. as he was trying to pull the tube out for the tenth time. His nose was so sore from them putting it back in. I went to the cafeteria and bought a small container of Jell-O. I was going to try it, even though the nurses were against it. They said he can't swallow and he would choke. He was swallowing though. I watched him in the past week, and he definitely did swallow. I was only going to rub some Jell-O on his lips so he could taste it. I felt pretty safe with Jell-O, as it would dissolve, and he wouldn't choke. I rubbed a bit on his lip, and his tongue went crazy so I gave him a little more. I didn't tell anyone that I had done it. I thought every day we would practice and give a little more until he was good at it. Then we would show them. When I got home, I told P.J. what I had done and said, "It's our little secret." He was very happy to keep our little secret.

Every day, I went a little further with the Jell-O, until the third day when Bonnie caught me. She just laughed and said, "Good for you." Brent was doing better too; he now had his eyes open. Watching J.J. progress, gave Bonnie so much hope. Finally, on the fifth day, I could give J.J. a little Jell-O on a spoon and he just smiled and ate it up. He never choked at all and swallowed without even thinking. I got a new container of Jell-O and laid it on his night table. When Rudi came, I thought I would show him first, which I did, but J.J. wanted more. Rudi went to get the nurse, who was quite leery, but watched as I put the spoon of Jell-O in J.J's mouth. He actually chewed it, as if he knew the nurse was watching and he had to be convincing. The nurse smiled and left, but returned a few minutes later with ice cream and a spoon. She said, "Try this." J.J. was so thrilled. He loved ice cream. He ate the whole bowl. I had done the usual phone calls to my parents and Elaine, telling, them the good news. I woke P.J. up when I got home and told him the good news. He was so thrilled; our secret was working.

The next day, the doctor watched and being surprised, said, "Take the tube out and start him on puréed food." I brought P.J. in the next morning with me, so that the two of them could eat breakfast together; ice cream. The days became more exciting. Brent was now using the standing frame, so at lunch times, both boys were in their frames and I could feed J.J. his lunch. One day at lunchtime, my dad showed up with J.J's favourite ice cream on cones–one for J.J. and one for himself. They were already partly melted. My dad helped

J.J. eat his, while he ate his own. I said that I would go upstairs and get a cup of coffee because I saw the tears in my dad's eyes as they ate, and I couldn't handle that. It was the togetherness that my dad got back with his first grandchild, but it was so emotional for him. The therapists started coming at lunchtime to plan how to make utensils, which J.J. could hold and be able to eat on his own, eventually. They brought me an "anchorman." This is a piece of jelled, thin rubber, so that his bowl could sit without sliding.

At ten weeks after the accident, the doctors called a meeting with all of us and suggested that this is probably as far as J.J. could go with the damage incurred on his brain. We should consider now moving him to a place like St. Amant Centre. Rudi and I refused to listen and said that we would not even consider this. They then said that they were moving him down to the end of the hall to be in a ward with other kids. They figured maybe the stimulation would be good, so we agreed. They said that J.J. would never walk or talk again, but we ignored them.

No one could tell me what functions J.J. was getting back. Right from day one of the accident, all the top specialists said they just didn't know what to expect, exactly, when it was a brain injury. J.J. was moved into the ward. Rudi asked if there was a chance we could bring him home. We were sure that home would make his recovery faster. It would be good for all three kids if we could get back some normal life. Their reply was, "No," because J.J. really needed intense therapy, and it just wouldn't be good for him to go home. For one thing, they said he would be too much work for us. I didn't listen to things like that. I didn't look back.

I held close to my heart my son J.J, who grew up with curly blonde hair and ran around with so much energy, talking a mile a minute. But I knew he was gone and that I still loved the J.J. who was here, now, and trying so hard to please. I looked ahead to J.J. taking his first steps in the future, his first words. I thought of the song by Billy Joel, "Everybody Has A Dream." The words were so right when he said,

> *"While in these days of quiet desperation,*
> *as I wander through the world in which I live.*
> *I search everywhere for some new inspiration*
> *but it is more than cold reality can give.*
> *If I need a cause for celebration*
> *or a comfort I can use, to ease my mind,*
> *I rely on my imagination*
> *and I dream of an imaginary time."*

To keep my hope from crumbling away, I would dream of J.J. walking and talking. All these fantasies I was keeping to make the empty hours easier to stand. For every little new thing he could do, like hold the spoon in his hand by himself, trying to aim for his mouth with the food, then missing and spilling it all over. The mess didn't matter. The excitement was in that he tried. I thanked God for every new little thing that we were given back.

Murray's wife, Jan stopped in to see me. I thought this was her first time seeing J.J. since the accident. But no, she had been keeping tabs on his progress; after all, she was a nurse in the hospital. She sat and talked for a while and told me she was the nurse on duty when they brought J.J. in. She said that she didn't come to talk to me that day because the doctors had informed her that he would be dead by midnight. She couldn't deal with the devastation I would be in, if that happened. After she left, I thought back to the day of the accident when I had asked the priest to let J.J. live. I thought, "See, He did have more pull." Then I thought of all the prayers Margaret's mother had going for J.J.

Rudi and I were both lying on the bed watching the news, when the phone rang. It was the nurse on duty at the hospital. She was so excited; I barely understood what she was telling me. She said that the doctor had walked into J.J.'s room to see another patient.

As he walked by the bed, he noticed J.J. was still awake, so the doctor said, "Hi J.J." The doctor stopped in his tracks and walked over to the bed, thinking he was just hearing things. He asked JJ, "Did you say something to me?"

J.J. nodded his head and with a smile, said, "Hi." This doctor then called in others nearby along with the nurses, to make sure he wasn't hearing things.

She said, "J.J. must have said, 'Hi,' about twenty times, but he didn't say anything else." She went on to say that he was sleeping now, and I should wait until morning.

No way, Rudi and I were out the door and at the hospital within twenty minutes. J.J. was sleeping, but I woke him up anyway. He smiled when he saw me, so I said, "Hi J.J."

He said, "Hi." We then let him go back to sleep.

All the way home I kept saying, "I knew it, I knew it," as I thanked God many times before I fell asleep that night.

The next morning, I could hardly wait to get to the hospital. I told P.J.

that I would phone him when I got there and J.J. could say hello to him. I knew that if the word, "Hi" was there, more words would follow.

I helped J.J. eat breakfast, and then got him showered and dressed. It was a beautiful day, so we went out in the front of the hospital to sit in the sunshine. I was reading J.J. a story, and he was sitting in the wheelchair, when a friend of ours came by. Howard worked for Rudi. Whenever he would come over to the house, he had a game he played with the kids.

He would ask, "Who is your favorite uncle?"

They were trained by him to say, "Uncle Howard." He wasn't really their uncle, but definitely played the part. Usually after they answered correctly, he had a treat for them. He apologized for not coming by sooner, but didn't think he would handle seeing J.J. in a coma. At the risk of being emotional, he just called all the time to see how J.J. was doing. Howard said he was leaving that afternoon for an exchange program in England. He looked at J.J. and said, "Hi."

Of course J.J. smiled his half smile and said, "Hi."

Then Howard knelt down and said to J.J., "If you can answer this question correctly, I will bring you back the biggest double-decker bus that will fit on the plane." He then asked, "Who is your favourite Uncle?"

I was a little upset thinking that was a bit much to expect from J.J., but he just smiled his smile and answered very clearly, "Uncle Howard."

Then he asked him if there was anything he could get for him before he left.

J.J. said, "Ice cream."

All day we tested him. Anything simple, that was routine before his accident, he could repeat. He knew, "Cookie Monster" and his "ABC's." My parents came in to hear him talk, but when Rudi came, he couldn't believe it. When Rudi had dropped me off in the morning, all J.J. could say then, was, "Hi."

The next morning, the doctors came and talked to us. They wanted to send J.J. to Children's Rehab Hospital. There, he would get intense physiotherapy, occupational therapy and speech therapy. We both agreed. So that afternoon we made the move. We said our goodbyes to all the nurses and promised to come back and visit. Bonnie and I did have a problem parting company. We had gotten to be good friends and held each other together. Brent was standing now, but didn't talk yet and still couldn't see.

The Rehab Hospital was quite different than what we were used to at the Children's. The nurse's Station was in the centre of a large circle of beds.

There were a few rooms on the sides but, for the most part, all the patients were in this circle. Leading away from the circle, there was a long hallway, which went down to the therapy rooms. When we first came in, there were only about five patients in the place. We knew that J.J. would receive close to undivided attention. Out back, there was a huge deck, which overlooked the river and out front was Wellington Crescent, where all the old Victorian dream homes lined the riverbank. What a great place for J.J. to heal! It was the beginning of August, and the weather was beautiful.

We got J.J. settled in one of the beds on the river's side of the circle. He appeared quite content, so we went home. It was a longer drive home now, but we felt like it was such a step in the right direction. We had come so far.

The next day, I started to feel we had outgrown the Children's Hospital and were now at the starting point of the Rehabilitation Centre. When we went down the hall to meet the therapists, I was shown how much damage there was to J.J's body. All of which had to be worked on, in order for him to start to walk again. His legs were so crooked, his feet had dropped and he had no idea of what it was like to stand without the standing frame. They soon built a special toilet seat for him to try. Now, everything was so much more technical. The therapists watched how he ate, how he drank, how he sat in the wheelchair and then built him everything he needed to get through the day as close to a "normal" person as they could. They built splints for his hands and did exercises, putting balls in his clenched fist to try and loosen his grip. J.J's right side was obviously much more damaged than his left, but not with physical damage; the side of the brain which operated the right side was damaged and wasn't working as well as it should. Special shoes were made which could go over the splints, which were holding his feet in place, fighting the foot drop.

The therapists were so positive minded, and so were the nurses. The people at Children's Hospital had played their part and had taken J.J. as far as they could; now it was time for Rehab to take over. J.J. even went to a classroom, set up down the hall, and they had a teacher who spent many hours with him, seeing what he was capable of and what they could do to help him learn.

A one armed wheelchair was set up so that J.J. could use it himself with the one good working arm. They built an insert so he could sit up without falling to one side. This was all so astonishing for me as I thought it was tough enough waiting for him to open his eyes and speak. Now this was like walking the second mile. It took so much more faith to get through and believe that J.J. could eventually walk with everything being so crooked.

They put him on a huge medicine ball and rocked it back and forth. I never really knew what that was for. They laid him on a mattress and then put his favourite things a small distance away. It was such an accomplishment to see him try to reach and get them for the first time. This was the beginning stage of trying to get him to crawl. Did I ever learn through this about how little things in life could be taken for granted so much!

While J.J. napped, I would take coffee outside on the deck and watch the river. It was still warm outside, and this was a real treat. I would sit and dream of taking J.J. home, but I never did put a time on it. It was safer that way. Rudi had his own way of dealing with it. He was planning to buy a house and was keeping his mind open to the possibility of J.J. coming home in a wheelchair. So it would have to be a bungalow to accommodate the chair. The doors had to be wide enough because the one handed wheelchairs have an extra bar on the outside of the wheel for balance.

It was now the beginning of September. One morning, I came in later than usual because I had taken P.J. and Tammy for their yearly check-up. Dr. Weidman kept me in his office for so long, questioning me about J.J.'s progress. He was so pleased at the way J.J. was recovering. I told him, "It isn't over yet."

Later, when I got to the hospital, J.J. was sleeping on top of his bed with a blanket thrown over him. My mom had knitted the blanket for him when he was quite young, and it was now, "his blankee." He never consciously lay down without it. At the bottom of the bed, taking up half of it, was a teddy bear, a huge one. I asked the nurse where J.J. got it, and she said that a lady had come to visit and brought it for him. I asked what the lady looked like, thinking Elaine had been in to visit. She told me, but I didn't know who it was.

She said, "Oh, I wrote down her name in the day book, I will get it for you." As she was walking back to the desk, she said that this lady had taken J.J. for a walk down Wellington Crescent for over an hour, and that was why he was so tired. They weren't able to get him up for school or therapy; he was just too tired. When she told me the name, I went wild. I was so upset and I didn't hesitate to voice my concerns to the nurse. She was quite surprised at the angry side of me, which she hadn't seen before. It was the girl who was driving the car that hit J.J.

I asked, "How dare you let this girl take my son for a walk for over an hour? Could anyone just walk in and take my son out? Did I have to stay at the hospital for twenty-four hours a day to make sure nothing like this could happen?"

She apologized profusely, but I felt that wasn't good enough. How could this happen? I hated that girl and didn't have one ounce of forgiveness for her. She put my son in this situation, and now she gets to take him for a walk?

I went out on the deck, so I could calm down before J.J. woke up. I was thinking to myself, "I am guilty for not being there to stop J.J. What if someone were to say to me, now, 'You can't take him for a walk because you weren't there to stop him from being hit by the car?'" I put that out of my head fast and went back inside.

I made it very clear to the staff; I did not want this girl to be anywhere near my son. I had already been informed by the police a couple of months before that I had to get a lawyer and sue on behalf of J.J. He would have to be taken care of financially for much of the expenses incurred due to the accident. Being his mother, it was my responsibility. I had gone to my dad's lawyer, who then referred me to another lawyer who specializes in accidents similar to J.J.'s. The driver of the car had since been charged with a list of crimes. I don't remember them all, but there were a few which I will never forget; driving with an unsafe vehicle (no brakes), driving with bare feet and driving without prescription glasses, which her license called for.

At first, I avoided going to a lawyer. I felt it didn't matter what you sue for; I couldn't replace my son. Then we received two ambulance bills in the mail and were told that our medical insurance doesn't necessarily pay for his hospitalization when caused by an accident. The bill for the Intensive Care Unit alone was close to $50,000, so I thought I had better take the advice and call.

I finally got over the frustration of J.J. going for a walk with the girl and for another month, went daily to his therapy and school. He was just learning to bring the spoon from the plate to his mouth, but he would still forget to open his mouth. He still couldn't crawl and toilet training was really not registering with him. I was really getting impatient. There had been no new improvements for so long, and I was getting scared.

One afternoon in the middle of September, I came back after having coffee and J.J. was crying and moaning. I asked the nurse what was going on because J.J. always smiled whenever he saw me, in the past. She said that he had a bad infection in the urinary tract. I really wasn't surprised. He had a catheter in for so long at the other hospital, which couldn't have been good.

She said that he was now on antibiotics, and it should clear up in a few days. When I proceeded to change him, I was floored; his penis was three times the size of normal and he was having a problem urinating because it hurt so much. I was so frustrated. I probably wasn't so much frustrated at them as I was being impatient, and this just added to it. By the time Rudi came to pick me up, I had J.J. packed and dressed to go. I was taking him home.

Rudi just looked at me and was obviously in shock. "Who said he could go home?"

To this, I replied, "I did."

He gave me a look of, "Oh, oh, she's lost it!"

When I showed him J.J.'s infection, he winced as if he felt the pain himself and said, "Okay, let's go." Rudi picked up J.J. while I gathered up his personal belongings, and we walked out the door.

The nurse ran behind us saying, "You can't do this, you are not equipped to look after him properly."

Rudi answered, "And obviously neither are you!" It was so good to have him in the car. He was sitting on my lap and looking out the window. It was like he was seeing the world for the first time.

When Rudi walked in the door carrying J.J., P.J. started to dance and was running around yelling, "J.J. is home! J.J. is home!" J.J. just laughed at him, and we both knew it was right. Rudi's mother was so glad to see J.J. and was hugging him and speaking German. With every little cuddle, she was speaking to Rudi in German, and I could tell she was very concerned about what we had done. She said that she would stay and help me look after him. It didn't take long after we arrived, when the doorbell rang and there were two police officers standing there with the new social worker that had been assigned to us previously. We convinced them that J.J. was fine for the night to stay with us. Rudi and I would come in first thing in the morning to discuss us keeping him at home. P.J. was really the one who convinced them. He pretty well let them know they weren't taking his brother away again. He still had that certain glow when he talked and could convince anyone of anything.

We made do for the night, but when morning came, we knew we needed all the equipment from the hospital to make this work. J.J. couldn't crawl, and I couldn't put him on the toilet. He really needed his standing frame or all the good done to now, wouldn't take long to backtrack. I got him bathed, but even that was difficult without the equipment they had made for him. J.J. wasn't a big boy, but was solid. Dr. Weidman always referred to the boys as "prime beef, no unnecessary fat." We took J.J. to the Rehab, and once there, went into the meeting room. The therapists had his wheelchair ready. I stayed with the chair because I was afraid they would run off with him because of what I had done. They came right out and asked why we were doing this.

Rudi then told them that we wanted what was best for J.J. "Being at home with the family is what's best." He told them, "We should all co-operate with each other in this and if you let us keep him at home, we will bring him for therapy every day if we have to. We will do whatever you want, but just let us keep him at home."

To our surprise they didn't disagree. They said their only concern was, "It would be a lot of work." I didn't care and asked for them to give me the chance. They said they would give me four days to try this out, and then we would get together again to discuss what is best for everyone. We, at least, got the door opened a bit more than a crack. They would send home all they could to help over the four days, and if that worked out, they would set up the house with what was needed. We were to bring J.J. in for therapy every second day for the four days, and the rest would be done at home. Before we left, the therapists helped us load the car with the standing frame, toilet seat, wheelchair, inserts, splints and his utensils for eating. The car was packed full.

When we finished loading the car, the therapist told us, "I agree that J.J. would have a much faster recovery at home, and I will be praying that God gives you the strength to handle it."

Chapter 9

J.J. COMES HOME

When we got home, Margaret met us at the door and helped us unload all of J.J.'s things. When she left, she told me, "Any time, night or day, if you need help, just call." She also said, "Just bang on the wall, I'll come." Then with a big smile, she left, saying that she was going to phone her mom, tell her the good news and catch her up on what she had to pray for next.

It felt so good and so right to have all three kids at home together. For four days, we did the routine but for J.J., it was so different. After Rudi went to work in the morning, I would put J.J. in the standing frame in front of the television. He and P.J. would watch "Sesame Street" and "The Friendly Giant." P.J. talked constantly to him and explained everything. JJ would then repeat it. During breakfast, lunch and supper, we all sat at the table and P.J. would show J.J. how to put the spoon up to his mouth. We would all laugh every time he told J.J, "Open your mouth now." P.J. would go to the bathroom and show J.J. how to do it, then we would put J.J. on the toilet seat, and he would say, "Now." Both the boys were together again. J.J. was so content. I realized after the second day, it wasn't that J.J. needed to be at home, he needed his brother. P.J. came to therapy with us while Oma looked after Tammy. She had gotten to be pretty close to P.J. over the past four months and was finding it a little hard to share him with J.J.

On the fourth day, the therapists came to the house with the social worker. We were more than ready. They were shocked to find that in just four short days; we had J.J. at home, he was toilet trained, could eat anything with a spoon (we had already started to use a fork) and that the best part was; we had him crawling. They said, "No doubt, he can stay home." We would still be going to therapy every second day, but they would start to equip us better at home, now that they knew he was staying.

Rudi and I did some serious house shopping. We weren't very comfortable with J.J. sleeping downstairs. We installed an intercom system to the upstairs and showed P.J. how to work it. P.J. insisted that he stay in his room.

He promised us he would call us if they needed anything. We discussed this with the therapists, and they thought it would be good for both boys.

In November, we finally found a house. It didn't really exist yet; it still had to be built. We saw the display home, which was affordable and the set-up was perfect for what we needed. It definitely wasn't what we originally had planned for, but we couldn't wait anymore. We had to think smaller as we ran out of time to save a bigger down payment. The house would be built over the winter. It was kind of fun because we could watch it being built. It wasn't too far from our present house on Treger Bay. It was in a new area called "All Seasons Estates." The area was a young community and had good schools.

The first week J.J. was home, we celebrated Tammy's third birthday. She had almost white shoulder length curly hair and was so petite. P.J. started kindergarten. The school was only two blocks away. J.J. was booked to go to therapy every Monday, Wednesday and Friday. We showed up on the Wednesday and were told we wouldn't have to bring J.J. to therapy anymore. He was really supposed to be in kindergarten, and there was an opening at SMD (Society for Manitobans with Disabilities) preschool program. He would be picked up five days a week with a wheelchair van around noon and driven there. He would get all the therapy he needed all afternoon and be brought back around four. This was such a blessing. He started the following week. After so long running to the hospital, I didn't know what to do with myself. Oma went to live back home, but she was open to coming anytime we needed help. I think she got very attached to the kids in those few months she lived with us.

J.J. would be picked up by the van around ten past twelve, and there was time left for Tammy and me to walk P.J. to school. Tammy then had a nap. We would go back and meet P.J. at school at three-thirty and be home in time for J.J. to be brought back between four and four-thirty.

Rudi and I did buy the house in All Seasons Estates. They said it would be ready to move in January. Margaret and I would normally get together for coffee in the afternoons. She was a little upset that we were going to be moving even though it wasn't very far away.

One day at the beginning of March, we were all settled in the house when the driver was dropping off J.J. at home, she asked if I had any interest in driving one of the vans. I would be driving the same times as J.J. was on the van and would have to do one morning run at around eight. The pay was $100 per week. It sounded great. I would only have to take the test for my "chauffeur's license." I told her that I would think about it and talk to Rudi.

I ran it by Rudi when he got home but he really didn't want me to go back to work. He asked, "What would I do with Tammy for that time?" I didn't know. He asked, "What will P.J. and J.J. do in the mornings?" I didn't know, but what I did know is that this was a great opportunity. If it worked out well, maybe they would consider taking me back in September. What a perfect job while I had the kids–summer, Christmas-break and Spring-Term break, off.

I said, "If we can just 'tough it out' until June."

He said, "Find out answers to my questions, and we will talk about it again."

The next day, I asked Shirley what she did with her own kids. They were in school full time. She said that I could take Tammy with me for the day and that if I did start, I would be taking J.J. home anyway. I phoned the Social Worker and told her about this job, and she said that she thought it would be a great idea and would look into it some more. She said that she would call me back. Within the hour, she called. She stated that she thought it would be possible to do. If I took Tammy with me during the lunchtime run, I could be home for two hours in the afternoon. Then, the only problem would be P.J. coming home from school. I wouldn't make it back for him in time. Oma offered to look after them. But she had her own life, and I really wanted to do this myself. My parents still lived in the other side of the city, so that didn't help. It would have been good though, because my sisters were old enough to handle it.

By the time Rudi had gotten home, I was already frustrated and confused. I really wanted to do this myself, but the three months until summer would be crazy. Rudi finally said that he would wait until I got back before he left for work. If I did the morning run, I would be home by about ten past nine. He would stay with the kids until then. If I could figure out the rest of the day, then I could take the job. He told me that he would have to work the extra hour later to make up the time. I called the Social Worker back the next day and told her what I had sorted out so far. She informed me of a family who lived a couple of streets away who took in foster kids. They were willing to give P.J. lunch, send him to school and then the bus could drop him off at their place until I got back.

Rudi and I discussed it again that night. It would work.

On the first of April, I had my baby blue van with the number sixteen painted on the outside. That was my number on the two-way radio. I had done all the testing and passed with flying colours. I was now a bus driver. My area was in the southeast corner of the city, and I had seven kids to pick up in the morning along with five in the afternoon. We could bring the kids in the school at eight forty five, so I was getting home by five past nine. for Rudi to leave. I left the house at seven-thirty, so he handled getting the kids up and dressed and fed. Everything clicked very well, and it was a great job. Besides, I now had extra money every month. That money went into an account for a sidewalk and eventually to build a garage.

Margaret and Brian moved into a side-by-side on the next street over from ours. She said that if I was still working, the kids could go there before or after school–whatever we needed. I could get everything done between my runs as if I wasn't even working. Rudi would get home around five-thirty, and I was so well organized. If it weren't for the fact that he looked after the kids in the morning, he would never even notice I was working.

Mother's Day came and went. Neither my mom nor I cared to cele-brate. It had been a year since J.J.'s accident. At the end of the school year, when I got my separation certificate, it said to return to work in September. Yes! I applied for unemployment cheques the next day and was now on holi-days for two months with the kids.

Tammy was really acting up. We thought it was due to all the commo-tion in our lives over the past year. P.J. and J.J. stuck together like glue. J.J. progressed from crawling to pulling himself around on his rear end. He didn't get any use back from his right hand or arm; so when he pulled himself, he was pulling his full weight with his left hand. He could scoot across the floor so fast. His shoulder and arm became solid muscle. His foot was still dropped so he was having a problem standing. The therapists at the school had set up surgery to lengthen the tendons in his heel, and then he could learn how to stand. The surgery was done in early July. He was only in the hospital for three days. He came home with a cast on one leg and foot, but still could pull him-self around on his rear end.

Rudi signed P.J. up to play soccer and took him to all the prac-tices. We all went to watch him play the games. No matter what P.J. did, he did it well. We still took the kids to church every Sunday. There was no wheel-chair access, so someone would just help Rudi carry the wheelchair up the steps.

The sod was all put in and we planted some trees. We really wanted to put up a garage in the back because Rudi wanted the convertible parked for the winter. There just wasn't enough time. We spent a lot of time playing cards on weekends with Ron and Carol. Their kids, Jason and Lesley, were close to the age of our kids so it was always a good time.

He ran the business out of the house and I helped him by taking calls and doing payroll for the guys. I had finished the Bishop Sewing Course, so friends started to ask me to make their wedding dresses for them. It was really busy for us, so when Rudi had to work weekends, I went painting with him. I learned pretty quickly, even though there really isn't much to learn painting. If he was texturing ceilings, I was his "shmuck." I would have to scrape the walls after he was done with the ceilings. He tried to teach me how to spray, but the hopper and gun were just too heavy for me to hold. (The truth was I just didn't want white texture speckles all over my hair and face.) Soon enough, J.J.'s cast was taken off. It was time for the kids to go back to school and for me to go back to work. J.J. was starting full days at Lord Roberts School. It was on the other side of the city, but there, he would get the therapy he needed during the day along with specialized education. The part of the brain which memorizes was still damaged, so learning had to be routine. If they taught him something, they went over it day after day until it was so imbedded in him, he would never forget. He was picked up early in the morning by bus and dropped off around four-thirty in the afternoon. P.J. started grade one at Springfield Heights School. Margaret would keep him until the bus came, and he would go back to her house after school until I got there. Both boys ate lunch at school. Tammy spent the day with me, so Rudi could go to work at his normal time. None of this affected him.

Tammy was really stubborn when it came to talking. She had developed quite a lisp. The social worker suggested I see if there was a space available for Tammy at the speech program at SMD. That was the pre-school program, which I drove for. The director, Thelma Reid, was a wonderful English lady. When I spoke to her, she said, "Yes, I'm sure there's room for Tammy. Tammy started right away in the morning program. When I took the kids in from my morning run, Tammy also stayed there until my lunchtime run. Then I would take her home to nap in the afternoon, until it was time to go back to get the kids again.

The house was completely re-painted during the first year, and we built a huge rec room and laundry room in the basement. The rec room became the favourite room in the house.

P.J. decided he really wanted to play piano, so we found a lady nearby who gave lessons and gave it a try. She told us we needed a piano. Without knowing whether P.J. would keep going with the lessons, we rented one "with option to buy." After the first six months, P.J.'s teacher told us, "He's a natural," so we purchased the piano. Every day after supper, while I did dishes, P.J. would practice. I never knew how to play piano but had enough of an ear to tell whether he was doing the right thing or not. I played guitar and clarinet when I was younger but never kept it up. I always wanted to play piano, so I tried to learn along with him.

A boy moved in a couple of doors down from us who was the same age as P.J. They became best of friends. They were a Mennonite family who were very church oriented. They said that they were "Christians." So was I but I don't think in the same way they thought. After a while, if Greg wasn't at our house, then P.J. was at theirs. Sometimes he would go to their church with them.

Rudi signed P.J. up for hockey, and it became a big thing in all of our lives. Because they were so young, the team got mostly outdoor ice. There were so many mornings when we were in snowmobile suits at six, outside in thirty below weather, watching P.J. play hockey. Because his birthday fell at the end of the year, most of the boys on the team were almost a year older than he was. This made P.J. a fair amount smaller than the rest of the team. It was to his benefit though, as he could maneuver in and around the bigger boys. At first, he played mostly the Centre position and became a real goal scorer. I definitely could score points for being "Hockey Mom." We served our time volunteering in the concession stand at the community club, and I never missed a game, not so much out of dedication, but more so, for the thrill. P.J. and his team were a real joy to watch.

Tammy continued to go to SMD for speech therapy. By the time she was ready to start school, her speech had improved to the point where her lisp was almost undetectable. Her behaviour improved a bit, but she still acted like she was very spoiled. I was accused several times by the social workers of smothering the kids. In my opinion, I was just trying to keep them safe. When Tammy started school, she went to the same one P.J. was attending. They both took the same bus. .

When Tammy turned six years old, she had a problem one day, going to the bathroom. She said that "it" really hurt. I took her in to see Dr. Weidman, and he said that she had a bladder infection. He prescribed antibiotics and sent us home, telling us to return in ten days. The antibiotics worked fast, so ten days later, we went back. Dr. Weidman suggested that we send her to see a urologist. I was concerned as to why, because Tammy wasn't having the problem anymore. Dr. Weidman just said that he wanted to be safe and make sure the infection was gone.

When I arrived back home, I received a phone call from the urologist, Dr. Decter. I knew him quite well already, because J.J. was seeing him every six months. (J.J. had developed a problem with "strictures." That is, "a closing of the urethra." Apparently, because so many catheters had been used when he was in the coma, scar tissue had formed and this would block the urinary tract every once in a while. We always knew when this happened because J.J. would start screaming. There was way too much fluid in him, which couldn't be released. It always meant a trip into the Children's Hospital for a few days to have it reopened.)

We took Tammy in to see Dr. Decter, who suggested a series of tests on her. I was getting nervous by this point, thinking something was seriously wrong. Dr. Decter told me, "Don't worry, it's just a precaution." We had to go to the Health Sciences Centre for the tests, which took most of the day. She was put into scanners, had I.V.P. tests and several others I had never seen before. We then had to wait a week for the results. Rudi and I both went in to see the specialists who showed us different X-rays and explained, as best he could, that there was a problem. He told us that when Tammy was born, she had a vessel wrapped around her kidney. There was no reason for anyone to look for or find it, so it slowly choked off her kidney over the next six years. He showed us the difference between her two kidneys, which was unbelievable. The bottom part of her kidney was totally deteriorated but the top was still good. He said that he had to operate. He told us, "A person can live with one kidney, but I would like to try to save the top half if I can." He said, "One and a half would definitely be better than one kidney." He showed us in great detail how he could remove the bottom half of the deteriorated kidney and run a false urethra to the upper part. This hadn't been done before and he couldn't say it would work for sure, but he said that it was worth a try. The worst-case scenario was that it wouldn't work, and that the rest of the kidney would have to be removed. Rudi and I both agreed to try the surgery, which meant a six-week stay in the hospital.

Tammy was admitted the following week. It was a good thing that we were on summer holidays and I didn't have to go to work. I could stay at the hospital with her, as I don't think she would have stayed alone while I went to work. She was quite attached to me and really didn't do too much on her own after school. Her love was her bicycle, but she only rode it on the front street.

She never went far, she would always rather stay home and help with supper or bake with me.

Oma came to stay at the house again while Tammy was in the hospital. The surgery took quite a few hours, and when she got back to the room, she had a tube, which ran into a hole in her side to drain the urine. This had to stay that way for four to five weeks until the procedure could heal enough. It was hard to be patient waiting for all that time to see if it worked. She had a surgical scar that ran from the front of her belly all the way to the center of her back. Rudi commented that the good in this was; he wouldn't have to worry about her wearing bikinis when she got older.

After the first week, Tammy had taken quite well to the nurses. She was such an adorable tiny girl, and she talked so sweetly. She was in a room across from the nurses' desk, so I could eventually take some breaks from the hospital without worrying too much.

After the second week, I could even go home after supper. After the fifth week, the tube draining the urine was taken out. Then we had to wait. She had to start to relieve herself, by herself. It was really tough on her. She finally did it, and we were told that all was well, so far. If she kept doing well for the next week, we could take her home. After that it would be testing every six months for two years, then once a year for three years. If all was still okay, we had this thing beat. A week later, we took Tammy home.

J.J. had several surgeries over the next couple of years. He first started to walk with a "Quadra-pod." He had special shoes made from time to time in order to accommodate the splints. He stayed at Lord Roberts School for his elementary years, so he had to be on the bus for an hour each way. He received his therapy at the school along with special education. He was able to sight read close to twenty words: Men's washroom, exit, stop, etc., words that could get him through life. They taped a number board on the top of his desk so that numbers could be drilled until he could say them front wards, backwards and inside out. He could write them, say them and even add some of them. His walking got better and better until after a couple of years, he didn't need even a cane.

In the summer, our favourite time was spent water-skiing. We had purchased a new boat and it was a blast. We would put the kids in the front seats of the boat and they would sit for hours just riding around. I was so hooked on water-skiing that we were on the river most evenings in the summer for a couple of hours. The kids just loved it.

Chapter 10

OFF TO THE RACES...

The year after J.J's accident, Rudi and I started going to the speedway to watch the races. Rick was racing in the Late Model class. He was engaged to a really nice girl, Joy. Many times we would sit close to Rick's parents or sisters. It was always good to see them; they were just a very nice family. Even though they were related to Jeffrey, they never had any hard feelings and always treated both Rudi and me well. They always asked how the boys were, especially after J.J.'s accident. Rick was the top racer at that time, and even though Rudi didn't like him much, I still rooted for him.

I always wanted to be the first female driver at the speedway, but whenever I talked about it with Rudi, his comment was, "It's no place for a girl."

Over the course of the second year, Rudi decided he was going to race a car. He was going to show all of them how it's done. I am sure every guy who went to watch the races felt that way at one time or another, but Rudi was determined. That winter, he ventured out and found some companies who said if racing became a reality, they would sponsor him. It took two years, but his determination paid off. For the first year, Rudi said that he would run in the Super Stock class, just to get used to the track, then he would consider moving up to the Late Model class, where Rick was. Late Models took a lot more time during the year to run. Those guys raced in Winnipeg, Fargo and sometimes in Grand Forks all in one week. It would involve a lot of time and money to travel and to keep the car "up to speed."

Rudi was in charge of the mechanics, and I was in charge of making the car look good. We started to attend the monthly meetings for the club, where I met Janet Scholz. Janet was the secretary of the club, and we hit it off right away. Her husband, Henry drove a Late Model at the track. He had been at it for a couple of years by this time. Janet wasn't only secretary of the club; she also worked at the track itself. The more I watched her, the more I wanted to be the kind of person she was. She was involved with her husband's sport but had her own part in it. She wasn't just "the racer's wife" who scraped mud off the car after each race.

My first year in the club, I just observed. I had to look after the home life and get the car looking good for the first race. It was christened with the number 16, from the wheelchair van I drove. It was "fire red" with gold numbers on the doors. We had found enough sponsors to do everything for the car to make it look good.

The Speedway was owned by a little Dutchman, known to everyone as Pete. When Brookland's Speedway closed previously, he decided to build a speedway on his land. It was a tough business to run, never knowing if it was going to rain on race night. If it rained on the day before the race, they couldn't get the track ready in time. The track was made out of clay and was only used from May to September. The idea was to have the track packed to be the best before race time. Occasionally it was too wet, sometimes too dry, and most of the time they just couldn't please everyone.

Most of the drivers and pit crews were good to deal with. Every race night, the odd driver would be hard to get along with. That was where Janet came in; she could handle any situation which arose, with tact. "Whatever works," was her motto. Rudi spent most evenings in the garage working on the car. I think that was the same with all the racers.

It was a great hobby for all of us, if it only would have stayed a hobby. The first year went by without too much of a problem, but I knew racing had become serious to Rudi when he made the decision to sell the Cougar. He then bought a small box Chevy Van. It was supposed to be used for pulling the racecar. I'm sure all racer's wives agree that it's great when the last race of the season is over.

J.J. was still attending a special program at Lord Roberts School. Tammy and P.J. were still being bused to Springfield Elementary and I still drove the van for Specialty Transportation. That year, I was asked to work in the classrooms, replacing any teachers who were sick. If I came in from my run, they would let me know if they needed me and would pay me thirty-five dollars for a half-day shift. It was a really good addition to my paycheque.

My parents moved once again that year. They were offered a job in Calgary. J.J. was completely out of the wheelchair by now. We kept it around in case we were going somewhere and had to walk a long distance. Other than that, he could handle walking without a problem. He really wanted to skate like P.J and to play piano like P.J. The problem was he only had the use of one hand and arm. He never got the use out of the right arm back. His right leg was also quite weak, but he just learned to carry on with what he had. He had such a wonderful personality.

Before we knew it, May long weekend had arrived, and it was time to race again. (Most of the time after Christmas was spent getting the car ready to race.) I was offered a job at the track getting the racers and pit crew to sign in at the back gate. I was paid twenty dollars and didn't have to pay to get in. There wasn't much to do before the races anyway.

The first part of the season, Rudi blew up the motor. That was very costly. I knew he wasn't winning enough money to keep up with the damages, but I wasn't the one to look after the bills; he was. The money I made paid for groceries and the kids' expenses like shoes and clothing. Some of these bills were quite high due to J.J. needing special shoes and other needs. The lawsuit from his accident was still on the go. They said that I would be reimbursed for everything, but it could take years. I didn't have to ask Rudi for any money. We didn't race in the States at all during that year either. Rudi just wasn't doing as well as the first year.

The kids didn't see too much of Rudi that summer. He had a lot of contracts painting, along with the racing. It was so busy, half of the time he would get his mother to come to look after the kids so I could work with him. (I got to be a fairly good painter and learned to hang wallpaper too. The joke always was, "I knew way too much about the business and could probably open my own company.") In the evenings, he was mostly working on the car in the garage.

Sundays remained church day. Rudi was pretty good at keeping that priority. Part way through the summer, he made a suggestion to me that he could do the payroll and accounting on his own. I was surprised when he said that I had so much to do and that he could handle it. I believed him and didn't argue.

If I were to describe Rudi through the years we were married, I would say he was always a fair, honest and reliable person, unlike his brothers. From what I had heard from their wives, Rudi was very unique in the family. Many times, I received phone calls from collection agencies asking me how to contact a couple of his brothers. Their problems were their problems, and as long as they didn't make them ours, we were fine.

J.J. was going into grade seven that September. He was tired of traveling across the city for two hours every day to get to school, and I couldn't blame him. He wanted to go to school with everyone else in the area. I went to the school in our neighborhood, Chief Peguis Junior High, and discussed

J.J. going there for grades seven, eight and nine. They explained to me that they didn't have the teachers or the facilities to accommodate him. So, I went to the school board and put up the, "My son has rights," fight. After a month of staying on top of them–along with Rudi and me going to numerous meetings–we won. A teacher would be hired, and J.J. would be integrated into "normal" Junior High.

When it was time to go and buy new clothes for the kids for school, P.J. helped J.J. pick out all the up to date jeans and tops so that he would fit right in. For the first time, we could also find a pair of high top basketball shoes, which his splint would fit into. Finally, he wouldn't have to wear those "Fosters black leather oxfords," though they definitely served us well and got J.J. walking for the past six years since his accident.

One evening Rudi was doing the accounting and payroll, so he could pay the guys the next day. Payday was every second Friday. It was late already, so I offered to give him a hand. He was very quick to close all the books and say, "No, I am too tired and will get up early and finish." I then offered that he could go to bed and I would finish for him. He became quite angry, so I backed off right away and chalked it up to; he was tired.

The next morning, I got up and Rudi had been up for a couple of hours getting the payroll done. He poured me a coffee and said he wanted to talk to me about something. He then informed me that he was moving the business into a shop. He had found a unit in an industrial part of the city, which was quite a drive away from the house. It was expensive, but he figured the business was ready to handle it. I was surprised and gave my opinion. It didn't make sense to me to have the extra expense, and we didn't see much of him as it was. He then let me know that he was moving all the equipment and racecar to the shop. Apparently, there was a big overhead door in the back to bring the car in. It was more heated than our garage, even though he had installed a large heater the year before. He said he could move all the paint, ladders and junk there, so the garage would be free for me to park. I thought, "Pretty extreme plan just to let me park." That was a lot to swallow already, but when he told me he was selling the racecar and building a Late Model car for the next season, that was "the straw that broke the camel's back." I asked him if he had won a lottery that I didn't know about. That's when he made me feel very guilty saying that he had always given me what I wanted and now it was his turn. He had always given me what I wanted, that was true, but he still wasn't "hard done by." I never really ever wanted that much, but he did mention the convertible and the boat. I left it alone; he was right, so I just had to be quiet.

Rudi had to go to Regina for a while to paint a huge building called The Lunchbox. There was another one in Calgary, so he suggested that we go to visit my parents on Boxing Day, and then he could go to the job and check it out. He had already moved everything into the shop. At first it wasn't too bad. He wouldn't be working on the new car until after the New Year.

We did take the kids to Calgary on Boxing Day, December 26th. It was great! My parents were now looking after a huge complex of three-story apartment blocks with an outdoor pool in the center. We had our own one bedroom suite, fully furnished while we were there. It was next to my dad's office. The kids stayed with Mom and Dad, but still we all ate together. For Christmas, they surprised us with a brand new built-in dishwasher. It was still in the box. They noted that we probably wouldn't have the room to take it home in the van, so they would have it sent to us. Up to that point, I had never owned a dishwasher. What a treat this was. We *did* fit it in the van. It was a tight squeeze in the back for the kids, but I surely wasn't going to leave without it.

I really wanted to go skiing. I had learned how to ski in Europe when I was younger. Rudi thought that strapping your feet to two boards and going down a mountain was the stupidest thing he had ever heard of. Needless to say, we never went, but I still loved to visit Calgary and the mountains. There was such a "free" feeling when we were in the mountains. I never really could explain it. We had a great visit with my family, but I always hated the drive home on the boring plains. We arrived back, just in time to celebrate New Years.

Chapter 11

BACK TO AL-ANON

I was really in a state of shock when Rudi told me he was combining his company with his brother Horst's. That really wasn't good news. In my opinion, Horst wasn't a very responsible person, and from what I had heard, his drinking had gotten worse. The shop started out to be a very nice place where everything was stored neatly. That was typical of Rudi. Everything was in its place and was always clean. I had to go there quite often to bring Rudi supper, and the shop was always immaculately kept.

About a month after he and his brother combined forces, I cooked supper along with Rudi's favourite pie. I thought I would surprise him and bring him supper and desert without him asking. He hadn't asked for a while, and I felt that it was because he thought it was a long drive for me. When I walked into the shop, I could almost cut the air with a knife, the cigarette smoke was so thick. I walked into the office, and Horst was sitting at the desk. There were four other guys and the place was a mess. There were rye bottles all over the desk along with dirty cups and glasses all over the office, on filing cabinets and on the floor. I had to look twice to make sure I was in the right place. Horst yelled for Rudi to come to the front, "Your old lady is here to see you." When Rudi came in, the guys said to him, "No women allowed here." I was stunned and embarrassed so I walked out, laying down his food on the way.

In a state of confusion all the way, I went straight home. What was happening? Rudi walked in the door about five minutes later and then I started to cry. I asked him, "What was going on?" He defended Horst. I knew we were in trouble. I just went to bed, thinking the words, "drunken hangout." The next day, I thought so much about what I had learned in Al-Ateen about, "the alcoholic and the enabler."

Between my morning and afternoon runs, I phoned AA and questioned them about the situation. They suggested I go to a meeting and ask some questions there. They told me where the closest meeting was to SMD, and that there was one the next afternoon. I went home after work, fed the kids, put them to bed and out of frustration, waiting for him to come home, cleaned the house really well. I had put new placemats on the table and fresh doilies on all the living room tables. He walked in after I had just finished and was pouring a cup of coffee for myself. He looked around, and I thought he was going to comment on how good the place looked. But the bucket full of water I was cleaning with was still on the counter. I forgot to empty it. Instead, he made a comment about that being a good place to leave a bucket of dirty water. I thought it best if I just take my coffee and go to bed before I say something I would regret later.

The next afternoon, I went to the meeting. I found it hard, but I know it was eye-opening. I was renewed on what I had learned in the past and believed Rudi was an "enabler" and was like a dry alcoholic. Oh sure, he drank socially, but he was a very light drinker; maybe one or two at the most, a couple of times a month. I wasn't about to go through this again. I had been "an enabler" for my first husband already. No, Rudi definitely wasn't him, but it didn't matter who it was. I remembered going to Al-Ateen when I was younger and didn't want to fall into the same trap again. I had no idea what to do, but I was quite comfortable going to this meeting every week. I wasn't about to tell Rudi that I was going. He didn't need to know, I was doing this for myself.

It was good for me. I cried many tears and talked multitudes to the other people in the program. I learned very quickly to, "Let go and let God." God was my higher power. By the time I got back home at night, I had peace. I realized this mess in the shop and what was happening in Rudi's life was his problem, not mine. I could only help myself and not let him put the problem onto me. When he wanted to talk about it, I learned to listen but tried to have compassion and not be accusing. I wasn't perfect but learned very quickly I wasn't expected to be. To forgive and forget was so important to me but not necessarily to just forgive Rudi. I spent more time asking to be forgiven and trying to forgive myself.

I found so much peace in the program that I went twice a week. The other one was in the morning between my runs. I went with a family member. The rule was, "What is said here, stays here," so I will respect her anonymity and only speak for myself. I did the "twelve steps" over and over. I started to feel much better about myself. Sometimes Rudi would look at me like he knew something was up. I am sure he noticed the peace in me. I wasn't about to tell him, unless he asked me. I wouldn't lie to him.

P.J. and J.J. were still going to the Boys' Brigade group at the

Mennonite Church with Greg. They loved it. P.J. would always come home with a glow on his face. He still played lots of hockey, and his games became addicting for the rest of us. Tammy was playing ringette. I would get the kids ready for the games and take them. Usually, if Rudi was still working, he would come to all the games by the time they had started. The kids on P.J.'s hockey team were pretty well the same ones who had been on it for a few years already. The parents had all gotten to know each other over the years just by talking at the games and the year-end parties.

I never went to the shop anymore without being invited. That was because of the comment made, "No women allowed." Rudi asked me one morning, why I never came. I told him I wasn't invited and left it at that. He came home for supper that night and told me that I didn't need an invitation. I just smiled. I was finding that the less I said, the less of a chance I would fall into complaining. Sometimes, I felt like Rudi would start to talk about things which bother me, just to get a reaction and make me angry. If I allowed him to make me angry, it seemed like he would be justified to go sit at the shop with his brother. He could fit in to the, "Woman are nothing but naggers" club with the other guys at the shop.

I really liked my peace, and if something was said to make me angry, I quickly learned to let go of it and let God handle it for me. He did handle it for me, so quickly that it was gone right away along with the hurt feeling. I almost felt like I was being tested. Rudi would go out in the morning, leaving me with a crummy comment. I would be rushing to get out the door myself, so it wouldn't be a good time to get my books out of the drawer, which were hidden, to deal with the comment. I sure couldn't let it brew though, so I would just tell him that I was sorry he felt that way and hoped he would go out the door. I then would have a chance to deal with it before I saw him again that night. I found that if I dwelt on anything which was said that was negative, it would be like never letting a wound heal.

My Al-Anon books became my bible, and I never wanted to leave home without them. It wasn't too hard to talk to people from my group on the phone for support because Rudi wasn't around much. He came home one day at supper and asked me why I never phoned him anymore to find out when he was coming home. I told him he was a big boy and I trusted that when he was finished his work, he would come home. For some reason, that answer really bothered him. I tried to make it very clear to him that I missed his company in the evenings and on weekends, but understood that he had to work. I was being honest and felt that if he wasn't really working and just hanging out at the shop, it was his problem and I really didn't want to hear about it. I tried very hard to not open the door to negative conversation with him.

Elaine and I were good friends, but sometimes I felt like she was just calling me to get information from Rudi on what her husband was doing at the shop. I finally had to tell her I wasn't going to talk about what they were doing anymore because it really bothered me. I told her to ask Rudi if she wanted to know anything.

After a couple of months, I saw that Rudi was trying to change the situation. Leaving him to handle his own problems was really good. I didn't have to remind him of what was wrong at the shop or with what was going on. He didn't need me to heap burning coals on his head. I could see his confusion and how he bounced back and forth. He tried so hard to straighten the mess out. Going to work everyday with guys who speak so negatively about women and not having positive input was very destructive. If he came home for a couple of evenings a week and did something with the family, he would have to go back to work the next day and listen to them tell him he was a "wife pleaser" and how he should be a man and do what HE wanted. It didn't seem to matter that what he wanted most was to be home with the family. The negative draw seemed pretty powerful, and he seemed to be pretty weak

One thing I did notice was that he wasn't the happy person everyone used to know, and people started to ask me what his problem was. I said that he was fine. I tried very hard not say anything about Rudi or to him unless it was positive. I wasn't going to be a doormat though. If he did or said something I didn't like, I tried to quietly tell him how I felt then left it alone. I told him that I was lonely at night and that we missed him at the supper table.

It was getting pretty close to Christmas. Rudi suggested we have Christmas as usual with his family on the twenty-fourth, then our own on the twenty-fifth, then take off in the evening and drive to Calgary to have Christmas with my family on Boxing Day. I was thrilled and so were the kids. I had Christmas Break off from work and the kids were off from school. He said that he would take a week off. I knew it was going to be good. I could spend some time with my dad talking about the situation. He was very understanding when it came to AA.

When we arrived at my parents' house, they had supper ready for us. It was now Day three of turkey with all the trimmings. The whole family was there, which was great. My parents had set dinner up in the banquet room. We had long tables and all the grandchildren were there. There were my three kids along with Grant and Louise, who had a son and a daughter, Shanna and Dax.

Jimmy and Janet had their two kids, Jamie and Tina. I wished so much that they would all live in Winnipeg. I wanted all the nieces and nephews to come to my place on weekends. During supper, we planned to have a family reunion at our house at the beginning of the following summer. Everyone would come for a week and on race day, the whole family would go and watch Rudi race.

It was a wonderful visit. I was just so glad to be there, and it was nice to have Rudi back to normal. I once again tried to talk him into mountain skiing, but there was no way. He had never tried to water ski either. He was just not an athletic person; give him anything with a motor and he was happy, but the two words, "physical" and "fun" didn't go together in his books.

The main message my dad emphasized to me while I was there was, "Easy does it. Don't analyze or try to read too much into things. Stay positive." I really missed having my family in Winnipeg.

It didn't take long for things to return to normal. When we got home, Rudi was planning a trip to Minneapolis to pick up some new racecar parts from a company where most of the guys from Winnipeg went. He was buying the latest and the most expensive car chassis available, The Howe Fifth Stage Design. I had no idea what this was costing and wasn't about to ask. Rudi asked me to come with him to Minneapolis to buy everything. I told him I would, but wasn't sure if I really wanted to.

I didn't know how much strength I would have to make it for three days, trying to stay positive. I finally came to the conclusion that it would be fine. He was always more positive when he was away from the guys. He made arrangements for his mom to come and stay with the kids while we were gone. He arranged the hotel, so we were ready to leave.

I was told that morning that Rick, was coming with us. It seemed strange bringing Rick when he was my ex-husband's cousin. That was all in the past and now Rick was just a benefit to Rudi. He could put together a winning racecar, and that seemed to be all Rudi was interested in.

When we got to the border, he told me we had to stop to declare the money he was bringing. I laughed and said, "Only if it is over $5,000 in cash, so we don't need to worry."

He said, "We have to go in." We did and when he declared the cash, I almost needed to be held up. He had $10,000 in cash. That was a quarter of the cost of our house. I had no idea where this money came from, nor was I about to ask. I didn't say a word; I didn't have to. I'm sure the look on my face said multitudes. As we were driving, I was glad Rick had come with us because it helped me keep my mouth in check and not say anything I would regret later.

When we arrived at the hotel in Minneapolis, I went straight to bed because I didn't want to open my mouth and start to nag. I wished I could phone someone from Al-Anon. I wished I had brought my books. I just prayed for peace and soon fell asleep.

The next morning, we went to the racing company where we were buying all the parts. It took a while to load everything up, new tires along with tons of car stuff. The roll cage chassis went on the trailer, and while all of this was going on, I was sitting there trying to remember what was in my books–still trying to find peace. For a while, I wondered, "What happened to my responsible husband? Spending a fortune to have this racecar, but for what?" I got over that kind of thinking pretty quickly. I felt like I was trying to open that can of worms again.

After we were loaded up, we left right away and headed for Fargo.

As we were driving down the highway, Rudi tried to tuck some paper up in the overhead console for the stereo. It was a button tuft box above the front windshield, which had a built-in Pioneer stereo and speakers. I asked him what that was, and he told me, "It's probably better you don't know until we get home."

We arrived at the border about nine o'clock. The guy came out and asked where we had been and for how long. Rudi told him and showed him the hotel receipts as proof. The guy then asked if we had purchased anything. Rudi said, "Yes" and pointed back to the trailer. The crossing guy then took a few steps toward the trailer and said quite loudly, "Wow, a Howe Fifth Stage Design offset chassis."

All of a sudden, from the back seat, I heard a quiet, "Oh no." Rudi turned and gave Rick a look.

I said, "Oh no, what?"

Rick said that someone had probably phoned and warned the border that we were coming through with this. He said this guy would never know what kind of chassis that was unless someone had warned him.

I asked, "So?"

He looked at me and said, "That means he probably knows what it's worth."

Again, I asked, "So?" I couldn't see what the problem was. Rudi knew that he had to declare it. By then, the guy had started back towards Rudi's window. We kept quiet as Rudi handed him all the receipts.

The guy looked through them and said, "You will have to pay duty on this, park the van and all three of you come inside.

Rudi parked and said, "Come in, it should only take a few minutes."

Rudi had to fill out papers, so I phoned home to let them know we were on our way. Finally, all the papers were filled out, Rudi paid the money for duty and taxes and I said, "We have to stop and get something for a headache." I knew if I didn't get something soon, it would only be a matter of time before it developed into a migraine. I turned to leave and the guy told us to wait. He told us that we had to answer some questions. I thought, "Now what? I have a headache." They told us to follow them.

The three of us were put in separate rooms. I couldn't figure out what was going on, Rudi had declared everything, gave him the receipts and paid the money. What was the problem? I sat by myself in the room for a long time. I tried the door, but it was locked. The overhead lights were florescent, so my head started to pound. I was getting quite worried when a guy finally came in and said, "We just finished questioning your husband and his friend. It could be a long day if someone doesn't start telling us the truth. He said, "Do you realize you could lose your van and your trailer and everything you bought?"

I was angry and asked him, "What is the problem? What did we do?"

He asked me why I was so angry. I told him, "I am locked in a room away from my husband, being questioned, and I don't know why. Mainly though, it's because I have a headache and if I don't get something for it soon, it can turn into a migraine."

He said I could have something when we are finished and left the room again. I sat for about another hour. I started to cry, and the more I cried, the more my head hurt, the more my head hurt, the more I cried. My stomach started to get upset too, but that was normal when I was getting a migraine.

Finally, the guy came back in. I must have been quite a sight. He said that if I answered his questions, he would get me something for my headache. I was really angry by then, so began to cry even harder. Through my sobs I told him, "I'm not about to say a word unless you tell me what's going on and if you don't tell me what's going on, then I want to call my lawyer. I have rights too."

I guess he took me seriously because he started to tell me what the problem was. He said, "You came into the States with $10,000 and came out with $1,100. The receipts only add up to $5,900. What happened to the other $3,000?"

My head was hurting too much to follow the arithmetic so I just believed him. I told him to ask Rudi. "He was the one who had the money, not me. He was the one who bought the parts. I was sitting in the van when all this was happening."

He asked me how much the car parts came to.

I told him that I didn't know.

He said, "Your husband spends $8,900 and you can't account for where it was spent?"

I laughed and said, "Yeah, well, that's the way it goes. Did you ask my husband where the $3,000 went?"

He answered, "Yes."

So then I asked what his answer was.

Instead of answering, he asked me what I did when I was in the hotel in Minneapolis.

I replied that I slept.

He then asked what Rudi was doing.

I said, "I don't know, I was asleep. Why?"

He told me that Rudi had said, "We went out and got some hookers."

I knew it was a lie, but for some reason Rudi was short $3,000. I didn't have a clue as to why or why he was telling this guy that. I said, "Well if he said they did that, then I guess they did."

The officer got really angry and asked if I would really let Rudi go out with a hooker.

I said, "Let him? My husband is a big boy and he really doesn't come to me for permission to do anything, so it has nothing to do with, 'Let Him!'"

He left the room again and I reminded him, as the door was closing, that he had promised to get something for my headache.

I put my head on the table and dozed off. I woke up about fifteen minutes later and felt a little better. Three hours had passed since I had gone into the room. The door opened and another guy came in carrying a bottle of Tylenol. He gave me the bottle and told me to take whatever I needed. I shook out three and asked if I could use the washroom. He told me to follow him. As I walked down the hall, I looked around to see if I could spot Rudi or Rick, but they were nowhere around. The guy was waiting for me when I came out of the washroom and led me back to the room.

He said, "It shouldn't be much longer."

It didn't take long before my friendly officer came back in the door. I remembered for a moment my dad saying to me, "You get further with honey than vinegar." I thought I would try and give it a shot. My headache was lightening up, finally. Big tears started to roll down my cheeks and I thought I could use them to my benefit. He asked, "What's the problem? I didn't even say anything yet."

I told him, "You come in and lay on me that my husband was out with a highly paid hooker for the night. I'm only human. How do you think I'm feeling? I was wondering where he was that night. I woke up and he was gone. I thought maybe, he had gone for a drink to his friends room." I had outright lied but was at the stage that I didn't care anymore. I just wanted to go home.

He said, "Your friend had eight hundred dollars on him. Rudi said that he had 'given' it to him, but Rick said that he 'owed' it to him."

I was lost. I told the guy, "I really don't know what is going on. We have been here for five hours, and I have three children waiting at home." I then asked if I could take a bus and the guys could handle it.

He said that they were tearing apart the van, doing a search and I could go and watch if I wanted to. We went outside. At least it was something else to look at, other than the four walls.

Almost everything was out of the van including the table and the cushions. The bed was taken apart. The guy doing the search was really big, appearing to me to be about three hundred pounds. The van wasn't very big. I noticed my suitcase was lying on a bench and my clothes were in a pile on the ground. Rudi and Rick were standing and watching, both with their hands in their pockets. I could see a, "very big sorry" on Rudi's face as he looked at me. He asked if I had gotten something for my headache. I nodded my head and didn't say a word.

It was really cold outside so I almost went back in, but the guy had gone in the passenger door and was trying to open the console where the stereo was. He pulled it open a bit and took a peek inside. I remembered Rudi sticking the paper in the console through the other side. This whole thing started to become very clear. "I bet that paper was the real receipt for all the parts he bought, and the company gave him a fake one for less money so that Rudi wouldn't have to pay so much for duty and taxes." I felt ill. If they found that paper, they could take our van and trailer away. I looked at Rudi, and I think he knew that I had figured it out. The guy went around to the driver's door, and I thought, "Oh no, we are finished."

Rudi spun around and quietly mouthed, "sh. . . ." Rick just shook his head and looked at the ground. At that instant, I thought to myself, "Oh God, forgive him for this. 'Let go and Let God' handle it." I turned to walk away.

I heard the guy swear, then say to Rudi, "Is there something wrong with this door?"

Rudi replied, "There wasn't before I got out of it when we went into the building."

I came back as the guy was pulling the door again. It opened just a crack but then got stuck. He asked me to get inside and push. I went inside and pretended to push but was barely touching the door. It was a really tight squeeze to get out the sliding door, so I said to the guy, "You can get in through the sliding door in the back." I knew he was too big to get to the front of the van through the sliding door. He came around and got in, but knowing it was hopeless, tried to reach for the console, which was just at his fingertips. He was angry and embarrassed and said when he got out, "Clean up this mess and get out of here."

We threw everything in the van, just piling it up on top of the benches. We then jumped in and took off. Not one word was said by anyone for the first five miles, and then Rudi pulled over. I asked him what he was doing and he said, "Just putting everything at least kind of back into place." Rick and I both said that we would do it and for him to just keep driving. Rudi then opened his door fully and the three of us just looked at each other and laughed. Nobody was able to figure out why that door wouldn't open for the officers. Now there was nothing wrong with it. I just said, "Thank you Jesus!"

When we got home, Rudi showed me the real receipt hidden in the console for $7,000. The one they had given at the border was for $4,000. I was laughing a bit when I asked, "So, where did you guys get the money for the hooker?"

He was embarrassed and just said quietly, "Oh, he told you I said that."

It didn't take long before the racecar was well on its way to being built. It was a big job. It was up to me to decide the colour and the number. There was already a number sixteen registered in the Late Model class so I chose number fifty-five, the year he was born. The car was going to be painted red, white and blue along with the lettering in black. It was a very impressive car but still, extremely expensive.

The body shop that sponsored the painting on the racecar was owned by two brothers Mike and Toni. Their sister had come to stay with them from Austria. I didn't really catch the story on her because she couldn't speak English very well. Her name was Helena. She had two daughters who were in their early teens. I was told her husband was in jail in Austria; I don't know why. I didn't know how old she was, but she always wore a babushka like they do in Europe. She also wore an apron all the time. Whenever I went to the shop, I felt sorry for her because she was always in the back, sanding shuffle-boards. It was a side business they had started so she could have a job. She was now living with her parents. She was quite a bit shorter than I was and had a very masculine face with no make up. I always wanted to be able to speak to her and take her home. I thought I could dress her up and show her how to put make-up on–sort of, the before and after deal, where she comes out beautiful. She was always thrilled when Rudi came in because she could speak to him in German.

One afternoon, Rudi and I were both sitting in the body shop. We had just taken a break from working on the racecar. Helena walked in with a roaster. She opened it up on the desk, and scooped out pork chops, sauerkraut and potatoes onto two plates for her brothers. She then sat down, put the roaster on her lap and started to eat the rest with her fingers. I said that I had plastic forks in the van. We always carried them under the seat. Rudi translated and she kept saying in English, "It's okay. It's okay."

We left right away saying that we had to get home for the kids. I said to Rudi, "I wish I could speak German enough to help her get settled properly in Canada. I should go home and go through my closet, get out the clothes I don't wear anymore and give them to her." I was pretty sure I had some jeans in my closet that would fit her. I said that I knew the jeans would be too long for her but that I had the technology to fix that.

He replied laughing, "There is no hope."

I was a little angry about that comment; I didn't think it was necessary.

The car was painted and taken back to Rudi's shop to do the finishing touches. I barely saw him in the evenings. I had extra money and really wanted to sign up at the Fit Stop for aerobics and to work out. I knew Rudi wouldn't like the idea. He thought I would end up muscular and always said he didn't want a muscle bound wife, so I didn't ask. I just said, "You are busy most nights and I am lonely so I'm signing up at the Fit Stop for aerobics."

He got the message that I wasn't asking anymore as much as telling him. He asked, "If you have time to do that in the evening and between your runs, then why aren't you coming to the shop to help me?"

Wow, how that got turned around. I just said, "I wasn't invited." That was the end of that conversation.

The next day, I signed a one-year contract at the Fit Stop. I could go between my runs to work out when I wasn't at Al-Anon, running to the kids' schools, substitute teaching or running around for the race car. There were ten "between run breaks" in a week. "Heck," I thought, "I can probably add one more thing."

Racing season came fast. The kids were so excited with the new car. I have to admit that so was I. It was very impressive. While Rudi was out working on the car, I was getting ready for our family reunion. Grant and Louise bought a truck with a camper on the back, so that four people could stay in there. The boys wanted to sleep in the tent next to Uncle Grant's trailer. Their cousin, Dax, was going to sleep in the tent with them. Tammy was invited to stay in the trailer with her cousin, Shannon. That freed up two bedrooms in the house.

Jimmy, Janet and the kids couldn't make it because Jimmy had to work. That was really too bad, I would have loved to see them too. My two sisters could stay in the boys' bedroom and my parents could stay in our bedroom. Rudi and I could make do in Tammy's room. It was tight, but it was only for five days. How do you cook for thirteen people in a small kitchen like mine? Rudi bought a huge barbecue and said that I could do the vegetables in the house and he would barbeque the meat outside. I really had a good laugh at that offer. The idea of the barbeque was great. It even had a burner on the side that could be used, but Rudi barbeque? He couldn't even make toast if his life depended on it.

The week before everyone came, Rudi had the new dishwasher hooked up. It had been a year and a half already since we brought it home, but hooking it up just wasn't a priority in life. If I had known it would only take my family coming to finally get it done, I would have had the reunion the year before.

Rudi had a few races in under his belt in the new car before the family arrived. My job had just finished for the summer, and the weather was stifling. We had been in the high nineties for over a week, and it wasn't about to quit any time soon. Rudi was getting used to the new car, but the speed was a bit beyond him. It was much different than he was used to, and I could see he was feeling intimidated. The uneasiness he had lived with for the past years only added to his confusion. He had taken some time to clean the shop before everyone came. He wanted my dad to come and see the car before the race. He came back feeling pretty good about the whole thing. He said that I should go and see how the shop could be so immaculate. I told him that I could stop by in a couple of days.

I had taken a drive over with the kids on the Wednesday, pulling up at the same time as Rudi. He didn't look very happy and still had the car on the trailer from the night before. He said he was taking the car home and putting it in the garage to work on while my family was there. I went into the shop and understood why. The place was again starting to look like a dump and a drunken hangout.

Rudi just said, "It was spotless on Friday. Obviously over the weekend, Horst had his gang over. I can't have the family see it like this and don't have time to clean it again."

Everyone arrived on time on Friday. They had all traveled together. Grant and my dad did all the barbequing, while Rudi was the foreman. We all agreed that it was safer that way.

My parents came to church with us on Sunday while the rest stayed home and cooked breakfast. After church, I told my father, "I didn't get much from the sermons and didn't have much peace from church."

He said, "It doesn't matter about going to church. There are too many people who just go to church on Sunday and for the rest of the week, forget and not live by the rules. 'Religion' is religion but 'Spirituality' is a walk with God one step at a time." He went on to say, "Church is good for the kids. It gives them some tools for when they get older, some understanding about God to build a foundation for them to make decisions for themselves."

I told him about Helena at the shop and how she dressed. I added that I thought I could be friends and help her as she was new in Canada but we didn't speak the same language.

He said, "She has to learn English from someone and you shouldn't just think about it; you should at least offer to help in some way. Giving her some clothes you don't use anymore is probably a good start." He reminded me, "When we moved to France, I was always impressed how you could get along with other people even though you didn't speak the same language as them, until later." Then he told me how my mom and he relied on me to get them through the language barrier.

He told me that if I was praying at all for love, God usually gave us "problem people." I definitely was praying for that. He said, "If you are asking for favour, God gives us opportunity. Don't expect to receive what you want, God usually gives what is needed." I never forgot that. As for the kids going to church, I believed what he was saying because every Sunday when we were growing up, my parents took us to church. No matter where we were living or staying, we always traveled around, but we always had church and God as our solid foundation.

Tuesday came–race day. It was sunny and really hot. I was so glad it wasn't raining because Rudi really wanted my family to see him race. We all went out early and it was great. Rudi had his very own fan club in the stands, and they were an awesome cheering group. They let everyone know who they were rooting for. My mom was the leader of the pack. We had arrived early. I took Janet to the stands before the race started and introduced her to the whole gang. They had heard so much about her up to then. We both laughed in the pits throughout the whole race, watching them have such a good time. Henry, Janet's husband, didn't meet them until after the race. Racecar drivers' brains shut off until after race time, they only have a one-track mind.

Since we were there so early, my family was front and center. The announcer in the tower, Pat Mooney, had a lot of fun using them as a focal point for the night. He was referring to them as, "The cowboys who came in from the west and never saw a race before." I watched him race when Brooklyn Speedway was around. He and I were close to the same age, but I always looked at him as a big brother. He had a natural born talent when it came to announcing. Rudi did really well in the heat race, which set him up to start the feature in a decent position. The feature was a real disappointment to him. Something broke on the car in the middle of the race, and he had to come off the track. He never did make it back on.

After the race, the family went down to the pits. Rudi said that it was a stupid bolt, which shook loose in the bell housing, but they hadn't seen it right away. My dad then said to him that the next day, he would spend some time with Rudi, showing him little tips to help, so that problem wouldn't happen again in the future. My dad had spent his adult life as an airline technician and said, "Vibration can really throw things out of whack." He told Rudi to torque all the bolts to where they are supposed to be, then to draw a line with a bright coloured nail polish across it and a bit further. That way, they just had to look in the motor and they could see if the line was separated, it was then out of place. Rudi was so impressed.

I hated to see my family leave. I really loved the talks I had with my parents. I have to say that when they all left, my house seemed to have grown to twice the size. Meals got far easier to cook.

Rudi went back to work and seemed to be working longer hours. I was sure the racecar was costing him a fortune. He wasn't winning much money, at least not near enough to keep the car going. It seemed to have grown into a vicious cycle for him. He would race and not do well. He was so tired. He would then have to work to try to cover the costs. He started to work weekends to get enough money to race, then he was really tired when he raced and didn't do well, so had to work more hours to support the sport. It seemed like it was never ending.

So many times, he would come home and sit and stare off into space and say quietly, "Why did I ever start this? What happened to our good life?" I told him that I was still walking "the same walk," it wasn't me who had changed. The only thing I had changed was my attitude towards Rudi's problems. Lots of friends asked me what was wrong with Rudi. It almost seemed like he was having a burnout. Everyday, I worked on the weddings in the morning and then the kids and I would go to Birds Hill Park to lie by the lake all afternoon. A couple of evenings a week, I would go to aerobics. We didn't ski anymore that summer. "There was no time," Rudi said. Rudi told me that life was moving too fast for him and he needed some time off. He asked me to talk to my parents and see if it was all right to go visit during the second week of August. Of course they said "yes."

I packed some of my clothes that I didn't wear anymore and got brave enough, one afternoon, to drive over to the body shop to offer them to Helena. Rudi said that he would meet me there, and we could go for coffee after. I arrived before he did and left the box in the car. I thought I would ask her first if she minded. I went in and she was in the back as usual, sanding shuffleboards. I was really glad I had come. She was wearing the usual babushka and apron along with a thin polyester dress down to her ankles and runners. I said as simply as I could that I had some clothes, that I didn't wear anymore and asked if she would like them. I don't think she understood because she looked past me, saying something like, "I vant heme." I didn't know what a 'heme' was, so I tried to say it again, pointing to my clothes. She seemed frustrated and again said, "I vant heme," pointing past me. I turned around and Rudi was standing there, behind me.

He said, "Come on. Let's go."

I said, "I don't understand what she is saying." Then it hit me. She wasn't saying anything in German to me.

She was saying, "I want him." She wanted my husband–blunt and straightforward. She wanted him. I laughed a nervous laugh, thinking how much gall she had.

I said to Rudi, "I'm leaving now," still laughing. He asked me where I was going. I told him, "To take a box of clothes to the Salvation Army," and walked past him.

He said, "You aren't leaving me here, alone, with her?" We walked out.

I had a hard time getting over this. I definitely wasn't threatened by her but was shocked at how she could just bluntly say what she had said. For the next week, while we were getting ready to go to Calgary, it became a joke between us. I would say to him, "I vant you." I told him that she desperately needs someone who speaks her language and who can look after her and her daughters. I said, "I sure hope I didn't ever come across as being that desperate."

Rudi just laughed and said, "No, I really did 'vant' you."

The week before we were to leave for Calgary, Rudi blew his motor at the races. A new one was going to cost him a few thousand dollars. I spent a lot of time on the phone to people at Al-Anon. I couldn't take in too many meetings in the summer because the kids were home. I had my head together enough by the end of the week just in time to get another blow. Rudi had to work; there was no way he could take the time off. He had to get another motor. The car was too expensive to stop racing in the middle of the season, and he had to work as many hours as he could to get the new engine. I said that I was sorry to hear he wasn't coming with us. He was obviously shocked that I would even consider going to Calgary without him. I made it quite clear that my parents were expecting us, and I was really excited to go. If he changed his mind, we would definitely be thrilled, but we were still going.

Chapter 12

MILES APART

"and no terrible disasters will strike you or your home.
God will command his angels to protect you wherever
you go." Psalm 91:10–11

I knew for my own sake and for the sake of the kids, I still had to go to Calgary. I also knew this was going to be a real test for me. I had gotten the chance to take in two meetings before they made it clear; it was totally up to me. If I were to do it, it should be because I wanted to go, and not to spite Rudi. I phoned my parents and talked to them. They still really wanted us to come. They said that they were disappointed Rudi couldn't make it, but they were glad I was still bringing the kids. They were concerned it was a long trip to make with the kids on my own. I replied that I was concerned too, but it would definitely be one step at a time. They told me to phone collect while I was traveling, so they could keep tabs on where I was. They also told me if I got tired at all, to stop at a hotel and they would pay the bill. I promised I would. My dad said as I got off the phone, "Remember your serenity prayer." It was so nice to have that unspoken understanding. I could pretend that everything was wonderful, but my parents knew what I was going through and what it took for me to get to their place on my own with the kids.

I felt bad while I was packing up. By the look on Rudi's face, I felt that I had really depressed him. I told him that if he changed his mind or if he finished his work early, I would gladly buy him a plane ticket to come and meet us for a few days.

I was surprised at the angry tone I heard back saying, "I can buy my own plane ticket," he added, "You won't make it without me, you know."

I asked him what he meant by that.

He answered, "You can't do a trip like this with the kids without me."

I told him I didn't want to but I really didn't have a choice.

He said, "Of course you have a choice, you don't have to go."

I asked him if he really wanted us to sit in the house and do nothing

155

while he was working twelve to fourteen hours a day to make the money for the motor. He walked out of the room and didn't answer.

Rudi helped me load up the van. He asked if I was sure I had enough money. I told him not to worry, and I would call him while I was on the highway. If he wasn't in the shop, I would leave a message on the answering service as to where I was. He took the lawnmower out to mow the lawn and was standing, leaning on it as we all got in the van. I felt really bad about the sad look on his face, so I got back out and went over to him. I whispered, "I will really miss you on the trip and sure wish you would change your mind."

He half grinned and said, "I will take the day off today and take you water skiing if you stay."

I just smiled and got back in the van. He knew that water skiing was my weakness, but I still felt I really had to leave. What I really wanted to do was to get on my knees in front of him and beg him to come. I drove away thinking of step eleven in the program; "Praying for the knowledge of Gods will in this and the power to carry it out." The van didn't run out of gas or get a flat so far, so I figured God's will was that I make the trip, without Rudi.

When I arrived at the city limits, I started to cry. How was I ever going to do this? Rudi was right; I couldn't do it without him. I stopped just past the perimeter highway and phoned a friend from the program. I was only three minutes out of the city and already I was out of control. She reminded me that everyone was praying for me in this situation and, "Letting go and Letting God," was tough right now but would get easier with every mile. She said to stop looking at Calgary and start looking smaller, "One step at a time." I went back into the van where the kids were all in the back bed with their Walkmans on. They all had different tastes in music, so Walkmans were very important on our trips. I decided I was only going to drive to Portage la Prairie, which was about a half hour away.

I arrived in Portage la Prairie and thought, "Alright, that was easy. Now I will attempt a bit harder step and drive to Brandon." It was working. I could handle thinking that way, but if my mind drifted to the fact that Calgary was so far away, I would quickly say the serenity prayer in my mind: *"God grant me the serenity to accept the things I cannot change."* I couldn't change the fact that Rudi was not coming on this trip. I could have tried a guilt trip on him, but that wasn't fair. He seemed to have plenty on his mind without me throwing guilt on top of it all.

"The courage to change the things I can." I could change my way of

thinking; I had my higher power, God with me. Who better to make the trip with? I had the kids with me, who were great travel companions.

Each of them took a turn in the front seat to keep me company, and each of them fell asleep shortly after they did. I thought, "Was this called 'generation gap,' or was I just a boring mother?" They would talk for about ten minutes before they fell asleep. The deal was that the person sitting in the front seat keeping me company could play his or her cassette in the overhead stereo. I became very educated on music on that trip. I heard everything from Elvis to Twisted Sister to Michael Jackson.

"And the wisdom to know the difference." That was sometimes pretty tough, to know if what I was doing was for the right reasons or did I have a hidden agenda. Lots of times, I would put myself in the other person's shoes to see how I would feel if I were in that situation. Quite often I could feel their hurt or guilt, and it would help me to know how to be compassionate in the situation. It didn't always work, though.

I found out that driving on a trip like this was great for thinking. Memories and good times would come flooding in. I didn't allow myself to think of the problems. If they popped in my head, I would quickly think, "Let go and Let God." It was always "eye opening" to me as to how fast the problems were gone and good thoughts would replace them.

I thought of some of the things that P.J. had been telling me for the past few months and started to realize just how much wisdom and knowledge he had and how right he was. P.J. was best of friends with Greg. They were both very involved with the church programs and always included J.J. in whatever was going on. Every Thursday night, they still went to Boys' Brigade where they went on hikes, canoe trips and camping programs. It was great for the boys. P.J. arrived home one night from the program and he was so excited. He couldn't stand still as he told me that there was a speaker at the group that night. He "accepted Christ into his heart." He was only ten years old at the time. He was bursting with joy.

After that, he would preach to me. When I was upset, he would quote a scripture from the Bible. I had talked to Greg's mother and asked, "What is this all about?"

She said, "We are Christians."

To this, I replied, "Well so am I, but I want to know more details on "accepting Christ," like P.J. said." I just wanted to make sure he wasn't getting into this "born again" stuff that I had seen on television.

She took the time to explain to me in detail that they believed, "Jesus died on the cross so our sins would be forgiven. By accepting Christ into our hearts, we were turning our lives and our will over to God for him to lead us in a daily and personal walk with Him."

It reminded me so much of the Al-Anon Program's third step: "To make a daily decision to turn our will and our life over to God." I thought, "Well that sure won't hurt me." It seemed like P.J. and J.J. had found their own program.

One day, we were coming home from church when P.J. asked if I knew what he wanted to be when he grew up. I replied, "Maybe, a world famous hockey player."

He smiled and laughed, as he said, "No."

I said, "A painter?"

He laughed even harder and said, "No way."

I said that I give up.

To which he replied, "A youth pastor."

I was surprised but thrilled. The way kids are into drugs nowadays; I could handle my son being a youth pastor. I chalked it up to our church where P.J. always got the lead in the Christmas and Easter programs. He was a natural with no fear of getting up and playing the parts, and he always did very well.

We drove to Regina, and I was still feeling pretty good. I didn't want to stop yet for the day, but I really was tired. I asked the kids if they wanted to do a bit of shopping for junk food for the trip. They informed me that this is considered a really dumb question. We never have junk food in our daily lives. It was always saved for times like this so that it was extra special. We shopped for about an hour. Then we bought ice creams because it was close to ninety-five degrees outside, and we didn't have air-conditioning in the van. I phoned the shop and Rudi answered. I told him that we were in Regina, munching on ice cream cones. I almost felt like there was disappointment in his voice when he asked how the van was running. He said that he had checked the weather and there were thunderstorms coming from the west in the late afternoon. He suggested we shut it down in Regina and find a hotel with a swimming pool. I told him it was very tempting but I really wanted to get as far as I could today, so that there would be less driving the next day.

We continued on through Moose Jaw and just kept on going. It was so hot and we were now in the long stretch of highway, which is so boring, heading to Swift Current. The kids all dozed off after stuffing themselves with junk food, so I cranked up the ABBA tapes and just kept on going. (Rudi and I really liked ABBA when we traveled, and the sound on the Pioneer Stereo was great.) J.J. started to complain that it was too loud and he couldn't sleep. I felt sorry for them in the back of the van. The vent in the roof was open all the way, but only the two front windows opened so it was really hot in the back. I turned the stereo off and turned on the CB radio to see if there were any truckers talking. That was always entertaining.

The radio was quiet, so I thought about the twelve steps in the Al-Anon program. The first step was, "To realize I had become powerless over a problem and life had become unmanageable." I thought of how good life was. I had a great job, which gave me time off with the kids in the summer. I thought of how lucky I was to have met Rudi. He was a good husband and father. He was just in a slump, but he was smart and wouldn't let it get the better of him. He would figure it out and fix the mess we were in. I was powerless over the problem. I couldn't say what I really wanted to say. If I could, it would come out something like, "Rudi, I know the race car has created major debts in our lives. It isn't a secret anymore. I think if you sold the car, then you wouldn't have to work so many hours anymore. Then you wouldn't need your brother to share the costs of the shop and be a partner anymore. Come to think of it, you wouldn't even need the shop anymore." Well that sure is a "controlling" thought, isn't it? I then thought to myself, "If he really does love racing, then he will figure this out. As for the shop and business sharing with his brother, I had no right to try to change that. He would get fed up on his own time and deal with it. If he didn't, I wouldn't let that affect our lives."

I then thought about steps four and five in the program: "To make a searching and fearless moral inventory of myself." And, "To admit to God, to ourselves and another human being, the exact nature of our wrongs." I wondered if something is wrong with me. I chuckled to myself, thinking, "Something I have done wrong? How could that be possible? I didn't do anything wrong." After a good laugh, I did some serious thinking. "Am I right in not sharing with Rudi the fact that I was going to the program? Maybe it's time to tell him, so he has the option to go too if he wants." Then I felt guilty that I hadn't told him yet. I was wallowing in the guilt but couldn't help thinking, "The reason I went to the program was because I knew it was a *personal* journey of recovery. Personal? Did that justify me not sharing with Rudi, so he could choose if he wanted that personal journey for himself?" I then thought that this was too hard for me at the moment, and I would talk to my dad about it when I got to Calgary.

When I arrived in Swift Current, the kids woke up. There was no sign of rain yet, and I still felt pretty good. So we stopped for gas, washrooms and cold drinks and then kept on going. I wish I hadn't. We were half way between Swift Current and Medicine Hat when the sky turned a strange shade of green. I knew that meant trouble. I told P.J. to look at the map and see if there were any bigger towns coming up, so that we could stop for the night. The next couple of towns were off the highway, but in fifty miles, it looked like there was a fair size one on the highway. I said, "Alright, that's where we are stopping. We will get a bite to eat for supper, then find a hotel." I kept looking at the sky and worrying, but I didn't want the kids to know we had a potential problem brewing over the horizon. The wind started to pick up and Tammy asked me if a tornado was going to get us. It then became quite dark, and I could see the kids were worried.

I tried to keep the conversation light. I told P.J. to turn on the CB radio and see if there were any truckers in the area. He kept calling, but the radio was silent. We tried to get a radio station to hear the weather, but all I could find was the CBC, which didn't help. It then started to rain so we had to close the windows. The wind was blowing the rain in on us. It was so humid that the rain felt good, but I didn't think the velvet seats would take to it so well. I must have said the serenity prayer over in my head about ten times during the next few minutes. I thought that God probably heard me the first time, but it sure wouldn't hurt to reinforce it a few more times.

The kids were very quiet and I knew they were scared. But I had to just keep going to get to the town. It started to rain so hard; I had no choice but to pull over. I couldn't even see where the road was anymore. I couldn't see where I was pulling over. It felt like the shoulder, but I was only guessing. I thought what if I am still out on the road a bit and a semi hits us. I was losing control of myself. I picked up the CB microphone and started to ask, "Is there anyone out there? Can anyone hear me?" No one answered.

Then the van started to rock quite hard sideways from the wind. I told the kids to come up by the table and do up their seatbelts. I figured if this van is going to go flying through the air or if it is a tornado and it starts us rolling, we have more hope if we are strapped in. Suddenly I heard a very clear voice over the radio. It was a man's voice, and he asked, "Was someone calling?"

I picked it up and replied, "Yes." I started to cry and told the man what was happening. He asked me where I was and I told him that I didn't know.

I gave him a rough idea and he said, "Not to worry, it's just one of those prairie storms; short but not sweet." He said that he was heading west and had already been through the storm. The worst part would be over in about fifteen minutes.

P.J. said, "Fifteen minutes," turning to Tammy and J.J, "There is only about eight minutes left, so let's time it."

I realized that God had taken over. He gave me the trucker to settle me down, and P.J. to settle the other two down. The trucker started to ask me questions. I am sure he was just trying to keep my mind off the storm. He asked me where I was coming from and where I was going. He asked how old the kids were and why was I traveling alone. (Why do guys think women can't travel without a man present?) We talked so much that I almost didn't notice the van stopped rocking and the rain lightened up enough for me to see the highway again. P.J. then commented on how I was parked so perfectly on the shoulder when I couldn't see. We both looked at each other as if we knew it was God who parked the van. Neither of us said anything.

I continued on while still talking to the trucker. He suggested I carry on to Medicine Hat if I was looking for a hotel. There was more of a chance to find a vacancy there and better hotels. He said that it was only a half an hour away.

That's what we did. We carried on to Medicine Hat, picked up Kentucky Fried Chicken and got a hotel room. We munched on chicken and sat on the beds watching television. I left a message on the shop answering machine, letting Rudi know where we were. He called back an hour later. I didn't tell him anything about the storm. He talked to the kids after he talked to me, and Tammy said, "Daddy, there was a big storm and Mommy started to cry and talked to the man on the CB radio." When she handed me the phone, I got reamed out for not telling him, myself. I just said that I didn't want him to worry. Later, I fell asleep realizing that we only had a couple of hours drive left to get to Calgary. I talked to my parents the night before and they said they would have a nice lunch ready when we arrived.

When I pulled up in front of my parents' place, I shut off the van and sat back, feeling pretty good and thinking, "I am physically exhausted but I did it." I thanked God in my head and said out loud, "I made it."

I loved to spend time with my mom and dad. It was always so relaxing. I did next to nothing most of the day except lay by the pool with the kids and jump in once in a while to cool off. I was already tanned and didn't think it was possible to get any darker, but I did. My sisters lazed around the pool with us as we listened to Thelma's ghetto blaster for the whole week.

One day it rained in the afternoon, so we all went to the Calgary Zoo.

Then another day, my parents took us to Banff for the day. P.J. loved the mountains as much as I did. I always said that when I look at the mountains or go through them, any problems I have seem to disappear, and I get lost in the beauty. I believe there is lots of truth in the saying; "It is God's Country." Rudi called every day, but we usually weren't there to get the phone. He would call back at night. I almost felt like he wasn't happy that we were having a good time. He said that I wouldn't make it without him, and I think he was disappointed when I did.

We were having such a good time; I really didn't want to go home. Part of the reason was, I dreaded the drive and part of it was because I was so relaxed. I told my dad and said, "I almost feel guilty."

He said that we are always welcome and could stay as long as we wanted. He said that both Mom and he loved having the kids and me there. Then he asked me if I was really enjoying myself or did I just not want to go home in order to stay away from the problem.

I laughed and said, "I will think about that before I answer." I sat back and thought about it, but Rudi called before I could come to a conclusion. He asked when I was leaving, to which I replied that I didn't know. I asked him how the work was going.

He said, "One more week of hard labour and I should be able to have the motor paid for. One good thing was I didn't miss the race on Tuesday because it was rained out." He didn't want to lose any more points.

I asked what he would think if I stayed another week while he finished the job. Would he be able to help me drive back?

"Oh," he said and sounded quite angry, "What's the matter? Did the world traveler lose some independence between Winnipeg and Calgary?"

My family was all sitting close by, so I thought I would try to lighten up the conversation with some sick humour. I asked if his cooking skills were getting better while I was gone. Obviously, that was the wrong question.

He answered with, "Do you think it is funny to come home every night to an empty house after working so hard? Do you know how hard it is to work fourteen hours a day while my family is sitting around the pool relaxing nine hundred miles from me?"

I said, "We are eight hundred and twenty miles away." He didn't laugh. I added that I would talk to him later when the kids went to bed.

He then told me not to call until I had decided when I was coming home. He seemed really bothered.

My dad was looking at me when I hung up the phone. He said, "I take it that didn't go well."

I responded, "You took it right, and I guess I had better go home."

I made some tea and got the kids to bed. My mom asked what I was going to do. I told her I was really hoping he would fly down and drive back with us, but he said he had another week to work on the job. My mom said they were talking and thought maybe they would take the camper and go to Moose Jaw for the weekend with the girls. It was a long drive, and I knew they were just trying to help out.

My dad said, "At least you will have company on the road. The kids can go in our car while Thelma and Estella can drive with you."

I phoned home and told Rudi what my parents had suggested. He thought that it sounded like a really good idea. My parents liked the campground in Moose Jaw, and we had even met there a couple of times previously. It was half way between Winnipeg and Calgary. Rudi would work late for the next few days so he could finish and we could spend some time together. He told me that he didn't like this vacationing thing without him. I became quite confused so I went to bed.

P.J. didn't want to leave because he had made a good friend there. My parents volunteered that he could stay for the rest of the summer, but I didn't think it was a good idea. I told him that if his grandparents agreed, he could spend some time with them the next summer. Of course, he asked them right away, and they said he could stay the whole summer if he wanted to.

We arrived in Moose Jaw in the early evening. We were staying at the hotel by the campground because there wasn't enough room in the trailer. We were still asleep at eight the next morning when there was a knock at the door. Thinking it was my mom telling me to come have breakfast, I opened the door and had to give my head a shake. Rudi was standing there with a funny smile and a cup of coffee in each hand. The kids began yelling to him.

P.J. said, "Good, now we have someone who knows how to drive." I noticed lately he was getting to be a bit of a male chauvinist. I was so glad Rudi came. All of a sudden, I had peace of mind knowing I didn't have to drive. I asked him how he got there. He said that he had worked really late the night before and heard one of the guys say that he was leaving for Vancouver. So, he asked if he could catch a ride.

"It was great," he said, "I slept all the way." He said that he was just talking to my parents, and we were supposed to go and meet them for breakfast. The kids got dressed and went flying out the door to Gramma's camper. I showered, got ready and helped Rudi load up the van.

Chapter 13

FACE OF CHANGE TO COME

"For he is the kind of man who is always thinking about the cost" Proverbs 23:7 (NIV)

The trip home was very talkative, but I found Rudi to be quite hyper. He was talking about selling the racecar and equipment after the season, and then he would get rid of the shop after the one-year lease was up. He would not be partners with Horst anymore and move the company home again.

I said, "Gee, maybe I should go away more often."

His reply, "Maybe it would be a really good idea if you never did it again."

He told me he was in such a bind during the past year because he rang up so much debt and moved the business out of the house. He thought that he could catch up and clean it all up before I found out. It backfired in his face, though, and got worse. Then he explained that was why his only choice was to get Horst as a partner to share the cost. He said, "It was a great partnership, I work day and night and Horst drinks." He told me he was really sorry and he just needed a little more time to straighten everything out.

I told him I had some money left in the bank and if he needed it he could have it. I had finished getting all the kids school clothes when I was in Calgary. My mom showed me a great store where they had some pretty good deals.

He smiled and said "No, we had a deal on who pays for what and that money was mine to do what I wanted."

I asked him if I could pay for us to go to the final race night in Fargo. It was a fun weekend, and it would be the last race with the Late Model if he was going to sell it. He agreed. I just chalked the big change up to him being on his own while we were gone. There must have been some truth to the saying, "Absence makes the heart grow fonder." Ten days was a long time for him to have to fend for himself.

The next two weeks were great; Rudi was like his old self again. We went racing and he even managed to come home early three days in a row. He took us water skiing on the river. I was really glad that he was back to his old self, but he still did seem to be a little hyper.

We packed up early on Friday. I had managed to get the last run off at work. I was still working driving the wheelchair van and working in the classrooms as a substitute when the teachers were sick. One of the drivers owed me a favour and said she would double up her own run. I had done it for her for two days when she got the flu.

Rudi and I left the city by one in the afternoon. His mom stayed with the kids. I was leery about going through the border because I felt the border crossing guys would recognize our van and give us a hard time. They didn't. We were cruising along nicely and calculated that we would get to Fargo in lots of time to grab a decent supper before we had to go to the track. I did manage to get a room at Kelly's Inn where all the other drivers from Winnipeg were staying. It was the last room they had available. We were traveling on our own, as our pit crew was coming down after work. Rudi seemed pretty proud traveling down the highway. Then I remembered, this was the first time we were going south to race with the Late Model car. That changed pretty quickly when Rudi looked at the gas gauge and said, "Darn, I was making sure I had everything ready to go this morning but I forgot gas."

"Darn," was right. I knew there were no gas stations for a long way. I asked how much gas was left.

His answer was, "The gauge says, 'not enough.'" No sooner did he say that and the van started to choke on its last fumes. I started to laugh. Rudi asked me what was so funny.

I told him, "Here we are with a smart looking van and thousands of dollars of race car, hauler and equipment, sitting on the road out of gas."

He laughed as he got out and said, "Part of the thousands of dollars worth of equipment includes two Gerry cans full of gas. Isn't that the way? Forget to fill up the van, but remember the gas for the racecar. Go figure!" It was really too bad the gas tank was on the same side of the van as the highway. Rudi was caught standing with the bright red Gerry can tipped up pouring the gas when a voice came over the CB radio.

"Hey fifty-five, do you have a problem?"

I picked it up and asked who it was.

He just asked, "Do you guys need help?" while he was laughing. A few seconds later, a red truck with a car on the back went flying by. I saw "-Coca-Cola" written all across the sides and knew it was Ron Powers along with his pitman, Dave Brown. Ron raced in Winnipeg against Rudi. They could see him pouring gas.

I just answered back, "Very funny Ron." I could tell Rudi was embarrassed when he got back in the van.

He just said, "Great."

I told him not to worry about it. Ron was a real nice guy and just had a lousy sense of humour. I told him it could have been worse.

As usual, the city was full of racecars. We both agreed it felt a little different being on the high side of the racing world, running Late Model. There were Late Model cars in from all over. Rudi still had to qualify, and we weren't really sure that he could against all the stiff competition. Besides, the track was a lot bigger and faster than Rudi had ever raced before.

The first night went all right. He qualified by the skin of his teeth. That gave him starting position Saturday in the back of his heat race. We both thought, "As long as the car doesn't suffer too much because we wanted to sell it." Part of me was really glad of that because of our situation. I knew selling it would take the financial pressure off of Rudi and get him away from that shop. The other part of me had been a racing fan since I was a teenager, and I knew I would miss it. I didn't know how Rudi would be, becoming a fan again after racing for the past three years. Things were back to normal since the trip to Calgary and "normal" seemed to be really good. He still appeared to be overly nervous lately, but he did have a lot on his mind to deal with. Normally his blonde curly hair was clean cut and he was always clean-shaven, but for the past few weeks, he had definitely failed in that department. I just figured, "It didn't take us overnight to get into the mess we were in, and it wouldn't take just overnight to fix it."

After Friday's race, we had a drink and some pizza with Janet's family and the rest of the gang in their hotel room but then went to our own room. Saturday went by pretty quickly. We went shopping as usual and stocked up on the kids' favourite foods.

We arrived at the track pretty early. It was still quite warm. When the heat races started, Rudi was more than ready to race. I took my lawn chair on top of the van where I could see what was happening on the whole track. There were so many haulers and racecars in the pits that standing on the trailer, like I usually did, just wasn't working. I could only see the first corner from there.

Rick wasn't racing anymore but was still at the track. He was actually there helping Rudi. He had a really bad accident earlier in the summer driving

Rudi's car. I can't recall why he was driving Rudi's car; maybe it was to see how it was running. But as he was going into one of the corners on the track with one of the Americans beside him, the back of the Americans car swung over and hit the door of Rudi's car. It was such a freak accident. It looked to be very minor, but the roll bar, which sits where a bumper sits on a normal car, had put a hole in the door. Then it managed to go in between the roll bars in the door and into Rick's side. It was quite severe. They had to cut the roof out of the car and hoist him out, seat and all. He was in the hospital for quite a while and decided it wasn't a good idea to race Late Model for a while. I went to see him at the hospital the next day and hardly recognized him because there was so much swelling.

Most of the Canadian Late Model drivers were at this race. All of them parked together in the pits and from top of the van, I could see everything that was happening. This just happened to be the one race that I wish I wasn't able to see so much. The feature started, and our car was close to the middle. After the green flag was dropped, I couldn't believe the speeds these cars were running. It was just a really fast track that night. I was facing the stands and there was not one empty seat. It held about seven-thousand fans.

Rudi was doing quite well. It almost seemed like everything was clicking for him and he was really liking the track. He had passed quite a few cars and was closer to the front where all the top racers were running. One of the cars had a flat tire and pulled into the pits to change it. After changing the tire, the car then headed for the entrance back onto the track. The racecars were coming down the front straightaway, so I thought for sure the car at the entrance would wait for them to go by. But for whatever reason, he thought he could get on the track before the cars got to him. The front of his car was just nosing out on the track as the cars were approaching him. Rudi was on the inside lane passing a car, and I could see that there was no escaping. He had no choice but to hit the side door of the car dead on and at the speed they were going, it was really bad.

Rudi's car flipped end over end three times. I wasn't really sure it was Rudi until the car then hit the concrete wall and flew up in the air. It flew quite high, and was turning over as it was coming down. On the roof I could see the number fifty-five. I almost fell off of the van trying to get down. I started to run towards the turn. As I ran, the car rolled sideways another three times. It had stopped before I got there and the ambulance was soon on its way. It normally sits in the pits, ready throughout all the races. I was just about up to the car when Rick started running with me.

When we arrived at the car, we saw that it was sitting on all four wheels but it really didn't look too much like a car. Rudi got out on his own and looked fine. The ambulance attendants asked him to get into the ambulance just as a precaution, so they could talk to him and make sure he really was okay.

He ignored them and said to Rick, "The harness is broken. If we can fix the harness, I can finish the race."

Rick and the ambulance attendants just looked at me as if to say, "We have a big problem. Not with the car but with Rudi." There wasn't really a car left to race.

I suggested quietly to Rudi to go in the ambulance to pacify everyone and that Rick and I would get the car back to the pits and check it out. I said we were now on a red flag stop, so it would be a while before they could start the race again.

He said, "Okay, I will make it fast," and almost ran into the ambulance with the guys. The ambulance went to the pits with him in the back and I could see the attendants checking him out from our hauler. Rick helped me pack everything up and get ready to load the car.

It was quite a while before the tow trucks brought the car and then they pretty well picked it up off the ground by the roof and dropped it onto the trailer. It was a sad sight. What a mess. I went over to the ambulance to see how Rudi was doing while Rick tied down the car. Rudi was getting out of the ambulance when I arrived and looked angrier than I had ever seen him before. He grabbed me by the arm and said, "Lets go." He was going so fast, he was almost dragging me. I looked back at the ambulance attendant who nodded his head that Rudi was okay. He opened the passenger door and put me in and asked Rick, "Is everything tied down?" Rick then told him that everything was loaded and ready. Rudi jumped in the driver's seat and took off. When we passed Janet, she motioned to me that she would phone me.

Rudi didn't say one word and neither did I. He just left the track and headed straight for Winnipeg. It was a long drive and it was already quite late. I wasn't about to have any opinions. I had never seen him look that way before. It really scared me. We arrived at the border where the guy came out and asked, "How did you do?" Rudi just motioned with his thumb to look at the car. The guy did go and look and soon came back saying, "Ouch. Go home." That was it. Rudi never said another word to him or all the way back to the city for that matter.

He parked the van with the trailer and car on the front street and went in the house to bed.

In the morning, he unhooked the van, leaving the trailer and car where it was and drove his mother home. I thought, "Okay, he will come right back and move it in the garage." We lived in a very young community where there were lots of young kids and the car was definitely too beat up with too much torn metal to leave it where it was.

He didn't move it. He didn't move it that day or that week. He didn't want to talk about it. Racing and the accident didn't exist. He was so angry. I finally just bought one of those winter covers and covered the car up completely and left it where it was. I didn't know what else to do. I didn't know how to hook up the trailer and move it. It was crazy for the next few weeks. He just came and went, saying only what was absolutely necessary.

I just worked and went to as many meetings as I could fit in. P.J. started Junior High School that term and was in the same school as J.J. Tammy was in her last year of elementary. They were all doing really well. We bought Tammy a new bike for her birthday, one of these fancy pink ones with a banana seat. Her favourite thing in life was riding her bike. P.J. was going for tryouts for the top hockey team in his age group. The tryouts were scheduled for October 24th. He wouldn't have a problem. He had over a month to get ready for it and was an excellent player.

We didn't see much of Rudi and when I asked him anything, he didn't want to talk about it. On my birthday, he left before I even got out of bed. There was a large gift-wrapped box in the kitchen with a small one on top. There was a card attached and when I opened it, all he wrote inside was, "I am so sorry, I never meant for things to turn out the way they did." I opened the big box first, and it was a feather quilt. I had always wanted one. In the small box was a sapphire pendant for my gold chain, which I always wore.

Several times I tried to talk to him about the Al-Anon program, but we would just get into an ugly fight. I knew there was a really big problem. It seemed like he couldn't handle me talking to him or for that matter even doing anything for him. I didn't understand what was happening and didn't know how to fix it. Elaine had called me at the beginning of October and said that she asked Horst to leave. He got an apartment. I had asked Rudi about it and all he said was, "Yeah."

October 24th came and P.J. was so nervous about the tryout. I went to work in the morning and told him to give it to God, and he said that he already did. I told him not to worry then.

Chapter 14

Torn Asunder

"I won't leave you like orphans. I will come back to you."
John 14:18

I came back after my lunch run and was surprised to see the van in front of the house hooked up to the racecar. Surprised, but I was really glad that Rudi was finally dealing with it. I got an even bigger surprise when I walked in the house.

Rudi was standing in the kitchen and all he said was, "I am leaving!" He was crying and said that he loved me since he was twelve years old and will always love me, but he couldn't live with me anymore.

I asked him, "Why?" by then crying myself.

He didn't answer, he just said that all his clothes were packed in the van, and he had bought P.J. new hockey pants for his tryouts. I asked him where he was going, and he said, "To Horst's apartment," and handed me the phone number written on a piece of paper. He walked out the door and didn't want to talk anymore.

I couldn't understand it. I was so upset and had to go back to work. The kids were going to be devastated. I phoned Elaine, and she was shocked. I finally got myself to go to work, but I cried through the whole run. When I got home, I went to pick up the kids from Margaret's. She too, was shocked. I took the kids home and sat them down and told them as gently as I could that their dad had left. I was right; they were devastated. I felt so sorry for P.J. I was really angry that if Rudi had to do this, why couldn't he at least have waited till the next day. I took P.J. to the tryouts and the poor guy spent the whole time on the ice trying to wipe away his tears, so that the other guys wouldn't see. He didn't make the team. I was really angry with God and with Al-Anon and with everything. I just couldn't understand why. Couldn't we get a counselor and work it out? Couldn't we talk about it? Why so cut and dry?

I didn't call Rudi. I was hoping that if I just left him alone, he would come to his senses. Two days later he came in while the kids were eating supper. I asked him if he was hungry. He wasn't and neither was I. I just couldn't eat. I couldn't go to aerobics; I couldn't do anything. I was just existing and doing what was absolutely necessary. He said he was just there to get all the tools and stuff out of the garage. I said to him that I was hoping he was there to talk about it. He said there was nothing to talk about and went to the garage. P.J. was so upset; I had to cancel his piano lesson at the last minute. When Rudi finished taking stuff out of the garage, he just drove away without saying good-bye to the kids or me.

The next day I went to work. I was in pretty rough shape. When I picked up David, one of the boys on my morning run, his mother asked me what was wrong. I told her and she asked me to come back for coffee after my morning run. Her name was Ruth. I had gotten to know most of the mothers quite well. I usually sat and talked for a few minutes everyday with them when I picked up the kids. I said I would come back. I was supposed to go to the program, but for some reason, I felt I wanted to talk to her. I went straight to her house after I dropped off the kids, and she had coffee ready when I got there. She was a nurse but was off work because she just had a baby. I told her everything that had happened. She asked where I was with my belief in God. I told her about the program and my upbringing. She told me she was a Christian, to which I replied, "I thought I was too." I found out we had different ideas as to what a Christian was.

She told me, "Jesus died on the cross so our sins could be forgiven."

I told her I knew that.

She said, "Well if you believe that, that is all you need to accept Jesus into your heart. If you would turn your life over to God, He will guide you and help you through the mess you are in."

I asked, "Why didn't He just help?"

She said, "He is a real gentleman and is knocking on your door, but He won't come in without an invitation."

I told her that is what P.J. was telling me and he was a Christian in her sense of the meaning.

Time flew by and eventually I had to go back to work. She asked if I minded if she prayed before I left and I said, "Not at all."

I felt better than I had felt in a long time when I left and decided I had to try to put my life back together for the kids' sake. Halloween was coming on the weekend, so I picked up a couple of pumpkins in the afternoon and thought I would cut them up with the kids that night. When I got home, P.J. said he had to go to hockey practice, so I told him to do his piano practice before he left. We would cut up the pumpkins on the weekend when all three kids were home.

The next day, I felt a bit better about myself. I kept thinking about what Ruth had said. I was thinking that I sure couldn't fix what was broken in my marriage, but God could. I didn't know what was wrong with Rudi and why he was taking this to such extremes. God knew. I went for breakfast the next morning with the other drivers. We usually did that a couple of times a week. While we were eating breakfast, my mind was somewhere else. I was thinking about how to handle the whole situation.

At the table next to us, there were a bunch of hydro guys having breakfast and were all talking back and forth. The conversation they were having was answering my questions on how to handle the situation. It was so weird. That isn't what they were talking about; they couldn't read my mind. It just happened that the answers were coming from them.

When I dropped David off at lunchtime that day, I told Ruth what had happened. She laughed and said, "God uses people to answer prayer." She said that she had been praying for God to guide me and that this was an answer to her prayer. Then she said she had a gift for me. She handed me a Bible. I told her I never read the Bible though there was always one in the house when I was younger. She explained that the answers to any questions I had were in the Bible. She said, "Consider it the roadmap to life."

At suppertime that night, I told P.J. what happened and showed him the Bible. He was really excited and asked me if I was going to become a Christian.

I said, "Who knows?"

To which he replied, "God does."

We started to laugh and as we did, the door opened and Rudi walked in. The kids were so glad to see him. He looked terrible. He obviously hadn't shaved all week, and his hair was in desperate need of a haircut. He got angry that we were laughing. It was ironic that it was the first time we had laughed since he left, and he walked in at that very moment. I guess he thought he wasn't missed. I asked him if he wanted a cup of coffee, and he said that no he was just there to pick up the boat. I asked what he was doing with it.

He said, "Selling it to fix the race car." He said that his brother Heinz was buying it. He asked me for the bills that came in the mail. He said that he would pay them. I gave him the bills, and then he hooked up the boat and left.

The next morning I went to my meeting and told them what was happening. They let me talk and I realized that every time Rudi was taking something and leaving, I would fall apart. It would take me a couple of days to get back on my feet. When I was back on my feet he would be back for something else, and so I would fall again. I almost felt like what was happening was to keep me down. "Misery likes company."

Halloween was on the weekend. I had already made new costumes for the kids. Tammy was a pink bunny. J.J. was Zorro and P.J. was Dracula. When they were all dressed, I wanted to take a picture, but there was a slight problem. P.J. was so blonde; he just didn't cut it as Dracula. The only thing I had in the house to colour his hair was shoe polish, so we smeared black shoe polish all over his head. They all looked great, and I got the picture.

While the kids were out trick or treating, I spent my time running to the door to give out candy and back to my bedroom to clean out the dresser drawers. For some strange reason, anything I pulled out that was the colour red, gave me such a frustrated feeling. It was so bad, I started to throw the items of clothes in a bag to give to the Salvation Army. I came across sweaters, turtlenecks, socks, even long underwear. If it was red, it was going. The more I cleared it out, the more upset I was getting. I thought maybe the colour red related to anger. I thought maybe I was cracking up. How could a simple thing like a colour upset me? When I finished with the dresser drawers, I started on the closet. The red dress I had worn to church the year before, in the bag it went. I stopped for a moment and stared at Rudi's side of the closet. It was totally empty. What could be so bad to possess him to leave like he did? If there was a good reason, maybe it would be easier to accept, but I went over it so many times in my head and I couldn't figure it out. I heard the door open and the kids walked in. I ran into the bathroom to wash my face, so they couldn't see I had been crying. I yelled to them, "no eating the candy until I check it."

After I checked the candy, I told P.J. to come and let me wash the shoe polish out of his hair before it decided to be permanent. I washed it once and it turned a terrible shade of green. I washed it a second and third and fourth time. It was lighter but it was green. I felt terrible. He thought it was funny and laughed saying it would be pretty cool going to school with green hair. I phoned Elaine and asked her about it. She said it would wear out with time and laughed at the fact I had even used shoe polish in the first place.

I took all the clothes to the Salvation Army and thought it was funny that the same evening I did, one of the mothers from the hockey team asked me if I wanted to go through a bunch of clothes she was getting rid of to see if there was anything I wanted. I had lost a lot of weight in the past month with

Rudi leaving, so she and I were the same size. Their son was a fair chunk bigger than P.J. and had outgrown some of his equipment, so they had brought it
over and said if there was anything P.J. could use, he was welcome to it. They
bought only the absolute best of everything, and P.J. was almost able to make
use of everything. I went through all the clothes and could use it all except one
red sweater. Red was bothering me more than ever. I couldn't get it out of the
house fast enough.

Rudi was always coming and going for some reason, even if it was
just to take P.J. to hockey practice. He came with a birthday present for P.J.
one day. He had bought him a new pair of skates. Kangaroo Tacks. P.J. really
wanted a pair. When he left, he took the feather quilt he gave me for my birthday. He said it was cold sleeping alone. I was really angry about it. He was
sleeping alone because he chose to. At least that is what I thought. I really did-
n't know the reason why.

I was so angry that when he left, I went into my bedroom and spent
the next two hours rearranging the closet and dresser. I put all the clothes
given to me in his side of the closet. Till then, I left it empty with faith he
would be back. I filled up his dresser with my clothes. I almost filed all my
clothes in alphabetical order; there was so much room to work with.

There was a dress in the pile of clothes, and I thought about the
Speedway Banquet coming up the next weekend. Janet was trying to talk me
into going. I didn't really want to show up alone, and Rudi hadn't mentioned
he was going. I thought maybe I would go. Now I had something to wear. I
phoned Janet, and she told me she would hang on to a ticket. I wanted to ask
Rudi to go, but I was scared to. I finally thought I would just go alone; I knew
so many people there. I was really uncomfortable with the thought of them
asking where Rudi was. If I wanted a drink, I would have to go to the bar
myself. I was old fashioned in that way, if a lady goes out, she should be
escorted and taken care of. A bar was not a place for a lady, and it really was-
n't appropriate for me to sit with any other guys when I was married.

One evening P.J. was playing hockey, and I knew Rudi was going to
show up. I dressed up in a new pair of slacks I had gotten from the box of
clothes and a blue sweater. I left my hair long but had it restyled. I took extra
care with my makeup and wore a winter trench coat that was also in the box.
I really felt good when I looked in the mirror but couldn't help to think that I
was doing it for someone who didn't really want me anymore. Rudi pulled up
at the same time as I did. I was driving the convertible and had washed it the
day before. It shined under the lights of the parking lot. He came and opened

my door and his eyes actually lit up. He asked if Santa came early. I just smiled and felt I owed no explanation as to where the clothes came from. He chose not to be at home so that was the rule. I don't know why he left, so why should he know every detail about my life. We walked in together and when I took my coat off, he asked if I ever eat anymore. I ignored the comment. He was really attentive that night and asked what the plans were for J.J.'s birthday.

I said J.J. really wanted a bike. He couldn't ride one but he really wanted a bike. I said I was seriously thinking about buying one. Then he could have it equipped with training wheels and whatever else it needed before summer. It could go to the school and be used in therapy. By the time the snow went, he maybe could ride it with help. He agreed and asked if I wanted to meet him at the Bike shop on Tuesday. I told him I could meet him on Tuesday afternoon. Tuesday morning I was busy. He asked me what I was doing on Tuesday morning. I wasn't about to tell him I had an Al-Anon Meeting. He was obviously angry, but it really didn't matter.

On Tuesday, I got up extra early and put on another new outfit. When I was putting on my make-up, I threw the mascara and started to cry. I was really angry with myself that I put such an effort in every time I was seeing Rudi. He noticed, but there was no talk of ever working this out. I washed my face and started over with the make-up. This time I was doing it for me. I would do it whether I was seeing Rudi or not. I just felt I had put so many years into caring. And now if he chose not to be here, then all the extra time I had would go to the kids and me.

When I pulled into the parking lot at work with the load of kids at lunchtime, I was ten minutes early, so I sat in the van with them until it was time to go in. My door opened and one of the drivers jumped in. Lots of time the drivers got in each other's vans and talked. Rod was just hired to work. He was somehow related to the boss. He was single and fairly good-looking. Rod had asked how things were going. Everyone knew what had happened. I answered, they were going.

He stated, "When Rudi first left; we were all worried about you. You seemed so depressed. You must be handling it quite well because you look great."

I thanked him and thought about what my dad always said. "Fake it till you make it."

Rudi pulled up, and it was time to take the kids in. He yelled to me, "Do you want to go for lunch first?"

I shook my head yes and continued on into the school with the kids. I was really glad they didn't need a substitute. I would of had to tell Rudi I couldn't go. I wanted to tell him I was going to the banquet that Saturday.

He took me to McDonalds, and I just had a coffee. I didn't talk. I let him do the talking. He commented again how good I looked then asked me why Rod was in the van.

I laughed to think he was actually jealous and questioned, "Why?" I didn't stop there and didn't give him a chance to answer. I just continued, "You chose to leave me. You give me no reason why, and then you have the nerve to ask me about something I am doing in my life. Where do you get the right?" He looked so surprised. I don't remember ever talking to him like that. I continued, "In your world, I always felt like a woman was at a lower level and was there to cook and clean. Whether you came in from work at five or ten at night, the meal would be put on the table. The house was always clean; not lived in, but clean, a showpiece. It never really bothered me because you were always a hard worker and a good provider, so I did my part the way you wanted it. You and the kids were always first." Now I was tired of it. "Where did it get me?"

He told me to cool down. He just asked me a question.

I continued, "You want your cake and to eat it too, and it isn't going to happen. What have I got to lose by being myself and being honest? You? You are already gone, so I have nothing to lose." I got up and put my coat on, threw a dollar on the table for the coffee and went to leave.

He smiled and reminded me, "You came in my van, remember."

I answered, "I will walk."

I walked back to my van; it was about a mile and a half. I cried most of the way, partly because I had left my gloves in Rudi's van and my hands were really cold, and partly because I felt like I blew it with Rudi. How could I lose it like that?

The next day I went right after my run and bought J.J. the bike. Rudi was still paying the bills, and I was still responsible for groceries and the kids. The grocery bill was almost cut in half since Rudi left, so there was plenty of money to spend on the kids. Rudi was really angry that I bought the bike without him, but I really didn't show I cared.

He came over for J.J.'s birthday and was surprisingly quiet. J.J. was so thrilled to finally have a bike and understood it had to go to rehab for a while to be equipped with special gadgets so he could ride it. I had already made the appointment for the following week. I didn't see the van out front when Rudi came. He must have been dropped off. We had lots of company, so I didn't pursue it. He left before everyone else and I didn't see anyone out front to pick him up.

All of a sudden, I heard my convertible running. I grabbed my coat and boots and ran outside, but not fast enough. All I could see was the back end of it going down the street. That was the last time I saw it. He had sold it to someone. He apparently showed them during the day while I was at work. It was registered under his name, so he had the right. I couldn't believe he would go that far. So far in the past month he had taken the racecar, the boat, all his clothes, my car, and all the equipment from the garage. I was slowly being cleaned out.

The next day I went to the meeting and discussed this whole issue. By the time I went back to work, it was quite apparent that the reason this was happening was to try to get me to react. If I reacted and got angry, Rudi could be justified for his action. But it was so frustrating to not know why. I never mentioned the car. It was only a car. He was taking away all the gifts he gave me. I was so confused. I wasn't without a vehicle. I could use the work van until I could buy another vehicle.

We had a social worker assigned to us through Family Services because of J.J.'s disabilities. They had offered me respite for one weekend a month now that Rudi was gone. (Respite is a break for parents of children that have disabilities. Usually the disabled child and siblings go out of their own house to stay at the respite worker's house for the designated break.) We met the respite worker; her name was Diane. She didn't live too far away from us. All three kids would go to her house on Friday nights at eight and come home at nine on Sundays. She offered to keep them an hour longer on Sundays because I bowled. I offered to pay her for the extra hour. The next weekend was the first weekend she had them. The kids were really excited about going. Diane had kids close to their ages.

I spent Friday evening and Saturday morning cleaning and changing the rooms around. I got new lacy curtains for the kitchen and changed the living room so the sectional was in a square in front of the fireplace. I bought some candles and put them around the house. It felt really good to do things the way I wanted them done.

It was still early when I finished, and I didn't have to be at the banquet until six-thirty. I looked in the newspaper and marked off some cars I would be interested in seeing. By two on Saturday afternoon, everything was done, and I felt great. I took a hot bubble bath, and then got dressed to go look at cars. I couldn't buy one. I didn't have enough money, but at least I could look to see what I wanted. I hadn't mentioned a word to Rudi about the convertible, and he didn't know Elaine told me it was sold. I just finished getting dressed and was ready to go when Rudi walked in the door.

He asked me where the kids were and I told him about the respite program. He didn't seem pleased with the fact I had a weekend to myself every month. As we talked, he looked around the house. For a moment, it crossed my mind; he was probably looking to see what he could take next. I was almost sarcastic thinking, "Gee, maybe you want the sapphire pendant back that you gave me for my birthday or the ring you gave me the year before." I didn't say it though. When the next question came, I figured I didn't wait long enough to answer.

He asked, "Where are you off to?"

I should have answered, none of your business like I wanted to, but instead I picked up the newspaper and said I was just going to look at a couple of cars. His face looked like someone had just opened his mouth and poured in a gallon of guilt.

With a nervous laugh, he asked, "What do you know about cars?"

I answered, "I know what I want. I can't afford it right now, but I want to see what I am looking at price wise." He asked what I was looking for and I told him either a Camaro or a Firebird. He laughed and I reminded him it was for me and not for him, so it really didn't matter what he thought. I went to leave and waited to lock the door. (I had the locks changed on the garage and the house the day after he took the convertible. It was time to draw the line.) He looked at the new deadbolt on the door and asked if he was being locked out of his own house. I told him that I was pretty sure he had taken everything he wanted from us, and if there was anything he forgot then I felt he could phone and ask for it. He was evidently quite taken aback by my non-caring attitude. It didn't matter. I was really tired of not knowing if he ever planned on coming back and not knowing why he left. How could such a nice person change so much? He had then suggested he take me to look at the cars and then we could grab a bite to eat. I didn't take long in my decision to say yes, but (here was my opportunity to tell him I was going to the banquet), I have to be back to get ready for the banquet. He looked at me with a look you would have thought someone just punched him hard in the stomach.

He asked, "You are going to the banquet?"

I answered very innocently, "Of course, aren't you?" I didn't give him a chance to answer; instead I continued, "Well I really don't know too much about cars. I guess it wouldn't hurt to take advantage of your knowledge, but only if we take separate vehicles. It is too cold to walk today."

He laughed his old laugh that I missed so much and promised that if it got rocky with us I could take the van and he would walk.

"Yeah right," I laughed and got in his van with him.

The first vehicle we went to see was the one I wanted. It was a gold 1969 Firebird with gold interior, not very practical for the kids, but what the heck. I had the van most of the year and that was really practical. I tried to keep in my head that this was a car for me. What I wanted. The guy was asking $1,200. Rudi stated it was a really good deal. He asked the guy if he would take $1,000. He shook his head, no. It was a great deal at $1,200. It really didn't matter to me because I didn't have $1,000. I was honest with the guy when I phoned and explained I wasn't out to buy, just to look. We left and Rudi asked me if I wanted to go and see the other car. I told him no; I was stuck on the Firebird and would be buying it. He asked how I planned to do that. I reminded him he was there to help me by checking out the mechanics of the vehicle and how or why or what I do with the info he gave me was my department.

He was obviously upset by what he heard and asked, "Are you pushing me out of your life now? You aren't going to make it without me."

I couldn't believe that actually came out of his mouth since he was the one who left. Was this just a game to prove something to me? I always made it quite clear that I didn't want the marriage to end; whatever the problem was could be worked out. His answer was always the same. He loved me, always did and always will, but couldn't live with me and would never tell me why. It was so frustrating.

He dropped me off at home, and I never said any more about the banquet. He asked me as I was getting out of the van if he could pick me up for the banquet.

I was surprised and answered, "No." I would take my own vehicle in case I wanted to leave early.

He asked me to meet him outside at six twenty-five so we could go in together.

I agreed.

I felt good about myself as I walked out the door to go to the banquet. It was snowing a bit. I covered my hair, thinking it would be one big ball of fuzz if it got wet. (I had really naturally curly hair that would go in little ringlets if I just washed it and let it dry on its own. I always conditioned it and straightened it. It worked well but if it got damp, it would go really frizzy.) I pulled in the parking lot and Rudi was sitting in the van waiting for me. I apologized for being late. I told him fashionably late.

We went in, but he was like a time bomb. He kept looking at the floor. It almost seemed he was embarrassed because everyone knew what was happening. We sat next to each other at an empty table, but it didn't take long to fill up with people–other drivers and pit crew from the track. Matt Desjarlais and his girlfriend were sitting across the table from us. Matt raced Late Model for a couple of years and was really good.

We were joking around about me racing. I told him not to laugh; I just may show up with a racing car for the next season. He told me if I was serious, he had one for sale. It was stripped down, but the roll cage was there. I just laughed. The guys at the table started to bug me that I should be the first girl to race. I definitely wouldn't have to be convinced. I drove the powder puff (ladies race) at the end of the last two seasons with Rudi's car and won the trophy both times. I loved it. Rudi was noticeably bothered by the conversation. It didn't matter because I was having fun.

Rudi was called up for two trophies during the presentation. He insisted on leaving right after the meal. He looked to be really agitated. I was having a good time and wanted to stay. He said he wouldn't leave unless I did. I think that was just to save face.

It was still early when I got home, so I changed and called Ruth to talk. She told me to come over for coffee. We sat for two hours and I filled her in on everything that was happening. She suggested I give the car situation to God and let Him handle it for me. She believed God wanted to provide the car for me. He loved me and wanted the credit now for looking after me. She asked me if I read any of the Bible, and I explained that I flipped through it and it was like a different language I couldn't understand. She offered to write down some scriptures for me that would help in my situation and asked if I believed God would provide me the car. I answered, "Yes." She promised she would believe with me. I had no problem with that. I was sure God would provide in His time, but what was His time?

On Monday, I came home to get the mail from the mailbox. I had been doing that lately because I just didn't know what Rudi was taking when I wasn't home. He couldn't get in anymore, but I had a pension cheque coming. I just didn't have the same trust in him as I used to. There were some Christmas cards in the mail and an envelope from J.J.'s lawyer. (His claim was still ongoing and I thought it would never end. It had already been six years since the accident.) I opened the envelope and inside was a cheque written to me for $1,500. I couldn't believe it. The letter with it was from the lawyer and just stated that it was a portion of what was owed to me for out of pocket expenses for the past six years, and he persuaded Autopac Insurance to pay something toward the bill to help out with the situation. (I had let him know Rudi had moved out.)

I thought about Ruth and her prayer and could hardly wait to tell her. I phoned the guy with the car and asked him if it was still for sale.

He answered, "Yes."

I told him I had $1,000 cash and would bring it to him that afternoon if he would accept my offer.

He agreed.

I was so excited. I thanked God all the way back to work, picked up the kids and dropped David off first, so I could tell Ruth.

When I left, I told her I was going to go and pay for the car right after my run.

I picked up the new plates and paid for the car. There was still money left over for Christmas shopping. No one could burst my bubble that day. I was on top of the world. When Margaret's husband, Brian, got home from work, I asked him to take me to get the car. He drove it back to my place, and his comment was I got a really good deal. Coming from him, it meant a lot.

Rudi came by after supper to take P.J. to hockey. When he pulled up, I was sitting in the living room listening to P.J. practice piano. From where I was sitting, I could see him get out of the van. He was walking toward the house and kept looking back at this car. I was sure he was thinking that he had seen this car somewhere before. When he came in the door, he asked how I got the car.

I calmly answered, "Brian took me to pick it up."

That wasn't what he meant. It threw him off track though because he and Brian were no longer talking to each other. They had a falling out. (I didn't care though because a lot of people were having a falling out with Rudi. I think his attitude caused most of the problems.) Rudi didn't ask any more questions and I was really glad because I really didn't want to answer. He just asked the kids if they were ready to go to the game. P.J. wanted a ride in my car to the game. Then the other two followed. Rudi stated, "It is too small for all of us. We can all go in the van."

I told him we would meet him at the arena, I hadn't had a chance to drive the car yet. The door slammed pretty hard behind him.

Christmas was only three weeks away and I was really behind. I had finished all the baking, and it was in the freezer. Gifts were ready to be sent to Calgary; that was it. We were used to really big Christmas in our house. There were always so many gifts under the tree. I barely even started shopping. I hated to shop alone. It was something that Rudi and I decided together, and I guess I was hoping if I waited long enough, he would be home for Christmas.

I couldn't wait anymore. The next day, I started shopping between the runs and wrapped every night after the kids went to bed. I didn't buy any of the food, as I wasn't sure of what I would be doing for Christmas. I just turned that over to God. I laughed as I thought on the way to work one day, Jesus' birthday is the only one I know where everyone else gets the presents. At least I could let Him decide where he wanted me for Christmas. I did realize that wherever it would be, would be what was best, even if it didn't seem like it at the time.

I thought so much about what P.J., Ruth, and Greg's parents had told me about being a Christian. I wondered if it was really necessary to accept God in my heart. God was obviously trying to tell me something but I had already turned my life and my will over to God everyday in Alanon. It seemed strange that I was hearing it from three different people.

I went to get out all the tree decorations and couldn't find them. We had an artificial tree in a huge box in the garage; it was gone too. I was getting ready to take Tammy to her ringette game one day after supper and asked the kids if they seen the ornaments. I couldn't believe that Rudi would take the Christmas decorations. Some of them were from my parents. They were family memories. Besides, he was trying to get to me, he would never do that to the kids. How did he get them? The locks were changed. P.J. said they were all in the garage, not just the tree. Maybe he took them when he cleaned out the garage.

We were all standing with the other families watching the first period of the game, when Rudi walked in. J.J. came right out in front of everyone and asked if he stole our Christmas decorations. He was really embarrassed and told J.J. to just watch the game. J.J. asked how we were going to get gifts if there was no tree decorated. Rudi got mad and told him to be quiet. J.J. persisted and said he wasn't very nice to steal our ornaments. I stepped in to take J.J. out to talk to him, but I stopped when Rudi answered him with, "Your mother has lots of money to buy new ones." I couldn't believe my ears. He did take the ornaments. That was really low. What would he want them for, to put a tree up in his and Horst's apartment?

I told the kids not to worry, I would figure it out, and we would have a real tree, bigger and with more decorations. I didn't know how, but it sure wasn't right what he did. The following Saturday morning, the kids and I went to the Safeway parking lot and picked up a real tree. I had already bought a new stand. It was a really nice tree. I had no idea what to do with it, but we put it in the van and brought it home. P.J. was being really ornery and kept saying, "What is the use?" I asked him where his faith was. He laughed; normally that is what he was asking me. I said we would pray and believe that God will provide decorations for the tree. He was so excited to find out that I knew about the scripture:

"Warn the rich people of this world not to be proud or to trust in wealth that is easily lost. Tell them to have faith in God, who is rich and blesses us with everything we need to enjoy life." I Timothy 6:17

I phoned Ruth when I got home and told her what was happening. She laughed and promised she would believe with us. We have to bring the tree in the house and put it up. Faith without works is dead she said. I asked her if I were ever going to learn how to read the Bible to find all of these things, and she remarked I really needed a more simplified Bible to start off.

We brought the tree in the house and put it up. It looked pretty sad with no lights or decorations but at least it was up.

Margaret phoned and asked me if the kids and I wanted to take a ride to her mom's with them. She had to pick up a few things. I told her I would pick them up and we could all go in the van. We left just before noon, and I told the kids we wouldn't be that long and would grab something for lunch when we got back. They had a late breakfast anyway. It was quite a drive to Margaret's mom's from our house. With the snow, it took about a half an hour each way.

We got there and right away she had asked all the kids if they ate. Of course they were starving so she made them lunch. We were in the living room talking to her mom and dad after lunch. They were elderly people with Christian knowledge pouring out of their hearts. They were such positive people, and I always felt so good when I talked to them. They talked to me about becoming a Christian, and P.J. contributed his opinion.

I explained I was still unsure if it was necessary and was a little unsure about accepting Jesus into my heart and I had already turned my life over for His will to be done. I prayed for guidance and trusted He would clean up the mess and show me a good life. I understood it didn't mean everything was going to be wonderful, but at least I knew God would be with me all the time and I never would be alone.

Margaret's mom then handed me a more simplified Bible and asked me to phone if I ever had any questions.

I felt like I was confused all the way home. P.J. was thrilled that he had helped to convince me.

He stated, "Mom, you are so close, open the door and let Him in."

I knew what he meant by that. I told him to just let me think about it a bit longer.

We dropped off Margaret and the boys and went home. By then it was almost suppertime. There were two big boxes on the doorstep. The kids and I thought maybe Rudi broke down and gave us back the Christmas ornaments. We brought the boxes in the house and when we opened them, there was a note inside. One of the boxes was from the ringette team parents. Since J.J. talked so loud at the game, word got around about what Rudi had done, and the parents got together and each gave some of their ornaments. We opened the second box and it was from P.J.'s hockey team. Some of the parents of the ringette girls also had sons on P.J.'s hockey team so those parents did the same. There were new strings of lights and tinsel. There was everything we needed to decorate a beautiful tree.

Rudi came by that night to pick up the mail from the past few days. The look on his face was priceless when he saw the tree all lit up. It was so evident he was trying to prove to me I wouldn't make it without him, but I didn't tell him God would get us through.

As the days went on, I found more things missing that Rudi had taken. I would always cry my tears, and then carry on. Margaret's mother said they were called healing tears.

I felt like I was constantly wrapping gifts every night. I thought I would be pulling an all-nighter on Christmas Eve if I didn't keep up with the wrapping. Every year we always had the tree in the rec room, but it was so nice and cozy to have it in the living room where the fireplace was, and P.J. was already doing quite well on the piano playing Christmas carols.

The kids had rehearsal for the Christmas pageant at church. They had to be at the church for a couple of hours starting at two o'clock.

We were really late for rehearsal. P.J. had the lead. He was playing the part of God and the M.C. All the way to down Henderson Highway, he was telling me he was late. Tammy and J.J. had parts too. J.J. was one of the three wise men and Tammy was Mary. When we turned to go down Hespeller and over the bridge, I saw the light was green and speeded up to make it before the light turned yellow. I made the light okay. Then half a block past that, I could see a police car on the side of the road, and the police officer was standing beside it waving for me to pull over. I looked at my speedometer, and the needle was showing just over the speed limit, but not enough to be stopped. I pulled over and the officer asked me if I was going to a fire. Naive about his sarcasm, I answered no I was on my way to the church for the Christmas Pageant Rehearsal and I was late. (Never tell a police officer you are late for something when you are stopped for speeding, it only confirms your guilt). He wrote me a ticket and I left. I told the kids that now we were good and late but watched my speed the rest of the way. I went into the church with the kids and apologized for being so late. Of course J.J. and his innocence told everyone we were late because the police stopped mom.

That night after the kids went to bed, I was wrapping gifts on my bed and wondering when Rudi's game of taking things out of the house would stop. I looked around and thought about ways I would change the place. I would re-do Tammy's room all in pink. Her favourite colour was pink. I had finally caught up on all the wrapping, hid the last of the gifts in my closet with the rest, chucked off my clothes, and jumped into bed with the simplified Bible Margaret's mother gave me. As I was flipping through, it still all seemed complicated. I was wondering if it would ever make sense.

I came across Psalm 92:1 and it said, *"It is good to give thanks to the Lord."* That was so straightforward, and it wasn't hard for me to figure out what I had to be thankful for: the car, the money to buy the car, all the gifts finally bought and wrapped, J.J. doing so well in Jr. High–so much better than anyone ever had hoped for. I was thankful for all the joy, even though Rudi was gone, and for all the hope. I said a quick prayer, thanking God for all the good in my life and asked Him to show me if He wanted me to invite Him into my heart. I asked Him to fix my marriage.

I then turned over to go to sleep, and for some reason, I tossed and turned. I kept thinking negative things. I thought: What if I didn't start reacting to Rudi taking things out of the house. What if I didn't start to ask him to come back? How could he leave? I thought we had so much more than that. I started to think about the fact that I was only twenty-nine years old, and I was already married twice. What was wrong with me? What did I do to make my husband not want me? I thought about Rudi finding another woman and stopped myself there. I was getting ridiculous. How many times had Rudi told me, he loved me since he met me and would always love me? That was fine, but he said he just couldn't live with me. I did an analysis in my head to try to figure out what I was doing wrong that he didn't want to live with me. I wasn't the most immaculate housekeeper, but I did my best to keep up. I cooked his meals and don't think I was a bad cook. I didn't look too bad; at least I didn't think so. I smoked, maybe he didn't like a woman smoking, and well, I could try to quit. Maybe Alanon is making me into a person Rudi didn't like. Would I be able to quit? I was letting negative thoughts keep me awake. I asked God to show me what I was doing so wrong that my husband left me. I looked at the clock, and it was three o'clock.

I got up and went to the kitchen. If I didn't get to sleep soon, I would be really tired in the morning. I remember my dad telling me to not let garbage from the past ruin my future. I needed to start thinking about Rudi coming home and things straightening out. No, I had no control over his life. I really needed to think about making myself the best I could be and not thinking about what other people do. I can only change myself. Rudi just needed to sort out his life. He sold the car and the boat, so now he could fix the racecar and sell it. That would fix all his debts, and maybe he would have a peace of mind again. I needed to take my father's advice and to round off my shoulders and shake off the negative past. If I keep my shoulders squared off, then all the burdens just sit there and build up. That is what weighs a person down. I was so confused and my thoughts kept bouncing around. I finally fell asleep.

I didn't want to get up the next morning when the kids got up. I was really tired. Tammy was sitting on the bed beside me with her markers colouring a picture. The boys were downstairs watching a movie. I was kind of awake but didn't want to get up. P.J. finally came in the room and said it was time to get ready for church. He said he would help J.J. get dressed and asked what did I want him to wear. I told him, and then I strolled down the hall to go in the shower. I may have wanted to be the best I could be but was too tired to start that morning.

I dawdled and of course was running late for church. I went to quickly make up my bed and saw that Tammy left one of her markers on the sheet with the lid off. It had to be a red one. It had seeped into the sheet and looked really gross. It left a stain about two feet around. I wasn't too worried about it because it was a waterbed, and I knew it couldn't ruin the mattress. As usual the colour red was really bothering me, and I almost felt like I was having some sort of panic attack when I seen it. I quickly took the marker off the bed and threw the top sheet over it, so I didn't have to look at it. I would deal with it later.

P.J. was standing at the door, tying J.J.'s shoes saying, "Mom, we are going to be late again." I hadn't even cleaned up from breakfast or made the beds yet. Rudi had said he would take the kids to rehearsal in the afternoon, so I still had time to clean up after church before he came. We ran out the door and got into the car. We could still make it on time. I had driven that same route to the church in the past few weeks for rehearsals and church, and I chuckled as I was driving, thinking the car already knew the way.

The Firebird was so comfortable and easy to drive. It just had more power than I was used to in a smaller car and I had to watch my foot. I turned onto Hespeller where I had gotten the ticket the day before and watched my speedometer to make sure I wasn't speeding. I was right on the nose. I crossed the intersection and couldn't believe my eyes. P.J. said "Mom, not again!" The same police car, parked in the same spot, with the same police officer telling me to pull over. I pulled over and was really upset. He asked where we were off to today in such a hurry? I told him to church again.

He laughed and said "Yeah, right."

The kids all started to tell him we were going to church. I told them to be quiet.

The officer said to me, "You know the routine, license, registration." He then sarcastically stated, "If we keep this up, I will have it memorized."

I told him, "I know for a fact I wasn't speeding. I've only had the car for a couple of weeks."

He was very nice when he handed me the ticket and recommended, "It might be a good idea to get your speedometer checked; it might be out." He gave me the address of the place that does it and stated, "If it is out, take both tickets to court with proof that it was out, and they will more than likely let you off." Then he said, "Have a nice day." You know the tone police officers use to say that, as if it is a recording.

We still made it to church on time, but I was really frustrated. I tried hard to listen to the sermon, but it didn't seem to give me the peace I so badly needed.

I went home, pulled the sheet off the bed, and soaked it in the laundry room sink to get the red marker out. Just doing that frustrated me so much. I thought after Christmas I would discuss this with the social worker or phone Diane to find out if I was cracking up. I thought I would just let it keep soaking for a few days.

There were Christmas miracles that year, lots of them, but not the one I was looking for. Janet had called and asked if we could come and spend

Christmas Eve with her family. It was a yearly ritual, they serve hors d'oeuvres. I declined the invitation as we always spend Christmas with Rudi's family at Elaine's house. It was December 22nd in the evening and we went to the church for the kids' Christmas pageant. At seven o'clock Rudi walked in and sat down, right when it started. The kids were fantastic. P.J. of course, never forgot any of his lines, and he could have gotten a standing ovation in my books. He always was a natural. J.J. was adorable in his beard and staff but had a bit of a problem standing so long, so he sat down. They had a hard time getting him up to sing after because the long robe he was wearing was giving him difficulty. Tammy stole the show with her one word. They all asked where the baby child was born, and Tammy was supposed to say Bethlehem. She said it so loud everyone burst out laughing even Rudi. I just smiled because it was the first time I really saw a sincere laugh since he left.

After the show, goodie bags were given out to all the kids, and when we were leaving, Rudi mentioned he would come by with the gifts on Christmas Eve. I realized right away that we weren't invited to the family's by his comment and was very quick to say we were invited out for the evening, so he should call first to see if we were back home yet. He had a surprised look on his face and asked where we were going. I told him it was cold and I wanted to close the window, if he wanted to talk later he could call.

About an hour after the kids went to bed, the phone did ring. Rudi's first question was who invited us for Christmas Eve? I felt like saying it was none of his business, but I didn't. I didn't want to play the game. I told him we were invited over to a friend from the speedway and left it at that. He didn't ask me anymore. He suggested maybe I should consider staying home on Christmas Eve and he would stop by. I asked what time he was planning on stopping by, and he didn't know yet. I informed him when he knew, he could let me know and I would reconsider. I said goodnight.

The next morning I phoned Janet and told her the update. She suggested we wait until the last minute to decide if we were coming. That was the way Janet was. I appreciated her understanding in the situation.

One of the guys from the track had stopped by on the 23rd to drop off some papers. I was still secretary of the club though now it was a quiet time. Things would get more active after Christmas.

He asked me how I was doing (knowing Rudi had moved out).

I offered him a cup of coffee. (The kids were in bed, and I really wanted some company.) I asked him how he found out that Rudi had moved out.

He started to explain that he stopped by the body shop that sponsored Rudi one afternoon to pick something up. There was a girl sitting on Rudi's lap, and he seemed to be pretty drunk.

I almost threw up, and by the look on my face, he knew if there was anything going on, I didn't know.

He apologized for saying anything and asked if Rudi was seeing someone else.

I couldn't hold back. I started to cry. I couldn't believe what I was hearing. I had no idea.

He quickly recovered what he was telling me and started to say it was probably nothing. The girl that was on his lap looked quite old and was wearing one of those square things his mother wore when she went out.

I laughed through my tears and declared, "A babushka?"

He answered, "Yeah!"

" That was Helena," I explained. I was really surprised to hear she was on his lap, but I was even more surprised that Rudi seemed drunk. I felt a bit better about it but still was wondering who gave this woman the right to sit on my husband's lap.

After the guy left, I went to bed and spent the night very confused. I was definitely not threatened by Helena. She did say she "vanted" him, but there was no way. I finally fell asleep.

The next morning Elaine came in with gifts for everyone. She had a coffee, and I asked her outright if she knew anything. By the look on her face, she did know something, but said she had to leave. I was in hell. All day I was torn up but was able to keep justifying in my mind that there was no way Rudi would be with Helena.

We unpacked my mom and dad's gifts from the box. There were so many under the tree, and Santa hadn't come yet. Neither did Rudi. He phoned at three o'clock and asked if we were going out. I asked him quite sharply what time he was coming. He noted the coldness in my voice and asked what was wrong. I explained I wanted to talk to him and maybe he should come after the kids were in bed. He was adamant he wanted to come when they were up. I answered, fine! Come whenever, but plan a bit of time to talk. His voice seemed nervous when he asked again if there was something wrong. I hung up the phone.

He came by at eight and was quick to let me know he wasn't in a hurry and he could stick around for a while. We could talk after the kids were in bed. He had brought a gift for each of the kids and they were big gifts. I had a hard time getting through the visit he had with the kids. He just kept talking, and it seemed to me, he just wanted them to stay up so he didn't have to hear what I had to say. The kids finally went to bed and we sat in the living room.

He asked me what the problem was and I burst. He told me to cool down and talk. I told him it seemed to me that he had been trying to get a reaction from me for months. Now he was getting what he was looking for. I was reacting, and he finally found something to make me irrational. I looked at him with hate and cried out what I had heard the night before. I couldn't see the reaction on his face when I told him because the only lights in the living room were the lights on the tree and two candles burning.

He was quiet for a minute then started to laugh. It wasn't a real laugh, but one put on. He asked me if I really thought he would ever have anything for that woman.

I firmly stated that I asked the question and would really appreciate an answer, not another question.

He responded that she was an older lady and I saw how she was. He asked if he was ever to cheat on me, did I actually think it would be her?

I again reminded him, I didn't want a question for a question. He was obviously getting frustrated, and I asked him why she was sitting on his knee.

He explained that lasted about two minutes and he told her to get off. He then remarked, "Helena and me? Give your head a shake lady."

Then he handed me a gift. A small box, velvet box. He told me not to wait, to open it right away. I did and it was the sapphire ring I had wanted a couple of years before. I didn't know what to say. I was so emotional and so confused. I couldn't help thinking about another girl sitting on his lap. That wasn't the Rudi I knew. Being drunk wasn't the Rudi I knew. Who should I believe? He was leaving at about eleven and went to give me a kiss. It was like there was a concrete wall coming at me. I backed off so fast. I needed a meeting not a kiss. After he left, I just sat and stared at the tree for an hour. I didn't know what to believe. Finally at midnight I thought I had better play Santa and get the gifts under the tree and fill the stockings.

The kids got up at seven to open gifts. I just turned the whole mess over to God and made the decision I wasn't going to let this ruin my kids' Christmas. I loved Christmas with my kids. They had so much spirit. They loved the day. It was a wonderful day, but the whole time I had a pain in my heart. It almost felt like something had gone through my skin with claws getting a good grip and pulling constantly. We had turkey, and I said grace before we ate. P.J. had commented that it was the first time I said grace and didn't thank God for Rudi coming back. I never answered him, and I could see he was bothered by it.

P.J. had gotten a pair of jeans for Christmas and he wanted to wear them the next day. He asked me if I could hem them. They were really long. I went to get the sewing machine out. I hadn't used it since I finished the bridesmaid dresses in the summer. I couldn't find it. I thought for a moment, then started going through the house. Why would Rudi take my sewing machine? He wouldn't. He knew I needed it for weddings in the summer. It was brand new. I bought one of the Singer Machines that had a few of the fancy stitches. It was so new, when I finished the last dress in the summer; I packed it back in its box to make sure it was good until I sewed again the next year. I looked everywhere; it was gone. This whole thing was getting out of hand.

The kids went to respite that following weekend. I really didn't know what to do with myself. I hated to stay by myself in the house. I went to Janet and Henry's house on Friday and had a drink with them, and then I went back home. I slept on the couch in the living room when I was alone. I guess that gave me some kind of security if someone else was in the house, I would at least be close to the door, whatever that would do for me. It was an emotionally draining weekend.

I decided to go to MGT Auto Body and talk to Mike and Toni. Hopefully Helena would be there and I could find out what was on her mind. I went early in the morning and Mike's truck was outside the shop. He was surprised to see me when I walked in but smiled and asked me how Christmas was. I told him it was all right. He asked if Rudi sent anything over for the kids. I told him he had come and spent a few hours, and I showed him the ring he gave me. I think I only did that to see if there was any expression on his face. There was. He was surprised.

I asked him if he had seen Rudi lately and he said yes but only at his mom's on Christmas Day. I tried very hard to keep a straight face then I asked him what was he doing there.

He replied very nonchalantly that Helena had invited him. He said Rudi never spoke a word and was really looking sad the whole time he was there. He just sat on the footstool and watched everyone open their gifts. When he opened his, he managed to force a smile long enough to say thank you, but he couldn't fool anyone.

I asked what he meant by that.

He answered, "He is not happy without you."

I asked then, "Why is he without me?"

He replied as if I knew something that I didn't, "Well he screwed up and doesn't know how to fix it."

I had a fear growing inside of me. There was evidently something that had happened that I don't know about, but it seemed like everyone else did. I asked him what Rudi got him for Christmas. I said it as a joke and he took it at that, but really I was fishing for information.

He answered, "A bottle." Then he continued, "Rudi bought Helena a new sewing machine, and she doesn't really know how to sew."

I couldn't believe it. I asked if it was a Singer Machine.

He said, "Yes, a pretty nice one."

I left before I started to cry again. I was so baffled on the way home. My brain was spinning trying to figure out if something was up or if Rudi just went to their house because he had nowhere else to spend Christmas. I am sure he spent Christmas Eve with his family, but he wouldn't have anywhere to go on Christmas Day. As for the sewing machine, I didn't even want to think that it could possibly be mine that he gave her. Was he trying to turn her into me? Was she trying to replace me? I was just trying to justify everything that was happening. I think inside I really knew that this was not good, but until Rudi actually told me, then I would have to believe what he said. Nothing was happening. I got back on Main Street finally, after a couple of turns out of the way. It was so ironic, but Rudi was a half a block in front of me. I really wanted to talk to him, so I speeded up to catch up to his van. He was heading for a light with his signal on to turn left. I was hoping he wouldn't make the light and then for sure I would catch him. The light turned red, and he stopped. I changed lanes so I could pull up beside him. I was sorry I did.

I pulled up to the passenger side of his van and turned to smile at him and was face to face with Helena. She was in the passenger seat of the van. I just looked at Rudi and the light turned green. I went straight, and he turned. I was sick. What was going on? I thought this was so stupid. He couldn't possibly be seeing Helena. I just didn't think she could have anything in common with him, though I really didn't know Rudi anymore. He almost seemed to have turned into a sad, angry person. I could almost say he had become desperate. Stealing my sewing machine to give to her for Christmas? I couldn't even think about it. Maybe they did have something in common. No, I tried to justify it in my head. Maybe he was just giving her a ride somewhere. He probably got hooked into giving her a ride because he was invited to spend Christmas Day at their house. I cried to God, I didn't want to do this anymore.

I wanted my marriage back together. I didn't want my husband driving this woman around. Why was this happening to me?

I started cleaning my house when I got home. I had to keep going. The phone rang, and I was scared to answer it. I knew it was Rudi. He said we had to talk. I laughed with tears rolling down my face. He stated things aren't how they look. I didn't answer. He asked if he could come over. I told him I was really very busy and it wasn't a good time. The truth was I was so emotional; I had to get my act together. I declined, explaining the kids weren't home and I had plans. He said he had to talk to me and he was busy that evening. I told him that was too bad because I wasn't changing my plans anymore; I had a life. I guess that he knew I meant it because he said he would change his plans and come over whenever was good for me. I told him I didn't want to be alone with him in the house anymore, so we would have to meet somewhere else. I could swear he sounded like he started to cry. He asked if he could pick me up at five and go for a bite to eat and talk. I told him my appetite was trashed this morning, and I didn't think I could handle food that day. He pleaded to let him come. I told him I would see him at the house at seven. He could say what he had to say then leave. He agreed.

Chapter 15

ACCEPTING THE TRUTH

"You will know the truth, and the truth will set you free."
John 8:32

I called Ruth and Margaret. I needed prayers. I was so afraid of what he was going to tell me. I wouldn't allow myself to stop. I knew if I stopped I would have too much time to think. I just kept on cleaning. I baked cookies for the kids for when they got home the next day.

I went downstairs to do the ironing and remembered the sheet was still soaking. It hadn't been neglected for all that time. I just couldn't get the stain out. I threw it back in the washer for about the fourth time. I went back to the washer when it stopped and the sheet was as if I never touched it. I looked at the big red spot and felt like I was a time bomb ready to explode. I turned the washer on again and again that afternoon. Finally the last try, I opened the washer, pulled it out and the red spot was as red as it was when I had started originally. There was no hope. I started to cry, threw the sheet in the dryer and decided to use it for rags.

I sat down with a cup of coffee, and then it hit me. I was remembering J.J.'s accident. I remembered him lying on the road. I had thought of it so many times in the past few years but never remembered feeling so desperate or wanting to run away. This time was different. It was the red. J.J. was lying in a big puddle of blood. I never remembered it like that before. There was never any blood. I guess my mind blocked it out. I didn't want to remember it, but it was flooding me. I got up off the couch and started to run. I wanted to run out the door and away from the horrible memory. There was no place to go.

I picked up the phone out of desperation and called Margaret. There was no answer. I wanted to run to her house. I didn't want to be alone. I called Margaret's mom to see if Margaret was there. She wasn't, but Margaret's mom asked me what was wrong. I told her of all the times I thought of J.J.'s accident, there was never any blood in my memory, but there really was. There was so much blood, and I just remembered. She explained it had to be dealt with. I had to remember and feel the hurt then I could heal. I didn't want to remember. No mother would ever want to remember that. I had no choice. I kept going over it with Margaret's mom. She told me she would stay on the phone as long as I needed her and to remember that I wasn't alone, God was with me. It sure didn't feel like it. She said just give it all to God–all the hurt, and the terrible memory. She seemed to understand how devastating it was. I didn't realize it then, but Margaret's mother was like an angel sent to me by God to handle this horrendous situation.

I could never have handled this without help, and God knew it and made sure I wasn't alone. She asked me if I wanted to pray. I told her to pray for me. She did.

I turned my life over to God with her on the phone and invited Him into my heart. She told me Jesus died on the cross so that we could be forgiven and go to heaven. It was that simple for now and I was a Christian. She prayed again asking God to heal this terrible hurt. She asked Him to take it away and to replace it with peace, His peace beyond all understanding. There was such a flood of peace over me that I will never forget. The tears dried up, and I felt like I was on top of the world. I told her I hadn't been able to wear red or look at red for so long, and I guess it was the terrible memory brewing inside of me that I had blocked out so long ago.

She explained, "Now it is gone, and when you think of red or see the colour red, think of how God loves you."

I filled her in on the situation with Rudi, and she said not to worry. We must have been on the phone for a couple of hours. She told me that at seven she and her husband would be praying that God's will be done and that I would see good coming out of this whole situation. I might not see it right away, but I would see in God's time.

I took a bath and the peace didn't leave me. I still thought about the accident, but I didn't feel the devastation anymore. The emotions were there, but the pain was gone. I got dressed up nice and did my hair and my make-up. I was all ready and still had a half an hour before Rudi would get there, so I lit a fire in the fireplace and made a pot of coffee.

He arrived a few minutes before seven. I poured him a cup of coffee, and we sat in the living room. I was so peaceful like nothing could break through that peace. I was wrong. It was quiet for a while, and we both looked into the fireplace. I thought how he used to be so clean-cut and so blonde. He was in such good shape and cared about the way he was dressed. Now he sat there with longer hair, you know how curly hair stands up when it is long. His hair was quite dark and he had on jeans that looked like he had slept in them. His beard was very bushy and long.

He finally said to me, "You seen Helena in the van today, and it wasn't what it looked like."

I asked him what he thought it looked like? Little did he know that I knew so much more about this than I was about to let on. I wanted to see how honest he was willing to be about the whole thing.

He told me, "I was just giving her a ride home."

I answered sarcastically, "Her parents live in the other direction."

He answered so defensively, "No, her and her daughters got an apartment a few blocks from here. She doesn't have a license so I was just doing her a favour."

I asked him if he was doing her a favour when she was sitting on his knee at the shop? He got quite loud and reminded me we had already gone over that.

I crossed my arms smugly and stated, "Okay, then were you doing her a favour when you gave her the sewing machine for Christmas?"

He right away jumped and asked who I was talking to.

I ignored the question and asked if it was my machine.

He again said louder, "Who were you talking to?"

I asked then if he was doing her a favour when he spent Christmas day with her and her family instead of at home with his own.

He knew he couldn't fight it. He knew I knew too much, but I was about to find out just how much I didn't know. He got up and put his hands in his pockets and looked out the window. He almost whispered he was so sorry. He didn't know how he got himself into such a mess. My fear instantly took over my peace. I am sure it showed. I knew I was about to hear something that I didn't want to hear. He told me to just listen and he would tell me everything. He had been avoiding it for so long but knew this day would come.

He started talking about when I went to Calgary to visit my parents. He knew he had screwed up the finances. That is why he moved into the shop and started to do the accounting himself, so I wouldn't find out what a mess he made. He said the credit cards were maxed out. When I left for Calgary, he was afraid he was losing me and hated every day that I was gone. He couldn't sleep or eat and just wanted to fly down to meet me, but when the racecar got all smashed up, it was either concentrate on fixing the mess or risking me finding out we were so badly in debt.

He was at MGT Auto Body one day while I was in Calgary, and Helena was saying she moved into an apartment with the girls close to our house. She asked if she could catch a ride home. He didn't see any harm in it and put himself in my shoes and knew I would do the same if it were Mike or Toni. She was no risk to me. She had some boxes at the shop that she wanted to take to her place, so he threw them in the van. He drove her home and she was talking about a guy she had been going out with. He was a biker. She said she broke up with him. He thought it was kind of funny because she didn't look like someone who would go out with a biker. (I laughed because I couldn't see it either.) When he got to her apartment, he helped her carry the boxes into the apartment. He said it was clean but pretty grim–just the bare necessities.

She told him he had to stay, and she would make supper. He answered no. She insisted or he would have to take money for driving her home. He again replied no. She insisted and he thought about going home and eating alone. He was hungry, so he thought it wouldn't hurt to stay and have supper. She gave him a bottle of beer while she was cooking. She was telling him all about why her husband was in jail in Europe.

Rudi was still standing looking out the window as he was telling me all of this. I threw another log on the fire and he continued.

Supper was taking so long to cook, and she gave him another beer. Finally supper was ready, and he asked her where her daughters were. She answered they were staying the night with her parents. He felt like he was being set up by her and was just going to finish eating and leave. She had brought out a bottle of wine and poured it in the glasses set at the table. The meal dragged out, and she started to tell him how much she liked him and how terrible I was for going away without him. He was drinking the wine pretty fast with the meal because he needed the courage to tell her there was no way he was going to be manipulated by her, and he said she kept talking about how a wife should always be there for her husband.

I thought to myself, how dare she criticize me to my husband. He continued and explained he got pretty drunk and one thing led to another and before he knew it he woke up next to her at three in the morning. He was out of that house so fast and didn't go to work the next day. He was so confused and knew he had done something so stupid that he couldn't change. He said he kept tossing around on how to handle it. He knew he blew the marriage. He did something unforgivable. He was so sorry. He turned to look at me and I was devastated. I felt like those claws with the grip on me had torn my heart out, put it in the meat grinder, and then shoved it back in my chest. I hurt so badly, and the tears were flowing.

He started to cry and said, "You have no idea how sorry I am."

I told him to leave, and he answered, not until he finished. I had heard enough. I could never believe he would ever do this.

"For all of these months," I cried, "you have tried to make me react to stupid things you were doing, and all along you were just covering your own butt. You were hoping that I would react, and then you could justify leaving me because I was such a terrible person to live with. You wouldn't have to deal with the fact that you were responsible because you cheated on me. Leave now! I have heard enough!"

I was sobbing as he was leaving. He wanted to finish telling me, so it was all out. He would call me in the morning and maybe if I felt a bit better, we could talk again. He said sorry again and left. I must have cried for a few hours and fell asleep on the couch. It was too late when he left for me to phone anyone.

I didn't want to get up in the morning; I didn't want to deal with this anymore. I just wanted to stay in bed and it would all go away. The phone rang and it was Margaret's mom. She asked me if I wanted to come to church with them. I told her what happened, and I didn't want to go anywhere. She understood and promised to pray for me. I hurt so much, I just wanted to go to bed and live in denial. I thought this hurt would never go away.

The phone rang and it was Rudi. He asked if he could take me for breakfast. I asked him how he ever thought he could tell me all of this over breakfast in a restaurant with people around. He just kept saying how sorry he was and I didn't want to hear it anymore. He begged me to let him talk; he wanted to come over. I told him to give me an hour.

I really was very tired and just wanted to go back to bed. It was too hard being awake, and now he was coming back to load more on. I asked God, "Why? Why me again?" My first husband spent more time cheating on me than with me, and now Rudi. I don't ever remember pain like this when Jeffrey cheated on me. What was I doing wrong? Why did Rudi stay there to eat? Why did he drink too much? Why would he jump into bed with a woman like that when he doesn't even remember? What did I do to deserve this?

I just wanted my peace back again, that peace that Margaret's mother talked about, the peace beyond all understanding. I made coffee but really thought maybe I should have a drink to take the hurt away. I knew it would only last a little while. When the drink wore off, I would have to deal with the reality again, but at least it would stop hurting for a little while.

Rudi came in, and we pretty well started where we left off. This time he was shaved and in clean clothes. He sat on the coach and started to talk. He said when he met me in Moose Jaw, he was so glad to see me. He really missed me. He hated the fact that I was being so independent. He wanted me to rely on him and didn't want me to make it on my own. He wanted me to phone him on the road on the way to Calgary crying and tell him I couldn't do the trip without him. (I thought of how many times he had said that I couldn't make it without him.)

He told me he really thought we could make it without him telling me what happened (concerning Helena), but the guilt started to eat him up. He wanted me to need him, and every step he took in walking away; he wanted me to stop him.

I jumped in, "How many times did I tell you I didn't want this to happen?" How many times I told him I didn't want him to leave and that I missed him. I asked him what he wanted me to do–to get desperate and crawl to him begging him to come home?

He replied, "It would have worked."

I said, "You would have come home but not because you wanted to, only because I needed you to. Where would that have gotten us?"

"I am so sorry about what happened," he repeated again. "You can't possibly believe I would intentionally sleep with Helena."

I told him I was very surprised, but she "vanted" him and needed him. I continued, "I guess that is what you like in a woman. I definitely loved you and wanted you, but I don't *need* you. I can make it without you." That was just a shot on my part.

He went on to say he was living with Horst. Then Horst moved back home and took all his stuff. Rudi stayed in the shop, but there was no place to shower and it was a stupid way to live. He couldn't come home because he was too guilty about what he did. He felt like there was no hope anywhere.

Then one evening Mike came to the shop and brought Helena with him. "She told me this was a stupid way to live, and I could come and stay at her place. It was better than nothing," he said.

I was in shock again. "You are living with her?"

He answered, "Well, kind of. She cooks my meals, washes my clothes. She is my chief maid and bottle washer. That is all. I don't love her, but she is better than nothing. What else was I going to do? I just kept making things worse. I am so sorry, I loved you for so long and will never stop loving you, and I am so sorry I made such a mess."

He walked out the door. I didn't know what to do. I screamed, I cried, I hurt. I went into my bedroom and pulled the blankets up over my head and cried, and screamed, "God please help me! What am I going to do? Please stop this hurting."

I was so glad the kids weren't home. They weren't supposed to be home. How was I going to tell them? How could Rudi do this to the kids? Sure Rudi adopted J.J. and P.J., but no one would ever have known it to see them together. They were his kids. He didn't even tell the boys he wasn't their birth father until P.J. was six years old and J.J. was seven. He told them they had his last name because he was now their father. They only knew Rudi as their father. When he told them, they just said, "Okay, can we go out and play now?"

I didn't want to get out of bed the next morning. I couldn't believe this all wasn't a bad dream. The Christmas days were over, but we were still on a break for another week before the kids went back to school and I went back to work. I just turned over in bed and told P.J. to get the other kids their breakfast.

I went back to sleep, and then at about ten o'clock, I heard the doorbell ring. I just ignored it, thinking it was one of the kid's friends. I looked up sensing someone was standing at my bedroom door, and it was Rudi. I said quietly so the kids wouldn't hear. "What do you want?"

He had the nerve to ask me, "Why are you still in bed and the kids are making their own breakfast?"

Not caring who heard anymore, I yelled back at him "And who the hell are you to ask?" I jumped out of bed and was so angry that I didn't give him a chance to say anything; I just lost it. I said, "Oh, did Helena get up at the crack of dawn and run your shower for you and fetch the eggs from the back yard and make your breakfast and serve it on a silver platter to you in bed?"

P.J. came running and yelled, "Mom, what are you doing?"

I started to cry again and went into the bathroom. Rudi got what he came for, a reaction from me.

I heard him say to the kids while I was in the bathroom, "Now you know why I left; I don't want to put up with that from her."

I came running out of the bathroom to yell some more, but he went out the door. The kids were so mad at me for yelling at Rudi. They asked me why I was being so mean to him; didn't I want him to come home? I was so angry. He did that purposely to make himself look good to the kids and to make me look bad.

I knew I needed help and phoned around to find out if there was help out there. I still didn't tell the kids what happened. I figured they could be mad at me if they wanted. It wasn't as bad as the hurt they would feel and the hopelessness if I told them the truth. I had to find a way to get myself back on my feet. I had to be more stable before I could tell them, so they could see it would be alright. Watching their mother fall apart in this situation wouldn't give them any security.

The kids were downstairs with Greg. They were laughing and listening to Michael Jackson records. I think they were trying to moon walk. P.J. was pretty good at it and was trying to teach Tammy. I was watching them for a few minutes. J.J. was growing to be such a handsome boy. He was growing taller and was still very slim. P.J. was still so blonde and had one of those new haircuts. The kind that looked like you put a bowl over his head as a guide for cutting. He still had that adorable face that glowed when he smiled. Tammy was so tiny and so blonde. She had such long hair and very wavy. She was really looking more like Rudi. I thought to myself that we were so blessed with such great kids, how could Rudi just walk away? What did Helena and her daughters have that we didn't? I knew inside that the answer was "nothing."

Rudi and Helena's relationship was started by a malicious game on Helena's part, and Rudi got taken in out of being weak. Like he said, "She was better than nothing." How sad, and it was his loss. It was a bit of a good feeling to know he wasn't with her because he loved her, and he wasn't with her because he wanted to be there. He was desperate. It is a big difference.

It was really good to get back to work again, to get up in the morning with a schedule. Three weeks into January, I still didn't hear from Rudi. He didn't even come to see the kids or call them. I guess he figured my blow up the last time I saw him justified what he was doing. P.J. blamed me. I hated that, but what was I going to do? I still didn't have the heart to tell them Rudi was living with another woman and looking after her daughters. I guess I thought the longer I could keep that from them, the less time they would hurt. No mother ever wants her kids to hurt. I couldn't tell my parents either. Somehow I thought they would think badly of me–that here I was only thirty years old and had already blown a second marriage.

At the end of January, I got a letter in the mail from the bank. The mortgage hadn't been paid. I knew it was worse than that because all the bills were sitting and Rudi didn't pick them up. I met a good friend of Rudi's at the store one afternoon and he told me that he was really shocked at the whole situation and that Rudi had really changed since he was with that woman. (That is how he put it) He said he was talking to Rudi the day before, and he told him that he and Helena bought a house and were going to be moving into it in spring. I told him Rudi didn't pay the house bills and that is probably why. The money was going into that. He said no. Apparently part of the deal is that if Rudi stays with her, then her parents offered to pay the down payment on the house as long as it goes in their name.

I asked him what kind of house, and he said Rudi told him it was just a little Sugar Shack on a small street in Elmwood. Nothing special. "Sugar Shack" I thought as I said goodbye and finished shopping. He wasn't very creative was he? That was a term we used. Couldn't he at least have thought of something new for them? I went back to work and was really afraid of what was to come. Somehow I had to pay the mortgage and bills. I didn't make enough money to cover everything.

One of the parents from P.J.'s hockey team suggested I talk to a lawyer to see where I stood. Rudi did have a responsibility to the family, and I had to make the choice of enforcing that. I didn't want to get a lawyer; I didn't want to get a legal separation. I said I would talk to a lawyer anyway just to find out where I stood.

The next day, I called legal aid. They set up an appointment with a female lawyer for me to talk to. I went to her office between runs and told her the whole story. She had suggested I get a legal separation to protect myself and the kids from Rudi taking anything else away and to force him to pay for his responsibilities. I replied I would think about it.

It didn't take long before I called her back. The first of February went by, and the mortgage wasn't paid. I had no choice but to go forward on this. I felt bad because I was learning to be a Christian, and divorce was not part of this life. I made the decision, no matter what, Rudi was my husband and Helena had no right to have him with her. I couldn't let the house go, I had to find a way to pay the bills and get Rudi back. I could forgive him for what he did. It wasn't like he intentionally went out and slept with her. He was manipulated into it, but he allowed it. I was sure he learned a lesson from this.

I sat down and figured out all of my finances. I could catch up the mortgage and pay the bills up to date by the end of the month, but there was no money left for groceries. I checked through the cupboards and made a menu to make the food last. I could be careful, and if I didn't eat too much and I didn't eat at work, then I may have enough food to get us through to my payday. I had a fair amount of baking supplies, so I could do baking with what I had and it would help out. But most of all, I would quit smoking.

I brought the mortgage payments up to date and paid all the bills. I was pretty well totally cleaned out. Payday wasn't for another couple of weeks. I got up every morning and did my devotions (a time set apart for me to personally spend time in prayer) and prayed for God to show me how to get through the day with what we had. I took advantage of fasting. I believed if I fasted, not eating food or a certain kind of food for an amount of time my prayers were more powerful. I didn't know if what I was doing was really fasting, but God knew I had good intentions in my heart. The first week was really good. The kids were getting a kick out of the creative cooking. It was amazing how many ways you could make hot dogs and hamburger look different on the plate.

I didn't smoke but it was so hard. With all the frustrations, I could only do it with a lot of tears. I would go to work and whenever I wanted a cigarette; I would tell God to please take the feeling away. He did, but at first it was almost every minute I was crying out to him. After three days of this, it was getting better.

Coffee and milk ran out. I just quit with the coffee and drank black tea. I scrounged up enough change to get milk. There was a container of lemonade left in the cupboard from summer so I made the kids lemonade for breakfast to save on the milk. We made it till half way through the second week before were totally out of food.

I didn't know what to do. I had been praying to God to show me what to make for meals every morning. That morning as I was working, I got desperate and told Ruth when I picked up her son David what was going on. She told me to stop praying for God to show me what to make for meals that day and pray for Him to provide the meals. She said she would pray and believe too. Oh did I have it wrong. When I came back to drop off her son, at lunchtime, Ruth had a lunch packed for me with enough food for a meal for the kids. I thanked her, and she explained she was only giving me enough for the day because she prayed and wanted me to see how God would provide. I looked in the lunch, and there were two sandwiches and cookies and fruit and a can of juice. I didn't eat it because I could use it as back up if I had to.

The kids and I thanked God for the food and for providing for us what we needed. I cleaned up the dishes, and the kids went to hockey and ringette practice. They were picked up by friends. J.J. went along with P.J.

I finished cleaning after supper and put my shoes on to take the garbage out. It was thirty below and with the wind chill it was even worse. I was bad for not putting a coat on. I had on a turtleneck sweater and another ski sweater overtop that my mother had made me for Christmas. I was only taking the garbage bag down the side of the house to the back by the garage. I wouldn't need a coat and mitts for that. When I got outside it seemed all right until I got around the side of the house. The wind was deadly, so I started to run. I got to the side of the garage and it was solid ice. I threw the garbage bag next to the can and started to turn to run back. I slipped on the ice, my feet went out from under me and I slid into the side of the garage. My hip hit the concrete foundation. I just lay there. I was sure my hip was broken. It was so cold.

I thought as I lay there crying from the pain, that the kids weren't going to be home for a couple of hours, and I would be frozen to death by then. I cried out to God and asked Him what sense He made out of this now. I asked why He was letting all of this happen to me. I was really angry and so cold. I thought maybe I could crawl to the garage and get the door opened. At least I could be safe from the wind, but I knew the door was locked and the key was in the house. I was angry with myself for not putting on my coat and gloves to take out the garbage, and I was so cold.

As I lay on the ice, the pain in my hip started to numb and I found I could crawl without too much trouble. I crawled over to the fence and pulled myself up. I stood on my foot. It hurt, but I figured out it wasn't broken. I used the fence as my crutch and made my way up the side of the house. I could feel the tears frozen against my cheeks, and I could barely move my fingers anymore. I had managed to make it to the house and crawl up the front steps. I went to open the front door and thought maybe my fingers would stick to the door handle. I went to pull the sleeve of the sweater over my hand when the door opened. Margaret was standing in the door with a big smile on her face.

I asked when she got there. She said she was there for about twenty minutes and was wondering where I was. I told her what happened and she commented something about would I let my kids take out the garbage with no coat?

I replied, "Of course not."

She just got more sarcastic. She helped me into the kitchen, and I sat down. She offered to make me a cup of coffee. I told her I have no coffee. She answered yes I did. She found some in the cupboard and put on a pot while she was waiting for me. I thought how could I have missed a package of coffee; I went into the cupboard so many times to take stock of what I had. She poured me a coffee and went to the fridge to get the milk. I told her I was totally out of milk.

With a smile she asked, "Did you hit your head outside too?" Then she pulled a whole gallon of milk out of the fridge. She reached up into the cupboard and brought down a package of cookies and started to put some on a plate. I didn't know what was going on but just said I didn't want cookies–save them for the kids.

Margaret then stated, "There is more than enough food for you and the kids."

I got up and was so surprised; my hip wasn't hurting at all though I still felt cold. I went to the fridge and it was full. Full, like people's fridges are at Christmas time. The freezer of the fridge was full. Pork chops, ground beef, a roast, hot dogs. Full. The cupboards were full of soup, Kraft Dinner, macaroni. There was a whole new supply of baking goods. I asked her how she did that so fast.

She asked, "What?"

I knew it was Margaret and understood this was the good coming from me falling outside. The timing was unbelievable. She had enough time to bring the groceries in the house, put them all away, and make coffee. She finally caved and said she had gotten a big cheque and went to get groceries. She told me she was shopping and thought she would shop for me while she was there. She didn't know I was out of food. I never told her. I didn't want people to know what I had done. I told her I could pay her back on payday, but she wouldn't hear of it. I told her how I had prayed with Ruth that day for God to provide. She said she figured out why she was supposed to do what she did when she started to put the groceries away and the cupboards and fridge were all empty. When I was lying on the ground outside, I was crying to God to show me the good in this. He definitely showed me.

When the kids came home, as usual, they were hungry. They asked if there was a snack before they went to bed. I told P.J. to go into the cupboard and get the cookies, and I would make hot chocolate for them.

"Cookies? Hot chocolate?" P.J. said, "Mom got groceries while we were out."

I told them, "No I didn't." As they were eating, they heard the whole story of how we were running out of food and how I prayed for God to provide and how He definitely provided. P.J. suggested we pray for Rudi to come home. We did.

I could hardly wait to tell Ruth what happened that night. She smiled and said that is what Faith is.

I decided I couldn't let that happen again. I was responsible to put food on the table and to make sure my kids ate. I was determined to stand up to my responsibilities and trust that God would take care of Rudi and his responsibilities. I wasn't going to pay the mortgage anymore, even if we were going to lose the house. I was told there was a time to draw the line. I wasn't a doormat. Besides, I was only trying to defend myself. It was all so deceiving. I was feeling guilty. Yet, it was Rudi who was living with another woman while he was married to me, and he wasn't looking after his kids. He was in the wrong, and I had to keep it straight. I wasn't going for a divorce. I was just trying to get Rudi to stand up to his responsibilities, and I definitely knew there was nothing wrong with that. Once I had that straight in my mind, I gave my lawyer the okay to serve the papers for a legal separation.

I had to tell the kids. It was time. Of course they were so upset, and P.J. couldn't understand why I would go for a separation when we were praying for Rudi to come home. I was to blame again.

I knew the Bible was my roadmap, and I was ready to follow His plans. I just didn't know where to go to learn it. Little did I realize at the time that God was teaching me at His pace. I had spent some time with the lawyer getting ready. She had all the information she needed. After Rudi left, he took the convertible, the boat, race car, van, all the equipment from the garage, all the paint company equipment, the sewing machine, part of the furniture and the old money collection. Some he had sold and I never saw a penny of that money. The lawyer said she strongly believed he should have to pay for the house and utilities and help with the kids. Well I wish she had been the judge.

We went to court, and I met Rudi outside the courthouse. He told me I was a jerk to do this and he would fix me. I didn't bother to answer. His appearance helped because not only did he not sound like the man I had married, but he didn't look anything like the man I married. He looked so angry and had put on about forty pounds. I still had to believe that somewhere under that mess was the man I married. I had heard that your outside reflects how your inside feels, and as far as I was concerned, Rudi's outside was showing that he felt terrible on the inside. Love comes from the inside and it is the joy that is reflected. If Rudi really did love Helena and was happy with her, then he had a strange way of showing it and likewise if he really did love me he had an even stranger way of showing it.

.

Chapter 16

WAS JUSTICE SERVED?

*"Do you want justice? Don't fawn on the judge, but ask
the Lord for it" Proverbs 29:26 (The Living Bible)*

The court was called to order. As the judge sat down, it seemed to me
he looked kind of young to be a judge. He was obviously older by the hair
colour but was a very distinguished looking man. (God gave men that. They
could get older and turn grey and with no makeup or other necessities, they
can look handsome and distinguished. Women, on the other hand, got older
and grey, and when gravity got them, they just looked old. Women have to
fight it every step of the way. I wonder why God did that?)

My lawyer told the judge what the situation was in detail, and then
Rudi's lawyer got his chance. He said Rudi was struggling with a paint company and wasn't making any money. The racecar had been smashed up and
couldn't be sold until it was fixed. The car and boat had been sold to fix the
racecar, but it wasn't enough. He then said Rudi wasn't supporting Helena
and the girls. Helena's parents were supporting them. The house they were
moving into belonged to Helena. (At this point I felt that everything Rudi
expressed to his lawyer must have been a misrepresentation for them to take
that position in court). Then the clincher, Rudi's lawyer told the judge that the
boys were not his. What heartbreak. I was so glad the boys weren't there to
hear it. He said he was more than willing to take his daughter, and his girlfriend Helena would gladly help to care for her.

I looked at my lawyer and couldn't believe my ears. He had to be kidding. He thought he would take Tammy. After raising the boys since they were
babies, could he actually allow his lawyer to say they weren't his and he did-
n't think he should pay a penny for them? My lawyer had to almost sit on me
to stop me from opening my mouth. She wrote on a paper, he is only looking
for a reaction; don't give him the satisfaction. That toned me down.

The judge ordered Rudi pay $75 a month per child, starting the following month, and I had to pay the mortgage and the bills. I didn't react but was ready to blow.

I prayed all the way home for God to show me how to do this. I asked him to please not let me lose the house. The kids had established all their friends in this area, and their lives had been disrupted enough. If I lost the house, I couldn't afford to live in the area. The lawyer had said we would get together again to discuss the next step.

March came, and Rudi didn't make the maintenance payment. They were threatening to shut off my utilities. I couldn't tell my parents or ask them for help because I didn't want them to know I was having so much trouble. Every time I talked to them I made like I was all right. April 1st came, and Rudi didn't pay again. I was getting desperate. I couldn't do it anymore. There wasn't enough money to satisfy everyone.

The kids knew Rudi was living with Helena. The agreement was he could take them out every second Saturday. We were struggling so badly, and every second Saturday Rudi would pull up in front of the house with Helena and the girls and take the kids out and show them a really good time. All the kids were seeing was how wonderful Rudi was to them and how I had to keep struggling to put food on the table. Whenever they would ask me for something, I had to say no. There was no money. In the kids' eyes, Rudi was coming out the saint. I prayed so much and couldn't understand why this was all happening. I was really trying to be patient and to trust.

He now owed two months in arrears, and I was definitely losing the house. I had to do something desperate to pull things together. I was really confused that I was now responsible for paying the mortgage, and Rudi was responsible to pay me maintenance. Because he didn't pay the maintenance, I couldn't pay the mortgage. Somehow I still felt responsible; yet I wasn't willing to deprive the kids of their food. I really didn't know what was right and what was wrong. I read in the Bible that Rudi was supposed to put me first and definitely not sleep with any other women. He didn't have the beliefs I did though he did believe in God.

We were at hockey one night, and one of the parents and I got talking about the whole mess. They had offered to buy the piano from me for $1,500. I said there was no way I could do that. P.J. was in fourth year piano, and he would be devastated. I said I will talk to Rudi and tell him about the offer, and I knew as bad as it was, he didn't have it in his heart to let that happen to P.J. He had always meant so much to Rudi. They said if I change my mind, the offer holds and I could buy it back anytime for the same price.

I didn't want to phone Rudi. Anytime I did, Helena always seemed to answer the phone and hang up on me. I phoned the shop and left messages, but Rudi wouldn't return my calls.

I actually got fed up enough that I went to the shop between runs one afternoon. All the way there I was praying for God to give me the strength to walk in, to take the fear away. When I got there, I thought it was better that I just do it and not sit and think about it.

I opened the front door and walked in. I heard a vacuum cleaner in the office so I just went in. Helena was standing there wearing an apron and her babushka, and was holding the vacuum cleaner nozzle in her hand. She was vacuuming the top of the filing cabinet. I asked her if Rudi was there. It was apparent she was really surprised to see me. She said, "No." I asked her where he was and she shrugged her shoulders. The place was totally spotless. It smelled like Javex.

I went into the warehouse and looked around. The racecar was in the back all fixed. It was sitting on a brand new hauler and looked really good. Beside the racecar was a candy apple red corvette. Even the warehouse was clean. I turned to leave and Helena was standing behind me. I told her she forgot to clean the tires on the racecar. She looked at the racecar. I just laughed and walked out.

As I was pulling out, a new red half-ton truck blocked the back of me. I got out to see who it was and was surprised to see Rudi standing there. He asked what I wanted. I just started to tell him when Helena came out and started to yell in German. I thought she was yelling at me, but when I turned to see, she was yelling at Rudi. He whispered to me, "You better go now."

I explained "I came to talk to you about something important."

He replied, "No, you better go now." He jumped in the truck and moved it. I just sat and watched while he parked the truck. They were talking so fast in German to each other as they were walking, I couldn't understand. I sat there for a few minutes thinking about what to do and decided I really had to talk to him and there was no other way. I got out of the van and headed for the door again. The office had big windows. I could see them talking. Helena looked really angry. She saw me coming and ran and locked the door before I got there. Rudi was still standing in the office and picked up the phone and motioned to me that he would call me later. Helena didn't see. I just got back in the van and went back to work. I replayed what happened in my head a couple of times and thought what a weird situation.

Rudi did call me at suppertime and asked why I would do a stupid thing like come to the office. He stated I should have known it would cause trouble.

I asked him, "How was I to know the maid was on duty?" I told him if he didn't make the maintenance payments up to date, I would have to sell the piano.

He answered me with, "Oh, so what you are saying is you can't make it without me."

I said, "I am making it without you. I don't have a choice."

He answered, "Then you will have to sell the piano." He then tried to explain, "Just take a look at what is happening here. I bought a house, a new truck, and a Corvette. My racecar is ready to race, and I am moving into a house while I build a new one. It must have been right to leave. You are losing your home, and can't even put food on the table properly."

I said, "Can you honestly tell me it doesn't matter that this piano is sold and P.J. can't keep up with the lessons?"

He started to laugh and said "I sure wouldn't do it to him, if it happens, it is you doing it."

I just hung up the phone. I was confused. He didn't make any of the payments. I have to survive somehow, and now it was my fault. He left me and cheated on me. How can I be guilty of trying to survive? I knew P.J. would blame me. For some reason Rudi managed to pull the wool over the kids' eyes. I was the rotten parent and poor Rudi. Now he sold the van, bought a truck and Corvette, the racecar was ready to race–a new hauler? He said the business was sinking. I couldn't figure it out. I called Elaine and talked to her. She was not pleased with what Rudi was doing, and she and I (I thought) were still very good friends. We still got together for lunch between runs once or twice a week, and we saw each other at church. I told her what had happened and she said it was really sad. She said from what she has heard from the family, Helena's parents are so glad she has Rudi and will pay whatever they have to in order to make sure she keeps him. I said surprised, "It sounds like Rudi is being bought."

I knew I had no choice. What good was the piano to P.J. if we couldn't live in the area close to the teacher and if we didn't have a house to put it in? What was worse was after fighting the school board for so long to have J.J. integrated into a normal setting Junior High, I would have to leave the area. I couldn't let that happen. I picked up the phone and made arrangements to sell the piano to the couple who made the offer. They reminded me that I could have it back any time even if it only took a week. They said to pick up the cheque right away, and they would figure out a way to get it moved.

When P.J. got home, I sat him down and told him. He was really upset and so was I. He cried that wasn't fair. If Rudi was still here, he wouldn't have to lose his piano. He was right, but Rudi wasn't there because Rudi chose not to be there. I told P.J. Rudi was gone because he slept with another woman and believed it couldn't be straightened out. P.J. asked me if it could be. I told him to pray and believe, and it could if it were God's will.

He was surprised and said, "You would take him back?"

I thought about it, and marriages aren't supposed to end. Yes, it would take some time to fix it, but I did believe I would take him back. P.J. was very smart and I knew it was time to be as honest as I could with him. I told him that Rudi made the mistake of sleeping with Helena while we were in Calgary and that Helena wanted it that way. Rudi felt it was like she set a trap for him. I tried to explain that Rudi's priorities and what was important to him had changed since we were first together but P.J. then concluded that none of this was Rudi's fault. I explained Rudi was a big boy and chose to fall for it. Yes he regretted it afterwards but thought it was too late. I was totally honest with P.J. telling him yes I was hurt, angry, felt very devastated and more, but Rudi didn't tell me right away. Instead of telling me and going somewhere else for a while, he got desperate and moved in with her. That was just more fuel added to the fire.

P.J. then said, "God says you should love everyone."

I agreed and said if I really thought about it hard, I could say I love Helena, but I really didn't like her. God did not want Helena and Rudi to sleep together, and when someone knows they are doing wrong (like Rudi said Helena did–manipulating him into bed when he was drunk), then that relationship wouldn't be blessed. There could not be God's peace in it. There may be happiness eventually, but that doesn't hold. There will not be the joy on the inside, which was very obvious whenever I saw Rudi. My vows said till death do us part.

He said, "Then you should try to get him back."

I answered, "I waited and he went with Helena."

P.J. then made another excuse, "Rudi didn't know you would take him back."

Like I thought, he didn't understand and blamed me. I was thinking, after P.J. and I finished talking, of how much I had prayed for the words to explain this all to him and how that prayer was just answered. I could never have told P.J. all those things on my own. God definitely had given me the words. I really wished that I could live the Christian life, so I would go through my days remembering God was always there to help me do it all. But too many times I would forget.

I promised P.J. I would do whatever I could to put the marriage back together. I could see it happening to a point. But then Rudi would do something that I would let hurt me again, and I would get angry. Rudi seemed to be waiting for that anger, so he could be justified for all he had done.

I promised, "We can buy the piano back anytime. I called the piano teacher and told her. She said, 'That was really a sad situation, P.J. was really good.'"

That weekend the piano was moved while Rudi had the kids. It took six guys to get it out of the house and put it on the truck. When P.J. came home, he saw it was gone as he walked in the door and started to cry.

He said, "Dad said that was really cruel for you to sell my piano."

I was really frustrated, and it was a good thing Rudi was gone already because I probably would have reacted in a way I would have regretted.

I used the money to catch up all the house bills, and I paid the mortgage up to date, minus what Rudi owed me. He was responsible for that money, and if he didn't want to lose the house, then he would have to catch up the maintenance payment. I knew it would just happen again if I didn't do something. I couldn't change jobs because I would have to pay for someone to watch the kids all day during the summer holidays and Spring and Christmas breaks. I made the decision to pay my portion of what had to be paid and to leave the amount Rudi owed as debt. I couldn't struggle anymore; it was not fair to the kids or me. Even if Rudi did pay the maintenance, it wasn't enough to pay for P.J.'s hockey and Tammy's ringette. It was pretty expensive. It was bad enough that P.J.'s piano was gone. He would be totally distraught if I couldn't afford for him to play hockey.

My neighbours across the back lane and I had gotten to be pretty good friends. Gail and Bill had one son, Keith, and he was close to Tammy's age. He and Tammy chummed together quite a bit. Bill was a mechanic and Gail was a secretary with Bombardier. Gail had suggested I put the word out for some kind of extra work I could do at home or between my runs. Sewing would make sense, but I didn't have a sewing machine anymore.

I was at aerobics one morning between runs and got an idea. I asked the instructor what I had to do to become an aerobics teacher. I thought if I was going to do aerobics anyway, why not be paid for it. She said she was making $15 for a one-hour class. I usually managed to go about five times a week. That would be an extra $300 a month, and it wouldn't affect the kids. The instructor told me there was a course I would have to take at the Y downtown. She said it was pretty intense. I could do it; I knew I could. I was excited. I went to the Y the next day between runs and got all the information. I had to pay for the classes, but it would pay off the first month I would start to teach. The course was a couple of months. I could start in two weeks.

Rudi and I had to go to court again. It was to determine the terms of the legal agreement. This time when I pulled up in front of the courts, Rudi was getting out of the Corvette. I had to laugh because there was still snow on the ground, and no one drives a Corvette with snow on the ground–unless they are trying to show off or make a point. I looked at the car but couldn't determine what year it was. It was an older one but was nicely fixed up.

I met my lawyer in the courtroom, and she asked if I received any money from Rudi yet.

I replied, "No, he owes me $900."

That would serve us well right now. My lawyer told the judge there was a problem with the maintenance payments. He asked what the problem was.

She explained, "There weren't any payments made."

He seemed surprised, "None?"

She repeated, "None."

The judge then asked Rudi what was the problem. Rudi stood up and started to explain to the judge that the racecar still wasn't fixed enough to sell and he was now supporting another woman and her two daughters.

I whispered to my lawyer, that wasn't true, the racecar was all done, and he even had a new hauler for it.

Rudi then went on to say that the business was doing really badly. He really wanted to pay, but it was just not possible at this time and was asking the court to give him a break. He promised he would still pay the money but was just asking for time to get back on his feet.

I then whispered to my lawyer that he was driving a Corvette, sold the van and bought a new truck. She got up and told the judge all of this. Rudi denied it. Then the judge granted him six months grace from paying the maintenance payments. I couldn't believe it. I felt like, "What am I doing wrong? Why are the other woman and her kids so important, and we don't count? Rudi shook his lawyer's hand and walked out the door.

Driving home I was so frustrated and upset, I thought how it usually took something like this happening to remind me to look to God. I remembered some of the people from Al-anon that really had it together. How they could let go and trust God in their situations was way beyond me. I have to be honest to say that there were many times I forgot to start the day with God. Margaret's mother once told me that as time goes on, I will learn to trust God more. With every day that goes by, He will guide me, give me peace and joy, and after a while, I won't want to wait for something stupid to happen to acknowledge Him. I won't want to get out of bed in the morning without making sure God's will is going to be done when I get up. I look forward to that day.

Chapter 17

BACK IN THE RACE

"Therefore, since we are surrounded by so great a cloud of
witnesses, let us also lay aside every weight, and sin which
clings so closely, and run with perseverance that race that
is set before us, looking to Jesus the pioneer and
perfecter of our faith." Hebrews 12:1–2
(The Revised Standard Version)

Easter weekend came and the Saturday and Sunday were respite weekend. The racing club asked me to volunteer to stay at the auto show in the Convention Centre for part of the weekend. There were three cars from the track at the show. I told them I could. On Friday night I helped the guys set up and made sure we had everything we needed. I just went home afterward, though the guys were bugging me to go for a drink. I didn't enjoy going into bars.

I got up early the next morning. It was too early to go to the Convention Centre, so I got ready, sat down with a cup of coffee and started to write a letter to God in a journal my parents had given me for Christmas. I told Him how I felt, asked Him to forgive me for different things I had done wrong, and turned my day over to Him, asking for guidance, including not to let any evil in. I thanked Him for the good things that were happening in my life (It was amazing how many good things there were when I put them on one page together), and asked Him to bless the people I was angry at. (Surprisingly, that had gotten to be a fairly long list.)

As I finished getting ready to go, I found myself singing a song from church on Sunday and whenever Rudi popped into my head, I would just shake it off. Not that there wasn't good in Rudi to think about, I really believed that somewhere inside of that man was the person I fell in love with but I wasn't strong enough to see that right then. I sure wasn't bringing the good out in him lately. I didn't think it was just me bringing the bad out in him because anyone I had talked to since he left told me that Rudi just wasn't the same guy anymore. He seemed to have turned into an angry, bitter, very unhappy person I guess taking our belongings one at a time was supposed to fill the void, but material things didn't seem to make him any happier. It seemed to me he would sell it and use the money for whatever. But he still didn't have the peace he was looking for, so would come back looking for more. That went on until there was nothing left to take. I was sure the only satisfaction he had been looking for in all of this was he thought that I couldn't make it without him. I do believe I was learning that with God, I *could* make it. I just had to trust Him even if it looked like things weren't going my way. He had a plan, and if I were patient, I would see it.

I felt so good going to the Convention Centre, like I could walk on air. I had peace and joy. I didn't worry about anything. There was a time in the past I would have had a real problem going to the Convention Centre on such a morning. I would have felt like I wasn't good enough, didn't fit into the group and would be very shy and quiet when I first got there, afraid if I opened my mouth I would say the wrong thing and embarrass myself.

I was the first one to arrive in the Speedway display so I sat down at the table and drank my coffee. A couple of the guys from the track finally showed up. By the looks of them, I was glad I didn't go to the bar with them the night before.

The guys decided to spend the day trying to talk me into racing a car that season. I was taking it as a joke, but after a while I realized they were serious. I always wanted to race, but I didn't want anything to do with the car except race it. The guys were telling me I should race and Matt Desjarlais had a car that could be used as a hobby stock. It was the rolling chassis with a roll cage but needed a body and a motor. I just laughed. I told them not to even think about it, I was having enough trouble trying to pay for my house with Rudi not paying.

How was I going to race a car? I turned the whole situation over to God and said He could handle it, and if it were His will, He could build the car. Of course I prayed this without anyone knowing.

Janet and Henry came to the show and joined in. They thought it would be great for me to race. As guys came through with different companies, they were trying to convince them they should sponsor me. By the time the day ended, I had eight different sponsors: the car, motor, body and a way to get the car to the track. My neighbour, Bill, and Margaret's husband, Brian both said they would be pit crew and get the car ready.

The guys were willing to help, even the ones I would be racing against. They figured I wouldn't be a threat. I was considered a lady. I left the Convention Centre feeling scared, excited, nervous and unsure all at once. I guess that was confusion. I finally agreed to do this as long as there was no expense to me. I couldn't afford to even put gas in the car. I also didn't have time to spend on the car either. It was just going to be a fun thing. I went to pick up the kids and told them about the day. They were thrilled. The kids thought it would give me a connection back with Rudi. I never thought of that.

We all seriously jumped into it. Brian and Bill picked up the first part of the car from Matt. I went between my runs to get more sponsors. I needed the car painted, and parts to get this motor running.

I picked up more sponsors. Some offered cash, and some offered parts or some kind of help to get this off the ground. It was almost too easy walking in and ask these different companies for their help. Being the only girl racing was what sold them. I definitely didn't have the courage to ask, but before I walked in any door, I asked God for the strength, courage and words to knock down the wall of fear that would stop me and carried on. *"I've commanded you to be strong and brave. Don't ever be afraid or discouraged! I am the Lord your God, and I will be there to help you wherever you go."* Joshua 1:9 Sometimes I surprised myself at what I had been saying to these companies and would walk out quite amazed at how easy this had become. With the cash we received from the sponsors, we managed to get what we needed to get through the rules.

I had called my parents and filled them in on what was happening. They were upset hearing how bad it was going with Rudi but were thrilled about the racing and said they would be in some time in the summer to watch.

By the time we went to the May meeting for the club, the car was pretty well ready except for the lettering. I had to find out at the meeting what car number I could have. I actually got number 1, the first girl. We decided that since my last name was still Hardt, pronounced heart, where the rules said we had to put the car number in a circle on the doors, they let me put my car number in a heart instead of a circle. The car was painted all white and the lettering was black and red. The sponsors' names were painted on and even the names of my pit crew: Brian, Bill, Margaret and Gail. Across the side of the car was my main sponsor, Molson Canadian.

They supplied me with a cheque and a case of beer every week for the pit crew after the races. Ram Messenger Courier Company paid for a proper helmet, and I put the company name on the rear quarter panels. They even had Patricia with a heart put on the side of the helmet. The other racecar drivers had given me a proper seat, 5-point harness, and lots of parts. The ease with which this car went together showed me without a doubt; it was God's will–though I found it hard to believe God really wanted me to race. I was given a one-piece fire suit by one of the drivers, but I took it apart and redesigned it to be more of a ladies style jumpsuit. Since I didn't have my sewing machine, Pro-Am Sportswear did all the sewing on it. They were the company I dealt with to have all the jackets made for the racers and pit crews at the track.

At the time I was taking orders from the club and having their jackets made by Pro-Am Sportswear. They were taking the pictures of the cars and embroidering them on the backs of the jackets with cross flags on the front and car numbers on the sleeves. They did a great job. I went to Pro-Am to pick up the jackets the week before the races.

I was helping bundle up the jackets when Gabe, the boss I always dealt with, came out of the office and said "I have something for you." He handed me a jacket with my car number and a picture of my car on the back. My name was on the front with the cross flags.

I laughed when I saw the car. It had Pro-Am Sportswear on the front hood as one of the sponsors. I told him I couldn't just put his company name on the car like that, but it could be on the jacket.

He then brought me out a black leather jacket exactly the same. He asked if he could have his company name on the car now.

I told him I couldn't.

He went back in the office and brought me out a pair of black leather pants to go with the jacket and said they were custom made. He explained one of my pit crew had brought him in a pair of my jeans to copy.

I couldn't believe it. I went into the washroom and tried them on.

He said the "only girl" had to dress the part–all leather.

I felt like a biker but loved it.

Finally, he promised he would make jackets for the whole pit crew and the kids. I told him he would have to make them for my family in Calgary too. He agreed, and I went back and had Pro-Am Sportswear put on the front hood of the car.

By the time the first race day came, my kids and pit crew were all in the jackets. We looked pretty good, but I was a nervous wreck. Janet was the track official that lined up the cars and kept them straight on the track. She ran the show on the front straightaway. She had been psyching me up for the past month, getting me ready for the first night. I didn't eat that day. I was too afraid that if I ate, I would end up throwing up from nerves in the first lap.

We pulled into the pits and found a place to park. I got out of the truck, and we started to unload the car when I found myself face to face with Rudi pulling in with his race car. Obviously he hadn't sold it. He was pulling it with his new truck and worst of all; Helena was sitting next to him in the seat. I was glad I hadn't eaten. For sure I would have been sick. I couldn't believe she was actually at the track and more so, I couldn't believe he brought her. I don't think Rudi believed I was going to race. I know P.J. told him I was having the car built, but I don't think he ever thought it would happen. When P.J. told him, he just laughed.

We went to the drivers meeting, all the drivers and pit crew had to go before the race. The guys were all great. They treated me like a real lady, and I think most of them knew the scoop about Helena and so were doubly nice. Rudi didn't take Helena to the drivers meeting.

When we were walking back to my car after the meeting, Helena was standing next to the truck. She looked better than when I had seen her before. She wasn't wearing a babushka, and her hair had been dyed the colour of mine. She was wearing a pair of slacks and a T-shirt that hung down over the slacks. I thought at least it was much better than the dresses and aprons. She looked better but still had that hard, angry look on her face. I thought to myself; if I were in her shoes, and had to influence a married man into my bed with a bottle of wine, I would be quite angry too, but at myself. I shook that thought off and smiled and said hello to her as I went by, and then prayed for God to bless her. She didn't acknowledge my hello but quickly opened the door of the truck and got in. I had to race, and I didn't need Helena on my mind.

First we had to pack the track and I just stood by and watched. The cars would go around in reverse direction slowly to pack down the clay.

Hot laps started and I had to drive the car for the first time. I climbed in the car and did up my belts, and then put on my helmet. They showed me how to start the car. (They laughed; because being a woman I had to have help with that.) Really it was much different than driving a normal everyday car. Brian told me to just do a leisurely drive around the track to get the feel of the car. I did just that and got really nervous when I found it was very hard to steer the car around the corners. My arms were actually burning from being so tense from steering by the time I pulled in.

I found my worst pressure was being unsure of what I was doing,

221

where I should be, and how to line up to get started in the right position. I had seen it done a hundred times before but never really paid attention to it. There was no reason to. I was terrified that I would do something stupid and get in the way of the guys. I didn't want to become the woman that was such a pain in the butt to the guys, always getting in the way.

Janet had come and asked me how I felt. I asked her if she carried any barf bags. She told me I'd be fine.

I dumped the responsibility on her and said, "You can't let me make a fool out of myself out there, you have to keep me in line." As if she had any control over what I was going to do on the track. Her label was the Track Controller.

The first race came and I just pulled out and took another leisurely drive around the track. I was driving like I was out for a casual drive in the country. It was a little uncomfortable watching all the cars go by me the first time, but when it came to the same cars passing me three or four times, it was highly embarrassing. I came in last. But at least I didn't so anything stupid, and the car was still in one piece. My arms were really sore. I just wanted to build up some confidence. I think I was praying the whole first race. The guys had commented afterwards that it would get easier with time. They told me to go and work out more so my arms were strong enough to steer around the corners. After the race, I went to the back concession with Janet and got ribbed by the announcer, Pat Mooney. Like I said before, Pat was always like a big brother to me, so it didn't bother me.

I didn't let the kids go to the race that night, they were still in school and it would just be too late for them. I told them they could come when school got out in a few weeks.

When I was leaving to go home that night, I knew I wasn't going to get a cheque of any kind for racing. Pete, the owner handed me $100. I was so surprised. He whispered, "Just keep coming back. You are good for business." I definitely knew where that blessing came from.

I found it pretty hard getting up for work the next day. By the time we left the track and towed the car back, it was really late. I was looking forward to the summer break when I could take the kids to the track and it didn't matter what we were doing the next day.

I started the aerobics course. I found it to be pretty tough. I didn't know if it was because I hadn't had to study for a few years or if it was just a tough course. The classes were once a week for three months, and then I had to teach fifteen classes with a licensed instructor in order to become a qualified instructor.

I kept doing my devotions every morning when I got up, but I was finding my letters to God to be getting dry. I was really craving more wisdom and knowledge. I wanted to learn the Bible and find the promises and the truths that I was told about. Margaret led me to a church that was running a *Life in the Spirit Seminar.* It was on Sunday morning. The kids could go to the Sunday School while we were in the Seminar, and we could all go to the service afterward. I was hoping this would satisfy the craving I seemed to be having.

Race day came again pretty quickly. I thought maybe my nerves would be a bit better this time. They were worse. I guess I knew what I was getting into this time.

Rudi passed us on the highway, and this time he didn't have Helena with him. I felt it was a wise move, and that he wasn't comfortable with her there the last week. No one acknowledged her. It was too bad. I felt she just didn't fit in. If I hadn't been there, it might have been different, but I felt she was trying to tread on my territory. I felt she had gotten her claws into Rudi, but that is where it was going to stop. She was not going to take over my life. I would stand my ground on that. I thought about a scripture I had been shown in Ephesians 6. *"So put on all the armor that God gives. Then when that evil day comes, you will be able to defend yourself. And when the battle is over, you will still be standing firm"* Ephesians 6:13. I asked God to give me the armour to defend me against such things as someone trying to tread on my territory. I sure hoped that I could live my Christian walk enough to be able to know some of the scriptures by heart, so I could pull them up as I needed them.

As soon as we got the car unloaded, Rudi showed up and checked out the motor. This was my chance to keep my promise to P.J. I stood beside him and asked what he thought?

He had a smile on his face when he said, "Well, there is nothing wrong with the car." Then he gave my arm a little squeeze and said, "I will bring you something that will help next week."

I told him I found it really hard to steer compared to when I raced his car in the powder puff.

He started to laugh and said he had a Late Model.

I said to Brian, "Okay then, let's just build a Late Model."

Rudi laughed even harder and told Brian to watch out that I probably would do that for next year. He asked if it had power steering, and Brian told him yes.

That night ended up worse. During the heat race, my arms were so tired, I thought I was just going to let go of the steering wheel at one point and give up, then I looked out my side window at the pits when I was going into number 1 turn and saw Rudi standing there motioning for me to go faster. I prayed so hard and I think I actually started to cry at one point. Can you imagine if the guys knew that? At intermission, one of the Late Model Drivers had asked Janet if he could take my car for a spin around the track just to check out the steering. She said sure. It was great to see what the car could actually do. He did a couple of rounds and had the car humming until the third lap–too much power in the driver and not in the car. He was going into the Number 1 turn when all of a sudden the axle broke. The rear tire and axle went flying through the air. It was in a way a disappointment, but at the same time a relief that I was finished for the rest of the night. When he brought the car back, he said it was no surprise I couldn't steer. It was so stiff, he could barely steer. That's when I realized it hadn't just been my imagination over the last two weeks.

Some of the drivers came over to the car and offered some parts to help fix it for the following week. Rudi came and offered to get an axle. I couldn't believe it. He was actually offering to help keep me racing. Ron, the Late Model Driver that was driving when it broke, told my pit crew to take it back to his place, and they could get the axle done there. He felt badly that this happened while he was driving.

With everyone helping, the following weekend I took the kids over to Ron's, where they were fixing the car. We spent the whole day with Ron and Shirley. It was great! They had no kids themselves but were naturals with the way they treated mine. They had a dog named Benji, and that was their kid. By Saturday night the car was all fixed and ready for Tuesday.

Sunday morning I started the Life in *The Spirit Seminar* with Margaret. It was really eye opening for me. It was just what I was looking for. I learned how to pray for wisdom and knowledge in the Bible and about some of the scriptures that told me what I was looking for. I realized how God's spirit would lead me and how to listen for answers. Faith was everything. We went to the service afterward. I found it to be a little steep, but the outcome was that I felt so much peace.

Tuesday night was definitely better. I could control the car and got a little braver. When I pulled in, Rudi came over right away and handed me a brick. He said to put it on my gas pedal, it will help. At the drivers meeting he came over and told me he thought it was pretty neat that I was racing. I was really surprised at how relaxed he was talking to me. I was still angry about him not paying me, but that wasn't what was important now. He looked much better. He had his haircut and was clean-shaven. Was this for me?

The six months grace was up, and I hadn't been able to pay the mortgage for the past three months. Everything else had been paid. Rudi would pay me the money he owed. There was a lot of equity in the house, and I knew he didn't want me to lose it.

But I shouldn't have gotten my hopes up. We had to go back into court. Rudi told the judge I refused to sell the house and there was a lot of equity in it. He asked the judge to force sale on the house. He agreed and gave Rudi a paper giving him permission to sell the house without my signature. It was so strange. It was like dealing with two different people. At the track Rudi was great, but when he picked up the kids or was in court, the word "Jerk" comes to mind.

It didn't take long. The next day Rudi had the "For Sale" sign in front of the house. That Saturday was an open house and I was to be gone out of the house for the day. The kids were at respite. I couldn't let this happen and I had to try to open Rudi's eyes. I cleaned the house, baked a pan of brownies, made coffee and set it out with my good dishes. Then I got ready for aerobics. I put on my one-piece aerobics suit with the leg warmers and headband. I felt pretty good in that outfit. The house looked very different than what Rudi remembered. I was given a sectional for the rec room and a new set of tables. I had changed the bedroom colour. The bathroom was done more modern with more feminine accents. I had burned candles before and the house smelled like cranberries. I prayed for peace beyond all understanding, and God gave it to me.

When Rudi walked in the door with the agent, his eyes were evidently opened. He was looking at me all the time I was getting ready. I was no raving beauty but sure felt good that I could get his attention. I kind of knew already that when this happened I should duck because he would come back swinging for a response again. I told the agent and Rudi to help themselves to coffee and cake. The agent thanked me and Rudi just stood speechless. I am sure he was expecting me to be crying and hysterical and for me to purposely mess up the house to block the sale. Little did he know at that point, I had a better plan.

I smiled and said, "I have a class to get to, so have a nice day."

I heard the agent say to Rudi as I was leaving, "You left her?"

The open house was planned from one to four, and I was to stay out of the house. My aerobics class was from noon to one. I could get back before any damage could be done and the house be sold. As I drove down the street to aerobics, I pulled every sign out of the ground that gave directions to the open house. The judge could give Rudi the right to sell the house without my name, but I really didn't think I could get in trouble for taking the signs out. I was going to do everything I could to prevent our house from selling. It just wasn't right!

I did the aerobics class, then changed. I knew the Open House was advertised in the paper so my pulling out the signs wasn't enough. When I got to the house, there was a strange car parked in front. I panicked. I knew it was someone looking at the house. I sat in the car and started to cry. I thought I could get back fast enough to stop people from going in by telling them my story. Then the door opened and a couple walked out. I waited till they were off the property, and then approached them in tears telling them what was happening and to please don't put an offer in on the house. It worked. They not only listened, but surprised me when they said they were so sorry for all the trouble and would be praying for me. God did have this under control.

Rudi came out of the house yelling at me. He said he would call the police.

I told him to go ahead. What could they do to me? There was a court order saying he could sell the house without my signature, but there was no court order saying I couldn't try to stop it.

The agent came out and said they may as well leave; there was no sense in trying to sell the house if I was going to do this.

I told them the house was theirs for the afternoon to try to sell. If they gave up and left, that was their choice.

They left. I knew it was only a matter of time before the next blow, but at least I managed to buy a little more time. I would try to keep paying for it. There was a chance I would lose the house, but I wouldn't lose it without a good fight.

The court was telling Rudi he could have half of the profits of the sale of the house and that was why he was pushing. He wanted the money. I really felt this wasn't fair. He already had all the money from selling everything else. I couldn't understand why the kids and my share of the marriage weren't considered in the court. I felt that there was a conspiracy going on, but on the other hand, maybe I was just a little paranoid. I had to believe that God had control over the situation. Even though it didn't look like it was going right,

God had a plan and I just had to learn to be more patient. I learned that He *did* know the desires of my heart. His plan wasn't necessarily the same as mine. He knew so much more what was best for me.

I didn't hear anything more about the sale of the house before the race on Tuesday. I helped Janet at the back gate while I waited for the racing to start. I got a kick out of talking to the drivers. Especially the ones I was racing against.

When Rudi pulled up, he was alone. It was so hot outside, and when he opened his window, the air-conditioning came flooding out. It felt so good. He told me to jump in, and he would give me a ride into the pits. I did just that, and he put a cassette tape in the machine and smiled as the music started. It was ABBA. We always listened to ABBA. It felt so right. He dropped me off at the car and I thanked him. He got out and asked how the car was doing. I told him the car was fine but the problem was in the driver. He told me to come for a walk with him and left his truck and hauler sitting where it was. We walked over to the number 1 turn, and he told me what I was doing wrong going into the turns. He made some suggestions on what to try to cure my problem. As we walked back to the car, I told him I was sorry I had to do what I did on the weekend, but I didn't want to lose the house. He said he didn't expect any less from me and smiled. I was so confused but knew I had to pick up on the good times and let the bad go. He was still my husband, and the fact that he was living with Helena was really his problem and not mine. From what I saw, he was really very miserable with her and was quite normal to me whenever he had the chance.

In the first race, I tried what Rudi said to do going into the turns, and it worked. I actually passed a couple of the cars. I could see Rudi on the side smiling and his head shaking, saying go, go. The guys didn't like it though. They started to get rough. If I passed them, they would hit me. They even admitted that when they saw that heart with the number 1 on it passing them, something happened to their egos, and they had to try to stop me. I got knocked around and hit so many times over the next few weeks, and the guys didn't treat me like a lady anymore. Oh sure, they were still very nice to me, but I was now considered one of the guys. Pete kept paying me every week to keep me coming back, but the damage to the car was getting worse every week. Pat Mooney kept telling the crowd that my problem was the Ram Messenger Logo written on the side of the car. The guys just had to hit me when they saw the word Ram.

My family was coming in for a visit. I knew I would have to tell them the truth about the house when they came in. I was really excited that they were going to see me racing. When they came, I gave jackets with the car embroidered on the back to everyone.

The kids had just finished school and were on summer break, so they could start to come to the track. Both their mother and father were racing. I had to get someone to take them all the time to sit with them in the stands. I never let them in the pits during the race since I didn't think it was safe. I couldn't watch them well enough while I was racing. After the race, they always ran to see Rudi. He would let them sit in the racecar while he loaded it up. That was safe enough.

Helena and the girls never did come back to the track. That told me that they didn't have the right to take that part of Rudi's life. They didn't have the marriage and the racing and the kids. From her, Rudi had the financial support, the meals cooked, the clothes cleaned and the house cleaned. He told me that he would love me forever. He said the only way he would ever consider marrying her was if we got a divorce and I got married again. Then he said he knew there would be no hope to ever save our marriage, so he may as well marry her. He did say she was bugging him to get a divorce though. Even if he was really mad at me during the week because of court or something that happened, he always came over to the car before and after the race to see how I was doing. He was always his old self then.

He had put on so much weight that he had to buy a new racing suit. According to him, the other one wouldn't zip up any more. I asked him why he was gaining so much weight, and he said because Helena made two suppers a day, one at lunchtime and one at supper. I couldn't help the sarcasm when I asked if she force-fed him too. He would just snicker and walk away. Both of us really tried to avoid having her in the conversation when we were at the track. I found that if I pretended that she didn't exist, we got along a lot better. Rudi tried to make like she didn't exist when he was around me.

It was so much fun when my family came to visit. They could hardly wait to see me race the car. I gave them all their jackets to wear to the track even though it was a bit too warm when we went. I gave them all calendars too. Bill's dad owned United Pharmacy in Saskatchewan and had calendars made with me in front of the racecar in my fire suit. He sent a whole boxful as a gift. I gave them to the family and to the sponsors. My mom and Janet got together with the kids and made a huge banner that ran about twenty feet long. On the front, they drew a big red heart. Then after the heart, it said, "GO MOMMY GO," followed by another red heart. They kept it a secret. I wasn't to know about it. When we went to the speedway, I knew something was up. No one would tell me. They would just laugh. I climbed into the car and was ready to do the heat race. I got into line with the rest of the cars, and we started to pace waiting for the green flag to be pulled. I was still quite nervous. I don't know if that ever changes for the drivers. The green flag was pulled and we were racing. I always figured coming down the front straight away with the crowd yelling, the sound of the car and the helmet muffling it, left me with the sound of pigeons gurgling. This time it was louder. I turned as I stepped on the gas, to see if I could see into the pits. The kids and my family were front and center. I almost drove off the track when I looked. Here was this huge banner that said, "GO MOMMY GO." I didn't have to wonder who it was for. I was the only mommy on the race track. I could see Janet laughing and giving the kids the thumbs up sign from where she was at the finish line in the pits. I just kept going. I didn't do anything too exciting in that heat race. I did manage to stay in one piece though. That was always exciting to my pit crew.

The feature race was a little bit of a different story. I really wanted to do something exciting that the family could take home with them. I got a little braver and started to pass a couple of the cars. Apparently, I was told afterwards that Pat was telling the crowd that someone lit a match under my butt. I was going along fine and passing the other cars. Then I noticed the little oil pressure gauge that I was always supposed to keep my eyes on. It was dropping to zero! As I came out of turn 2, I noticed my mechanic standing on top of the mound with a smile on his face telling me to keep going. I put my hand out the window between the screen and showed him the zero sign with my thumb and forefinger then pointed my thumb down to show him the oil pressure was dropping.

He didn't understand and showed me the zero sign back as if to say, "Perfect, excellent, now keep going."

The power didn't seem to be dropping. I was still passing cars, but the gauge was really dropping. I knew something was wrong and didn't want to blow my engine. I came back around, and coming off number 4 turn, something really changed. I couldn't keep my foot on the gas pedal. It kept slipping off. I pulled over to Janet, which I knew was a real no-no, but being the only woman on the track, I usually could get away with some things that the guys couldn't.

One of the Late Model drivers came running over and asked me what the problem was. I knew they had to pull the yellow flag because I pulled over like that. I could almost hear Pat up in the tower saying something like, "That has to be a woman," to the crowd. I showed the driver the gauge and told him 1was sliding. I lifted my helmet to find out what he was saying and he told me I would have to get out and have the car towed in.

It was nothing major but the line to the gauge broke and pumped oil all over the inside of the car. I was covered in oil and couldn't get up. It was like something out of a comedy! They tried to get me out, but I was too slippery. Finally they towed the car back to the pits with me inside. They got me out when we were in the pits.

I laughed all the way home; it was so funny. I sure didn't like the feeling of the oil squishing between my toes though. I had ruined my fire suit and my shoes and socks. Pete still paid me, and my family still really enjoyed themselves.

I told my parents that I was losing the house and was planning to go to the Winnipeg Free Press to tell the story of how unfair I felt the courts were to not force Rudi to make his maintenance payments. The Maintenance Enforcement Officer told me it was really tough trying to force Rudi to pay. They couldn't garnish his bank account because he kept it empty. Since he owned his own business, they couldn't garnish his paycheque. I was in the Maintenance Enforcement office so many times, and they understood, but they just couldn't seen to do much for me

It seemed like Rudi was trying to play a game with me to prove to me I couldn't make it without him. I could see it happening to a point. He was trying to get to me, but I couldn't understand why he was doing it to the kids. Why take their house away? What did they ever do to Rudi to deserve losing their house? Even if he did say the boys weren't his. What did his daughter ever do to deserve this kind of treatment from her own father? Helena's daughters weren't his. To have just one child in life, I would think he would want to give her all he could. How could I be so wrong?

The bottom line was I knew the Maintenance Enforcement office was doing the best it could. It wasn't their fault that Rudi was getting break after break in court. For whatever reasons the judge came to the conclusion that Rudi was hard done by and deserved all the breaks was beyond me.

I had tossed it around so many times, really unsure whether I should try to make the mortgage payments myself. I couldn't bring myself to do it. I had helped Rudi build the paint business, and he walked away with the whole thing clear and clean–all the equipment and contracts. I helped build the race business, and he walked away with all of it, the car, equipment, van, hauler, and tools, clear and clean. The convertible and boat were gifts to me. He took those, sold them, and never had to give me a penny. We had to sell the piano to pay for his responsibilities. Sure I was left with the house, but only half of the house. I was expected to pay for the house, yet whenever it sold, half of the equity in the house was Rudi's. The fact that he had to pay $225 maintenance was just a joke. We couldn't enforce it. I had a really tough time seeing how justice was done in this.

Wasn't it ironic that I had made the decision to not take care of Rudi's responsibility, even if it meant losing the house, and the very next day J.J.'s claim finally settled in the court? An annuity was purchased, so he would be secure for a lifetime. Until he was eighteen, I was to receive $250 a month to help with special shoes, special camps and anything else he needed to be as close to normal as he could be. It was a temptation to use the money to catch up on the house. But there was no way I would ever even consider it. I knew the kids would be very upset when they found out we had to move, and I didn't even know where. I was hoping with a good fight and by getting it in the newspapers, the situation might change, and we could move back in the house.

I had made arrangements for J.J. and Tammy to go to Lakeside Camp. It was owned and run by SMD. I knew they would be cared for there. My mom and dad had suggested P.J. go back to Calgary and stay with them. Of course he was thrilled to do that. I didn't want any of them to be dealing with the media or the courts, or for that matter, sleeping in a tent. I knew the day was getting closer. It was inevitable. I was going to lose the house. I fought the best I could with the courts to get it sorted out before it was too late, but for whatever reason, it wasn't meant to be. The bank manager called me several times. They really wanted to help, but were up against the big guns and couldn't do anything about it. I let them know that I appreciated all they had done to help me sort this out and for going over the line of time on repossessing the house. They were so understanding and compassionate. The manager actually came to the house and warned me on the Thursday that the house would be sealed off on the following Tuesday so I could have the weekend to get everything out.

On the Friday, my family left with P.J. all packed up for the summer. I was sure going to miss him! He was part of my strength. He was so excited; I tried not to cry until after they left. I also knew that he would love staying with Gramma and Grampa. I was told they would keep him as long as was needed, even if it ran into the school term. I said I would phone. I knew they couldn't get in touch with me once I moved out of the house, but they had phone numbers given to them from all the neighbours to call and they would give me the message. Before they drove away, my dad gave one last ditch effort to give me money to save the house. I told him, it would work for now, but it would just keep on keeping on unless the problem was fixed for good. He understood and said the offer holds indefinitely and as usual they would stand by me, whatever my decision.

After they left, I loaded the other two in the car with all their equipment for camp. It was really tough. I drove them down to SMD to meet the camp buses. They were really excited as they left, but I knew I had my work cut out for me.

Chapter 18

CLOSING OLD DOORS AND OPENING NEW ONES

"And God is able to provide you with every blessing in abundance, so that you will always have enough of every-thing and may provide in abundance for every good work." II Corinthians 9:8 (Revised Standard Version)

The neighbours had each made a plan to take a portion of my furniture or boxes. We had to have everything out before they sealed off the house, or I would lose it. Boxes went in people's garages and basements, and furniture was added to their own furniture. I was so surprised at how fast it went! There were so many people to help me! People came from the speedway, neighbours and friends. There were people helping that I never even knew.

By Saturday noon, the house was empty. Some of the neighbours had come with a lunch for all the people who helped. I really felt like I was blessed and knew by the way it went that I was doing the right thing. It seemed really weird when one of the guys from work lent me his small camping tent–one of those lightweight ones. He put it up right in front of the house.

Everything moved so fast, I really didn't have time to think too much about what I was getting into. The weekend was pretty quiet. Gail and Bill offered to let me sleep at their place for the weekend until the house was sealed off. I accepted their offer. I could have stayed in my own house, but it was empty. I just couldn't bring myself to do that.

Over the weekend we got the oil line fixed in the racecar. I felt strange losing my house with a racecar parked in the back garage. Still it never cost me anything to race. The day that it did would be the day I would quit. I occupied myself with aerobics and studied the rest of the weekend in the tent. It was raining and was really quiet there, so it was a great way to study. I saw Rudi drive by a couple of times. I think he knew what was coming. He could see the house was already empty, and I am sure that he was trying to figure out what the tent was doing there as well as where the kids were. I never told him they were leaving. I didn't care what the court thought. They made the decision to take part of my life away from me and give it to Rudi and Helena and the girls, so I felt I had to do whatever I could do to survive the court's decision.

I had to write my aerobics exam the following week. I thought what a lousy time to have to do it when I have so much on my mind.

I noticed there was construction going on across the street from the mall, which was only five minutes from the house. So, I asked the manager of the grocery store what was being built. He said he really wasn't sure, but he heard it was an apartment block of some kind. I was surprised because when our house was being built, there were no plans for any apartment block to be going up in the area.

It was raining on Tuesday, so the race was cancelled. People from the bank came to the house to seal it off around noon. It all felt so strange. My kids were farmed out, my furniture was farmed out, and I was living in a tent. I felt like someone shook my life into a hundred pieces, and I had to put it all back together again. I called the newspapers and TV stations to tell them what was happening. Gail helped me write a letter telling the story to the editor of the Winnipeg Free Press. Now I just had to wait. It rained for the next three days, and the tent was wet beyond repair. I couldn't stay in it anymore. Another friend offered a big tent. It was much cozier to sleep in.

Finally the Free Press came to interview me and put the story with a huge picture on the front page of the paper. The three local TV channels also ran the story. I guess Rudi didn't like the publicity because as expected, I was served with papers at the tent to appear in court again. I thought, "This is it! Rudi will now have to make all the back payments of the maintenance, and I can move back into my house." To my surprise, the whole thing backfired in my face. We got into court and the same judge seemed not too pleased with the whole situation. I was told I had to have a dwelling to live in by the time the kids came back from camp or Rudi would be able to take Tammy. I don't recall anything being said about the maintenance. Driving home, I ran through the whole scenario in my head. I wasn't paid the maintenance that Rudi was ordered to pay. Because he didn't pay me, I couldn't pay the mortgage. Because I couldn't pay the mortgage, I lost the house and moved into a tent. Because I did that, it seemed like I was looked at by the court as a terrible person and could lose my daughter to the man who didn't pay me the money to look after the kids properly. It seemed like I was obviously in a no win situation with the court!

Word got out pretty fast about the state I was in. I had a message the next day from Janet. She called Gail and told her I was supposed to call Matt Desjarlias. I did call and he said he had bought a house in Transcona and it was empty. He offered for us to move in and stay as long as we needed to so they wouldn't take Tammy. He was going to move into the house, but said he could stay where he was for now. It was more important that I not lose Tammy to Rudi. I asked him how much he wanted, and he said nothing. I only had to pay for the utilities. I couldn't believe it! I knew Matt was a very kind hearted person, but this was way beyond the call of duty. I accepted the offer and made a plan to move in on September 1st. I went to see the house to see how much furniture I would need to get through at least a couple of months till I figured out what I would do. Janet had suggested I think about garnishing Rudi's paycheque at the Speedway. I had never thought of that before. I don't know why it never crossed my mind.

The kids came back from camp and were sent out on the next bus for another two-week session. The camp director had organized that. They would get back in just enough time to move into the house. I arranged with the school that the kids could still attend even though we were temporarily living out of the area. It normally would be over $1,000 for each of them to do that, but they made a special request on the condition that we were planning to move back into the area. I thought about the apartment going up across from the grocery store.

I checked to find out when they would finish building it, how big the apartments were, and how much it would cost. I really wanted a three bed room on the main floor for J.J.'s sake, and that is unusual in apartments. With it being brand new and considering there was only what looked to be twenty-four suites in total, the chances weren't very good that I would find all I wanted.

I was amazed when I went to find out the details. These were actually low-rental apartments, and the families had to qualify to get in. They had three bedroom apartments on the main floor. I was told I had to go to apply downtown at Central Mortgage and Housing, which I did right away.

I was sent to the office of a very kind English fellow who had been following our story in the paper and on the news. He told me that I definitely qualified for a suite, but there was quite a waiting period for that apartment because it was brand new and everyone wanted to move in. He then told me I would be moved to the top of the list because I had a son with disabilities. I asked him what it would cost, and he said he would calculate it according to my income, and I should come back the next day to see if I could have a suite. None of the suites were assigned yet.

I called everyone I knew that night that had any belief and asked them to pray. It would be so perfect! I thought about the scripture *"I promise that when any two of you on earth agree about something you are praying for, my Father in heaven will do it for you."* Matthew 18:19.

I went in the next day, and as I'd hoped, he informed me the three bedroom suite in the back by the parking lot was mine and would be ready for me and the kids to move in on November 1st. He said the parking space right behind my suite was mine. It was like it was too good to be true! He handed me the key and said you can probably get in a little earlier. Just talk to the workmen as they are working on it and they would let me know the exact date. If it was ready earlier, I could move in, but my rent wouldn't actually start until November 1st. There was a laundry room on the second floor. The suite came with a fridge and stove so I would have to sell mine, as we wouldn't need it.

He showed me the layout of the suite. The back entrance of the parking lot came off the balcony. Since we were on the main floor, it could be used as our door. The other door ran off the hallway and there was a security beeper for people to get in. When you came in the back door, you were in a very large living room leading into a dining room. You turn left into a galley kitchen then carried on to another large room that was a den, then down a hall to the bathroom and three bedrooms. The master bedroom was so large; there was another door on the other side of it to go back through to the living room. Everything would be brand new! There was a very large storage room with big sliding doors that could be used as another bedroom or a sewing room. I still didn't have a sewing machine so I planned to place my deep freeze in there for the time being.

Now the royal question, "How much was this going to cost me?" He smiled and said he couldn't take J.J's money into consideration because it was tax-free money. They didn't take my wages into consideration either because I was on UIC for the summer, so they wouldn't take that amount. The kids' pension cheques came under their names, so those wouldn't be considered. So he said with everything included (I hadn't started to teach aerobics yet) for the first 6 months, they would charge me $135 a month.

"Is that for all of us for the whole month?" I asked.

He just laughed and answered, "Yes."

I couldn't believe it! It didn't really matter if Rudi paid anymore! We could still live and eat properly and have Christmas and live in the area, and the kids could stay in their own school. I was so excited! I hadn't told any of the kids we lost the house yet, but now at least when I told them, I could give them good news.

I left there and went to the Maintenance Enforcement office and suggested to them we garnish Rudi's paycheque at the Speedway. She said she would draw up the garnish order and give it to me instead of sending it to Pete the owner of the track. That way if Rudi didn't have a good night of racing, I could just hang on to it and use it the next week. I must have thanked God one hundred and fifty times that day! I knew it was His fingers bringing about good in the whole mess.

I went in to write my aerobics exam. I wasn't sure if I made it or not and had over a week to wait for the results. I just put it in God's hands and put it out of my mind. There was so much more to think about, and there was nothing I could do about it any more.

I called Janet and told her I had the garnish order. Normally Janet wrote the cheques for Pete after the race, and he would sign them and hand them to the guys.

I told Matt what I was doing when I went to pick up the key for the house and that I would only need the house until November 1st. He said however long I needed was fine.

I went to the track on Tuesday and raced. Rudi didn't come over to see me. He looked very angry and bitter. I was really hoping no one told him I had the garnish order. He owed me a lot of money, but in one good night of racing, he could make quite a bit. I found out who was working the back gate knew what was going to happen. She hung on to the previous week's cheque, telling Rudi they couldn't find it in the pile. He said it was alright, he would check with Pete after the races. That cheque was for $800, but he owed me a lot more than that. I don't remember ever cheering him on so much as I did that night! He was leading! Everyone seemed to leave him alone up front and fought for second place. He won! I was thrilled! I wasn't concerned about my own racing and it helped because for the first time, I came in third and earned a legitimate paycheque on my own.

When the races were over, I let my pit crew load up the car and all the tools, and I went to the front concessions right away with my garnish order. The plan was that when Rudi got to the front window for his turn, Janet would write the cheque including the previous weeks' winnings. The old cheque would be torn up. She would give it to Pete to sign. I would take it from there giving Pete the garnish order.

It went perfectly. I stood inside the concession with Pat Mooney and Janet's dad, Jim and just ignored what was going on. It didn't take very long before it was Rudi's turn. He seemed to get pushed up to the front. I heard him say he needed his cheque from the week before too.

Janet asked him if it was alright if she just added it in with this one.

He said, "Sure," smiling and saying, "Money is money." I looked at him and caught what I thought was a really smug Ha-Ha look from him.

I just thought to myself, he who laughs first, gets the last laugh.

Janet finished writing the cheque and handed it over to Pete, but not taking her hand off of it, she turned and looked at me.

My heart was beating fifty miles an hour, but I walked up and as soon as Pete finished signing it, I reached out and took it without even giving him the garnish order. Rudi came across the concession to get me but the other guys held him back. I didn't even look at the cheque; I just stuck it in my fire suit pocket. I threw the garnish order at him and said he could have that instead.

He read it and said he didn't owe me that much money.

I replied, "Well for once you are paid in advance."

He was furious but I really didn't care.

I was escorted back to my car. My pit crew got in the truck they used to haul my racecar and suggested they take the cheque with them, so I wouldn't have any trouble with Rudi. I still had my copy of the garnish order, so I wasn't too worried. If he tried anything, I wouldn't hesitate to phone the police, but I gave the cheque to Brian anyway. I told him to hang on to it till the next day. I was still sleeping in the tent, so I didn't want to chance sleeping with the cheque. I still didn't know how much it was for. Bill had come over to the tent after I got settled in and suggested I come in the house and sleep. I didn't have to make my point anymore; Rudi's maintenance was paid more than full.

I wasn't sure of what to do the next day except to pick up the cheque and take it to the bank. I asked God if He wanted me to catch up the mortgage with it. I got a really loud answer to my prayer when I got to the bank. The manager informed me the house was auctioned off a half an hour before I had walked in. That was good enough for me. I could move into a place I could afford on November 1st where I could make it without Rudi. I almost fell over when I looked at the cheque. It was for just under $2,000. No wonder Rudi was angry. I just didn't care anymore.

J.J. and Tammy came home from camp. I had made arrangements to meet my parents in Moose Jaw at the trailer park to get P.J. We were going for the long weekend in September and celebrating my parents' anniversary and Tammy's birthday while we were there. Tammy, J.J. and I traveled out in the work van that I had picked up for my job, starting work after the long weekend. P.J. was so tanned and blonde, and he had such a great time with my parents in Calgary. It was hard for him to leave because he had made a best friend while he was there. My parents tried to convince me to come for Christmas with the kids. I said I would try, but I hated to drive out there in the winter. My dad suggested I look into going VIA Rail. I said I would check into it.

We moved into the house in Transcona. We only had the bare necessities with us. Everything else was gathered up from other peoples' houses and stored in Gail and Bill's basement getting ready to move into the apartment when it was ready. I was back to work and drove the kids every day to Gail's house before work, so they could catch the school bus from there. They would go back there after school so I could pick them up

I kept tabs on the apartment all week to make sure we could move in on the first of November. I didn't need the fridge and stove so I told Matt I would leave mine for him. Bill, Gail and Rod from work offered to help me move. (Rod and I started seeing more of each other and did a lot of cross-country skiing together.) Gail would be at her house giving Bill and Rick the furniture and boxes, and I would be at the apartment receiving. I decided to just make my bedroom the storage area for all the boxes and unpack them as I had time. I was surprised at how smooth everything ran. All was moved and somewhat settled by midnight. My own apartment.

Over the past few years, I had gotten to know Sharron and Rick Sobey, who owned Ram Messenger. They had two sons, Sean and Sherritt. Their son Sherritt had been on the same hockey team as P.J. since they were very young, so we had become pretty well acquainted. At one of the hockey games, Sharron asked me if I wanted to make some extra money–that was always of interest to me.

She was going on a cruise and wanted me to make her wardrobe.

I wanted to but I didn't have a sewing machine.

She said she had won a machine, and it wasn't even out of the box. I could take the machine and work it off.

I agreed.

She dropped off the machine and I couldn't believe it was still in the bubble plastic. It was a really cool Kenmore that had the discs that did embroidery and had a detachable buttonholer–every sewer's dream. Sharron bought the material, and I started to do her clothes. I set up the sewing in the storage room in the apartment and used the deep freeze lid as a table to cut out the patterns.

Christmas was coming and the kids really wanted to go to Calgary. I knew the car wouldn't make it. It was alright but not to travel too far. Gail and Bill offered me their car in exchange for mine while I was gone. I accepted their offer and the kids and I decided to go Christmas Day after we opened the gifts. We would drive as far as we could then stay in a hotel and drive the rest of the way on Boxing Day. We were all off for Christmas break, so we could stay for a week and not have to rush back. P.J. would miss a hockey tournament, but he didn't care. My parents were willing to have Christmas Dinner on Boxing Day instead of Christmas Day. I bought mostly gifts that could travel well so the kids could take them with them–lots of occupying games.

Rudi didn't buy the kids any gifts. He didn't even send them a card. I heard he had moved into the house and sold the racecar. The kids had bought gifts for Rudi. I took them shopping and let them get what they wanted. They even bought something small for Helena and the girls. We wrapped them and put them in a box. I pulled up to their house, but not too close. The three kids went to the door. J.J. was having such a hard time trudging through the snow but insisted on going with them. I could see Rudi answer the door and I could hear Helena yelling in German in the background. He told the kids he couldn't accept the gifts. All three of them were crying as they came back to the van with the gifts. I couldn't believe anyone could do that at Christmas time. I really had to concentrate hard on forgiveness. Naturally I wanted to give back evil for evil. I knew revenge wasn't mine to give, and that God would do a far better job of handling it than I ever could. So "I Let Go and Let God" and tried to put it out of my mind. I knew as long as I thought about it and let it bother me that I was in the driver's seat, so I tried hard to forgive and forget. When we got back home, I suggested we change the tags and add them to the gifts we were taking to Calgary. The kids seemed pretty happy with that idea.

We made it to Calgary by one o'clock on Boxing Day. Bill and Gail's car was nice to drive on the highway.

My parents had given me a ski trip to Sunshine Village. Both of my sisters and I were going together. Thelma had been skiing before but not Estella. We had a lot of fun but Thelma and I spent most of the time waiting for Estella to get back up after she fell down. By the end of the first day, she was getting better. We figured out that maybe we should have started her on the bunny hill rather than the top of the mountain.

The week flew by so quickly, and it was time to leave. I was having problems with a tire going low on the car, so my dad suggested he take us out for breakfast and then get the tire changed. He took us to a Husky Station for breakfast that was on the way out of Calgary. We sat for over an hour talking over coffee and breakfast. I could have very easily stayed. We discussed that too. The tire was fixed as we ate, and my dad filled up the car. We finally did leave, joking that after all the coffee we would be visiting a lot of service stations on the highway for the bathroom. As I pulled away, my dad quickly drove onto the overpass going over the main highway we were traveling on. He stood on the bridge and waved goodbye. I had a strange feeling as I looked in my rear view mirror at him still waving behind us. Was this going to be the last memory of my dad? I tried to shake it off. He did have a bad heart but was so active and health conscious since he quit drinking so many years before. He even quit smoking.

I talked to my friend Patti when I came back home, and she was telling me she was helping co-ordinate the Blue Brigade (the Winnipeg Blue Bomber Football Team Cheerleaders) with a friend of hers. I thought about it for a while and told her I wanted to try out. With the aerobics I was in fairly good shape. I was older, but not as old as some of the girls in the group. I didn't really think I could make it but would sure have fun trying, and it would be good to build up my self-confidence. She said the tryouts were starting in April. I told her to count me in.

March 18th came, and I phoned my dad to wish him a happy birthday. My parents had moved out of the block and into a side-by-side since I had been there at Christmas. My mom answered the phone when I called and said that Dad was now working with the Commissionaires. He was at work. I was really disappointed that he wasn't home for me to wish him a Happy Birthday, but my mom said he took his racing jacket and calendar to work to show the guys. I was surprised! She said that Dad was really proud of how I handled all the heartache I had in life and for him to take those things to work really showed that he was proud. I knew she was right and knew both my parents loved me. They didn't hide it, and I didn't hide the fact that I loved them. I really wanted to move to Calgary so I would have family around, but I was so established in Winnipeg.

In April I went to the tryouts for the Blue Brigade. I was really intimidated when I went in but met one of the Stanwick girls there that I knew, so I stuck with her. The Stanwick family was a very unique family. All of them had hearts of gold. I met the parents at the Speedway. They were dedicated racing fans that volunteered to sell the programs every week and to handle the 50/50 draw. They were always a pleasure to talk to, and lots of times, they would have their kids there with them. Everyone at the track loved the Stanwick family! The girls were all raised to be dancers. Mostly tap and jazz.

For the first tryout day, we were to learn the routine that we would be doing. We had two weeks to memorize it. The song was The Conga. I learned the routine with everyone else and went home and practiced and practiced. My kids kept clearing out because they couldn't stand to hear the song again after about the hundredth time. It was spring term break, and they were home and I was off. I would do the routine over and over again then fall into bed and get up and do it over and over again. I rehearsed it in front of friends to try to get more confidence.

I even became tired of the song and the routine! It really was very daunting, but I didn't want to give up. The day came for me to do the actual tryouts. I felt all day like I was pushing down walls to get there. By the evening I was really relying on God to get me in the door. I went to the change room and there were over one hundred girls trying out. I didn't feel that I was anywhere near worthy of being on the Blue Brigade, and as each minute went by, I felt more and more like I was making a fool of myself. I suddenly developed a fear that people I knew might think this was a vain attempt to build up my self-esteem. I shook it off knowing this was just the enemy trying to discourage me. This was a test to see if I could build up enough confidence to even try. I knew I could never try anything remotely close to this without God giving me the strength and courage. What if He was allowing me to do this to prepare me for something He planned for my future? I was number eighty-eight on the tryout list. We stood in a line that wound all the way up the staircase according to our numbers. After about an hour, I was at the top floor and didn't care any more. If I made a fool out of myself, then so be it. I was committed.

I started to recall when I was just seven years old and I was taking tap-dancing and baton. I wasn't any great dancer then but did what all-little girls did at that age. Just got up on the stage and was cute. Of course my mom and dad were in the audience, and to them, I was just the cutest, most intelligent dancer and was on my way to the big time. I think all parents were like that. The truth is, God never gave me rhythm, and if He did, then He never gave me the confidence to use it. I didn't seem to have too much of a problem with doing aerobics or with leading a class, but even after a couple of years of aerobics, I still felt intimidated at times.

They finally called number eighty-eight. Number eighty-nine was called at the same time. Two girls had to try out at the same time. The girl trying out with me was shorter, so I thought it would help to make me look better. The music started and the routine was so drilled into me that I could do it without thinking. I was glad because at that moment I couldn't think. We were dancing before a table of four judges just staring at every move we made. I found it really tough to get through. The girl dancing beside me was really good. I was so glad when it was over. I quickly changed and left. I really didn't care if I made it. I was just feeling very satisfied that I tried. We had to wait for over a week for them to decide whether we would make it or not. Patti called to inform me I was part of the five-girl spare. Apparently the spares were used very regularly and had to be at the practices to learn all the routines. I was very pleased to make it that far.

Chapter 19

Insurmountable Heartache

"He renews our hopes and heals our bodies."
Psalm 147:3

My racecar was ready and the kids were getting anxious to go to the races. They were also real Bomber fans so they were excited to watch the football games too.

Suddenly life came to a screeching halt and did a total change for all of us. The last week of April–it was a Thursday around suppertime–I got a phone call from my older brother, Grant, in Calgary.

His words to me were, "How do you tell your little sister that both Mom and Dad are in the hospital?"

I was sick at the words. Of course with the two of them in, I thought it must have been a car accident.

Grant explained, "No, Mom has temple arthritis and has to have treatments right away. Without the treatments, she could go blind. Dad took her to the hospital. He stayed with her for a while but left to pick up Estella from school and took her home. His plan was then to grab a bite to eat and go back to the hospital to watch the hockey game with Mom."

The Winnipeg Jets and the Calgary Flames were in playoffs together and we had the sea of white (all Jets fans wore white) and Calgary had the sea of red.

He went on to say Dad bought a bouquet of red roses to take with him to the hospital and had a red T-shirt for both Mom and himself.

Estella had gone to her bedroom and Dad yelled to her to see if she was hungry. He was going to make a tuna sandwich.

She said, "Yes."

They lived in a bi-level, and Estella's bedroom was on the lower level. He went on to say that Estella heard a clunk, then my dad snoring. She just thought it was Dad putting back the recliner and having a nap. (Snoring was normal with dad.)

"It wasn't this time."

Estella had come upstairs a few minutes later and found Dad lying at the top of the stairs. The snoring was the sound of his breathing. She called 911 right away and the ambulance raced him to the hospital. He was in intensive care around the corner from my Mom's hospital room, but she didn't know yet.

"How is he?" I asked.

"Unconscious," Grant replied. "They were doing tests on him."

I asked, "What kind?"

He said, "Brain scans."

I told him to keep me posted and hung up the phone in a daze.

I cried, pleading with God not to let him die and to take care of my mother. I didn't know what to tell the kids. They were so close to Gramma and Grampa. I cried myself to sleep that night hoping everything would be alright. Dad was sixty-three, and my mom only fifty-four.

I was really glad we were off for the break. I didn't think I could work with this going on.

Rod had come over in the morning and offered to take the kids on a fishing trip. They would be tenting and his friend and their kids were going, so it would keep them all occupied. He promised he would phone regularly from the closest town to keep up on the progress. I accepted his offer and packed up the kids. They were really happy to go.

No one knew how bad the situation really was. At first, I only knew Dad had an aneurysm. On Saturday, Grant called me back and told me Dad was brain-dead, and we had to make a decision whether to shut off the machines. I was overwhelmed by the news! But I was eight hundred miles away and had no intention of making any decision like that. I would trust whatever he decided because he was there to ask all the questions. Grant reasoned that Dad wouldn't want to live like this. I knew he was right.

Rod phoned. The kids were having a great time. They caught fish and were cooking it for supper. They took lots of pictures. I was glad they didn't know what was going on yet. I gave him an update. He said they would be back Sunday around supper, but he would call me before they left. It was about a two-hour drive.

Grant phoned again. He had made a decision. They were disconnecting the machines on Sunday morning. I was sick! My dad shouldn't die so young! He was such a good person. Why? I didn't sleep much that night. I drank coffee all night. The phone rang the next morning around ten, and Grant said the machines were shut down and Dad kept breathing. He said Mom went in and sat with him and told him it was okay for him to go; she would be alright. Right after she told him, it was as if he needed to know she was alright; then he died. I told Grant I would call him back later. I didn't want to talk anymore. Rod had called and told me it was raining so they were on their way back. I told him my dad had died. I just wanted to crawl in a hole and make the hurt go away. I cried for about two hours then phoned Grant back. The funeral was going to be on Thursday.

I tried to keep from crying long enough to tell the kids Grampa had died, but they all started to cry at once. I didn't know who to go to first and just stood paralyzed, sobbing my heart out. They wanted to go to the funeral, but I just didn't think it was a good idea. I didn't have that kind of money. Gail offered to look after the kids. I felt like I was in hell.

I went back to work on Monday and made arrangements to take off. The boss re-routed all the kids on my run, so it would be possible. I was leaving Tuesday after work and would return on Friday.

The plane did a stopover in Regina. The stewardess came and asked me if I would like a drink, and I told her I would like a cup of coffee. I had a window seat just behind the wing. I don't know what kind of a plane it was. My dad would have known.

I had flown on planes so much in my life with my dad being in the Air Force. After we took off, I was looking out the window. I thought about when I was in France, and my mom and dad took my two brothers and me to see the bunkers. We found a potato masher beside one of the bunkers, and my dad called in the military police to come pick it up. They were left over from the war but still had been known to blow up. I remembered playing on the slide in France in front of the block, and a French teenager burned me purposely with a cigarette. My dad had seen it happen from the window and came after him. My dad couldn't speak French but he definitely got the point across. I reminisced about our trip to England. My parents took us to the Tower Big Ben and Madame Tussauds, and my dad tried to convince me the statues were breathing. I still don't know if they were, then afterwards we went for a walk, window shopping, and I fell in love with a stuffed white French poodle that had on a red rhinestone collar and leash. It was under the Christmas tree that year with my name on it. I thought of all the misery I put him through when I got older and how much he helped me, talked to me and gave me advice even if he knew I wouldn't listen.

We got word from the flight attendant to do up our seat belts. We were about to land in Regina. It was only supposed to be long enough to let passengers off and some to board, and then we would be off again for Calgary. I laughed quietly as I recalled my dad taking us to the base almost every week to tour the airplanes he was working on. Every time he came home for lunch driving the mule (a mule is like a jeep that is used in the military), we would always get a ride, even if was half a block. I thought of when he taught me how to ride my first two-wheeler in France. He took me to the top of a very slow sloping hill next to the school, and I started to coast down. He kept yelling, "Now pedal backwards! Pedal backwards!" I started to cry as the bike got faster, and I was trying to tell him you can't pedal backwards on those bikes. I didn't realize that was how the brakes worked. I crashed hard at the bottom, and even as young as I was at the time, I definitely recognized the guilty look as he picked me up off the ground and brushed me off. I had a great childhood–compared to some–with great memories.

We started to descend into Regina, and I found I was really uncomfortable. I watched the wings as the back of them changed position for landing. I felt like I was panicking to the point that I grabbed the shoulder of the man in front of me through the seat and asked him if all of this was normal, meaning the way the plane was landing.

He turned and asked if I was afraid of flying.

Surprised I replied, "I guess I never was until now."

When we landed, the guy must have told the stewardess because she came to talk to me. She brought with her an older lady that said she would sit with me for the rest of the flight. The lady's son was a sports announcer in Winnipeg, and she was just coming back from visiting him. She was very sympathetic when I told her I was on my way to my dad's funeral, and said that was probably a big part of my flying problem. She showed me pictures of her son and her grandchildren and asked me about my kids. I had almost told her my whole story by the time we landed in Calgary. She was so sweet to help me like she did. She was probably looking forward to a nice quiet flight.

I got off the plane expecting to see my brother Grant waiting to greet me. He was nowhere in sight. I went to have him paged, but he didn't respond. The attendant suggested he might have thought I was coming in on a different airline. Since they were under a major renovation, I had to go outside and walk quite a ways to get to the other terminal. I did, hoping that was the case, but I didn't find him. Maybe he was just late. I returned to the Air Canada Terminal just in case. I was hauling my big suitcase with me the whole way. My feet were already killing me so I decided to phone his place knowing that was stupid because he wouldn't be home. To my surprise he answered the phone.

"Hi Grant."

He replied, "Oh, hi Sis, are you watching the game?"

I said, "No, as the matter of fact, I am standing at the airport waiting for you to pick me up." There was silence from the other end. I knew he forgot or whatever, but he wasn't on his way.

He thought I was coming in the next night.

I asked, "Well I am here; now what?

He barely finished talking promising he was on his way and the phone hung up. I figured as far as he lived from the airport, it would take at least half an hour. Was I surprised when he pulled up in front apologizing even before he was out of the car and it had only taken 15 minutes!

I asked if he grew wings and flew.

Laughing, he said, "No, I am a cop, remember."

We finished watching the game when we got back to his place. I wanted to go to see Mom right away, but he told her I was coming the next day. He thought we should wait until morning, and we would surprise her. She was still in the hospital, but they said she could leave for the day for the funeral.

I asked Grant, "What are the plans?"

He said it was in the paper, and they were expecting a fair amount of people to show up.

I asked if anyone had made the arrangements for a reception after the funeral.

His answer was, "Well, they could come to the house." I thought that would be pretty crowded, but he said, "Mom would be more comfortable with that."

I then asked, "What arrangements were made for food for the people after the service?"

He looked at me with that look that says, "Oh do we have to do that?"

I looked in my wallet and had $98. I didn't want to ask Grant for any money because I knew he was handling the expenses for the funeral. I asked him to take me to Safeway the next day after we saw Mom so I could put something together. I looked in his cupboards to see if there was any food we could use. There was lots of stuff for baking. I made a list, and then sat down with my brother.

We put on the home movies of when my dad took Grant camping in

France and of all the trips we took in Europe. We laughed at how prim and proper I was always dressed with little coats and hats. We laughed and cried as we saw the whole family had the same coats when we were in England. We spent the night laughing and crying. I don't think we had slept too long when it was time to get up.

It was so good to see my mother, but so hard to walk into her room knowing that now she didn't have Dad. They did everything together for so many years. I really didn't know what to say to her, so I said nothing. I just gave her a hug.

She said she was so glad I came. She asked how the kids were. That was like her–always concerned about everyone else. She asked if everything was organized for the funeral.

Grant answered, "Yes."

She asked if any food was arranged for after the service.

I told her, "Everything is under control."

Grant gave me that look, and I gave him a kick so Mom couldn't see. He just smiled and said, "Oh yeah, under control."

We told Mom we would pick her up in the morning for the funeral, and that I would come early to bring her clothes. She told me what she wanted to wear, and we said we would stop to get it from the house.

Grant and I left. He dropped me off at the Safeway store to get the food. I prayed on the way into the store for God to show me what to buy and to provide me with enough food with the money I had. I borrowed a calculator from Grant, so I knew exactly what I was spending. I got pickles and cheese, different cold cuts, crackers, buns, and with the rest, enough stuff for baking. I ended up with over four dollars in change.

My sister Thelma helped me bake and set up the trays. Louise stayed on top of the cleaning, and Estella was just plain miserable. We just let her be, as she had been through quite the ordeal, finding Dad the way she did. We finished everything quite late in the evening, but Thelma and I were quite pleased with the outcome. We kept joking that Thatti's Catering Service did the job.

The next morning was like reality hitting us square between the eyes. Mom said Dad would want me to drive the white angel. (That is what Dad named his new Le Baron when he got it.) Nobody drove that car but Dad, and I was naturally nervous. The crazy car talked and told you when your door was ajar and let you know when the gas gauge was getting low. Mom suggested that the rest of the family would all go in the limo behind the hearse and I should drive the Le Baron behind the limo. What Mom said, went. None of us were going to argue, so I asked Thelma if she wanted to come in the Le Baron with me. She really wanted to go with Mom, so I took Estella with me.

The agenda was to go to the funeral home for the viewing, and then follow the hearse to the church for the service. The family was to sit in the back of the church until it was time, and then walk in behind the coffin to the front. The Commissionaires Dad worked with were pallbearers. They wore their uniforms and Dad was wearing his.

We got to the funeral home, and we were sitting outside the room where the viewing was taking place. Mom went in with Grant and came out like a zombie. I knew she wasn't doing well. Grant suggested I go in, but I didn't want to go. I preferred not to see Dad like that. I knew my dad loved me and he knew I loved him. I was quite happy with the memories I had and didn't want to add to my memories, an image of my dead father. Grant was insisting, and I was getting irritated with him. Then he said the guilt words. Dad would be very upset if you didn't say good-bye. I got up from my chair and walked in the room telling Grant I didn't need him to come with me. I looked in the coffin and saw Grant standing on the other side. I turned and walked out. He came to talk to me.

I spoke sharply, "That is not Dad. That doesn't even look like Dad, and I will remember him the way I want to."

He was okay with that.

We were looking at a fountain where there was a statue of a boy pee-ing. Grant's partner on the police force, Egan, had come and was standing with us. We had known Egan for years. He was always part of the family and a great friend of Grant's. I started to giggle as I looked at the statue. Grant raised his eyebrows and winked, "Are you thinking the same thing I am?"

I said, "I wouldn't be surprised if Dad thought it funny now to have the fountain go out of control and pee all over us."

"Exactly," agreed Grant. "It would be Dad's way of letting us know he's still with us." Grant went over to Mom and told her. I could see a bit of a smile on her face, but it just didn't hold. I felt so sorry for her.

It was time to leave, and I went to get the car while Grant got Mom into the Limo. As I pulled up behind it, the Le Baron told me I was short on gas. I just looked at Estella. At that point the processional started moving. I had to follow, as neither Estella nor I knew where we were going.

I asked her if she had any money on her.

"No," she replied smartly. "What are you going to do, motion for them to stop at a gas station?"

I started to laugh. Estella was in her late teens and had a major attitude problem that most of us learned to either ignore or make excuses for. I continued, "Well, I hope this church isn't too far away." The car started insisting I stop and get gas. It was really starting to get to me. I had just over four dollars in my wallet, but didn't know how I would break formation to refuel. Finally, thankfully, the hearse pulled off into a church parking lot, and I knew we would be all right.

We were taken into a room in the back of the church while we were waiting for the other people to be seated. A gentleman came and told us it was time for us to proceed. We lined up behind the coffin. That had to be the hardest part. The Canadian Flag was draped over the coffin and Dad's medals were lying across the top. The choir started to sing "Amazing Grace," and I went out of control. We barely could walk up the aisle to the seats. I sat beside Mom, and she put her arm around me while I sobbed. I don't remember the eulogy or anything that was said. I just remember the choir singing. I don't even remember the coffin being taken back out, but I do remember asking Grant where the burial was because I had to get gas in the car. He looked surprised, "Didn't you know dad wanted to be cremated?"

The pastor announced there would be a get together at Grant's house and gave the address. Estella and I stopped and put four dollars worth of gas in the tank and got home before everyone else. There was just enough food, I think we had one piece of ham left and two pieces of cake. I thanked God. Grant drove Mom back to the hospital. I promised her I would come and spend some time with her before I left for the airport the next day.

I didn't get a window seat this time. I was sitting in an aisle seat. When the plane made the first turn after takeoff, all I could see was the ground out of all the windows. I was really nervous again. There was a guy sitting next to me and asked if I was from Winnipeg. I was glad to make conversation with him, so I wouldn't think of the flight. He asked me if I was nervous.

I said, "Yes." He asked if it was my first time flying and I laughed. The guy across the aisle got into the conversation, and before I knew it, the supper was being put on my tray.

The flight attendant asked what I wanted to drink.

I said, "Just a Diet Coke."

The guy beside me told me to have a glass of wine with the meal, and it would take the edge off. I never drank on a plane before but heard one glass on the ground was equal to three in the air. I couldn't handle three on the ground, and besides, I didn't have any money left. I had money in the bank at home, but bank machines were non-existent then.

I said, "I don't know," just to be polite.

He said to let him buy me a glass of wine. The flight attendant gave me a really small bottle of wine and a glass. It was really good. I always did like white wines. The flight seemed to go by so quickly. I finished my meal and sat and sipped the rest of the wine, and carried on a conversation with the two guys. Before I knew it we were told to do up our seatbelts for landing.

I remember saying, "Already!"

Both guys laughed and said, "See, that is the secret to flying."

I felt really bad that I didn't take the kids to the funeral with me, but I just couldn't afford it. (The truth was, so much had already happened that hurt the kids and I just wanted to protect them from being hurt any more.)

The first thing they asked me was, "How was Gramma?"

By Monday, it was good to be back to a normal routine at work again. Life did go on but with a feeling that someone was missing. I found it hard to believe I wouldn't see my father again. I couldn't phone him and talk to him.

The weather was warming up. The snow was gone, and I was getting spring fever. I bought a dresser for Tammy's room and was supposed to pick it up. I told Tammy I was taking the old dresser out of her room, and after the room was cleaned, we would go and pick up the new dresser. J.J. was watching TV and P.J. was invited to spend the night at Greg's house. They were together most of the time when they weren't at school. Rod was doing an evening run on the other side of the city for a social for the adults. He said he would give me a call in the morning because it was going to be a late night.

Tammy wanted to go and ride her bike. She never went very far. She pretty well just rode around in the back parking lot. Sometimes she would ride to Gail and Bill's, but that was just up the street a couple of blocks. She almost always told me when she was going. Tammy was eleven years old and very small for her age. She looked just like Rudi. She was really adorable. Everyone said she would definitely break some guys' hearts when she got older.

She asked if she could go out and ride her bike.

I told her, yes, and I would call her when I was ready to go.

It didn't take very long to finish getting her room ready. I told J.J. to get his shoes on and get ready to go. I went to the door to call Tammy to tell her it was time to lock up her bike. She wasn't there. I went to the phone and called Gail. When Gail answered, I asked her to send my blonde rugrat home.

Gail said she wasn't there; she didn't see her at all.

I said she must be on her way to her house could she please turn her around and send her back before she gets in the door.

She said, "All right."

I fixed my make-up and got my shoes on expecting that Tammy would walk in the door any minute. The phone rang and I was sure it was Gail telling me Tammy was on her way home. It was Gail but she called to let me know that Tammy never showed up. I started to panic a bit and went to look out the front of the block. I couldn't see her and went to the back of the block. I told J.J. he could still watch TV. I was getting very concerned.

I thought about the social workers telling me I was being way too overprotective of Tammy and P.J. because of what happened to J.J. and that I wasn't being fair to them. I told them I would listen to their opinion, but take it for what it was worth. I drove the kids to their practices or sent them with other parents. The social worker said I had to let go; it wasn't healthy for the kids.

After another five minutes went by, I picked up the phone and called our local police detachment. The officer that answered the phone had an attitude that was as expected. He asked how long she was gone. I answered about fifteen minutes.

He laughed and said, "She will probably walk in the door any minute, relax."

I hung up and waited another ten minutes and the phone rang. It was Gail. I was hoping Tammy had shown up there. She just called to see if I found her.

I started to cry and shouted, "No and the police won't listen to me!"

Bill would be home any minute, and they would go out and see if they could find her. I picked up the phone and called the police again.

The officer said, "If you insist, then call the downtown office," and gave me the phone number of missing persons.

I called right away and told them Tammy was missing. They asked what she was wearing. I told them a turquoise tracksuit, and she had laces in her shoes that said "Tammy" with a heart beside it.

The officer said, "Transcona detachment knows more about that girl than we do."

I almost threw up. Something *had* happened. The officer realized I was missing something in the conversation and told me he was transferring me back to the Transcona department. I was put on hold for a few minutes then the first officer I talked to came back on the phone. He told me to just sit tight and asked me for my address. I was getting out of control and asked where she was and what had happened. He very calmly told me it was okay and two officers were on their way.

I called Gail back and told her.

Gail said, "Calm down, they're probably wanting her picture." She told me to get one of Tammy's pictures while I was waiting for the officers.

I was barely off the phone when two officers came in the apartment door. I didn't remember buzzing them in the block. J.J. was still watching TV, and I turned to get Tammy's big picture off the bookshelf in the living room. The officers followed me, and before I could turn around, one of them put his hand on my shoulder and told me to sit down. I looked at him and knew what he was about to tell me was not good. I ran. I ran out the patio door and headed for the parking lot with the two officers after me. I had my hands over my ears, so I didn't hear what they had to say.

I ran right into Gail, and I will never forget the look on her face. She grabbed me and said, "What happened?"

The officers tried to get me back in the apartment and said, "You have to listen to us."

I bargained with them, "I will if you tell me Tammy is still alive!"

They quickly answered, "Yes, she is, but she was hit by a car, and we have to get you to the hospital right away."

Gail said she would stay with J.J. I don't remember getting in the police car, but I remember sitting in the back seat talking a hundred miles an hour. I told the officers about J.J. and about Rudi leaving and about my dad dying. I told them anything that was on my mind, but I didn't want to hear about the details of what happened. One officer turned around and listened to me, but I could tell he didn't believe everything I was telling him. I asked if I could smoke. The one officer handed me a cigarette and lighter, and said I could do anything I wanted to. They asked me where her dad was, and I told them it didn't matter. They said they really wanted to have him picked up and brought to the hospital right away. I then realized it was really bad. They wanted to get us both there before she died. I was sobbing and gave them Rudi's address. They radioed it in and said a car was on the way to pick him up.

It didn't take very long to get to Children's Hospital, and when I got out of the car, the two police officers started to run with me. They ran me up the stairs to the Intensive Care Department. A nurse came out to meet us, and they said to her, "This is the mother of the little girl." But they had already figured out who she was. Apparently when the accident happened, the police had arranged to put bi-lines on the television saying, "Looking for a mother or father of a little girl approximately six years old, name Tammy." J.J. was watching television but couldn't read. I didn't look at the television set, and anyone we knew who was watching didn't relate it to us because Tammy was eleven. She was just so small.

I asked if she was still alive and the nurse said, "Yes, you can go in and see her, but she is hooked up to a lot of machines." I asked how they found out who she was, and they said they sent for the urologist when they found her kidney scars to find out what kind of surgery she had undergone. They needed all the information they could get on her. Dr. Decter came, and as soon as he saw her scar, he said this is Tammy Hardt. The police were already on the way with me by then.

The neurologist was there. Dr. Fewer just looked at me and said, "Tammy is in a coma. Need he tell me any more? You know the answers to all the questions; it is not much different than with her brother."

I couldn't believe what I was hearing. Tammy was lying on the bed and was so hooked up with machines. They were breathing for her. I was asked to go to the family room and the two officers came with me. They asked if I wanted to talk to a pastor, and I said, "Yes."

They informed me that Rudi was on his way. That didn't give me much comfort. I hadn't seen him in a long time. I must have been in shock because I don't remember too much, only that I wanted my daughter back. I didn't want to do this again! Maybe she would wake up right away.

The pastor came right away to talk to me, and the nurse said she would come in a few minutes to take me back in to see Tammy again. The two police officers said they were going and as they were leaving said the Winnipeg Police Department would be praying for us. I thanked them.

The pastor had just started to talk when the nurse came back in and said I could see Tammy again. I went right away, and the doctor that was leading the team came to talk to me. He told me he understood I have been through this before, but I should know in the nine years since J.J.'s accident, there has been a lot of new technology. There was hope. Of course there was hope! Where there is breath there is hope. I sat with Tammy for about five minutes, and then was asked to leave again.

I was on my way down the hall to the family room when Rudi came through the door. I thought he was going to hit me, so I backed up. He grabbed my arms and said, "How is she?"

I told him she was in a coma.

He just looked at me and quietly said, "Oh my God."

We both went to the family room–familiar even though it had been nine years. We had both commented at the same time that it was again Mother's Day weekend.

I told Rudi my dad had died the week before, and I just got back from the funeral. He told me his dad had died a couple of months before. We both went in to see Tammy. It sure didn't look like her. This shouldn't have happened. Rudi asked me what happened, and I told him I didn't know. He said he had seen the bi-lines on TV but never dreamed it was Tammy they were talking about. He asked how they knew her name was Tammy. I told him the laces in her shoes had her name all over them.

I called home and talked to Gail. She said she would just take J.J. home with her. She asked about P.J. I phoned Greg's house and talked to his mother. I asked her to make sure P.J. wasn't near the television to hear the news until I could get a chance to talk to him. She told me they would be praying for us.

I talked an awful lot to God. I had wished I had more knowledge at this point. I kept reminding Him that He promised not to give me more than I could handle. I just kept crying; I wanted my little girl back.

Rudi and I talked all night in between going in to see Tammy. It was funny how we had so much to say.

At one point, I had said to the doctor that it was quite possible Tammy would just wake up. Normally yes, but they had her in an induced coma to keep her relaxed, and that would help stop the swelling in the brain. He said they would probably keep her that way for at least three days. That gave me hope. She wasn't waking up, but it wasn't necessarily because of the injury, but more because they were keeping her out. Remembering I was not given more than I could handle, I felt much better knowing they would take her off the medication in three days, and she would just wake up,

Morning came and Rudi asked me if I wanted a ride home. He would take me home to shower and change and bring me back. I agreed, knowing Tammy was not going to wake up while I was gone. He talked all the way to my house. I realized I didn't have the key to get in. Gail had locked the door when she left, and the key was on the inside. I went to the caretaker, and he was very understanding and let me in. Rudi had a cup of coffee while I showered and changed. I got dressed and asked if we could stop at Greg's house so I could tell P.J. what happened.

P.J. was sitting at the breakfast table when we walked in. He was so happy to see Rudi and me together. He hadn't seen Rudi for a few months. I told him vaguely what happened, and he started to cry. I told him to have faith and remember that God wouldn't give us more than we could handle. He was so upset, and asked if it was the same as when J.J. had his accident. I just wanted to believe it wasn't and wanted to ease his mind, so I said, "No, not near like J.J.'s accident." Greg's mom said he could stay as long as I needed. I gave them the key to the apartment and told them they could get what they needed. P.J. asked if he could come with us to see Tammy, and I told him that for the next three days they were keeping her out, so to wait. He decided he would go over to see J.J. at Gail's after breakfast.

I got back to the hospital and nothing had changed. From the tests they had done, the doctors confirmed that Tammy did have a lot of brain activity. She had a broken leg. Apparently it was quite bad, but they just put on a floating cast since she wouldn't be moving around much for the next few days. A normal cast would come later.

The nurse let us know Rod was in to see Tammy. Rudi wanted to know who Rod was. I didn't answer. They told him I went home with my husband. I just smiled and said, "Oh that must have gone over well!" Rod and I had started to date. We were just friends in the beginning. Like a personal trainer, he helped me get physically fit. I think he was really closer to my kids at first, but it ended up that we enjoyed each other's company. He wasn't around in the summers. While we were on summer break, he was a fishing guide in Ontario. So we would grow closer together, and then he would leave again. It was almost like we weren't supposed to be close together. I really did keep in mind that I was still married.

The rest of the day went by pretty slowly. There were a few people that came in to see us that had read the story in the newspaper. The police came back to give us the details. Tammy had gone to see a boy she liked from school. The chain fell off her bike, so she was walking it. She got to the corner where there was a six way stop with train tracks in the middle. (All the families were fighting to put lights on that corner. It wasn't safe.) She had made it to the stop sign and her helmet was hanging over the handlebars. An elderly gentleman was stopped at the stop sign. He motioned for her to go not seeing the car coming across the tracks from the other side. Tammy did go and was hit by the other car. The impact threw her into the air, and the driver didn't realize he hit her until she fell back on the windshield then on the ground. She landed on her head. The police officer said there was a saving grace in this. At the other stop sign was an ambulance on coffee break. She was attended to immediately and didn't go very long without oxygen. They took her to the Concordia Hospital because it was closest. Then, she was immediately transferred to the Children's Hospital at the Health Sciences Centre. I called everyone I could think of for prayers. The police gave me the name of the guy that hit her. His name was Dennis, and he was only twenty-five years old. He was in the car with his girlfriend.

Janet was in Vancouver when her mom and Henry heard what happened. They weren't sure whether they should call her to tell her what happened. They knew she would be really upset, and no one was out there with her. It was a business trip. They also knew that she would be very upset if they didn't tell her and she came back a few days later and found out then. She and Henry had become quite close to the kids over the past year. Janet and I did aerobics every Saturday together, and we saw each other every week at the track. Janet's mom finally found it in her to break the news. Janet caught the next flight back. She showed up at the door of the family room holding a thermos of coffee. She had really become my strength. I had no doubt God gave me Janet as a friend to unload on. She was the kind of friend everyone wants in life. I could say anything to her, and she just listened. She never judged.

Rudi had left for a while. He promised he would be back soon. I still didn't have my own vehicle at the hospital. I came back with Rudi. I was too tired to drive.

I told Janet I hadn't called anyone in Calgary. I hadn't even called my mother for Mother's Day. How could I tell my mother this happened? I wanted to wait till there was good news to add to it like, "Mom, Tammy had an accident and was unconscious but is awake now." That would be good. I knew Tammy was in critical condition but kept remembering that God wouldn't give me more than I could handle.

Janet suggested I give Grant a call. He was Tammy's Godfather. She said to let him handle this in whatever way he thought was best. I didn't think that would work since my mother would wonder why I wasn't calling on Mother's Day.

I did call Grant and let him know what happened. He couldn't even speak. He said Mom was coming over for Mother's Day and he would play it by ear. He suggested I call back later in the day to give him an update.

Janet tried to persuade me to get some sleep, but I couldn't. I know I should have, but I was only allowed in the room for such short periods that I didn't want to miss my opportunity.

Rod came back. He asked what he should do. I didn't know. He said he was going to pick up the boys and do something with them. I told him to watch what he said and be very vague. He left and promised he would be back to pick me up.

Rudi came back. The family room was like a swinging door. One would leave and another would come. It was like it was all timed so I was never really alone. Rudi and I were going in to see Tammy every chance they gave us. In between the times, we just talked and talked and caught up on all the news. He never talked about Helena, and I didn't ask. I just decided that this was my husband and what he was doing was his problem, not mine. We talked as if he had never left. He caught up on the news of what my family was up to, and I caught up on the news of what his family was up to. We were just killing time waiting for the doctors to take Tammy off the medication that was keeping her out. It was funny how Rudi and Rod kept missing each other. Rudi suggested he pick up something for both of us and bring it back and we could have supper together. I wasn't hungry. He said he would go home and eat and get some sleep then would meet me here in the morning. He was gone about five minutes when Rod walked in. He insisted I had to sleep. I hadn't slept since the Thursday night and was a zombie. The nurse agreed. There was nothing I could do for now, and they promised to phone if there was any kind of change. While we were pulling out of the parking lot at the Children's Hospital, I exploded. It was like someone pulled the pin. I was so out of control with tears, at one point Rod just pulled over and tried to calm me down.

When we finally got home, I was sitting on the couch just staring out the window. Someone knocked on the door and Rod answered it.

I could only hear him say, "Not now, she has to sleep."

I asked who it was, and I could see he was getting angry.

It was Patti. She came in and promised she would only be a minute. She heard what happened on the news and was trying to get in touch with me all day.

I told her I just got back. I filled her in. She promised that she and her husband Warren would be there for anything we needed. She left right away, and I think I was asleep before she got out the door.

I woke up on the couch, and Rod was asleep on the other side of the sectional. I decided I would take my own car back to the hospital and would pick up the boys for lunch. It was Mother's Day. I did get brave enough to call my mom. Actually, I gave Grant a call later in the afternoon. Louise answered and asked how things were going. I told her there was no change and they would be taking her off the medication on Monday. I asked if Mom knew. Mom was sitting next to her and was waiting for me to call. As soon as my mom answered, "Hello," the conversation was total emotions. I even forgot to wish her a Happy Mother's Day. I think we had an unspoken understanding that it was a dumb thing for anyone to say to her or me anyway. I promised her I would keep her up to date with any news. We both agreed it would be good news.

Rudi spent a lot of the day with me. It seemed strange; we were so comfortable together, as if he had never left. In the afternoon, he said he was going over to Horst and Elaine's house for a Mother's Day Supper. He asked me to come with him.

I smiled "Do I get to sit next to Helena?"

He laughed, "Not if I don't pick her up."

I told him, "No, but thanks for the offer."

Both boys were busy at lunchtime, so I let them know I would meet them at Gail's at suppertime. Rudi pulled out and Rod pulled in. They passed each other and didn't even know it. Neither one had ever met the other one before. I told Rod I wanted to run up and sit with Tammy for a bit; then I was going to Gail's for supper. He asked if he could take me to Gail's.

"Sure," I replied.

I really had to watch my emotions when I got there. I didn't want to upset the boys. I didn't want them to worry. They handed me a little gift-wrapped box with a bow on the top. I thought it was something they made. It was a gold medallion of three hearts intertwined to go on my chain. P.J. said it stood for my three Hardts: Tammy, J.J. and P.J.

I went back for a quick visit after supper and picked up my car. I really wanted to get a good night sleep before Tammy woke up. They were still planning to pull her off the medication the next day. They kept reminding me that she was stable, but there was a chance she was in a coma and wouldn't wake up. I reminded them that God wouldn't give me more than I could handle. Tammy not waking up the next day was, I believed, more than I could handle.

I didn't do my run the next day. I talked to my boss, and he was sure he could hire Handi-Helper for as long as he had to. He told me all their prayers were with me.

When I arrived at the hospital, Rudi was already there sitting with the kids' social worker. She came to see how Family Services could help with all of this. According to her, it was very important that J.J. and P.J. have as close to a normal life as possible through this crisis. She suggested they find a worker to come into the home and take care of them after school and on weekends until Tammy was better and out of the hospital. I really appreciated this. She asked if I knew of anyone who could do it. I had told her I would talk to Patti. She was looking for work, and I was sure she would be interested. I knew the boys would love having her around. They knew Patti and Warren since they were small.

The medication was stopped, and it was explained to me that it would take time to come out of her system. That night there was no sign of Tammy waking up.

The neurologist came and again said, "You know the routine. You know the answers to all the questions. Tammy is in a coma."

I didn't want to hear that. Not again! Not Tammy! All the hope I had hung onto for the last three days was gone. Tammy was in the same kind of coma as J.J. had been. Not my little girl!

I screamed and cried, "I want my daughter back!" I cried out to God, I believed so strongly Tammy would wake up. How would I ever tell the boys? The neurologist reminded me that there was a possibility that she would never come out of the coma. I went in the washroom and threw up. I was sitting on the floor with my head on the toilet crying and begging God to please not take my daughter away. My world had caved in and I couldn't even get up off the floor. Rudi and the nurse kept knocking on the door asking me to open it. I told them to go away. I finally washed my face and opened the door. I went in to see Tammy and told her she had to wake up.

They took me out of the room. I didn't know what to do with myself. Patti came in and tried to help talk to me. They had called in the pastor from the hospital. I knew it would be another long haul and thought of the boys. I asked Patti if she would help out by working for Family Services in this. She said, "Absolutely," and she would call the social worker first thing in the morning.

Rudi left after supper and looked pretty drained when he promised he would see me in the morning. He then stopped at the door and asked if I wanted him to stay.

I told him, "No." No one could help.

I just sat in the chair and talked to the pastor. I tried to convince him to talk to God. I was convinced he had more pull than I did. He tried to explain to me that it wasn't God that did this, and I told him it was God who allowed it to happen.

Rod came in and left after a short time. He was trying to be strong for me but obviously was having a hard time with it. Tammy thought the world of him.

In the morning, I tried to find enough energy to gather up some of Tammy's favorite things. I picked up her Wrinkles the Dog puppet and a book she was in the middle of reading from her Babysitter Collection. I couldn't find Wrinkles' stuffed bone that was supposed to be in the pocket of the dress. I had to find it! She was very particular about her things and would be very upset if Wrinkles lost her bone. I sat on the floor beside her bed crying. I asked God, "Where is the bone?" I thought of the saying in the Bible, *"Be still and know that I am God."* Psalm 46:10 (*NIV*) I stopped crying and remembered I had packed up all the things on the dresser and in the dresser because we were picking up her new dresser. The bone was on her dresser. I opened the closet door, and on top of the box was the bone.

At the hospital, I would sit and read the book as long as the nurses would let me. Then I would sit Wrinkles on her chest, and she would talk to Tammy. She would keep telling her to wake up. Wrinkles and I got to be good friends over time. She would say to Tammy what I wanted to say but couldn't. I told her I was so sorry this happened.

Patti did come and look after the boys. I eventually went back to work. I would pick up the kids in the morning and drive them to SMD. I would leave the van parked there and walk across the street to the Children's Hospital. At lunchtime, I was ready for a break after spending all morning with Tammy, talking to her and reading to her and doing her therapy to try to keep everything limber until she came out of the coma. I would go back and spend the afternoon with her until it was time to do the last run. Then I would have supper with Patti and the boys and go back to the hospital for the evening. Rod usually came in either the morning or afternoon or both while he was between his runs. Rudi popped in and out during the day but mostly in the evenings.

Margaret's mother came in and prayed for healing for Tammy. I just prayed that God would send whatever we needed to get through this and for Him to please heal Tammy. As usual, I could never get a straight answer from the neurologists. I prayed that God would give me an answer—that He would confirm to me that Tammy was going to be alright.

One evening, I had just come out of the Intensive Care Unit when I realized it was later than I thought. I had to get home so Patti could leave. I went to the stairs and started to run down.

One of the neurologists passed me as he was going up. He said, "Hi."

When I got to the bottom of the stairs, he was at the top and called me. I turned around and looked at him. It was strange because the light on the wall looked like it was at the back of his head, and his head was glowing. He said, "I don't know why I am telling you this. It is against all my rules, but Tammy will be alright. It will take a long time, but Tammy will be alright."

I told him I knew why he told me that and thanked him. That was the confirmation I had asked God for. I danced down the rest of the stairs and held those words in my heart as I drove home. I never did see that neurologist again. The next day Dr. Fewer was back in the picture.

Janet came in with my supply of caffeine and told me I had to phone her office and hear her new secretary. Her name was Donna, and she was from Oklahoma. She said her accent was priceless. I did call and ask for Janet, who of course was standing next to me, so I knew she wasn't there. She was right. Donna had such a pleasant voice and such a down south accent. I asked Donna to give Janet a message that I called so it would seem more legit. To my surprise, Donna asked me how Tammy was. She said everyone in the office waits for Janet to come to work in the morning for an update on how Tammy is doing. She said my family and I are praying, "We are believing for God to heal Tammy." She blew me away! I thanked her and agreed with her.

Janet came to have lunch with me in the cafeteria and said that Donna had told her that her husband was an Eastern Rite Catholic Priest and would like to come to meet Tammy and me. I was thrilled. I knew it was an answer to my prayer. God actually moved this family from Oklahoma to Winnipeg and gave Donna a job with Janet so I could meet them. I knew God's hand was in this, and I was feeling much better. I agreed to have lunch with him the next day.

The next day I came out of the Intensive Care Unit and stopped by the family room. There sat Donna's husband. He stood up to shake my hand and introduced himself. He was dressed in a black suit with the black shirt and white clerical collar. His accent was really different, and he was such a distinguished looking gentleman. He told me to call him Father Ron or Pastor Ron, whichever I was most comfortable with. Out of respect, I called him Pastor Ron. We went to the cafeteria and ended up talking for three hours. He prayed with Tammy and me before he left, and there was so much power in his prayer.

There was a peace that came over me–that peace beyond all understanding. He handed me a Bible as he was walking out and told me we would talk again.

I sat flipping through the Bible thinking of all the things we talked about. He showed me scriptures backing up all that he believed in, and he was pleased to hear I was already a Christian. If it was God's will, Tammy would be healed, and I had to keep believing it. He showed me scripture. Isaiah 53:5 *"But he was pierced for our transgressions, he was crushed for our iniquities: the punishment that brought us peace was upon him and by his wounds we are healed."(NIV)*

He explained it wasn't God causing all this chaos in my life; it was Satan. This was spiritual warfare and God was the Almighty Powerful that could heal Tammy. I should keep my focus on God and pray for Him to give the doctors the wisdom and knowledge to help Tammy. He showed me verses I had heard said so many times but never knew where to find.

These verses are from Mark 11:22–25 *"Jesus told his disciples: Have faith in God and don't doubt, you can tell this mountain to get up and jump into the sea, and it will. Everything you ask for in prayer will be yours, if you only have faith. Whenever you stand up to pray, you must forgive what others have done to you. Then your Father in heaven will forgive your sins."*

And James 1:6–8 *"But when you ask for something, you must have faith and not doubt. Anyone who doubts is like an ocean wave tossed around in a storm. If you are that kind of person, you can't make up your mind, and you surely can't be trusted. So don't expect the Lord to give you anything at all."*

He told me how important it was that I forgive the driver of the car that hit Tammy. I didn't know if it was possible. At that point I didn't think I had ever forgiven the driver that hit Jeffrey. He explained all I had to do was to say it, even if I didn't feel it, and God would handle the rest. I could have sat and listened to him for hours. I thanked God for sending Pastor Ron and for giving me the wisdom and knowledge I needed to get through this. I knew I couldn't get through this on my own. Not again. I couldn't even imagine doing this over again. I wanted Tammy back. Tammy was moved to a room, the same one across from the nurse's desk she was in when she had the kidney surgery. Now I could spend more time with her.

The next day I stopped at Dennis' house. He was the driver who hit Tammy. I got the address from the phone book. His mother answered the door, and I told her who I was. She asked me to come in and called her husband to come right away. She wanted to know how Tammy was. I told them she was in a coma. They were really upset. I wanted to talk to Dennis. His mother seemed concerned. I told her I just needed him to know I forgive him for what happened–for his peace of mind and my own. No one could do anything to change what happened. She told me her son was totally devastated about what happened. She said he was at work. He drove a lawn mower, the kind you sit on, and was on Henderson Highway close to McIvor. She explained I would see more than one lawnmower, but I couldn't miss Dennis; he was the only blonde. She asked me to let them know how Tammy was doing and told me they were praying for her.

I drove down by McIvor Mall right away before I went to the hospital and saw a blonde guy sitting on a lawn mower drinking a coffee in the parking lot. I parked in front of the lawnmower and left the car running. I got out and said, "Are you Dennis?"

He answered, "Yes."

I told him I was Tammy's mother, the little girl he hit. His face turned white as if he was petrified. Then I said I just wanted to let him know I forgive him for what he had done. He started to cry and looked away. I got in the car and drove away.

When I got to the hospital and walked into her room, there was a huge purple teddy bear on the bottom of the bed. It had its ears pierced and was wearing really cute earrings. The kind of earrings Tammy always wanted when she got her ears pierced, but I didn't get for her. Rudi came in, and I asked him if he had brought it. He said, "No."

For the first time Rod came in at the same time as Rudi. It was a little uncomfortable. Rudi was standing at one side of the bed and Rod was standing at the other. I was at the foot of the bed and introduced them. They managed to reach across and shake hands with each other, but I could have cut the tension with a knife. I asked Rod if he brought the Teddy Bear and he answered, "No."

The nurse came in and gave me the update on Tammy's visitors. Pastor Ron had come in earlier with his teenage daughter; she said she was a beautiful girl. She brought the Teddy Bear for Tammy.

Rod made an excuse he had some errands to run and would be back later. I knew he was just uncomfortable with the situation.

Rudi stayed for a while. I wanted to tell him what Pastor Ron had said, but I knew he would think I was cracking up. I remembered what my dad always told me about a personal relationship with God and knew it was alright to keep this all between me and God for now. Rudi asked me to walk him out when he was heading back to work. He asked me how long I had been seeing Rod.

I told him it was none of his business.

His response was, "Well the guy has really good taste."

I asked him what he meant by that and he told me I looked great. I just smiled at the compliment and went back into the hospital. He yelled out the window that he would be back after work. He wanted to know if I wanted to grab some supper with him. I told him I wanted to go home to have supper with the boys. He just smiled and drove off. I was finding the situation to be very confusing. Rudi was still my husband and I was feeling guilty for seeing Rod, yet Rudi was living with another woman.

Pastor Ron came in for a coffee that afternoon, and I filled him in on the whole scenario. I wanted to hear what he thought. He asked me how I felt about Rudi. I told him I still loved him but I hadn't liked him too much for the past year. But now, I was kind of liking him again. He seemed to be more like his old self the more I saw of him. He was still living with Helena though and not supporting us. We hadn't been to court for a while. He hadn't seen the kids for a long time. He reminded me Rudi was still my husband. I was confused and said now I felt guilty about Rod. Pastor Ron just smiled and shrugged his shoulders and said, "Well you know who to give the problem to."

He prayed again and thanked God for healing Tammy and for my peace. He counselled me before he left; that when I pray for something, I shouldn't keep praying for it over and over. Ask God to do it once, and then just keep thanking Him. That is how I demonstrate faith. Then he told me to look up James 2:26 *"For the body without the spirit is dead, so faith without works is dead also."(KJV)*

When Pastor Ron left, I sat with Tammy for another hour pretty much daydreaming. It was really hard to believe it was almost a month since Tammy's accident. There was no sign of her opening her eyes. I couldn't take Tammy out for walks like I did J.J. I tried really hard not to compare the two. The neurologist told me that Tammy had a blockage in the top of the spinal column right under the skull and so they hooked up a temporary shunt to relieve the pressure on the head with hopes that she would wake up. They were hoping the clot would break through on its own. They would give it more time, and there was still hope. I couldn't get her up to give her a shower. All I could do was talk to her and read to her and let Wrinkles talk to her. There was no kind of response, but as Pastor Ron told me, don't go by how it looks. I tried to keep my focus on God; I did believe in my heart that Tammy would come out of the coma, so I tried to think before I spoke and watched what I said. When people asked me how Tammy was doing, I tried to answer positively.

Every day when I went home to have supper with the boys, I filled the boys in on what Pastor Ron said. They really wanted to go to see her, but I told then not yet. P.J. got very insistent and angry. He asked if it was the same as J.J., and I just kept saying no. I was upset when I left the house to go back to the hospital because P.J. was so upset.

Pastor Ron told me I could phone any time day or night. I went to a payphone and called on the way to the hospital. Donna answered. Pastor Ron was out but told me to tell her the problem. I explained everything to her, and she said very calmly in that Oklahoma accent. "Okay, let's pray," and she started to pray. I was always so mind-blown, the power they seemed to have in their prayers. When I got off the phone and continued on to the hospital, I was so much at peace. I could think of all that was going on and had no pain, just total peace. I thought back to just over a year before I became a Christian, how I sometimes doubted what was being told to me. It made me realize how far I had come in my Christian walk. Praying for God's peace could make me feel like I had been sedated. I developed a hunger to know even more about God. If I ever doubted what was being told to me, I was now convinced.

When I got to the hospital, Rudi was sitting next to Tammy holding Wrinkles the puppet. He had it bouncing on the side of her bed. When he saw me he held the puppet up and Wrinkles asked, "What took you so long?"

After reading to Tammy for an hour, Rudi asked me if I wanted to go for a ride since it was so nice out. I knew Rod was supposed to be coming, but he was busy packing to go to his summer job, fish guiding.

I phoned him and he told me he was right in the middle of a problem with one of his fish finders. I called it his cheater. He had taken me fishing so many times, and it was a new experience. It wasn't a question, do you catch a fish? It was, what do you do after you catch your limit in the first half hour? He was an awesome fisherman and would fill my freezer with enough fish that I could eat it every day in the summer. Most of it was Walleye.

When I got off the phone, it was obvious Rod would be tied up for a while, so I told Rudi I would go for a ride if he wanted me too. He drove me out to Lockport, a nice ride that ran along the river. The houses were so beautiful out there. He parked in a clearing beside the river and pulled out a thermos of coffee and two cups. I just laughed at how this had been planned. (I looked at the cup at one point and thought to myself what terrible taste Helena had in dishes. I knew I was just being finicky, so got rid of that line of thought pretty fast.)

We talked about P.J.'s hockey and how J.J. was getting along in junior high. Tammy had one more year in elementary, and then she would be going to junior high, and J.J. would be moving on to high school. That would be pretty hard for him. J.J. was so established at his school. He loved everyone, and everyone loved him.

After I finished my coffee, we went for a walk along the riverbank. At one point we stopped and just looked at the river. It seemed very awkward for a moment because I had the feeling he was going to kiss me. I had to feel that way for only a moment because he leaned over before I knew it, and kissed me long and gently. I almost fell in the river, and we both started to laugh.

As he drove back, I was very confused on how I felt. I was feeling guilty for kissing my own husband. This was so weird.

Patti left as soon as I got home. The boys were already in bed. I phoned the hospital to make sure Tammy was alright. I had just hung up the phone and poured myself a coffee, when the phone rang. I thought it would be Rod. At first I didn't recognize the voice on the other end.

It was Helena. She could speak a bit better English than before. I could at least understand her. She asked if Rudi was with me. I told her it was none of her business. She said she wanted to talk to him. I told her he was my husband and she had no right. I asked her what she thought God was thinking about this. I was just playing a game with her and that was really stupid. It was like revenge. I knew better than that, but I couldn't believe it when I heard her say she didn't believe in God. I told her I would pray that God would show her that He is real. She told me to stay away from Rudi. I just laughed. Then she told me that it was my fault Tammy had the accident. I was really quiet. She said our kids are like our eyes. We should never go anywhere without them. I let Tammy go on her own and now look what I caused. I told her I would pray for her and hung up the phone. She kept calling back so I took the phone off the hook. I was going to phone Rudi at the shop and ask him to stop her because I didn't want the phone tied up in case the hospital called. I decided it wasn't a good idea and after twenty minutes I put the phone back on, and it was quiet all night.

I just wanted to see Tammy. I was called into a room when I got there. Rudi was already in the room. Two nurses and the neurologists came in. They told us they would give Tammy another two weeks for the blockage to break through. If it didn't, they would put on a permanent shunt. This was something new to me. The doctor explained to me it was a little device that they attach to the side of her head under the skin. A small tube would run along the main artery and into her stomach. That would be a bi-pass to drain the brain. Then they could take off the temporary shunt. The shunt would grow with her. We would be able to feel the shunt on the side of her head and see the shape of the tube running down her stomach. He said that would be a bi-pass to drain the brain. Then they could take off the temporary shunt. The permanent shunt would grow with her. Then he said the clincher–if all of this didn't work, then there was a good chance she wasn't going to wake up, and we should consider sending her to St. Amant.

Rudi stormed out the door. I sat thinking this was deja vu, remembering when I was told J.J. was a like a vegetable and I should consider putting him in St. Amant. At that time I went home and cried for three days before I was finally determined enough to go back to the hospital with a new hope J.J. would wake up. I wasn't a Christian then. Now, even though the circumstances were so similar, it wasn't the same. I didn't need three days to go home to find some strength. I already knew I could take the problem to God on the spot. He promised to meet me where I was, and I knew He would guide me as to what to do with this situation and give me all the strength I needed. I also knew not to believe any negative comments. The neurologist did say he was giving her two weeks for it to break through on its own. What I wanted to tell the doctor at that moment was I was not going to listen to him, instead I was going to get my Bible and refresh my memory on God's promises. I didn't for fear if he didn't understand; he may think I was a woman who only hears what I want to hear or believes what I want to believe. I did tell him we would wait out the two weeks and if it still didn't break through on its own, then to put in the shunt, but I refused to even think about St. Amant.

I called Pastor Ron to give him an update on what had happened. He said they would be praying for the blockage to break through. I spent the day thanking God for Him answering that prayer.

I went to the rehab hospital to get a second opinion from the doctor there. It was the same doctor J.J. had when he was there and he remembered J.J. He agreed there was always hope and told me to talk to him again after the two weeks were up and it was decided whether the surgery was necessary.

Rudi came back after lunch, and I filled him in on what happened after he left that morning. He wanted to know why I went to the rehab hospital to talk to the doctor. I wanted to tell him all about God. I didn't. I didn't think it was the right time. I guess I was in the driver's seat when it came to deciding that. He had already noticed and commented on the peace I seemed to have about the situation. I should have told him then. I just told him I didn't want Tammy under the care of a doctor that wasn't more positive about her recovery. I believed Tammy needed positive attitudes around her.

I thought about letting P.J. and J.J. come in to see Tammy on the weekend. It might help if they talked to her. So much time had passed and I couldn't protect the boys from the hurt of seeing her anymore.

I told both Rudi and Rod (at separate times) I would cycle to the hospital to get my car that night. By the end of the day, I was finding myself unable to keep up with all that was happening. I referred to it as lack of time to pray. I knew cycling would help me to exert some of that negative energy.

They both understood and were each glad that the other one wasn't driving me. I couldn't fit my bike in the car when I got there. Rudi pulled in while I was trying. He just smiled and picked up the bike and put it in the back of his truck. He said he would pick me up the next day after supper and I could pedal home. Of course it didn't work that way. He was pretty creative. He did pick me up after supper and after we finished visiting with Tammy, I asked him for my bike, and he said, "Oh never mind, I will take you and the bike home–as if that wasn't planned.

The weekend came and P.J. was so excited to see Tammy. I decided to do this one at a time. It would be hard for P.J. to ask tough questions if J.J. was standing there and he were comparing the accidents. That wouldn't be fair to either one of them. Gail and Bill asked J.J. to come to their house for the day. He was really excited to do that but wanted to go to see Tammy. He didn't realize it was a set-up. I told him Tammy would understand if he went to Gail's and I would take him the following Saturday to see her. He was happy with that. I told P.J. on the way that Tammy was still in a coma like J.J. I also told him to talk to her. He was so emotional! The doctor and the pastor from the hospital both said they would meet us there to help with any questions. P.J. was crying before he even got to her room. He hadn't seen her in seven weeks. I felt guilty about this but didn't know what else to do. He had been hurt so many times. I just wanted to protect him from any more hurt. I knew I couldn't justify trying to protect the boys from the reality. I guess it is just a mother's nature.

He stood by her bed and tried to talk, but he was sobbing so uncontrollably. It broke my heart. I'm so sorry, I cried as I ran out of the room. I couldn't stand to see him hurt anymore. I got myself back under control, and when I went into the room, he was asking the doctor questions. The doctor handled the answers very well, not crushing P.J.'s hope. P.J. asked if Tammy could be handicapped like J.J. The doctor nodded his head, yes.

P.J. cried out, "Tammy, it doesn't matter. I will help you; just wake up!" At that comment the doctor left, and even the nurse had tears in her eyes. It was a very draining day.

I took P.J. out for lunch and let him spend the rest of the day at the hospital with me. He read to Tammy and tried to get Wrinkles to wake her up. Every once in a while, I could see him wiping away the tears. On the way home, he shared with me that he missed Grampa and Tammy so much.

The two weeks flew by, but there was absolutely no response from Tammy. Work was finished, and the boys were off for the summer. They were getting ready to go to a canoe camp for a week with Greg's church. Tammy's surgery was booked for first thing in the morning. When I went into her room, the nurse had her propped up and was shaving off her hair. All those long blonde curls were being shaved off to the skin but only on the one side. She may as well have done the whole head. She was going to but changed her mind. We put the other side in a pigtail. They wheeled her out of the room.

I just said, "Thank you God for breaking through the clot," even though it was strange that she was being wheeled out for surgery because the clot didn't break through.

At lunchtime they brought her back in the room. Rod was there to say good-bye. He was leaving but just wanted to wait until after the surgery. He said he would try to phone, and if he didn't get through, he would be back for a visit in two weeks. Rudi appeared in the middle of the good-bye and shook Rod's hand, and with a malicious smile on his face said, "She will be fine." Rod just left. It was an odd situation.

The neurologist came in to talk to Rudi and me. He said it was strange that he got the shunt in, but the clot had already broken through. She really didn't need it. I thanked God in my mind for breaking it through. The neurologist just said the shunt isn't hurting anything being there even though she didn't need it. I looked at the incision and didn't agree. It was a big scar on her stomach that ran up and down. He told us we would wait for a couple of hours for the drugs to wear off to see if there was any response from her. I sat on pins and needles talking to her.

By supper, there was still no response. The next morning we were told if she didn't wake up by now, he didn't see much hope. I had called the doctor at the rehab hospital to make arrangements to have Tammy moved.

Arrangements were made to transport Tammy by ambulance to the rehab hospital in two days.

That morning I came in early and started to pack up Tammy's belongings. Most of the things from the hospital were to keep her entertained. It was pouring rain, and I was hoping and praying the rain would stop before she was transported.

The ambulance attendants showed up early, and as they were wheeling Tammy down the hall, it started to rain so hard, you couldn't even see the cars in the parking lot out front. There was an overhang as they took her out the doors, but it still didn't totally keep her from getting wet. They were loading her into the back of the ambulance. I was starting to get upset watching the rain hit her in the face. I guess she was too because all of a sudden, they had her half way in the ambulance and her eyes popped open, and she gave them a look that would scare even a grown man. I was so shocked to see her eyes open. They asked the nurse if she thought maybe they should unload her and let the doctor see her. I told them no. I wanted her transported. The doctor at the rehab hospital could see her when they got there. I asked if she was alright, and they said she was fine. She was just staring at nothing. I didn't want to hear at that time from any doctor that it was just a reaction because of the rain. They left and I followed.

When we got there, I parked and ran to the ambulance as they unloaded her. I wanted to see if her eyes were still open. I could swear she looked at me when they pulled her out. Then her eyes closed. The doctor checked her right away and just told me to wait and see what comes from this. I sat around so long waiting, but she didn't wake up. I had to leave to get back home with the boys. Rudi said he would stick around for a while longer.

The next morning, I was getting ready to ride my bike to the hospital. I called to find out if there was any response from Tammy during the night. They said they had a problem. She was in a private room right across from the nurses station, and the nurse was sitting doing paperwork. She said she heard Tammy scream. My heart stopped when I heard that. When she went to the room, Tammy was in a real state. Her blood pressure started to drop, and it was touch and go for a bit. They were now monitoring her very closely. I put the bike aside and jumped into my car. I drove there right away scared of what they told me.

I got to her room, and the doctor was with her. Her blood pressure had been getting better since the incident during the night. I asked what could have caused it, and he just shook his head. He didn't know. I asked if it could be because she was waking up? He shrugged his shoulders and shook his head again. He said they would be watching her very closely.

Pastor Ron came in and prayed again about her stay in the hospital. He prayed no evil be allowed near her and that she would be kept safe from any harm. He asked for guidance for all the therapists and doctors dealing with Tammy and that only God's will be done.

Janet came in and suggested I come and work at the speedway on Tuesday nights for a break. They would pay me twenty dollars to come and work the back gate and the tower. Racing had already started, but I put my car up for sale and it sold the same day. Rudi told me he had sold his car, hauler and all the equipment that went with it. I told Janet I would think about it.

I spent the next couple of weeks sitting Tammy up in her wheelchair with the tray on the front telling her that Wrinkles needed his bone; he was really hungry. Her eyes were opening most of the time she was up, but she wasn't staring at anything in particular.

I just kept telling her, "Tammy, Wrinkles is sooooo hungry. Give him his bone." Then I would put Wrinkles on my hand and let him talk.

He would beg her. "Tammy, I can't reach my bone. Can you give it to me, I am so hungry."

This went on well into July. Finally one day, I went in the morning, and in tears, put Wrinkles on my hand, sat him on the tray, put the bone in front of him on the tray and with tears dripping, got Wrinkles to again ask for the bone.

Tammy looked at Wrinkles and with the look as if to say, "Anything to shut you up," reached for the bone. She was shaking so badly. She managed to pick up the bone and put it in his mouth.

I yelled for the nurse and she came running with the doctor. I said to Tammy, "Don't make a liar out of me." I knew she understood me.

Wrinkles then said, "Tammy give me my bone, I am hungry."

She picked up the bone and put it in Wrinkles mouth. The doctor put Wrinkles on his hand and told Tammy to pick up the bone and put it in Wrinkles pocket. With deep concentration and effort, Tammy then picked up the bone and tried to put it in Wrinkles apron pocket.

The doctor then stood up and said, "She's on her way back!"

Those were the words I so badly wanted to hear. I just wanted to tell the boys, but they were on a canoe trip with the Boys' Brigade. She couldn't talk but the doctor said she wouldn't be able to talk because of when the respirator tube was pushed in her throat. It went through her vocal chords and damaged them. They would teach her another way to communicate. He suggested we not get ahead of ourselves.

When Rudi came in later, we sat all evening playing with Tammy and the Wrinkles puppet. We made Wrinkles do lots of crazy things trying to get Tammy to smile. She was focusing, but had no reaction on her face. It was hard to tell what she knew.

Rudi drove me home. We stopped and talked for a while. It seemed just like it was before. We were getting along great and were growing so close together over those three months. He was glad Rod was gone for the summer. There were lots of times he was taking me home in the evening when I knew he was going to kiss me, and I would either quickly turn away or just happen to think of something and start to talk again. It wasn't that I didn't want to. He was still living with Helena, as far as I knew, and I just didn't want to be thinking of that when I did kiss him.

I did start to work at the track on Tuesday nights. The first night I was there, I was up in the tower lap counting. A young blonde girl came into the tower. I just assumed she was going to be the trophy girl for the night. She was there to sing the American and Canadian National Anthems. Before she started she asked, who was Tricia Hardt? I looked at her surprised. I told her I was. She introduced herself and told me she was Staci, Pastor Ron and Donna's daughter. With such a down south accent, I should have known. She picked up the microphone and belted out the two anthems with such a voice that all of us stood in shock. She could really sing.

Yvonne, the daughter of the owner of the Speedway was sitting next to me and just said, "Beautiful and can sing too, how unfair is life?"

We all laughed. After she finished the song, she said she would be in to see Tammy more often now that she was on summer break. She leaned down and whispered to me that the whole family was in her prayers every day and to keep believing Tammy would make a full recovery.

She was just a young teenager but seemed so grown up spiritually, physically and mentally. She had come to the track with her parents, so during the intermission, I met Donna. I felt I had already known her so well; we had talked so much on the phone. The next day, Rudi came in early. He came everyday, normally in the evening. He had a lot of work and was having a hard time getting there during the day. He spent an hour watching while I propped Tammy up in the wheelchair and gave her a haircut. The hair was starting to grow in on the other side, and it looked so terrible to have the other side always in a braid or pigtail. I cut it off even and she looked like she had a crew cut. It would grow out even now. I brought her some of her own clothes and started to dress her every morning. I thought it would help. She was awake and focused, but I never really knew then if she recognized me.

When Rudi was leaving, he asked if I would consider coming with him. He was going to check out a job and would be about an hour. If all went well, he was coming back to spend the rest of the day with Tammy and me. I told him I wanted to get Tammy dressed. He waited.

The job was out on the other side of the city. As we were driving, I noticed he was wearing the aftershave I always liked on him. I hadn't noticed at the hospital, he was dressed so nice and not in paint clothes. His hair was cut and he was shaved.

Rudi was very quiet for the first ten minutes. I knew he wanted to say something but was afraid. Finally he just blurted it out.

"I still love you and really want to work this out."

I played dumb (wanting to make sure I understood what it was he wanted to work out). He said he was stupid to do what he did in the first place.

I asked what he meant.

He said, "Sleeping with Helena." He just continued talking and I listened. He was devastated that he got drunk and woke up in her bed. She manipulated him and if that wasn't bad enough, he was worse for having fallen for her game. When he woke up in her bed, he was sick thinking he had done the unforgivable. He cheated on me. He asked me if I could imagine how he felt living with a woman that would go after a married man.

I told him, "No," and wouldn't even want to think about how it felt.

He said he just wanted to turn back the clock and change it, but he always thought it was too late.

I never answered. He stopped by the river and poured us both a coffee from his thermos. I asked him if he really had to check on the job.

He admitted he had taken the day off to talk to me and just used that as an excuse to get me out of the hospital. He hated going home. He just wanted to work it out with me. He never loved Helena and couldn't love her. Even after living with her all that time, his feelings didn't change. She was still his maid and bottle washer, and she cooked his meals and washed his clothes. He said he would go to bed at night and leave his dirty clothes on the floor. When he woke up in the morning, they were clean and folded ready for him to put on.

I started to laugh and said, "Well that won't happen with me."

He was very quick to answer that isn't what he wanted from me. He said he loved me and the relationship was everything. He missed our conversations and the fact that I never ran out of things to talk about. He missed the friendship. He was never bored with me, and that I was always full of surprises. He then said he didn't want to not mention that I was easy to look at first thing in the morning. (I didn't know what he meant by that but I assumed it was a compliment.) He said he missed the kids and the hockey games and he loved the boys.

I asked, "Why then did he stop seeing them and why did you not help support them without so much hassle in court?"

He answered with "I just didn't want you to make it without me." He said he always just wanted me to call him and say, "Please come home, I don't want to live without you; I can't make it without you."

I told him that was really sick thinking. I knew it was time to tell him about my being a Christian and what that meant. I could make it without him, but I couldn't make it without God. I didn't know how he was going to react to that, so I looked at my watch and said I really wanted to get back to the hospital. I thought I would tell him on the way back, and if it didn't go well, at least with every minute, I would be closer to the hospital and wouldn't have so far to go if he threw me out of the truck.

I was quiet while we drove back and silently prayed for courage, wisdom and the words to say to him. I was clued out on how to do this. I have never really told anyone the details up to that point. Finally I just said, "I am a Christian."

He said, "What?"

I said, "I believe Christ died on the cross for our sins to be forgiven. I have received His sacrifice on the cross as payment for my sins. That makes me a Christian. I believe what is written in the Bible."

His answer really threw me. He actually used my statement as an open door. He said, "If what you say is true, then you have to believe that our marriage is not supposed to end. I am truly sorry for what I did, and you have to forgive me."

I said, "Yes, a part of me just wants to forget all that happened and pick up from where we left off. The other part of me is more cautious and wants to date first and insist you move out of her house and make it on your own, so you aren't bouncing from house to house."

He surprised me when he answered, "That is more than fair. I will move out of her house totally and get a place. We will date until you are comfortable and the trust is built up."

I agreed. We pulled into the hospital parking lot and with a big smile on his face he asked me for a date. He asked if he could take me out for supper to a nice restaurant.

I said, "Yes."

We both spent some time with Tammy. We watched her therapy, and then in the middle of the afternoon, Rudi had to go.

I said to him, "I thought you had the day off?"

He laughed and said, "I do, but I have a big date tonight so I have to get ready."

I suggested I would catch a ride with him if he didn't mind. I had to get ready too.

When he dropped me off at the house, I asked him if he wanted a cup of coffee for the road. He came in and checked out the apartment. He was surprised. He hadn't been there before and didn't realize how big it was. He said when his finances were straightened out; he would be building me the house of my dreams. I told him to slow down.

He leaned over and asked, "Is this too fast?" He kissed me. I didn't resist this time. I think I really wanted to know how I felt when he did. His kiss was very convincing–convincing enough for me to tell him to leave before I did something I would regret later. He just laughed and said, "It isn't like we aren't married."

I was very confused when he left and phoned Pastor Ron. I told him what was happening, and he was glad I was honest with Rudi about being a Christian. He reminded me that we were still married and belonged together. He warned me not to let the enemy deceive me. Helena was in the wrong not me. I had nothing to feel guilty about. She was living and sleeping with a married man. Rudi was cheating on me. It had to stop before I could have peace of mind about Rudi and me. He said what I was doing was being a woman and wooing the man. I felt guilty about not spending the time with Tammy. He told me Staci and him would spend some time with her and that I should have a really good time with Rudi that night.

I put on a dress and felt pretty good. Then I stood in front of the mirror thinking that maybe the dress was a little too inviting, so I took it off. Just before he pulled up, I thought of what Pastor Ron said about wooing the man and quickly changed back into the dress. I could tell by Rudi's reaction when he walked in, that the dress worked. We talked and laughed all evening. I made a comment about too much wine with dinner and asked if he was trying to take advantage of me. I said it very innocently but noticed by his reaction, he took it personally. I apologized, and he told me not to be sorry. He always used that line until it actually happened to him. I knew he meant that he drank too much wine and ended up in bed with Helena. I got brave enough to ask him why Helena would do that. It seemed so desperate.

He said she had come to this country with two daughters. She couldn't speak the language, so when she met Rudi, she figured he would be perfect because he spoke her language. To her it obviously didn't matter that he was married. He admitted that it was really his problem that he was so stupid to fall for it. He was very angry with himself. I told him before it would ever work out with him and me, he would not only have to accept my forgiveness, he would have to forgive himself.

I knew when he dropped me off, he wanted to stay. I didn't even ask him in for a coffee because I was afraid he would stay. It wasn't that I didn't want him to, but I just thought we should take this slow. I really thought he had to move out of Helena's before we took any more steps. It was like he read my mind. He asked me if I would come with him the next evening to look at apartments. He wanted to move out of her house right away. He said he knew the sooner he did it, the sooner we could work it out. The boys weren't going to be back until the Sunday, so I was quite free to do whatever. We agreed to meet at the hospital and go from there. He would look in the paper to see what was close to my apartment.

The next morning, I woke up feeling pretty sure everything would work out for Rudi and me. He was going to call me before I went to the hospital. I was leaving a bit later because I had an early aerobics class. Afterwards, I had come home and sat down with a cup of coffee to do my devotions. I thanked God for Tammy's progress and all the positive developments that happened with Rudi and me the day before. I asked God to forgive me for anything I had done wrong and to bring it to my attention if I didn't remember. I prayed for blessings over the boys while they were on their canoe trip and for God to send His angels around them to keep them safe and free from all harm. Then I finished by asking Him to bless Helena and her daughters Petra and Sandra. I asked God to put people across their paths to share His Word with them and draw them closer to Him, so they start to believe. I had just written "Amen," knowing with faith it was done and closed my journal when the phone rang.

I was sure it was Rudi and answered with a bubbly Good Morning. It was Helena. I was shocked; her first words were, "Stay away from Rudi."

With a bit of a laugh in my voice, I reminded her he was my husband,

and she had no right to try to keep us apart. She asked then if he was with me, and I realized he didn't go back to her house the night before. That was a good thing. I tried to explain to her nicely that we were married, and Rudi made a mistake letting her manipulate him, but I forgave him. Also, we were going to try to work it out. I told her I was going to pray for God to put a man across her path that would be good for her and her daughters, but I was sure it wasn't Rudi.

She asked a tough question, "If there was a God, then why would he let J.J. and Tammy get hit by cars."

I was getting frustrated. I asked her if she wanted to go for coffee and talk. I knew that was stupid, but maybe I could explain everything better if we were face to face.

She said, "You are a terrible mother. Where are your kids?"

I answered her but knew I was just trying to defend the fact that the kids weren't with me. She knew where Tammy was and I informed her the boys were at a Christian Canoe Camp.

She said, "Well, I would never send my daughters out without me with them." Her tone was so scolding.

I was honest and told her I had to get off the phone, I was waiting for Rudi to call.

I could hear the desperation in her voice with her next warning, "If you are going to be with him, don't sleep with him."

I laughed again and firmly let her know I wasn't about to discuss with her my sex life with my husband.

She had such a hard, deep voice, and it got harsher as she played her trump card. "If you sleep with him, maybe we will both be pregnant and then what will he do?"

I was sure I had heard her wrong and asked her to repeat it.

As if I were a little kid, she spoke slowly, emphasizing each word, "I–am–pregnant." She didn't leave it at that. She said she had a test done, and it was a boy. She hadn't told Rudi yet, but was planning to tell him soon. She said he didn't need my boys anymore, she would give him his own.

By then I was crying so hard, I couldn't speak anymore. I thought that was probably the cruelest thing she could say, but I was wrong.

She kept twisting the knife, "Rudi said you ruined his daughter. Now she is retarded like her brother. Now I will make sure his new son is looked after."

I hung up the phone. I was so overwhelmed. I couldn't listen anymore. She had me. I was sobbing and out of control. The phone rang again and I grabbed it to tell her where to go. That was just how I felt. I put it to my ear and yelled, "Go to hell."

It was Rudi. He wanted to know what was wrong. He sounded really concerned and said he was coming over right away. I just told him to go back home to Helena and to look after his responsibilities there. I didn't say any more. I didn't want to talk to him. He was about to find out he was having a little boy. He could have his own like she said. I was sick to think he actually thought of Tammy and J.J. as retarded. We could never work it out. Helena would always have a hold on him with his son. We would never have peace. I hung up the phone on him and sat on the floor and sobbed for about half an hour. The phone kept ringing, and I just kept picking it up and hanging up. It hurt so much.

I had honestly thought we had a chance. I cried out to God asking Him why He let this happen. I was really glad the boys weren't home for all of this. They really wanted Rudi to come home for so long. They would have had their hearts ripped out in this too. It was enough that mine was, and I didn't want them to hurt the same way.

Rod came in on the weekend. I told him part of what was happening but not everything. I told him we really needed to take a breather from seeing each other until I sorted out my feelings. I just wanted to concentrate on Tammy getting better.

Pastor Ron and Donna both sat me down and gave me a lecture. I was not to allow what Helena said about me being a terrible mother get to me. Janet had her turn too. They all said what happened to Tammy was not my fault and I was a good mother. Everyone could tell me that, but a mother is expected to be 100% at looking after her children. That would mean that since Tammy and J.J. were hit by cars, I was not 100%. I know no one is perfect, but why couldn't I just make the stupid goof-ups with my kids like other mothers and not so extreme mistakes. I really did let Helena get to me. I was on a guilt trip and even angry with God for letting this happen. I realized I finally could admit that.

When the boys came back, they had so much to tell me about the trip. P.J. was telling me how the canoe tipped over and all the food was in the lake and how he saved J.J. That woke me up to the angels I asked God to send to keep them from evil. I finally started to come back to my senses. I let the enemy get to me. He used Helena to do it. I didn't hear from Rudi, and he never came back to see Tammy. I just chalked it up to the fact that he found out Helena was pregnant and he was so thrilled. He didn't want me or Tammy or the boys anymore. He had all he wanted coming–a son.

Chapter 20

LEARNING TO LEAN ON GOD

"With all your heart you must trust the Lord and not your own judgment. Always let him lead you and he will clear the road for you to follow." Proverbs 3:5–6

Tammy still had the tube in her nose for feeding but did start to swallow, so we could put soft Jell-o in her mouth with a syringe. The doctor had set a rule that if the food wasn't thin enough to go through the syringe, then she couldn't have it.

On the weekend was her twelfth birthday. I asked permission from her doctor to take her home for a party, thinking if there were a few people over that she knew, it might help to jog her memory. The doctor agreed that she could come home for the afternoon. I asked Sharon Sobey, Janet, and Gail to come. At lunchtime the boys came with me to pick her up. The wheelchair had to come apart in six pieces in order to be able to load it in my car. P.J. helped me get the wheelchair in the trunk and Tammy in the car.

We thought it would just be a quiet afternoon.

When we walked in the door, we got a shock. Sharron had planned a big surprise party with a clown and fifteen people that Tammy knew. I was afraid at first that the commotion would be too much, but she seemed to take most of it in. Margaret was there with the boys, Janet came, Gail and Keith, and so many more. There were hot dogs, cake and ice cream.

The clown was great. He spent his time making different animals out of balloons. Tammy was quite taken by him. Her eyes just kept following him around. We gave her some icing from the cake on her lip, and it was gone quite quickly. Everyone had gotten together and planned the gifts. Her bedroom was totally redone in pink. She even got a pink alarm clock, a ballerina picture with a pink frame, bedding and lots more. Tammy just kept watching everyone, but really didn't have any kind of reaction–not a smile or a frown, just kept looking.

After everyone ate we all went into the living room to watch the clown do his magic. We took Tammy out of the chair and let her sit on the couch with everyone else. The time seemed to fly by, and before we knew it, it was time to take her back to the hospital. I told everyone they could stay and party longer. Tammy started to fight me. She grabbed my arm and shook her head, "no." She didn't want to go back. She knew she was at home and knew what was going on and wanted to stay home. I started to cry when she grabbed my arm and was insistent. That was the first sign that she knew what was happening. I didn't want to take her back. I phoned the hospital, and the doctor said she could stay for another hour but had to be back for the tube feeding. I explained the situation and she nodded her head "yes," and actually had a smile on her face.

The hour passed too quickly. I had a hard time getting her in the car because she was fighting me so hard. She just wanted to stay home. I kept telling her as I was driving that I would talk to them and see if she could come back home. She was putting her hands together as if she was begging me. I cried all the way to the hospital.

The doctor met us there to see just how respondent Tammy was. He agreed, she knew what was happening, and it was probably the visit home that stimulated her. I asked if she *could* come home, but he shook his head. It was too soon. He told Tammy they would make arrangements for her to have home visits on weekends, but the apartment would have to be set up for me to look after her there. He told her she would have to stay at the hospital, so she could get her therapy. I offered to bring her in every day. Tammy nodded her head. Dr. Cameron said it would take some time, but they would figure something out.

Tammy then motioned me to give her a pen. I couldn't believe this was happening! We gave her a pen and paper. She was right handed but her right hand was paralyzed. She took the pen in her left hand and shaking quite badly, managed to print on the piece of paper the word school. She wanted to go back to school. Dr. Cameron just scratched his head and said, "Wow!" She could even spell properly! He remarked, "It must have been quite the home visit!" I got her settled down finally and went home. I cried all the way home thanking God for Tammy coming back.

The next morning the boys and I skipped church and went in to see her. P.J. asked her what she wanted us to bring from home. She put her hand up on her shoulder and started to dance around in the wheelchair. We started to laugh! "Your ghetto blaster?" She nodded her head, "yes." She got really good at playing charades, and we got really good at figuring it out. We asked her what kind of music she wanted us to bring. She put her hand to her throat as if she was dying then made a line in the air. She really hammed it up. I didn't have a clue what she was trying to say, but P. J. guessed, Dire Straights, and she shook her head hard. She wanted us to bring the Dire Straights tape. Then it was the Twisted Sister tape. P.J. started to laugh and said we really had to catch her up on the times; she was a little behind on her music. She knew her favourite movies and her favourite music. She just couldn't walk or talk. She made it very clear that she wanted to come home when we left, and that she didn't need diapers anymore.

The staff taped a picture board to the tray on her wheelchair so she could point to the appropriate picture when she had to go to the bathroom and when she was hungry. The doctor said the tube could come out of her nose as soon as she was eating and swallowing well enough. That only took two days. Every day she pestered us to go home and to go to school. I told her to pester the doctor when he came in. She motioned. He just turned away and then he didn't have to listen to her.

Therapy was every afternoon. They had come to the conclusion she wouldn't talk. They said they could teach her sign language, but it would take two hands and she only had the use of one. A signboard was made specifically for her needs. Other than that, we just kept playing charades.

The therapists began to set up the apartment for her to come home to visit on weekends. They placed bars in the bathtub and installed a lift. I could now place her in the tub and the lift would hold her above the water like a sling. I could help her wash without her head going under the water. The apartment had plenty of room for a wheelchair. They equipped a chair so she could maneuver with one hand. She was a maniac in the chair. She would race up and down the hall of the hospital as we were on our way to therapy.

During this time, Tammy's teacher from school sent work for her to do with the teacher at the hospital. Tammy made it very clear that she wanted to go back to school. The doctor prescribed such intense therapy every day so it didn't seem possible. I finally convinced him she should at least go to the school for half a day. The principal was quick to agree with me that they would take her back. He thought it was good for the other students as well as Tammy. They determined that everything she needed was on the main floor of the school. There was no reason for her to go to the second floor. That would be a problem since there was no elevator. The school division agreed to send a bus to the hospital everyday to take her in her chair and return her in time for lunch. She would make it back in time to have her therapy. We started right away and were amazed how fast everything fell into place.

Tammy really wanted to come home but understood she would just have to be patient. I told her I would take her home on weekends first, and then we would start to work on the rest of the time. I would have to reverse the procedure; she would go to school, then to the hospital for therapy, and back home. We could; but it would be quite the shuffle. I was hoping to work it into my afternoon run.

Rod came back. We both returned to work. We talked all the time, but I didn't want to be more than friends.

One evening, P.J. had to go to sign up for the next season of hockey. I was behind Mr. Sobey in the line-up. He asked me if I wanted some extra work. I asked what he had in mind. He said his company, Ram Messenger, had the contract to deliver the boxes of orders to the managers of The Avon Company. I could do it twice a month in the evening. It would only take a couple of hours, and the pay was good. I told him, "Sure," and he told me to stop in the office and see him when I got the chance during the week.

He registered his son, Sherritt and left. It was P.J.'s turn to register. We gave them all the information and I took my chequebook out. I knew this would be a hefty bill, but had prepared myself for it by doing extra aerobic classes. (Things were a little tighter in the summer because I was on unemployment.) I asked how much and picked up the pen. They said Mr. Sobey had just paid the bill for P.J. If that wasn't enough, I got back to the apartment and Sharron had dropped off almost all of Sherritt's equipment from the year before! Sherritt had grown so much over the summer that they had to replace almost everything. P.J. was thrilled to have such high quality equipment even though it was second-hand, and I really appreciated it. I had been praying for God to supply what P.J. needed for hockey.

Tammy came home for the first time that weekend. Talk about tiring, but we were so glad to have her home. It was a relief not having to run to the hospital. The boys played games with her at the table and listened to tapes. I was a little nervous during the night and thought I would see if the therapists could come up with some sort of system that Tammy could call me if she wanted me. I was afraid of her trying to get out of bed because she couldn't call me. When I expressed my concerns to Tammy the next morning, she motioned I should give her a baseball bat, and she could hit the wall if she wanted me! She loved her new room. Everything was pink. My mom even knitted her a pink afghan for the bed. That was her blanky, but it was our secret. She took it back and forth to the hospital with her.

During the week, I stopped in at the Ram Messenger Office to see Mr. Sobey about the run. His wife Sharron was there. She worked a couple of days a week in the office. The dispatcher was in the front, and I had to get through him to get in to see "The Boss."

The dispatcher was about six feet tall and had curly blonde hair. He had the look of the distinguished Englishman but was harsh to talk to. The job obviously kept him very occupied. It was hot in the office, and he had on a dress shirt opened at the neck and the long sleeves were rolled up. I thought to myself, there is one good-looking guy. I asked him if Mr. Sobey was around. As if I wasn't even there, he called Sharron. She came out and invited me to come in the office. The dispatcher just kept on working. I don't think he looked even once. I thought to myself, he was too young anyway, and I was married.

I was introduced to the people in the office, and most of them asked how Tammy was doing. They didn't know us but knew of Tammy's accident. Sharron introduced me to the dispatcher. His name was Gord Kell. He took a quick second from the microphone to say hello, but with an attitude.

Tammy was sent to school half days. The wheelchair school bus picked her up every day and brought her back for lunch, and then in the afternoon she had therapy at the hospital. Every weekend she came home.

We never saw or heard from Rudi. I was left to assume he was into his life with his pregnant girlfriend. I wasn't surprised when divorce papers were served to me. I gave them to my lawyer and told her I couldn't agree. I was married for better or for worse, and I couldn't agree to a divorce. He would have to fight me in court, which he ended up doing. I talked to Elaine quite often, but we never talked about Rudi. It was kind of an unspoken agreement that he was part of her family, and we shouldn't talk about him. There were lots of times I wanted to ask her when Helena was due or how she was doing with the pregnancy, but I decided against it. She must have been pretty close to forty years old, so I didn't think it would be easy for her to have a baby.

I was Christmas shopping in the mall between my runs one morning. I didn't go to the hospital in the morning anymore because Tammy was at school. I ran into Gunther's wife, Linda. She wanted to know how Tammy was doing. She asked me if Rudi ever saw the kids, or if he ever went to see

Tammy. I gave her all the details of what happened. I told her Rudi and I were so close to working it out, but then when Helena got pregnant it all changed.

Linda laughed and said, "Helena had her tubes tied and can't have anymore kids."

I tried to tell her she was wrong and asked her, "When was the last time you saw Helena?"

She said, "A week ago and she *definitely* wasn't pregnant. Helena has put on a bit of weight, but it isn't because she's pregnant."

I just stood in shock! I couldn't believe she could be so desperate to lie about something like that. The truth is, I didn't think I could be so gullible to fall for something like that. She told me an outright lie to stop Rudi and me from getting back together. I couldn't understand why any woman would want to be with a man who wanted to be with his wife. I walked around in a daze for a while wondering what I should do. Now I was being divorced, and it wasn't because Helena was pregnant. It was because I shut it down. I wanted to call Rudi and at least tell him why I said what I said. I went back to my van and rethought what I did say to him that day. I wonder what he was thinking when I hung up the phone on him. He couldn't have known why I said what I said to him. He must have thought I just changed my mind. I was so angry with myself for having been so deceived! I felt I had to at least try to explain it to Rudi, the reason why it all happened. I was so confused. I was picturing Helena laughing, thinking it was funny that I was stupid enough to fall for her game. I was angry that Rudi hadn't seen Tammy or checked on how she was doing. No matter what happened with him and me, that should never have anything to do with his relationship with his daughter. I was once told, "When in doubt, don't do anything." I definitely wasn't sure on how to handle it, so I decided to just pray and wait for an answer. I hoped I didn't have to wait very long.

I was still sewing for Sharron. I had made her quite a few clothes. I wanted to continue my pattern-designing course that I had taken, but I couldn't with Tammy in the hospital.

J.J. was having a problem with walking. The doctors said it was because he was growing and one leg was getting quite a bit longer than the other. The ball and socket in his hip was being worn down and we would have to look at surgery in the near future to rebuild the socket, or it could cause major problems. They suggested we wait for another six months then look at the situation again.

P.J. was deep into the hockey scene.

The kids were at respite one weekend when the phone rang, and it was Rudi. He asked me to meet him for coffee. I had to do an Avon run for Ram Messenger but told him I could meet him at a restaurant that was fairly close to the office. We would meet early, so it would give us an hour to talk before I had to go. Traffic just got in my way, and I was running about five minutes late. I was hoping he wouldn't think that I changed my mind because I wanted the opportunity to explain what happened that day.

He was sitting drinking coffee when I got there, and I sat across from him. He told me I looked good and asked how things were going. I asked him what he wanted to talk about.

He replied, "The divorce, why are you fighting it? The marriage is over. To fight the divorce is only costing both of us money."

I laughed and told him, "I have legal aid, so it's not costing me any-thing."

He wanted to know why I was making it so difficult.

I asked him if he knew why I said what I said on the phone that day.

He answered that he figured I just really thought about it and realized I couldn't forgive him for what he had done.

I told him no and went right on telling him about the phone call from Helena.

He said, "No way," and didn't believe she could be that desperate to keep us apart.

I reminded him of how her desperation—and him being so gullible—ruined our marriage in the first place.

He was quiet and again shook his head, "No way." He then asked why I was now bringing this up. Why didn't I tell him back then? I told him I had my heart torn up enough times with him and Helena and I just didn't want to talk about it. Besides, what was there to talk about? If she was really pregnant and it was a boy, would he really have left her for me? Besides, I just found out that she really wasn't pregnant and it was all a desperate lie.

He then said she was too old to get pregnant. He was apparently hav-ing trouble believing Helena could be that frantic, and I really didn't care.

I cried all my tears over this situation and it didn't matter anymore. I reminded him I was a Christian and had accepted Christ into my life and with that I didn't have a right to divorce. God didn't intend for us to divorce. He was obviously having a problem grasping all of this, and I had to leave. As I was getting my jacket on, I made it clear that it really didn't matter if he believed me or not. I knew what Helena had told me on the phone and how desperate she was. "Helena knows what she said and the game she played to keep us apart, but most important is that God knows exactly, word for word what was said, so nothing else matters." I told him I had no intention of agreeing to a divorce, and if he insisted on following it through that it was his problem and not mine. I walked out quite calmly. I could see he was confused.

As I was driving to Ram Messenger, I again became angry with myself for allowing Helena to play me for a fool the way she did. At least I got the chance to tell my side of the story to Rudi.

When I pulled up to the loading dock, Gord was there. He was dressed quite rough compared to when I saw him in the office, but I don't think it mattered how he was dressed, he was still really good looking. He started to hand me the boxes to load into the back of the van. I was trying to keep the numbers in sequence because I was told it was easier to find the addresses that way. I couldn't keep up with him, and at one point I turned around to take the next box from him. He dropped it in my hands and let go thinking I had a grip on it, but it fell down between the loading dock and the bumper. I grabbed my finger because as the box slid down, it bent my fingernail back and it snapped off.

Gord just said that is what I get for letting my nails get too long.

I just answered "Whatever," and kept loading the boxes purposely getting faster to keep up with him. It was obvious I had been challenged and felt pressured into proving my ability. I don't think he noticed that he put me in a bad mood. I don't think he really cared either.

On the run, I got lost a couple of times and forgot to drop off one box, so I had to go back. All I had to do was call Gord and ask him where the address was, but I decided Hell would freeze over before I would break down to ask him for anything.

I survived and thought to myself, it would get easier every time I did it. Also, I just had to remember the extra money would help

Time flew by and before I knew it, it was time for Christmas shopping and the boys' birthdays. I had made arrangements for the hospital to have Tammy released for the birthdays and for four days at Christmas. She was getting better going back and forth.

At first it was such heartbreak to take her back to the hospital after having her home for the weekend because she always fussed to stay. She couldn't actually cry. She could make the motions that she would be upset but lost the ability to cry in the accident. There were never any tears. I prayed for

God to heal her in that area because I couldn't imagine a girl growing up and not being able to cry.

Her reading got better; she could pretty well remember everything she knew before but of course couldn't talk or walk. She loved being back in school even if it was just mornings, and her friends and the teachers were great with her. I bought her new clothes that were easier for her to put on with the wheelchair and take off to go to the washroom.

We were still running to P.J.'s hockey games. Tammy really wanted to go to one of his games, so I told her he was going into a tournament over the Christmas break and we would take her to some of those games when she was at home.

One weekend, Tammy was home and in bed sleeping already. P.J. came in and asked if he could stay out past his usual ten o'clock. He said he was at the rink with a bunch of the boys. I told him no, and he was really upset. I told him I had both J.J. and Tammy at home, and I didn't want to be fighting with him. Wrong answer.

I was astounded when he came back with, "Just because J.J. and Tammy were both handicapped, I am going to have to suffer for it and have to be treated like a little kid." It was surprising to hear this coming from P.J. I thought about whether my answer would be different if Tammy and J.J. weren't handicapped. P.J. was only thirteen years old, and I came to the conclusion "no." I still wouldn't let him stay out until eleven. He was aiming to put me on a guilt trip and did a fine job. I caved and let him stay out for the extra hour.

When eleven o'clock came there was no sign of P.J. I panicked. At eleven fifteen, I was getting sick with worry and anger. I couldn't phone any of his friends because it was too late. Finally at midnight I called the police. I told them the situation and said I couldn't go looking for him because I had Tammy and J.J. at home. The officer remembered Tammy's accident and promised he would mention this to the officers in our area and they would watch for him. That was all he could do for now as I couldn't report him missing for twenty-four hours. I thanked him and prayed that God would keep him safe no matter where he was. I called back at one in the morning and the officer said there was no sign of him yet. P.J. didn't come home and I didn't sleep all night.

The next day, he still wasn't home, and I phoned all of his friends that he normally hung around with. They hadn't seen him. I had to take Tammy back to the hospital a bit early. I was just too tired and was out looking for P.J.

I had to keep Tammy and J.J. in the car with me, and it was just too hard on them.

By suppertime, I had gotten pretty panicky and didn't know what to do anymore. I took J.J. with me and went down to the police station. They let me make a report a bit early, but only because I insisted and told them he was gone since seven the night before.

I didn't tell them I talked to P.J. later in the evening.

I did doze off some time during the night on the couch, but was sick with worry. I got up the next morning at about four and called missing persons again. He was only thirteen years old. He couldn't be gone for the whole weekend without someone hearing from him.

J.J. went to school. I tried to keep what was happening from him, but he kept asking where P.J. was. I had to do my run. There was no one to replace me so late. I was on my way into the Society with a full load of kids when over my two-way, I got a message to call this number right away about P.J. I called and was told P.J. was there, and he was all right. I dropped off the kids and went to the address given right away.

It was so good to see P.J. sitting there unharmed. I asked him where he was all weekend. I was relieved but angry.

A lady came out of one of the offices and told me to come in.

I told P.J. to come in too.

He said, "No."

I insisted. I asked what was going on and followed her into the office.

She introduced herself as a social worker, and then immediately began telling me what had happened. "P.J. had taken off with six of his friends for the weekend. All seven boys came in to see me this morning because they were too scared to go home and face their parents."

I thought to myself that they had reason to be scared if all the boys put their parents through the same as I had been through the last two days.

She then asked, "Why would he be so afraid?"

I was frustrated when I answered, "I can't speak for the other parents. I don't even know who P.J. was with for the weekend. He is gone for two days, and I have no idea where he is or if he is even lying hurt somewhere. I was so worried, I even reported him to the police as a missing person. Now you tell me he was just out hanging around some friends. In my opinion, I would think he has a good reason to be afraid to face me. He knows he will be disciplined for this."

"He will *not* be disciplined." She said with a very stern tone. "He is sorry for what he did, and you have no right to put fear into your child. P.J. has rights too."

I then told her I was taking P.J. home; he was going to be grounded. I then told P.J. to move it out the door. He didn't argue. He knew I was really angry.

When I got home, I told P.J. he was grounded for two weeks. He could go to hockey practice and the games, but I would drive him there and back. I asked him whom he was with for the weekend, and he named boys that I never heard of before. He told me he met them at school.

I had asked some of the parents at the game if they had heard of the boys P.J. had been with. They told me the ringleader, Chris, was really bad news and had been known to set cats on fire or to skin them. I couldn't believe P.J. could be a part of any of that. I asked him about this, and he just said he loved animals, and this was all a lie. I left it at that.

I had started to see Rod again. I saw him every day at work. He was coming skiing with me between runs. He also started to do different things with P.J. I was hoping it would help with the situation. It did. P.J. really liked Rod. They would go skiing together and Rod would take him to some of his games and practices.

One morning, I got a phone call from a friend of mine that worked for an auto spring company in the city. He said he worked on my old Firebird that day and put in new springs. I told him I had sold it to the transportation manager's son. He asked me why the car repairs were billed to SMD. I couldn't believe it. There was so much money donated to Society, and half of the time we were told there wasn't enough money for clubs and different things for J.J. And now Tammy would be in need of SMD. I asked if he was sure, and he said yes, he had done the work himself.

After the dispute I had just gone through with the social worker about P.J. and all the fighting I had done in court with Rudi, I had had enough. I thought about what I had learned in the scriptures about unfairness and could only come up with a saying I had heard several times, "Life isn't always fair." If I allowed these things to happen and didn't do anything about it, would that be right? What if it wasn't true? I could probably approach my boss one on one to see if these things were true. There was too much of a risk I would be fired. I couldn't afford to lose my job. I had to support my kids. I decided to call the newspaper and talk to a reporter. I explained everything I had heard to the reporter and told her I couldn't confirm it, but she could. I told her if it were true, something should be done. I also said I couldn't have my name mentioned because I had two handicapped children and was a single parent and couldn't afford to lose my job. She promised me she would look into the accusation, and if it were true, she would make sure my name wasn't mentioned. I left it at that.

Two days later, I was on my way to work. I noticed when I stopped for a red light, the two newspaper holders on the corner of the street. The Free Press caught my eye. It said something about Society for Manitobans with Disabilities on the front page. I looked for another newspaper box and stopped to pick up the paper. Half of the front page was covered with the story. I was sick when I read it. Yes, it was confirmed; it was true. SMD money was used to repair the car. As I read the article, I knew I was in trouble. They kept their promise and didn't use my name, but they had said a tip came from someone whose name couldn't be used because she was employed with SMD but had two handicapped children and couldn't afford to lose her job. They may as well have put my name in flashing lights.

I was scared to pull into the lot when I got to work. My boss was standing there waiting for me. She was the mother of the boy who bought my car. Once the kids were unloaded, all of my belongings were literally thrown out of the van on the parking lot and I was told I was fired. I started to cry and Rod got out of his van and started to pick up my stuff. He was told if he helped me or gave me a ride anywhere, he was fired too. I told him it wasn't worth it and went into the building. The teachers were all shocked. I had been there for nine years, and no one could believe this was happening. The teachers called me a cab. Rod handed me money and put my stuff in his van. He told the boss if she had a problem with that she could fire him. He didn't care. I told the taxi driver to take me to the Children's Rehab. I wanted to see Tammy.

She wasn't there when I got there. She was still at school. I was so shocked; I just needed to get myself together before she got back. The nurses were great. They got me a coffee and sat and talked. It was on the news. I was so angry with myself for going to the papers, but I knew if I didn't do it, the scam could just keep going on and that wasn't right. I asked God what the plan was for me now. Here I was with three kids. Two were handicapped and two had birthdays coming.

I convinced myself I was stupid to do what I did. I talked to the reporter and asked her why she would ever print it the way she did. She apologized and I could tell she was sincere, sorry I lost my job.

I managed to hold it together long enough to see Tammy. Rod showed up. He had just enough time to take me home before he had to be back for his lunchtime run. Janet talked to me on the phone for a long time that night to try to convince me there was a good reason for all of this happening and I just had to be patient to find out what it was. Pastor Ron and Donna said they would pray for God's guidance as to what He wanted me to do with my life and also for God to provide for the kids and me. They said when one door closes, another would open.

I spent the next three days in tears and stopped long enough to go see Tammy. I didn't want her to know I was upset about anything. She was doing really well. J.J. was just quiet and I could tell P.J. was worried about how we were going to make it. I kept telling him God must have something better for me to do in my life.

It was a real problem that I no longer had the van. I thought I could bring Tammy home soon and she could come with me in the afternoon and I could take her to therapy between my lunchtime runs.

I looked in the newspaper for jobs, but anything that I qualified for just was impossible. What would I do with the kids when they were off for summer and spring term break? I finally gave in and gave up. I didn't want to get out of bed in the morning.

Pastor Ron called and asked if we wanted to come to church with them on Sunday morning then go to their house for lunch, and make sure I bring Tammy. She was eating really well on her own, so I accepted their offer. He said the wheelchair wouldn't be a problem. They would handle it. Rod stayed in touch. He phoned me quite often and always told me I was too smart to stay down too long. I sure didn't feel it. Sharron must have passed the word around that I was off work because I started to get an awful lot of phone calls to make clothes for people. I thought about finishing my course on pattern design and take one on designing–learning colours, etc. I thought maybe I could paint. I kind of chuckled through my tears as I thought maybe I would go and apply at Rudi's company to paint for him.

I pulled myself together and brought Tammy home for the weekend. On Sunday morning, I put on her Sunday best, and the boys helped me get her and her wheelchair in the car. We met Pastor Ron, Donna and Staci at the Church. We took Tammy out of the wheelchair and put her in one of the chairs at the church, so the wheelchair wouldn't be a problem. The music in the church was exceptional and the kids loved it.

The sermon was on getting my eyes off of people and problems and putting them on God. This was a real turning point for me. I don't recall any of the scriptures that were mentioned, but I do remember the pastor talking about joy not being based on our circumstances. To quit looking at the problem and focus on God and see what He had in store for us. It was almost directed at me. Even in all that is happening, get my eyes off of it and look to God and He will show me what He wanted me to do. I will never forget that day. I was definitely in the place God put me. I was determined to put my confidence in God from that point on. When I walked out of the church, I was floating. None of my problems mattered anymore. I was focused, and I would be looked after and provided for.

We had a great lunch at Donna and Pastor Ron's. Staci entertained the kids while I talked and prayed with Donna. There was so much power in her prayer, and I wanted to be able to do that some day. I wanted to be an ambassador for Christ. I realized my foundation was just being built, and God wasn't finished working on me yet. As a matter of fact, I felt like He just started. I didn't want to just sit and be blessed anymore. I wanted to be a blessing in people's lives. I felt so good.

I started to be more constructive and thorough in my devotions in the mornings. I believed if I let God work in my life regardless of what He chose, it would always be for my best. Christmas was coming. All I really had left to do was sew and aerobics. I continued with that, but I had to stop delivering for Ram Messenger because I didn't have the van anymore. Money was starting to become tight. The rent didn't matter because it was on a fluctuating scale. If I made no money, I paid no money. Tammy's expenses were getting high so I had gotten a lawyer. This time I got John Scurfield. I was told he was the best, and I was glad when he said he would take her case. He understood the bind I was in and stepped on the insurance company to reimburse me intermittently, so I could at least keep up. I just kept my eyes on God and believed He would look after us and give us a good Christmas.

Sharron had suggested I come up with some designs, simple yet something everyone would want to buy for someone for Christmas. I went down to the fabric store and found a fleece material that was clearing out. I made a pullover top and called it "the cozy." It had a drawstring bottom and a rollover collar. I had a flower decal in the drawer and put it on the collar. I gave it to Sharon and made a pair of black tights to go with it. She really liked it. So did I, but the quality wasn't so good because I really needed a serger to finish the inside edges properly. The next day we went to see a dealer for the Bernina Company. The sergers were fairly expensive, but Sharron said she would buy it and I could barter it off in time by making her clothes. I agreed. Now she had suggested I make a few of the tops and tights in different colours, and some shoe bags, and then get a table at the craft show that was coming up in a week at the community club. The table cost me fifteen dollars I did just what she suggested. I made four different colour tops in a few different sizes and took them to the show. I had picked up a couple of pieces of remnants in velvet and made shoe bags. The people could order what they wanted in whatever colour and size, and I would guarantee them for Christmas. It shouldn't be a problem. I had lots of time on my hands. The orders would have to be paid, 50% up front and the balance paid when they picked it up. The things I made were quick to make and very simple, especially with the new serger.

On the day of the Craft Show, I got up early and packed everything. Sharron was meeting me at the show to help me set up. There were about twenty-five tables setting up when I got there. Mine was the first one. I became very intimidated as most of the tables were beautifully set up with Christmas decorations. I didn't even bring a tablecloth. I laid out the clothes I had and the shoe bags in rows on the table and that was it. My focus was really off and I didn't have any confidence sitting at that table. I just wanted to run leaving it all behind. I quickly asked God for mercy in this situation and thanked Him for confidence and peace.

Then the doors opened and the people started to come in. I was surprised how many people there were. I wasn't one who would go to Craft Shows, so I never really knew how it was done or how successful they were. I was just taking Sharron's suggestion on how to make extra money for Christmas. Since I was set up right in front of the door, the people came to my table first. It was a good thing that Sharron offered to help because everyone was ordering and I could hardly keep up with writing receipts for their deposits and writing down what size they wanted and what colour. By noon I was getting nervous. I leaned over and asked Sharron how I was going to fill all these orders in the next four and a half weeks till Christmas. She laughed and said not to worry about it.

I answered, "Alright." and just kept writing orders. There was so much money sitting on the table from the deposits, I finally asked Sharron to put it in her purse. I didn't have any idea how much there was. I told her I had to go and get material and supplies to do all the sewing. She stated that is what the deposits were for. By the end of the day, there was a lot of money and I had no idea how much I had, how much the supplies would cost, or how much of the money would be for me in the end. I just knew I had better get to work.

On Monday, I sat back and figured out how much fabric I needed in each colour and added extra to make Christmas presents for my family and friends. It was a lot of work. That afternoon, I bought everything I needed, so I would know how much money was left from the deposits.

I was surprised how much money was left after everything was purchased to make all the clothes that were ordered. I even found a place to buy serger thread quite inexpensively, and it was a good match to the fabric. I got started right away, cutting out all the tops and tights. I was running my own sweatshop, but I was the only worker and kept going from station to station to do the next thing. I worked all morning, and went to see Tammy in the afternoons then back on the machines right after supper. I usually only worked until around nine o'clock, but it was getting quite evident, at that pace, I wouldn't get all the orders done before Christmas. I had to work later.

Sharron and her husband Rick asked me if I would help with the company Christmas party. They were having the office staff come to the house for cocktails and hors d'oeuvres. Then they were going out to the theatre to see a show and back to the house for the dinner and an evening of entertainment. I was supposed to serve the hors d'oeuvres, and then while they went to the show, I was to clear up the dishes and get everything ready for the dinner to be served. They had offered to pay me quite well, and I accepted. It was made very clear to me that when all this was done, I was to join in on the party as one of the guests. I had one week to prepare myself for it.

I didn't have too much confidence in myself and also I had nothing appropriate to wear. I rummaged through material I had, found a royal blue jersey, and decided to make myself a cocktail length dress with a full skirt with long sleeves and very fitted on the top. I fussed with the dress for two days and got fed up with it. I found it amusing how I could do something like this for a customer without any trouble, but when it came to making something for me, I just never felt good about myself when I wore it.

On the morning of the party, I was desperate and worked on the dress again. I did finish it on time, but really didn't want to wear it.

There was no other choice. I knew by my lack of confidence, I had issues that had to be dealt with on the inside. I don't think I remember feeling that I was ever "Good Enough" when it came to dealing with people that I thought were "better" than me. It wasn't Sharron or Rick that by whom I was intimidated. They always made me feel comfortable. It was the proper protocol of serving a dinner like this that had me concerned.

Sharron came over in the afternoon to check it out and threatened if I didn't wear it, she would. She thought it was great and very appropriate. That helped. I went to their house early to make sure I knew exactly what was expected of me. I was quite organized when everyone came. I had met most of the people previously, so I wasn't as anxious as I thought I was going to be. Gord walked in the door. He was dressed in a blazer and casual dress pants. I thought he was good looking at the office but was really a looker now. He was pleasant enough, very polite, but he came across as if he had to be nice to me because I was a friend of the boss's wife.

By the time the guests were ready to leave for the program, I had finished setting out the dishes for the dinner and cleaning up after the hors d'oeuvres. So Sharron and Rick suggested I join them. They had rented a bus to pick everyone up to go to the program. I accepted though I felt a bit out of place.

I had to wonder if I was being set up by Sharron. I was sure that was what was happening when the seating arrangements in the bus and the theatre had me sitting next to Gord. It was fun. Gord was a real gentleman. Always holding the door and waiting till I sat first.

I cleaned up the dishes and joined everyone downstairs while they were talking and playing pool. I felt a little uncomfortable with the situation so just sat in a chair in front of the pool table to watch them play. Gord decided to play and every time he went to shoot, it seemed like he was facing me.

I just kept thinking, good looking and a gentleman. It was really too bad he was younger than me. Sharron told me he just finished taking agriculture at the university and started working for Ram Messenger after he graduated. I was thirty-three at that time and was sure he would be around twenty-eight. I was considered over the hill to him. At twenty-eight, I couldn't understand why he wasn't taken yet. He had never been married, and I was pretty sure he could have had any girl he wanted.

It was quite late and I thought everyone had already left. Sharron and I were sitting in the eating area nibbling on the leftover shrimp when the basement door opened and Gord and Rick came in. Gord joined us eating the shrimp while Rick poured him another drink. The four of us talked for quite a while. Then, Gord asked if I was ready to go. I looked at him surprised. He offered to walk me to my car. It was about thirty below outside, but it didn't stop us from talking for fifteen minutes outside. I was really hoping he would ask me to go for coffee, but he didn't. I just went home.

The closer we got to Christmas, the later I worked. I was pulling almost all-nighters to get through the orders. They were piled all over the apartment. The tree wasn't up yet, and I was in no way ready for Christmas. Some nights I worked in tears, I was so tired but had a big responsibility and had to get it done. I finally set a goal to have everything finished by the week before Christmas, including having the sewing room closed up and clean, and also to take two weeks off at Christmastime to spend with the kids. The goal was reached three days early, and I finally put up the tree. I sat back staring at the tree wondering how I ever made it in the past without a personal relationship with God. I could almost imagine what kind of mess I would be in if I didn't have Him in my life now. No matter what the problem was, big or small, I could ask for His help. I was learning that in order to have an intimate relationship with God, the desire had to come from the heart, not the head. I was really tired but still hadn't done any Christmas shopping, so I just prayed for more strength and wisdom and set the rule to "do the next thing." Whenever I thought I wanted a break, I just said no and did the next thing. It seemed to work.

I put money in the bank for January to secure myself and took what I had left to buy Christmas presents for the kids. There was a big smoke damage sale I had heard about at a warehouse. I went there to see if I could stretch the Christmas budget a bit further and put more under the tree. I got lots of good things, but the money was just not going as far as I wanted it to. I still had to buy groceries.

Five days before Christmas, I was taking stock of what was in the cupboards and pulled out some soup to give to the Cheer Board. The same afternoon, Gail told me the company she worked for was putting together a hamper for an unfortunate family, so I decided to add the soup to their hamper.

The next day I started to see the Christmas miracles happen. I was just getting ready to leave the apartment with my list of shopping when there was a couple standing at my door with two boxes. They said Merry Christmas and informed me the boxes were from the Cheer board. I started to cry and asked who put my name in. They said probably the Social Worker, if I had one. There was a chicken and cans of fruit and vegetables, soup, cookies, so much. There was even a gift for each of the kids. I looked at the cans of soup laying by the door waiting for me to donate to the hamper at Gail's work and remembered that whatever you put into life, God gives back thirty, sixty, a hundred fold.

"And the seeds sown in the good soil stand for those who hear the message and understand it: they bear fruit, some as much as one hundred, others sixty, and others thirty" Matthew 13:23

I thought about how good God was. I hadn't even given the cans of food yet, and He was already sending back more than I could ever imagine or hope for. I went through the boxes before I left to see what I could eliminate off my grocery list. Any little bit would help the situation.

My first stop was the Bombardier Company where Gail worked. When I was walking into the office, the receptionist asked if she could help me, and I told her I was just dropping off a couple of things for the food hamper. She smiled and said great. She started to tell me about the family they had chosen having really hard times for the past couple of years and the hamper was so full, they could hardly wait to deliver it. She then said that since they were a snowmobile company, they were providing the whole family with snowmobile suits, boots and all the accessories. I just smiled and told her that was great. I was sure the family would really appreciate it. I was going to ask if Gail was around, but I thought it might not be a good idea to interrupt her when she was working.

Three days before Christmas, Sharron came in with a big box. I thought she was dropping off gifts, but it was from Mrs. Anderson. Mrs. Anderson was an elderly lady the kids and I called Mrs. Santa. She was a friend of Sharron's but really did look like, and had the personality of, a Mrs. Santa. Sharron invited us to come and have Christmas dinner with them. I told her Tammy was coming home, and she said it was fine that she crawled around the house. They had no problem with that. When the kids came home, we opened the box from Mrs. Santa. It was full of food and Christmas baking, and there was a gift for each of us.

Janet and Henry came over that night and brought gifts, and my gift was a bar. Every time I went over to Janet's mom's and dad's, I always admired the bar. Her dad had built it. It was curved and button tuft with black imitation leather in the front and shelves in the back. Janet said he had built a new one, so that one was mine. It fit in the dining room corner perfectly, and I put the phone on it and could store lots of my books for work in the back.

The tree was getting so full and Santa hadn't even come yet. The next day we picked up the box from my mother at Greyhound and again there was another pile of gifts. I just kept thanking God for supplying us so abundantly for Christmas. Sharron came over with a big box of gifts on Christmas Eve, then the clincher–the miracle that topped everything off. I was actually embarrassed that I could think of doubting. The boys and I went to pick up Tammy from the hospital, and then we headed home to get ready to go to Sharron's for Christmas dinner.

Gail was in my parking space when I got home. She was standing with her trunk open, and it was full of boxes. She just smiled at me. There was another lady standing with her. I asked her what was up, and I needed to pull in my parking space so I could get Tammy out of the wheelchair. She said they were just delivering the hamper for the family. It took me a couple of seconds to realize what was up. We were the family the receptionist was talking about that was having hard times.

P.J. jumped out and helped them unload the car. There were two big boxes in the trunk, and they took them in the apartment. I thought then they were ready to go. I got out of the car to thank them when they opened the back door, and there were another three boxes in the back seat. My emotions got the best of me, and I broke down. How could I ever have doubted that God would provide for us? I thought of the scripture

Luke 6:38 *"If you give to others, you will be given a full amount in return. It will be packed down, shaken together, and spilling over into your lap. The way you treat others is the way you will be treated."*

We were all in tears before they left. I noticed P.J. was even wiping his eyes. We unpacked the boxes. There was so much food, and I had to laugh when we came across the cans of soup I had put in. There was Christmas cake and baking, a turkey, all the trimmings to go with it. There were even bread-crumbs for the stuffing, buns, cranberry sauce, potatoes, applesauce, roast, pork chops, macaroni, cheddar cheese, so much food. We put it all away and had so much fun trying to fit it all in the cupboards. Two of the boxes were full of gifts, all wrapped and labeled.

We just got it all put away when there was a knock at the door. It was Rod bearing gifts. It was all too much. We got ready to go to Sharron's house, and Rod helped us get the wheelchair in the car. He was heading to his mom's and said he would stop by the next day.

There was a lot of family at Sharron's house. They were all so accepting with the kids. Tammy crawled around the house dragging herself with her one arm. We all ate too much. Everything was so good. After supper I sat and had desert while all the kids went downstairs with Sean and Sherritt, their sons. They were shooting pool and watching movies.

When we got home, the kids were asleep before their heads hit the pillow, and I really wanted to do the same. But instead, I had to finish the wrapping I hadn't done yet. I never realized just how much there was to do and sat in front of the television watching Christmas movies and wrapping then throwing it under the tree. At one point I looked at the clock, and it was four-thirty-five. I was hoping the kids were going to sleep in so the wrapping would be done before they got up. I finally finished at five-thirty and got to lay down for a bit.

The kids got me up at 7:30. We could barely find a place to sit to open the gifts; there were so many. It was so much fun. Sharron and Rick had given me a new feather pillow. Sharron knew I was really practical, and it was a great gift–something I would never buy for myself. The kids got their favorite boxes of cereal with money taped to them and accessories from the Winnipeg Jets (Winnipeg's NHL hockey team). Rod had given me sapphire earrings, and Tammy got the same.

(The holes in her ears had closed from being in the hospital so she made the it clear to me with no words that she was going to take the money Sharron gave her and have new holes put in her ears to wear the earrings Rod gave her. I told her I would take her to have it done before she went back to the hospital.)

The gifts from the Cheer board and Mrs. Santa were socks and mitts and scarves. Tammy got a book. Mom had sent so many gifts. I got new clothes and so did the kids. She knitted me a sweater. That was always my favorite from my mom. She was always overly generous at Christmastime. Janet and Henry gave them new bags to go to respite, and Tammy got a backpack for traveling from the hospital to school. Janet traveled a lot with her job and gave me probably my most favorite gift. It was a little shopping bag from Macy's Department Store in the States with a set of ten pairs of different colored knee high nylons. I was really into coordinating my clothes, and this was great. I don't know if I ever told her the socks were a lot of fun, but the best part was having a bag from Macy's.

When we opened the gifts from The Bombardier Company, it was awesome. The three kids got two-piece snowmobile suits with boots, mitts, sweaters, toques, scarves and long underwear, all with the company logo on it. I got the same except my suit was a one piece.

I told the kids to make sure they thanked God for all the gifts. I reminded them that we were so blessed with these gifts and it was Jesus' birthday, not ours. Before I dropped off to sleep, I had visualized God with a smirk on His face saying, "Trish, Ye of little faith." Once again, He has done more for us than I could ever ask for or imagine.

I followed through with my promise and took Tammy to get her ears re pierced before she went back to the hospital. She wanted to put the earrings on right away–that Rod had bought–and it was a struggle convincing her she had to wear the studs the lady put in her ears for two months to make sure they healed right before she could put them in. It was really hard taking her back to the hospital. She got more persistent to stay each time she came home, but there was no way they were going to release her yet.

I got word in January that J.J. had to have his surgery right away for his hip. It had gotten worse. We made arrangements to have him admitted and he had to be in for a week. I knew it would be a struggle spending time with J.J. in the Children's Hospital and Tammy in the Rehab Hospital, so I worked extra long on the sewing for two weeks to lighten the load.

It seemed like for every outfit I finished and gave to the customer, two more new customers would call to order. It was mostly for Grad girls, getting ready to graduate in June. It was too early for them to be ordering, but when the grad orders amounted to twenty dresses, I was thankful that I had a lot of time to get it done.

Sharron had suggested I think about hiring someone to help. She would pass the word around and see if she could find someone. It didn't take very long. She had a Portuguese lady that cleaned her house and mentioned it to her. She knew of a lady that sewed. Her name was Judy Pacheco. Judy phoned me. I had a hard time understanding her at first, but we did arrange for her to come twice a week to give me a hand. We agreed on how much she would be paid and she could start the next week. Judy ended up being a real blessing in my life. She had learned how to sew the European way, and we worked well together. She showed me how to make dresses much easier than I was taught.

J.J. went in for his surgery. The doctor explained to me it was to save his hip socket from wearing down any more than it already had. They used bone chips from another part of his body to build up the socket. The operation went well. I sat with him in recovery until he woke up then got him settled back in his room until he was all right with me going over to the other hospital to see Tammy.

Tammy was overly pressuring me with her sign language to let her come home. I was really getting frustrated and talked to the doctor. He said she had to be at therapy every afternoon and he didn't think it was a good idea for her to go home yet. I had to think about getting a van so she could go back and forth every day. I told him I was going to talk to the lawyer about it.

J.J. had to come home in a wheelchair. He would be in it for two months–until his hip healed. When Tammy came home on weekends, it was tough. P.J. had most of his hockey games early in the morning and of course both J.J. and Tammy were his biggest fans. P.J. and I would have to start to get them ready early. He would help dress J.J. while I dressed Tammy. He would tie their shoes for them while I warmed up the car. It was a major ordeal to get both wheelchairs into the car, then both of them. It was a miracle that we could get J.J. in the back seat of the Camaro when it was only a two door. I was always hoping for a tie game, so it would go into overtime because I knew what it was like to have to load them again and get them home. The parents were great to help. We even had offers for parents with vans to come and pick them up. J.J. had to be picked up for the two months by a wheelchair van to get to school. The days were a break for me. Tammy had become even more persistent to come home because if J.J. was home with his wheelchair then why couldn't she?

Judy and I kept plugging away at the sewing. She was great fun to work with and she was teaching me Portuguese. I am pretty sure the words she was trying to teach me weren't exactly appropriate for a Christian woman to be repeating.

The lawyer was working on Tammy coming home. He looked into transportation options and came up with some different ones to approach the insurance company with. We had gotten prices from different wheelchair transportation companies, but the prices were surprisingly high to go back and forth every day. A good friend of mine from the Speedway, Shawn Holden, was working at a Hertz rental company and came up with a suggestion. They were selling their vans from the previous year, and they were going pretty reasonably. I took the price into Mr. Scurfield to add to the options. It was surprisingly cheaper to purchase the van and insure it, so I could go back and forth with Tammy rather than have a wheelchair transport company do it.

The day finally came that I had to appear in court with Rudi for the divorce. I went into courtroom, Rudi and Helena were already sitting there. Helena looked to me to be very tired. I had thought she was there for support for Rudi, but when the court started I found out differently.

I got called up to the stand by the judge and was questioned about the divorce. Rudi's lawyer asked why I was against the divorce.

I told him I married him and the vows said for better or worse, richer or poorer till death do us part and that I was a Christian and didn't believe we should be getting a divorce.

The judge told me to step down and Helena was called to the stand next. I thought that was odd but Rudi's lawyer asked her if she was living with Rudi.

"Yes," she answered.

Then he asked, "Are your clothes in his closet?"

She again answered, "Yes."

I was embarrassed for her when he asked the next question and thought how degrading. "Are you sleeping in the same bed as Rudi?"

She said, "Yes."

If that wasn't bad enough, the next question must have been totally humiliating when he asked her if she had intercourse with him.

She said, "Yes."

The judge just said he was granting the divorce.

I said out loud, "Then you can live with the decision." I did all I could do to stop it and that was all that was expected of me.

An amazingly free feeling came over me when I walked out of the courthouse–like I had walked into another dimension of total peace about the situation. I believe I did everything I possibly could and didn't feel guilty. I just gave my freedom to God and said He had control over my life and to do whatever He wanted with it. I didn't like being a single person. I knew that. The world had changed, and I couldn't keep up with the times when it came to dealing with men. I believed in "back in the good ol' days" when men asked women out and women didn't dare ask a guy for a date. It was hard. I was being invited to weddings when I had made the wedding dresses but couldn't ask any guy out with me because I didn't feel right about it. I didn't want to go alone either. It wasn't a comfortable feeling sitting alone. I just felt like a pick up. I didn't want strange guys asking me to dance.

P.J. was really upset that Rudi and I were divorced. He asked what happened to our prayers and the fact that God didn't want marriages to end. I tried to explain to him that God gave us freedom of choice and even if He didn't want the marriage to end, He gave Rudi the freedom to choose. Rudi would have to deal with it. I told P.J. we couldn't control Rudi. I don't think he believed me, and if he did, it didn't make him feel any better. He seemed to be getting more rebellious. I had talked to the pastor of our church about it. He suggested I try to get him into a private school for high school. P.J.'s grades had dropped some after Tammy's accident, and I didn't know if he could get them up enough to go to a private school.

The church pastor called me the following week and had gotten together a full bursary for P.J. to go to St. Paul's High School. Spring exams were coming and we had to see if his grades were high enough to apply. Sharron suggested I talk to Gord about private schools because he was raised in St. John's Ravenscourt at first, a private school in Winnipeg. Then when he got a bit older, he was sent to boarding school for a few years at St. Johns Boys' School in Selkirk, Manitoba. P.J. did pass his exams, but his grades needed to be brought up by the last term in order for him to make it.

The sewing was getting really busy. I found it really hard to believe how fast it had taken off. I managed to take a couple of semesters on pattern design. It was fun, but it really put the pressure on me to get all the work done with everything else happening.

J.J. was finally out of the wheelchair and we were down to the crunch on Tammy coming home. The doctor finally agreed with her going home as long as she was brought in for therapy five afternoons a week. We made the mistake of letting Tammy hear the conversation, and she really started to bug me to take her home. It was remarkable how she could get her point across without talking. Mr. Scurfield was pushing the insurance company to make a decision, but they were more determined to take their time.

It was evident; the cheapest way to go for the insurance company was to just purchase a van and insure it. The van for sale was a window van exactly like the one I drove for work at SMD, so I would definitely be in my comfort zone driving it. It was in immaculate shape and would serve the purpose very well. I didn't even have to change anything to handle the wheelchair. Just strap the chair behind the seat like I did when I was working. The more Tammy pressured me, the more impatient I got.

I asked Mr. Scurfield if I could go to the newspaper with the story and he said he didn't think that was a good idea but I would have to do what ever I thought was right. I did call the paper and gave them the story. They said they would meet me at the hospital. They took pictures with Tammy in the wheelchair and me kneeling beside her and asked me a bunch of questions about why she was in and how long she was in. When the reporter left, he said to watch for the story in the paper the next day.

I never thought too much about it the next morning until I got phone calls from friends telling me to get the newspaper and look at the front page–the front page? I was surprised; I expected it to be on page two or three. I am sure that would have been enough to get the point across. I ran across the street to the grocery store as soon as the boys left for school. I didn't even have to wait to pick up the paper to read it. I could see on the front page was Tammy sitting in her chair and me kneeling beside her. I bought the paper and on page three in large print across the top of the page it read, "RED TAPE KEEPS GIRL IN HOSPITAL" and in smaller print under that it said "AUTOPAC SHUFFLE PUTS FAMILY IN LIMBO." They did a really good job of getting the point across. Good enough to get Autopac to respond immediately to the request.

Within two days the van from the rental company was sitting in my driveway fully insured and waiting to go to pick up Tammy from the hospital. I put my car for sale in the paper, and the next day, The Winnipeg Sun came and did a follow-up story on how their article did get the insurance company in gear and how Tammy was now able to go home. I thanked God for giving me the strength to step out, as I never had the nerve to do things like that on my own since the newspaper write-up that got me fired from my job.

The car sold right away and was a nice little nest egg in my bank account. I thought maybe I would just leave it there to see if P.J. would get into St. Paul's High School. He would need suits if he did, and I would be able to get them with that money.

P.J. had to be at St. Paul's High School to write the entrance exam. I took him in that morning. He passed without any problems, but the principle told us he would have to pull up his grades in the last term at school if he wanted to be accepted.

Elaine phoned me when we got home to see how he made out in the exam. She suggested maybe I should think about P.J. finishing school living with her. He could have his own room as they had a big house and could study without the interruptions of his brother and sister. I would think about it. He was still six weeks away from the final exams and I didn't feel good about him going there for that long. I talked to him about it after supper.

P.J. said maybe I should consider him staying home for the next couple of weeks and he could go to Elaine's for the last four weeks before the exams. It wouldn't be so long and he could come home on weekends. I didn't like the idea at all, but I told P.J. we would think about it.

Tammy had heel cord lengthening done on both feet to fix the foot drop that had developed while she was in a coma. Both legs were in casts up to her knees for eight weeks. That made her hard to maneuver and really heavy to pick up. I knew it was just a matter of time to get used to the routine. Judy and I were down to deadlines of getting the grad dresses finished. We had to start to work together for three days a week instead of two, or we just would-n't finish them all on time. It was tough getting both Tammy and J.J. ready for school in the mornings. I had until lunchtime after they left, then had to pick up Tammy and take her to therapy, then back home and begin the evening routine. I had to rely on P.J. He never complained about helping me with both kids, but I was feeling guilty that he was a kid himself and I had to keep relying on him. I went to the social worker and had a talk one morning while Tammy was at school, and told her I really needed some help. She said she would see what was available.

Mr. Sobey called and asked if I wanted to do the Ram Messenger run again since I had the van. I told him I would. I talked to Gord, and he said they were stuck for a driver for that Friday. I told him I would do it, but I had to take all three kids with me.

It was Friday, May 13th, and we were all invited to Patti and Warren's daughter's birthday. I made arrangements to start a bit early doing the run, so we could make it to the birthday party. It was so hot and the kids were sitting on the bench seat sweating. I could see J.J. was having a really hard time with the heat, so I stopped at the store and got them all slurpees. P.J. and I really bustled to get the boxes delivered quickly so we could get out of the heat. We finished just in time to get to the birthday party.

Tammy was crawling around in the house visiting person-to-person trying to get them to understand what she was telling them. The joke was, Patti and Warren were going to play charades at the party, but it wouldn't be fair to everyone else because Tammy would win. P.J. was chatting with the girls in the kitchen and J.J. and I were sitting on the couch talking to Warren.

I was telling him about St. Paul's School when J.J. started to hit my arm interrupting. I turned to tell him to hang on a minute when he fell over on the floor. He was blue and started to make gagging sounds. I tried to get him up and kept calling him, but it didn't stop. I screamed at Warren to get an ambulance but he had already dialed 911. It looked like J.J. was dying. Patti and her mom quickly took Tammy and P.J. and the rest of the party into the other room. J.J. finally stopped fussing and shaking, but still didn't open his eyes. I just told him it was all right, but I really didn't know if it was. Warren told me to go and wait for the ambulance to show them where he was. I didn't realize until later he was just trying to keep me occupied, so I would settle down a bit.

The ambulance came and I showed them into the house with the stretcher. They checked J.J. and asked if he had seizures.

I said, "No." I never even knew what a seizure looked like.

They were sure he would be all right, but still took him to the hospital. He still didn't wake up. I went in the ambulance with them. Patti and Warren said they would look after the other two kids. By the time we got to the Children's Hospital, J.J. had opened his eyes. He couldn't talk and didn't seem to focus on anything, but he had opened his eyes. They ran a series of tests, and afterward came in to tell me he had a grand mal seizure. They said it could just be a one-time thing, but I should probably be prepared because it could happen again. I was scared. What could I do if it happened again? They said they would refer him to a neurologist, and they would monitor drugs that would help. They told me if it happened again that he would be all right as long as he didn't hit anything when he went down. At that point J.J. was back to normal.

When I came out of the room Warren and Patti were standing there. Tammy was in her wheelchair and P.J. was pushing her. I told them what happened. I asked how they got the wheelchair in the car, and Warren said he drove my van and Patti brought the car. I took J.J. home but couldn't sleep that night. I was afraid of it happening again.

We had the appointment with the neurologist and he prescribed medication. I guess it was helping because it was a long time before it happened again.

I was still teaching aerobics in the evening and sometimes in the morning. It was all getting to be too much, and I knew I was burning out. The social worker suggested she apply for a worker from Winnipeg Family Services. Anything would help. It didn't take long before I got a positive answer from them.

They sent an older English lady with the sweetest accent. Her name was Gwen. She came to the apartment four evenings a week. The kids loved her, but then she was an easy person to love. She came right after school from Tuesday to Friday and stayed until ten.

I arranged my Ram Messenger runs and my aerobics classes during that time. I got groceries and did most of my running around while she was there. Life got much easier. I did all the sewing in the mornings and in the afternoon took Tammy to therapy. It was also arranged that when summer came, J.J. and Tammy would both go to camp for a good part of the summer. I took the extra time left in the evenings to cycle and cross country ski or to just spend time for myself. I also agreed to let P.J. go to Elaine's for the month to study, so he could get into St. Paul's.

Chapter 21

Court Again?

"God cannot be seen—but his power is great, and he is always fair." Job 37:23

The first week P.J. was gone, he phoned me everyday. He missed his brother and sister and was so happy to come home on Friday night. I missed having him around. He was my hope in my life. Hope that he would make it and be happy. He was swaying back and forth still wanting to be a youth pastor yet was growing more interested in becoming a lawyer. I joked with him telling him that as many times as I have been in court with a lawyer, it sure wouldn't hurt having one in the family.

We were still going to church regularly but I already knew my spirit was hungry for more spiritual understanding and growth.

The church was supporting P.J. to go to the private school. They were providing the bursary. The second week, P.J. still called every day, but he was vague in his conversation and always cut it short saying he had to study. When the weekend came, he phoned and asked if he could stay there because they bought him a new bike, and he made some friends in the area and wanted to hang around them. I was getting worried. I agreed but didn't like the idea, J.J. and Tammy were both upset he wasn't coming home. We met him at church on Sunday, and he didn't even come to sit with us. He stayed by Elaine and the girls. After the service, he came to talk to us, and I commented on the fact he was wearing new clothes. They weren't only new clothes but Ralph Lauren clothes–what P.J. always wanted but I couldn't afford.

I called Elaine later that day and asked her what was going on and let her know I was not pleased with the fact she bought him a new bike and new clothes.

She said to give the kid a break. She just wanted to build up his morale a bit before the exams.

I asked her to stop. I felt like she was buying my son, though I didn't say it to her.

Exams were starting the following week. I didn't pursue it any further because I didn't want P.J. to get frazzled before the exams. I thought it was only another week and a half, and he would be coming back home.

I passed the time that week getting J.J. and Tammy ready for camp. They were leaving for the first session at Lakeside Camp right after school finished. Tammy was getting her therapy at the Camp. All the grad dresses were finished and in the girls hands. I had nothing pressing so I took the week off.

I changed around the apartment moving the sewing area totally into the den. That way it was out of the way and I didn't have to keep putting away the machines. The sewing got so busy, I was beginning to feel that with it being at home; I never got away from it.

Rod was getting packed up to leave for fish guiding. We were still seeing each other, but mostly he was stopping by after work or on weekends. I was just too busy to think about dating.

The following week, I was cleaning the apartment. I hadn't heard too much from P.J. He had phoned me a couple of times feeling pretty good about the exam he had written on that day. I asked him if he was planning on going to grad and what he was going to wear. He didn't want to go. I told him if he changed his mind, I would get him a suit. We had to go shopping for suits anyway if he was going to St. Paul's. That was the dress code. That afternoon there was a knock at the door, and when I opened it, there was a man in a nice suit standing holding an envelope. He asked me if I was Tricia Hardt and I said yes. He handed me the paper and said I had been served. I closed the door and started to open the envelope. I smiled a bit thinking what was Rudi up to now? We were already divorced and our ninety days were even up, so it was final. I thought maybe they serve final papers just to say we are legitimately free. I started to read the stack of papers and had to sit down. What had I done? I played right into the enemies' hands. I was sick and started to cry. The papers said I had to be in court the following week for a custody hearing. Elaine and Horst were taking me to court to fight for custody of P.J. Not only could I not believe that Elaine could do this to me but that P.J. would be any part of it. I immediately picked up the phone to call P.J. to tell him he was to get his stuff together; I was picking him up right away. Elaine answered the phone and said he wasn't back from writing his exam yet. I told her to get his things together, I was picking him up. She tried to convince me it was better that P.J. stay with her.

I told her she was blessed with three beautiful, healthy daughters. If

God wanted her to have a son, she would have one, but it was not going to be my son. I never dreamed she would ever pull this.

She said P.J. was far better off staying with them. He could have his own room, and they would buy him what he needed to go to private school. She said he shouldn't be in our home with two handicapped kids. It wasn't good for him. (This was his brother and sister she was talking about.) She went on to say–at least in her house–P.J. could carry on normal conversations with her daughters and wouldn't have to help dress them as they could dress themselves. He could continue his piano lessons as they had a piano for him to practice on.

I hung up the phone without asking if P.J. knew this was going on. I really didn't want to know the answer.

I pulled myself together before I went to get Tammy for therapy. I managed to get through the day, but I was starting to lose it again before I got home. Tammy kept pointing to me and showing me tears running down and shrugging her shoulders. I knew she wanted to know what was wrong. I kept telling her I was just tired and needed more sleep. It was a Monday and Gwen wasn't coming that night. I was glad because I didn't have anywhere I wanted to go.

P.J. did call after supper. He was obviously oblivious to what was going on. He asked me why I was so upset. He didn't believe me when I told him. He didn't know. I told him to get his things together and I would pick him up. He said he was staying until exams were over. He tried to calm me down and told me he was going to be coming home and not to worry. I just left it at that. We agreed to meet for breakfast the next day. He didn't have another exam until the afternoon. I told him I would meet him at the store on the corner by Elaine's house. I didn't want to go to the house. He suggested I bring my bike and we cycle to St. Paul's to fill out the papers. I agreed.

It was so hot that day. We cycled for a while, and then P.J. got a flat tire, so we had to walk the bikes about a mile to get it fixed. We still had another five miles to go to get to the school. We didn't talk too much because I could see P.J. was really confused about the whole situation. He didn't believe Elaine would ever do anything to hurt him or me so whenever I brought it up, he would get defensive. I was so angry because I could see he was being deceived by her. I realized I couldn't tell him; I would have to be patient and wait for P.J. to realize it himself.

We cycled the rest of the way to the school and talked to the principal. P.J. was borderline for acceptance, but he questioned him on his Christian beliefs and P.J. aced it. The principal was convinced that he would be fine in the school. I didn't talk anymore about what was happening. I didn't want to burst his bubble. Court was in a couple of days. He went back to Elaine's but said he would come home the next day to see J.J. and Tammy before they left for camp.

There was a message when I got home from Pastor Ron to meet him at the lawyers office the next day. I was referred to the lawyer by my divorce lawyer. The lawyer told me I needed letters from everywhere I could saying I was a good mother. He said he could have the case remanded.

I told him no, I wanted it over with right away. There was still enough time to get the letters I needed.

J.J. and Tammy were going to catch the camp bus the same day as court at nine in the morning. Court was at two in the afternoon. I spent an hour the next morning making phone calls to social workers, teachers, nurses, and doctors, everyone I could think of that could make a difference. Every one of them was happy to write a letter for me. They all pretty well had the same thing to say, that I was more than a good mother and it was ridiculous for the court to even think of letting this happen. By the end of the day, I had thirty letters all from people who had the authority to have their say in this matter.

P.J. did come home to say good-bye to J.J. and Tammy. They were so happy to see him. He said Elaine didn't know he was coming. I could see the confusion in his eyes and felt so sorry for him. He cared so much about his aunt and uncle and didn't want to hurt them. I knew in my heart he really didn't want to leave home. He was already so full of hurt from all that had happened in his life. I was so angry that Elaine would dump this on him. I didn't talk about it. I just let him know we were so glad he came home to see his brother and sister. Besides, I knew with all the letters I had, there wasn't going to be a problem.

I put the kids on the camp bus. They loved Lakeside Camp, but I knew it wasn't that easy for them to go for the first two weeks. I told them I would come out and visit them in a week, and they smiled and waved as the bus pulled away.

When I got to the lawyers office, Pastor Ron was already there. I really appreciated him coming for support. They were very impressed with the letters and said it should go smoothly. We walked over to the courthouse; it was only a block from the office. When we walked into the courtroom I was surprised to see P.J. was sitting with Rudi. Elaine was sitting in the front with her lawyer. We were about five minutes early, and those minutes dragged by.

The court clerk said, "All rise." Then when he said which judge was presiding, I almost fell off the chair. I couldn't believe what I was hearing. It was the same judge Rudi and I always had in court when we were fighting about maintenance–the judge that I couldn't ever seem to have on my side. I got myself together thinking God had far more power than the Judge. *"What can we say about all this? If God is on our side, can anyone be against us?"* Romans 8:31 Even after all the unfairness I was feeling this judge had passed to me over the years, I still believed with all the letters, he couldn't do it this time. Now the tables had finally turned.

The judge just sat down and started to read something. He suddenly had a smile on his face. He looked up and looked right at me. All I remember hearing after that was something to the effect of. "It is you again." He then said "I take custody of Patrick Hardt from you and give it to Elaine Hardt, and you will pay maintenance every month to the amount of $525."

Shocked, overwhelmed, distressed and distraught, devastated, I can't find a strong enough word. I don't think there is a word to let you know my feelings at that moment. Rudi was smiling, Elaine was smug and I could see tears in P.J.'s eyes. I was so out of control; Pastor Ron and the lawyer had a hard time getting me out of the courtroom.

When they got me outside, I sat on the floor against the wall and screamed. God wouldn't give me more than I could handle and this was way too much. I was suddenly so glad the other two kids had gone to camp. None of us deserved this. I couldn't believe this judge would even consider it. What right did he have to come to this decision? I don't remember Elaine or Rudi taking P.J. out. They must have walked past us, but I don't remember.

This judge was the one that let Rudi get away with such low maintenance payments and gave Rudi the court order to sell the house so he could take half of the equity. He is the same one that allowed Rudi to keep the business, car, boat, van, racing car, and all the equipment that went with it. Now he orders me to pay five times more than Rudi was paying for just one child. How could that be? There was no discussion of why he chose Elaine over me. I was P.J.'s mother. I didn't hear anything to justify his decision. I didn't hear anything about P.J. being able to come home to visit. Tammy and J.J. will be devastated. Pastor Ron and the lawyer didn't want me to leave on my own. They thought I was too upset. I insisted. I just wanted to run away.

When I got home, I sat on my coach staring at the walls. The phone rang and I let it ring. After it stopped, I felt bad because it could have been the kids calling from camp. It rang again a second time, and I answered it on the first ring. It was Elaine. She wanted to pick up the rest of P.J.'s belongings. I told her to get P.J. to phone if he wanted something. I would only talk to P.J. If he told me he wanted his belongings, he would get them, but I did not believe anything she said anymore. I did not believe that P.J. was any part of this. He was so close to his brother and sister and we had such a bond for so many years. I left it at that and hung up the phone on her. The phone rang again and I was praying it wasn't P.J. asking for his belongings. It was Janet; she didn't have to ask the outcome because she could hear it in my voice. She wanted me to come and stay with them for a while. I told her I would call her later.

Sharron called, Gail called, and P.J. didn't call. The phone just kept ringing. Pastor Ron called and said they were praying. He didn't know for what, just praying that something good would come from this. That prayer got answered. I was still sitting and staring at the wall a couple of hours later when the buzzer went for the front door. I didn't answer the buzzer; I just went to the front to see who it was.

There standing with tears running down his face, was P.J. holding a big garbage bag and his backpack. I opened the door and grabbed him. All he could say was he was sorry, so sorry and he didn't know this is what they were doing. I knew that. He said when he came out of the courtroom and saw me sitting on the floor crying, he knew he just wanted to go home. He never wanted to do that to me. I knew that too.

I told him it wasn't his fault. They were the adults and were just using him. Rudi got involved just to pay me back. He thought he could make me hurt. He knew how to do it. I was so thankful. I asked him if Aunt Elaine was really upset. I know it wasn't right, but I really wanted to hear him say she was devastated. She had no right to use my son to do what she did. I trusted her and she misused that.

P.J. said when he told her at suppertime he wanted to go home, she got really angry and told him if he went, he couldn't take his new bike or the new clothes, he could only take what he came with. She said she helped him get into St. Paul's and now this is the thanks she was getting.

How dare she put him on a guilt trip? I was so thankful that he couldn't be bought. He still left the bike and the new clothes and just took what was his and walked out her door. His spirit was right.

Chapter 22

STANDING ON HIS PROMISES

*"Don't get tired of helping others. You will be rewarded
when the time is right, if you don't give up." Galatians 6:9*

Rod came back to the city for a visit part way through the summer. He took me out for a nice supper, and we got into a conversation about our future. I felt very uncomfortable and I think it was around the time the desert was being served that I realized I didn't want a serious relationship with Rod anymore. I was sure he sensed what I was feeling because I was being so distant and wanted to make it an early night. He dropped me off and said he would call me in the morning. I couldn't sleep that night and spent a couple of hours praying for Rod and for answers. The one answer I did get is that I had already been married to a man that didn't share the same Christian belief as me, and it made life tough because I couldn't share with him how I really felt and who I really was. It made me feel lonely even though I wasn't alone. I knew if I were to find another man to share my life with, it would have to be a Christian man who believed the same way I did, so we could talk and share our experiences. I made the decision to break it off with Rod totally and made a list of what I wanted in a husband.

One He has to be a Christian; Two-He has to accept the fact that I have kids and that two of them have disabilities; and Three-He has to be physically active or at least stand by me being physically active.

I gave the list to God, telling Him with those three points alone, I may need a miracle to ever find someone who would be all three. I told God if He wanted me to add more to the list, to let me know, and it was in His hands now. I thought how Rod matched up to the last two on the list, but to be fair, I never did know what he believed spiritually. We never discussed it.

P.J. was really angry when he found out I broke it off with Rod. He tried to guilt me into changing my mind. I knew the kids really liked him, but I couldn't be serious about a man just because my kids liked him. His anger didn't stop. After J.J. and Tammy went on the camp bus for their second round of Lakeside Camp that summer, P.J. and I were supposed to go buy his suits for starting school. He didn't want to. It seemed like a punishment to me for breaking it off with Rod.

Finally four days before school started and the day before J.J. and Tammy were going to be back from camp, he came and asked if we could go shopping. We went, planning on shopping for the morning, and then I was taking him out for lunch. It didn't work that way. We couldn't agree on where to go. P.J. wanted the best of suits. He said all the kids were going to be wearing the best at St. Paul's, and if he couldn't match up, he didn't want to go. He said he would just go to River East Collegiate, the public High School in the area. I still had the money from the sale of the car in the bank, but it had to go a long way for his school. Blowing it all on two suits was just not an option. I knew his school was going to be expensive. I was willing to work extra so he could go, but I had to be realistic about it. I was willing to pay $300 for his suit, but he needed two and shoes. He was even fussing about the kind of shirt. I had to pay for the school gym clothes and tracksuit, and he wanted the school jacket. All of that would come to $1500, which I had banked. But that was only the beginning, and it left me with only $500 in the account to do whatever else came up. We tossed it around for two hours until the conversation was getting ugly. His decision was to go to public school, and I didn't argue. I just took him shopping for clothes for school, and I bought J.J. and Tammy new clothes for them to go to school. I was so disappointed, but there was no arguing with him anymore. It seemed like he was so angry and bitter, and I knew it wasn't one thing that made him that way but several issues. When we got home, I suggested we go to a counselor, but he was too angry. So I just said to think about it.

I got all three off to school the first day then met Pastor Ron. I told him I broke it off with Rod and showed him my list of what I was looking for in a man. He said I wasn't being very fussy, and we just laughed.

I took out a pen and paper and started to make a list and told him it was for him to take and pray over. I wanted a house and this is what I was looking for. I reminded him that he created the monster in me for making lists. He told me to write down my goals and give them to God. This was the list for my dream house.

One-Had to have an attached garage; Two-At least three bedrooms with a potential for four; Three-Fireplace in the living room; Four-In a nice area; Five-A swimming pool would be nice; Six-This was the clincher–I had to be able to afford it.

Pastor Ron laughed. I really wanted it but was joking. He said I didn't want a house, I wanted a miracle. I told him what better person to ask for that–a priest. He put it in his pocket, and I reminded him I was joking. He said he had to show Donna, and they would pray for it for me.

We both chuckled when I said, "It is a good thing God has a sense of humor."

I struggled but finished my course on making patterns and designing. I took another shorter course on colour coordinating and what colours different people should be wearing. I learned what cuts of clothing were good for different body types. I managed to pull off some good marks. Gwen was still coming four evenings a week. I still had my respite one weekend a month with Diane. The sewing was taking over the apartment. It was getting to the point where it was hard to keep my life separate from the work. There was always something to do with the kids, but I did have my breaks where I could have time to myself. Hockey started again.

Tammy wanted me to take her skating so she could play ringette. It was heartbreak. She was walking a bit better, but skating wasn't on the list of what Tammy could do. She was walking quite well with a cane by November. We finally could put the wheelchair away for when we went shopping. The school used it sometimes for outings.

I wanted to take the kids to Calgary for Christmas, but I just didn't want to drive in the winter with them. All my cheques from doing the Avon Run for Ram Messenger were saved in a drawer so we could go to Calgary. My mom suggested I try Via Rail and see what it would cost to go by train. I was really surprised when I called. I informed them that I had two kids with disabilities. It would cost $30 for a ticket for one of them and they could take an attendant with them for free. J.J. could take me and Tammy could take P.J. The total cost of the trip including return would be $60. I couldn't resist, but the kids weren't to know. I didn't tell the kids. I would pick up the tickets and wrap the envelopes to stick in the Christmas tree. We were to leave at noon on Christmas Day. It was a twenty hour trip, so we would get there Boxing Day in the morning. That was cheaper than gas one way in the van, and I wouldn't have to drive. When I was doing the Christmas shopping, I kept in mind different things that would entertain them along the way.

One afternoon, I had a bit of time to spare so I quickly went down to the train station to pick up the tickets. I sat down by the ticket booth after I bought them to check the to make sure I had everything I needed before I left. A gentleman sat down next to me and said, "Hi Trish, how are you doing?"

When I looked up, it was a lawyer that I had met quite a few times in the past but had never personally dealt with. I was surprised that he even knew my name. He asked if I had ever divorced Rudi? I told him the shortened version of the whole story and even included the fact that I got the same judge when I was taken to court for custody of P.J. He just smiled and asked if I had any idea why the judge would always seem to side with Rudi in court? I told him I just figured the judge didn't like me for some reason. His answer floored me. He suggested it may have something to do with the fact that Rudi painted that judges house inside and out. He then patted my arm and got up to walk away. I sat for quite a while in shock. After I came to my senses I believed there is no way in this day and age these things would happen in Winnipeg. I respected judges to be fair and unbiased by outside influences. I made the decision that it was over and what I heard would not be pursued any further.

We were again invited to spend Christmas Eve with Sharron and Rick. It was good to know we would still have a turkey dinner since we would be traveling on Christmas Day. My mom said she would hold off the family Christmas dinner until we got there. I was really excited and had a hard time keeping it from the kids.

Sharron had come over one afternoon while Judy and I were working. She said their company owned a building downtown that was full of large tractor tires, but it had a decent room in the front and suggested that I could run the business out of it. I had already hired another lady that Judy knew. Her name was Maria. She worked from her house. I would cut and serge the clothes, she would put it together and I would pick it up from her, fit it on the customer and finish it. Judy was taking work home with her, but we were still so busy. I had to get it all together or it would get out of control. I agreed that I would move the business into their building and asked how much it was going to cost.

She said, "No charge, just make my clothes."

Moving day was going to be New Years Day, the day after I got back from Calgary.

I was asked again to come to the office Christmas Party. I was invited this time to be a guest, but Sharron asked if I could just help with the serving. She had set me up with a date for the party. His name was Leo. That was Sharron; she always thought of everything. I had met him before but didn't know him very well. I did know him well enough to know he wasn't the man on my list.

About a week before the party, I was still tossing around what I would wear when a parcel arrived. It was a sweater my mother had made. I knew God had His hand in this because the timing was so good. I threw together a winter white skirt in cocktail length and dusted off my cream shoes to match. The sweater was a pale turquoise, and the glitter thread that ran through was a cream. It shone like snow on the sweater. I felt pretty good when I was dressed and ready to go. I made a deal with Gwen that I would be late but however late I was, I would let her go that much earlier the following week. She just smiled and said she wanted to be home for breakfast.

I went over a bit earlier to help Sharron make sure everything was ready. This time I sat with everyone in the family room. I knew the staff from the office already because I would drop in when Sharron was working and from doing the Avon Runs. We were all sitting and talking. I was sitting on the edge of the base of the fireplace next to my date, Leo, trying to be a real lady. I wasn't doing too bad of a job until Leo dropped his drink on my foot. I jumped up to grab something to save the rug, but Sharron told me to go upstairs and rescue my pantyhose before they started to stick to me. I had taken them off in the bathroom and washed out the bottom and was trying to dry them with a towel, thinking wasn't this going to be a fun night. It would probably be a lot more fun if I weren't set up with Leo—not that there was anything wrong with him. I am sure he was a very nice guy, but I think he was drinking before he left the office. It would be better if someone were to offer him coffee.

The doorbell rang, and I heard Sharron talking to someone. I thought it was the bus driver ready to take us to the theatre. I got myself together fast and started to come down the stairs. Gord was standing talking to Sharron as she hung up his coat. He smiled and said, "Hi."

I thought to myself, now I wouldn't mind being lined up with him. He was so good-looking at the worst of times, but when he was dressed up, he was irresistible. I just chuckled to myself and walked by him and sat back down beside Leo.

He apologized, and I told him not to worry about it. We went to the program, and when we got back, I pretty well kept myself busy and out of distance of any drinks that might go out of control. Leo disappeared.

At one point Gord asked me how I ended up with him. He commented Leo didn't seem to be my type.

I took it as a compliment and told him, "Sharron set me up."

He asked me if Leo had driven me here, and I told him I drove myself and asked why. He said because Leo was in the driveway throwing up.

I didn't tell Sharron; I knew she would be really upset. I just smiled and said I guess it was a good thing I drove myself here and should change over to coffee since I was my own designated driver.

He laughed, and asked where I lived.

I told him around the corner. Gord and I were the last ones left after everyone else went home. We were getting a reputation for closing parties. We had a coffee with Sharron and Rick. I could have talked all night. It was getting really late and I made the comment that I promised Gwen I would be home for breakfast. I didn't want to go home yet and was really hoping Gord would come for a coffee with me. He was just great to talk to. He had a lot of interesting things to say and was obviously quite intelligent. He helped me on with my coat and walked me to the van again. We sat and talked in the cold for over a half an hour. I wanted to ask him to come somewhere for coffee but my old fashioned ways wouldn't allow it. I just said goodnight and went home.

My stress relief was in cross-country skiing. I wanted to train myself to do the Pinawa Race that year and get in shape for the Pumpkin Creek Mystery Tour. I would work hard all day and in the evenings when Gwen came to watch the kids, I would go to the trails and do the ten kilometer run, timing myself to see how much time I would cut off. Before I did the run, Christmas shopping was a priority. Keeping busy sure wasn't a problem while Gwen was at my house. I did whatever had to be done to have peace of mind when I was working.

Four days a week were for working, with one day left for running around. On that one day, I would schedule the kids' doctor appointments, have meetings at the school; buy my supplies, and anything else that would have to be done during the day. I started to do all my aerobics classes just before supper, so I would be able to come back home to shower and change while Gwen fed the kids. She would always leave me some supper. She was such a blessing in our lives.

I registered to do the Grand Beach Race before Christmas. The race wasn't until I came back from Calgary, but I got a discount for early registration. I had arranged that on that weekend, I would have a respite weekend, so I wouldn't have to worry about the kids. Judy and I worked hard to finish the work ahead of time, so I could take the Christmas break off with the kids, go to Calgary, and get moved into the new shop without being pressed to get any customers' clothes finished. Judy was going to start to work three days a week when we moved into the shop and Maria was coming four days a week. It was all coming together.

Christmas Eve was always a lot of fun at Sharron and Rick's. We again received the box from the Cheer board and from Mrs. Santa. Janet and Henry dropped off gifts. There were so many gifts, I was wondering if we would get them opened in time to get cleaned up and to the train station. The kids had no idea we were going to Calgary on Christmas Day and kept bugging me to drive out to Gramma's for Christmas. I could hardly wait to see their faces when they found out. There were a couple of slips at Sharron's house about going, but the kids never caught on.

I normally tried to get the kids to sleep in until at least seven on Christmas morning. I was behind on my wrapping again and packed during the night, so they didn't know. I finished at about four-thirty. I was so tired I was going to go to bed for a couple of hours but had a better idea.

If I made enough noise, Tammy would wake up and want to open her gifts right away. She would convince the boys to get up. I knew everyone would be tired but it would insure more time to get to the train station to catch the train. There was a better chance they would sleep on the train since we were in a day car and would have to sleep in the seats. The truth was I just didn't want to be excited on my own anymore about going. I wanted them to share in the excitement. I dropped my keys outside Tammy's bedroom door. Normally, she would wake up to that. She was a really light sleeper. After being at Sharron's the night before, she was tired and didn't even stir. I went into the bathroom that was across from her bedroom and first ran the water then flushed the toilet. That always woke her up. Not even a movement from her. Finally, I went into her bedroom and turned on the light. She turned around and looked at me with a questionable look then shrugged her shoulders, which meant, "What are you doing?"

I said, "Oh I am sorry, I didn't mean to wake you up. I was just checking to see if you were covered up and warm enough."

She nodded her head yes and turned over to go back to sleep. I gave up. I decided I wasn't being very fair and went into the living room and lay on the coach. It was the matter of two minutes when I looked up and all three kids were standing there smiling.

I said, "Do you know what time it is?"

P.J. said, "Time to open the gifts?"

I made them work at convincing me, but I think they were a little surprised that I gave in so easily. We had fun opening the gifts and got about half way through when I realized they were getting gifts to occupy themselves on the way to Calgary, and they didn't even realize it.

Finally, I told them to get the gifts out of the tree. They were so excited when they opened them and wanted to know when they were going. I told them noon if we got packed fast enough. That was the fastest I ever saw them open gifts, clean everything up and get packed. We were totally organized, showered, dressed and packed with enough time left to pack a lunch and a bunch of goodies to take with us on the train.

The trip was great for the first part. The boys totally occupied themselves and sometimes would wander together to the scenic car and sit and watch out the dome. I don't know what they saw; it was all woods or prairie. This was a new experience for them. They got to know people in our car, and I was just so thankful that I didn't have to drive. Tammy read most of the way or slept. It was a little cool, and I thought if I ever did this again, I would dress them a bit warmer for sitting. I had a hard time sleeping. It was so uncomfortable. Tammy was using me to get comfortable and J.J. was using P.J. We just sat staring at each other laughing. A man came around the next morning to tell us the train was running late. They kept bringing around free coffee, drinks, sandwiches and donuts. That helped.

A conductor came to talk to me when we were pulling into the station to let me know since they were so late coming in, I get free tickets for us to travel the same route as long as I use them within the year. I just looked at P.J. and said, "I guess we will do this next year too."

It was definitely different without Dad there, but it was sure good to see the family. There were many times I thought about moving out west with the family, but I always considered Winnipeg to be home. Whenever I would get to Calgary and see the mountains, I would give my head a shake and wonder why. After I got my papers for designing and patterning, I did seriously consider moving. Winnipeg was just not the place to establish yourself if you wanted a career in clothing design. The truth is I had done a check on Family Services and what they had to offer in Western Canada in comparison to Winnipeg for kids with disabilities, but there was no comparison. Winnipeg definitely had the best to offer. That reason alone, with both Tammy and J.J. in the system, was enough to keep me rooted in Winnipeg.

Mom packed us up a lunch, which was enough to feed us for a week when we left, so we wouldn't have to buy food on the train. We were running so late saying our goodbyes; we forgot all the food on the kitchen table. I felt so bad. There were leftover turkey buns–my favorite. She had given the kids these little computer games to play on the train. It occupied them all the way home. I never told her that I was jealous watching them play and wanted one too. I kept telling them it was my turn, but they just said no way and wouldn't let me have it. I told them I thought I raised them to share. It didn't help.

The train got in an hour late, which I am told, is really good for VIA in the winter. Bill picked us up, and on the way home offered to help me move into the new shop the next day. I asked him if he was sure. It was New Year's Eve, and who wants to move or even feels like moving after bringing in the New Year. He said the offer only holds after lunch.

I unpacked as soon as we walked in the door and started to pack up all the sewing room. It was surprising how much I had accumulated over the past year. I rented a leather machine that weighed a ton and didn't know how we were going to get it in the van. During the evening, I started to put boxes in the back of the van as I packed. The kids stayed up for midnight to bring in the New Year. They were having fun with the gifts we left behind when we went to Calgary. They got a lot of movies and were watching them. It was like Christmas all over again. We finally quit packing and brought in the New Year together. It was so much fun, I vowed at that point, I would always spend New Year's Eve with my kids.

The new shop was such a blessing. In the back of the sewing area was a large office with a desk and filing cabinet. I sat back in the chair with my feet up on the desk and felt pretty good about the whole situation. By six in the afternoon, the room was completely ready. There were enough machines for all the girls. I had picked up racks from a bankruptcy sale to hang the clothes. Sharron and Rick stopped in to check it all out. Again I had no way to thank everyone for their help that day except just to say it, and it didn't seem like enough.

On the way home, I knew who to thank, and that was God. He uses people as his angels to help other people. I went to sleep with a smile on my face that night.

It didn't take long to get comfortable with the new shop. It was nice to walk away after work, lock the door and leave it all behind. The work kept piling in. I had my phone hooked up and business cards made. We went right into the rush of grad dresses and weddings again. The only other person in the warehouse was Gerry. He was great to work with. The girls all got along with him, and he was spoiled. Whenever the girls brought snacks for everyone for lunch, they never forgot Gerry.

Patti had called me one morning and asked if there was anything she could do with my company. She was out of work and didn't know what she wanted do with her life. I told her to come and help cut out patterns. I would teach her how to serge, and it would give her some extra money until she decided what to do. She was still doing respite with my kids every once in a while.

She had been working for me for about a week when I got a phone call from Tammy's school telling me her one-on-one aid was leaving. They had to hire someone new. When I got off the phone, the first person I thought about was Patti. What better person than Patti? She was not a teacher and had no experience as an aid, but she could handle Tammy better than most people, so what better person for the job? Patti wasn't hopeful about it, but still said she would put in an application. I drove her to the school and introduced her to the people who mattered. The vice principal said there was a waiting list at the school board of qualified people that by law they had to consider first. I still thought there was no one on the list as qualified to work with Tammy as Patti. They interviewed her and called her back in. She got the job. She was thrilled and so were Tammy and I.

The year flew by fast. J.J. graduated to High School. He didn't go to the same High School as P.J.; they didn't have a program for him. He went to Miles MacDonnell High School. The girls in the shop made him a navy blue suit to wear for the graduation ceremony. It was a small ceremony but very emotional. There were some awards being given out to some of the grade nine students leaving the school, and then the principal was introducing the all around popular student. He spoke about how when this student first came into the school, the students and staff were very leery on how it was going to work out. He then said for three years this student was a shining light and his smile would light up the rooms and the hallways. Everyone would really miss this very special student. He then asked J.J. to come up to receive the award. He got a standing ovation, and I don't think there was a dry eye in the auditorium. I knew he was very special, but I guess I just didn't notice until then that everyone else knew too.

P.J. grew more bitter and angrier with God. His focus had turned to all the hard luck that happened in his life. I tried to get counseling for him, but he just didn't want it. He was turning fifteen that year, and it was hard enough for a fifteen-year-old to go through the teen years without carrying all the heartache he carried. I knew he would have to start to deal with it all but didn't know how to help him. The system wasn't much help. They seemed to still believe kids had rights, and very little or no discipline was the answer. I was pretty sure that all of these rights that were being handed out so freely to these kids would backfire one day.

It was hard to raise your kids with Christian beliefs when the system would tell them it was wrong and they could do what they wanted. Kids at that age needed guidance. They needed to start to make their own decisions but had to know that there were consequences that came along with them. Sometimes I had wonder if the people making the rules were book taught and didn't have kids of their own to experience what it was really like to raise children. I think I did the best I could, but it really started to show that my best wasn't good enough. P.J. was still playing hockey, at least he had that to work out his frustrations. It seemed to me that all the goals he set in life started to look too far away and too far-fetched for him to reach. I noticed he started to run away from the hurts he was dealing with instead of going through them. When I analyzed the situation, it seemed pretty grim. He lost his dad, watched his brother get run over by a car, his grandfather died, his stepfather walked away (being the only father he knew), and now his sister was in an accident. That was more than most people deal with in a lifetime, and he was only fifteen. When he asked me how I handled it all, I would tell him give it all to God and let him handle it, but it seemed to me like he wasn't able to keep that focus anymore.

J.J. and Tammy still went to Lakeside Camp in the summers, and P.J. went to Christian Athlete Hockey Camp. It did him good for a while, but there was too much peer pressure around to keep it going.

I got to know the people that worked in the offices at Ram Messenger. I seemed to have gained a reputation that I was available and I knew that came from Sharron telling everyone my story. The joke got to be how long it took for celibacy to turn a woman back into a virgin. I tried to avoid that joke. It was very embarrassing.

Gord and I talked quite often. It seemed he liked something about me. We had talked about the fact that I didn't believe in asking a guy for a date and didn't like to go to all the weddings I was invited to alone. Gord told me if I ever needed an escort to any of these functions to ask him. It didn't take long to take him up on the offer. Yvonne, the daughter of the owner of the speedway, was getting married. My company made the dresses, and I was invited to the wedding. The reception was at Tiffany's Restaurant. Tiffany's was a rooftop restaurant, and I heard the décor was a very Victorian design. It took me about four tries to get up the courage to phone Gord and ask him if he was serious about his offer. I could tell he really wasn't thrilled about it, but being the gentleman he was, he accepted. We had planned to meet for a drink at the Travel Lodge first, which wasn't far from the reception.

I had borrowed a dress I had made for Sharron that I thought suited the occasion, but I didn't feel like myself in it. It was very classy and elegant but made me feel a bit unnatural and uptight. I would have been better off choosing something with just a touch of class. I had my hair done for the occasion but hated it. My hair was past my shoulders. I never put it up, but to suit the dress, I did. I felt like I was trying to be a classy lady like Sharron. I was a few years younger than her, and Gord was younger than me. That left a big gap.

We met outside in the parking lot. My mother had come in from Calgary on the train that day for a visit. I only had time to pick her up between the wedding and the reception, drop her off at home, and leave right away. I left without realizing her suitcase was still in the back of the van. She was watching the kids and told me to stay out as long as I wanted to.

I pulled into the parking lot of the Travel Lodge, and Gord was already there sitting in his car. When he got out, he looked so good dressed up in his suit. As he started to walk toward my van, I suddenly thought I was going to have a panic attack, and I wanted to run. I felt like an old lady. I could have worn one of my dresses that was a little more stylish–not anything cheap looking by any means, but just more fun to wear. I could have left my hair down and just fluffed it a bit. I know Gord was being a gentleman taking me, but he shouldn't have to feel like he was taking his older sister to a wedding (I was going to say mother, but it wasn't that bad), I was in crepe and antique lace for crying out loud. He was gorgeous. We had gotten to know each other enough by then that when I got out of the van, I asked him if I could go home and try again. He looked surprised and said I looked great. I knew he was just being nice. He looked a little stressed, and I sure was not comfortable.

We talked while we had a drink. He went to private schools most of his life. He said he was boarded out to a school in Selkirk, St. Johns Boys School. I knew this from before, but he had the greatest stories to tell. He was disciplined by physical means to a great extent. Canoe trips from Winnipeg to other provinces with only the food you were rationed and fifty mile snow shoe races. No wonder he was such a gentleman. He was so fine-tuned. That was from the discipline. I told him it isn't like that anymore. That is the kind of school P.J. would have loved. He loved the challenge. But with the rules set for teenagers now and their rights, I was surprised a school like that was still surviving. Gord was on the Alumni Board for the school and said they were having problems keeping the school open, and it may be closing soon.

We took his car to the reception. He of course opened the door for me and when we got to the building where the reception was, he pulled up in front, opened my car door, walked me to the building, opened that door, walked me into the lounge and said he would just park the car and would be right back. (I checked my make-up while I waited and when I looked in the mirror; I thought maybe I could do like the girl does on television, pull a pin out of my hair and have it fall down perfectly. The only thing was with my hair as curly as it was, and with all the hairspray, it would just stay without the pins or it would end up standing up. Best leave it like it was.) It was the first time I was ever at Tiffany's Restaurant. It was on the top floor of an apartment block and when we got off the elevator, I was surprised at the class it had. The truth is, I was very appropriately dressed for the restaurant but only because it was Victorian. I loved the Victorian look (just not on me). The chandeliers were white with gold and had little flowers painted on them. The chairs were all done in brocade, and I commented how I would love to have those in my dining room some day. The ceiling was total heavy moldings painted with gold to give them the antique look. There was a dance floor in a separate room completely surrounded with windows that overlooked the city, and a door led outside to a huge balcony. I was surprised all of this was on top of an apartment block.

We went through the reception line. I introduced Gord to Yvonne and her new husband Gary. Pete and Tina were there. I told Gord they were the owners of the speedway. He wasn't a big fan but had gone out to the track on several occasions. Later he met Humphrey and Jamie, Yvonne's brothers.

We sat down at a table a ways from the head table. I can't remember whom we were sitting with, but I do remember the conversation we had all night. We started off discussing age–bad start. He said he thought I was the same age as Sharron–but only because we were such good friends. He then started to bail when he found out my real age and said I didn't look as old as Sharron but . . . The subject changed pretty fast. That was it. I was following Sharron's style, which is great for a lady like Sharron that has a lot of class, but it wasn't me. At that moment I made the decision that from now on to just be myself. (I wanted to tell him I was going home and I would try again another time.)

Then he told me he was supposed to be helping his stepsister move, and that was why he hesitated to say he would take me to the wedding. She gave equestrian riding lessons. She and her husband had built a new indoor arena with an attached stable and apartment for them to live in. It seemed strange to me, almost like living in a condo with horses as your neighbors, but what did I know. He said she suggested he should come to pick me up without any socks on, so when he crossed his legs, I would see he had he had bare feet in his shoes and would want to leave right away. Then he could go and help her move. I couldn't believe what I was hearing. He was joking but still why would he tell me that? I asked him why, and he said because he was glad he came. He was enjoying himself and didn't want to leave early to help.

We talked through supper then went out on the balcony. It was really cool out and he put his blazer over my shoulders. I teased him about it being a good thing he wore socks. He just laughed and said he already regretted telling me. He told me all about his mom leaving when he was a year old, and that she moved to California. His dad raised him. I was really interested in hearing more, but the music started and it was hard to talk even on the balcony. Besides I could see Gord was really cold. I could smell his aftershave on his blazer and hesitated giving it back. I just smiled and handed it to him. I wouldn't dare let him know what I was thinking. I was bothered by the fact he didn't really want to take me but said yes. I wouldn't feel comfortable asking him to escort me again.

He asked me if I wanted to dance. It was a long time since I had danced, but I said yes. I thought by the look on his face, he didn't really want to and was hoping I would say no. I was growing more and more paranoid or maybe guilty. It was a slow waltz, and I was surprised by how close he held me. I expected straight arm's length away. I was staggered by how good I felt being held so close by him. I enjoyed it thoroughly, and when the dance was finished, the strangest thing happened. Gord kissed me. Not just a little peck on the cheek but a full kiss on the lips. That was the kind of kiss girls talked about that they never forget. It was the kind of kiss that a girl wants more. We were the only ones still standing on the dance floor and he quietly asked me if I was ready to go. I think he was more surprised about the kiss than I was.

We said our good-byes to the Vernaus family and left. He drove me to my van. It was strange. I said goodnight and got out. He drove away. All the way home my emotions bounced around. He wasn't as young as I thought though he was younger than me. He could have any girl he wanted and was involved with all the pretty little equestrian riders–the entire society bunch where the daddies had lots of money. He was definitely out of my league. I felt really down on myself by the time I got home.

It was after midnight, and I was surprised my mother was still up and dressed in the same clothes she was wearing when I picked her up from the train. My mother was the type of person who always wore loungers if she wasn't going anywhere. I laughed and asked her if she was waiting up for me, and she laughed and informed me she wouldn't be if she had her suitcase to change for bed. That was when I realized I still had her suitcase in the back of the van. I stayed up after my mom went to bed and wrote in my journal. I wrote prayers for Gord. I asked God if he would guide Gord to be closer to Him and to put across his path a good Christian woman for him to fall in love with and marry. I prayed God would put people across his path with His word in their mouth to share with Gord. I prayed until three o'clock in the morning; then I fell asleep.

I avoided Gord for a while, and it wasn't easy to do since he worked in the next building over.

My mom stayed for a couple of weeks and got to be good friends with Gwen while she was here. She even had supper one night with Gwen and her husband Steve.

The following weekend, I did the Grand Beach ski race. It was brutal. I took out my frustrations on the track. I was more tuned to the race than I thought. I was doing fine until Nick came flying by me as if I was standing still. Nick was a guy that came to Winnipeg every year for the ski races. He was from Montana. I hadn't seen him for almost a year. He yelled back to me as he went by. "Hey, it's good to see you. I will meet you at the finish line. You are doing great, keep going." It ended up good. Seeing him going so fast gave me a second wind just at the right time. I was hitting the wall and fading and there was an uphill climb ahead of me. Coming down the final runway to the finish line, I could barely keep my feet going I was so tired, but everyone was cheering. I thought, gee, they are pretty excited. I knew I was missing something by everyone's reaction. I found out later I did far better than I ever dreamed. I found it hard to believe until I was handed the certificate that said I came in second in the ladies.

Nick suggested I do more traveling and racing but totally understood why I couldn't when I told him my story. He asked me if I wanted to go to the Yukon for a week-long race where people had a hard time keeping from freezing and they pulled sleds with their supplies. We just laughed about it. He showed me the article in a magazine and said as dedicated as he was, he had no interest in going there.

One of my customers had come by that week and showed me an article on a contest for designing patterns. It was from the States. It was a great challenge for me. I had finished all of my courses and came out with a B+ average. I never really got the chance to show my work yet. I had several designs I wanted to try out but never had the time or a good enough reason. I picked the hardest one that I thought I could wear to the Speedway Banquet. It had a V back with three pleats on each side. The front was a cross over and also had the pleats. It was synched at the waist with a triple pleated cummerbund, and fitted skirt with a split in the back. I made it out of sapphire blue velvet. There were many sleepless nights and a lot of tears trying to make the pattern work. It was really hard to fit myself. Every time I would make a change on the dress, I had to make the same change on the pattern. I finally made it work enough that I felt good wearing it.

To enter the contest I had to send pictures and the pattern. My hair and make-up were done professionally, and then I put on the dress and went to Sooters Photo Studios to have the pictures taken. I felt they turned out great. It always amazed me how a professional photographer can make you look better than you actually do. Janet met me at Sharron's house afterwards and took more pictures of me sitting in the solarium and standing in front of a fireplace. We were just hamming it up and had lots of fun with it. I won second prize. It was awesome. I felt like I finally could say I knew what I was doing. It proved though that Winnipeg was really behind in style. I had the design three years before it finally sold in Winnipeg.

Tammy was walking pretty well at that point. She didn't need a cane anymore. The doctor said she couldn't walk, so she was now learning to run. She started to try to talk, but her voice was very raspy. I had been praying along with a lot of people that God would heal her vocal chords so she could talk again. The therapists said it was not possible, that there was a big hole in the vocal chords. Tammy was having a problem blowing, and it would take blowing naturally to get the words out. The muscles in her mouth were too weak to talk.

Mom had suggested we give her bubble gum to help her learn to blow. We tried it. At first it didn't seem to work, but she finally got the hang of it. We let her chew gum all the time to strengthen the muscles in her mouth. Then I just kept thanking God for giving Tammy her voice back. She started trying to talk, but her voice was obviously very damaged.

The therapists told me not to let her do it because she could hurt it even more. How do you tell a thirteen year-old girl not to try to talk? It is impossible. She just kept trying, but we couldn't understand her. Over time, she had stopped trying to talk sentences and would just try one word. It worked. We could understand the one word. Tammy and I agreed not to tell the therapist she could say words until she got really good then we would surprise her. She was really good at keeping secrets. Sometimes, I would doubt whether I should let her try to talk. Her voice was so raspy. I knew that doubt was a sin, and I should just ignore that.

Dr. Weidman decided Tammy should see a specialist about her other arm and hand. There was a possibility that she could have a surgery that would give her back some of the use. J.J. had the same surgery, but nothing changed. It was really heartbreaking for him. He had the surgery and was in a cast for eight weeks, then the big moment. Take it off and see what would come of it–nothing, not a single change. I asked Tammy if she wanted the chance to see. She knew it didn't work for J.J., but she did want to try.

Dr. Weidman sent us to a Dr. Derkson. We were told he was the absolute best. He was only in Winnipeg part of the year because the other half he would be off in some country doing missionary work. He said he would do the surgery right away because he wanted to see the outcome before he left. The following week, the operation was done and Tammy was in a cast. Bathing was harder and it was like she carried around a deadly weapon with the cast, but we adjusted. Walking was a bit tougher because the cast was heavier than she was used to, and it threw her balance off.

I had the usual prayer group praying for the surgery to work and I thanked God every day for her getting back what was taken from her. *"But thank God for letting our Lord Jesus Christ give us the victory!"* I Corinthians 15:57

Finally, the cast came off. The doctor was looking at her wrist and hand and smiled. He said we wouldn't know anything for a couple of weeks because he wanted her to have therapy. Tammy asked if she could tie her own shoes now. The Dr. said to her maybe; we would see in a couple of weeks. Tammy jumped down off the table and tied her shoes. It was slow but she did it. When she stood up, Dr. Derkson told her to go home, she didn't need any therapy.

We left and she was happy. She did brag a bit too much to J.J. when she got home. It was really stupid how they compared their injuries. Her hand wasn't 100%, but it was sure a lot better. She could now hold a cup in that hand and drink. She could write again with that hand, but it was pretty shaky.

My company wasn't in the new shop very long when Mr. Sobey came to me and said they were moving into a new building. It was on Fife and

Church Street. All the companies would be put together in this building and I was invited to join them. There was a large room in the warehouse I could use as my shop. He suggested I go to see it. Sharron picked me up the next day, and we went down. I was thrilled to be included in the move, and it was great for me to get my Avon deliveries from the same building I was in. It was a huge building and our room was close to the front.

I can't remember how we moved. I do remember setting up. It was a big job. I bought a real cutting table from a company, and it was eight feet by sixteen feet and was a real ordeal to put together.

It was a very large room. There was tile floor and no carpet. I could paint whatever colour I wanted, and the only thing I would have to do is section off a small space for a table for the lunchroom. That weekend I went in to paint. I finished and washed and waxed the floor. There was a small storage room I painted and fixed up for a change room. I put up big mirrors for the customers and brought in all the machines. My desk was in the front with my own phone, and I put another phone on the other side of the room for when I was working. Everything fit in like a charm.

When I was ready to go to the shop to finish getting everything ready, I noticed I had a flat tire. I think it was just low on air but I didn't feel like fixing it then. Sharron offered to give me a ride. She brought the 1987 Grand National. It was black with all blacked out windows and black interior. Everyone drooled over that car. It was a limited edition.

There was so much commotion in the building when I got there. Everyone was there to help with the move. Moving a company like Ram Messenger was not an easy job–all the phones and computers, the office equipment, the tire business. Everything was being done over that weekend. My job seemed piddley compared to what they had to do. The kids were at respite with Patti so I could stay until I was finished.

The past year and a bit that I was in business, I collected pictures of the work I had done and put them in albums. They were sitting on the lunchroom table. In it was a picture of me in the dress I designed. Gord was taking a break from the moving and was sitting at the table. He started flipping through the pictures and then said, "Wow!"

I went to see what he was looking at expecting it to be one of the grad girls or models I sew for and was really surprised when it was me in the velvet dress. He asked who it was and I said very funny thinking he was joking.

Then he said, "It is you."

I told him not to be so surprised, I don't always dress Victorian. I save it for special people. He knew exactly what I meant by that, but everyone else in the room just looked at us strangely. We started to laugh.

I was finished the room and was ready to go. The girls just had to come to work on Monday and continue from where they left off on Friday. It was that organized. Sharron wasn't ready to go. I asked if they needed any help. I had nothing better to do anyway.

She pulled the car keys out of her pocket and dangled them in front of Gord. Her voice was persuasive when she said, "The keys are for the Grand National. Trish needs a ride home and a flat tire fixed on her van."

He said, "Let's go," as he grabbed the keys.

I wish if she were going to play matchmaker, she would have just asked him if he could drive me home and not used the car as bait.

While he was driving, he started to laugh and said, "Sharron is trying to line us up."

"Just ignore it," I told him. "She is only trying to get me a man, but I want someone who wears socks when he goes out."

He was embarrassed and asked if I was still upset about that. I laughed and promised I wouldn't bring that up anymore.

He did say he would drive me home even if it wasn't the Grand National. I didn't doubt it for a minute, but that car sure helped.

He fixed the tire on my van when we got back. I didn't invite him in. I let him go so he could play with the car a while longer. I had an aerobics class to teach anyway.

Working in the new building was never dull. The drivers and all the employees used the lunchroom, and the girls and I got to know them all. Gord would even stop in once in a while to see how it was going. There were windows in the front of the shop that looked out in the warehouse, and everyone could see inside the shop as they walked from the warehouse to the office.

Chapter 23

Friendship–Foundation
for Lasting Relations

*"A friendly discussion is as stimulating as the sparks that
fly when iron strikes iron." Psalms 27:17
(The Living Bible)*

The first summer in the new building, Gord and I had become really good friends. There were many times we would be working late, and he would ask me to run across the street to have supper with him. We both agreed we hated to eat alone. He and I could talk for hours. We never seemed to run out of things to talk about. He was like a best friend that I told all my secrets to. We had a lot in common. We both liked to watch figure skating and hockey games. It was never considered a date. We were just really good friends. He wouldn't hesitate to come into my shop during the day to tell me I looked really good in a certain outfit, nor would he hesitate to come in to tell me that what I was wearing did nothing for me. I respected what he had to say. He was always interested in my cross-country ski ventures.

I had heard from Nick later in the summer, and he convinced me that I should try one of the cross-country ski races in Montana that winter. I didn't know how I would do it, but I did say I would try. Hill training would be essential and that would be pretty tough in Winnipeg. I was told to go to the old dump hill, but I had to ski in the evening in the dark and wasn't very comfortable with being in that area of the city alone. Gord had suggested to me to try a hill out in Lindenwoods, a new area in the city that was well lit at night and set up quite nicely.

I didn't have to think about it yet. I cycled as much as I could in the summer to stay in shape. I still wanted to get into jogging, but jogging and I just didn't seem to jive.

One night I went home and Gwen told me P.J. didn't come home. He didn't come home all that night, and by the next morning, I was frantic. I reported him as a missing person. I couldn't even go to work; I was so sick trying to find him. I called everyone he knew, but no one knew where he was. That day went by and I called Pastor Ron several times asking for prayer. I just wanted him to phone and tell me he was all right. The second day went by, and I could barely function anymore. I gave it to God. He knew where he was. I prayed to let me know he was safe. I prayed to keep him safe and fed.

On the third day, the phone rang and it was P.J. He stated he was sorry he worried me.

I asked him where he was, I would pick him up.

He laughed and answered he was in Santa Cruz.

I asked if that was a pizza place.

He said no it was in California. I couldn't even speak I was so shocked. How could he get there and why? He told me that he went there to live out his dream.

I asked him how he got there. He hitchhiked. I couldn't believe what I was hearing. He then went on to say if his dad had any dreams; they were gone when he died. If J.J. had any dreams they were gone when he was run over. Tammy the same when she was hit by the car. He said if he were going to be hurt tomorrow, he intended on living his dream today. The dream was to surf. He refused my offer to bring him back. My hands were tied. I couldn't do a thing about it even if he was underage. I had to just beg him and pray and ask him to call me everyday.

After three weeks, he decided to come home. He was rough-looking when he got there but I was just glad he was home. He got to be a real handful after that. He couldn't seem to settle down. I got counseling for him, but he didn't cooperate. He grew more bitter and angry over the next few months. I finally found a group called Tough Love to go to.

The group went against the grain of any Christian Beliefs I had learned. I was getting really confused. What the group was suggesting I do didn't seem to be very loving. How do you throw your kid out on the street? P.J. hated me going. Pastor Ron had told me that sometimes the only way to help people was not to help them.

I still believed strongly that P.J. would be the Youth Pastor at some point and thought maybe he had to go through these rough days to be able to relate to the way youth were turning out to be. If he were hitchhiking and living on the street in California, he would be able to relate to a lot of problems. I was losing focus and felt like I was back in Alanon. I felt like I was being dragged into a pit. It is really hard to watch your son go through all this kind of garbage and turn your back on him, but that is pretty well the advice I thought I was getting.

I spent many hours having lunch or supper with Gord at work using him for my sounding board. I had to really watch myself. I felt like I was jealous of my friends' kids. Sometimes victory just comes easy to people. P.J. saw his friends get new vehicles for their sixteenth birthdays, and he knew he would be lucky if I could pay for him to get his driver's license.

The more I tried to help, the more guilt trips I would allow myself to be on. It wasn't my fault that Rudi decided to go with another woman, but P.J. didn't seem to see it that way. I hated arguing with him and knew for my own good and his I had to start to walk away, to keep my focus on God, and trust for the best. I was willing to work harder and to do whatever I could possibly do to help him, but I couldn't help him go in the wrong direction in life. I started to get arguments about my Christian beliefs, and our relationship was getting further apart in the process.

A lot of early mornings were spent doing my devotions, crying to God to please turn P.J. back around, to show us the good in this. I even tried to bargain. (I knew better, but that is how desperate I was getting.) I had tons of knowledge on how to handle head injured children and how to get through some of that hurt, giving it all to God, but when it came to raising a normal teenager, I found it to be overwhelming.

I kept Gord up on all that was happening, and he told me all the stories of how bad he was. That was part of the reason he was sent out to Selkirk to go to school. He sure turned out good, so I at least had hope. Gord would always say to me that there was something about me that was different. I hesitated and would never tell him it was my belief in God. As good of a friend as he had become, I would never tell him that. He may think I was some kind of wacko and not talk to me anymore. Yet, on the other hand, I was still thanking God for putting people across Gord's path with His word in their mouth to share the Good News. Totally being pulled and confused, I knew what was right, but I was having a really hard time hanging onto it.

I met with Pastor Ron one day and told him about the problem I was having. He just said I was on the right path. God had really good plans for me, but the devil was fighting to keep me from having it. I was being deceived, he said, and confusion doesn't come from God. Peace does. I backed off the conversation definitely believing strongly in God, but when it came to believing there was a devil, that put me in a worse spin.

Later, I went for a drive and thought more about it. It only made sense that without a shadow of a doubt, I knew there was God; God was as real to me as my kids were. If I believed that strongly in God, then of course there was a devil. I had always just referred to it as evil. Pastor Ron thought that was good. He expressed to never acknowledge the devil or talk about him. He thrives on the publicity, so don't give him that.

Staci had come to me that same week to tell me she was chosen to represent Miss Manitoba in the Miss Canada Pageant. Her talent was going to be singing a Christian song, and she wanted me to make the dress for it. I was thrilled but didn't have too much time to get it done.

It was dark coloured velvet and had tons of rhinestones set in around the neck and around a hole cut away in the back. There was a peplum of velvet that draped down into a partial train in the back. The sleeves were puffed and had scattered rhinestones set in. I had no fingernails left by the time I was finished setting a total of four hundred and forty rhinestones. Staci had left for Toronto and I had still not finished. My mom came into the city. She usually came to help with the rush at work. I spent most of the time visiting her while I was putting rhinestones in the dress. It was finally finished. Pastor Ron and Donna took the dress with them when they left for Toronto. There was no guarantee the pageant would let her wear the dress. There were so many sponsors involved.

The night of the pageant I was sitting at Sharron and Rick's in front of the big screen T.V. I wouldn't know until Staci came on to sing her song whether she got to wear the dress or not. Rick handed me a wine glass and was pouring wine when they introduced Staci. The curtain went up and Staci was standing in the dress. I drank the wine. I was so afraid during the whole song that a rhinestone might fall off and the lights would show it sitting on the stage beside her. It never happened. As a matter of fact, she didn't win the pageant, but she did win the talent. She sang the song, "I Believe." Sharron and Rick taped it for me and we must have watched it twenty times. It surprised me that I could do that fine work.

We all got along great at the shop, and the business had become fairly successful already. Staci's dress helped alot.

Janet phoned me one afternoon. She had two extra tickets to go to watch figure skating at the arena. She asked me if I wanted them. She, Henry, and her parents were going. I asked Gord if he wanted one of them, and he said yes. He suggested we go for supper, and then to the arena. Janet and Henry would meet us in the front. Gord and I went early to the restaurant and had a lot of time to kill, so I talked to him about why he hadn't found a nice girl when he could probably have whomever he wanted.

He explained to me, he dated girls from his stepsister's equestrian riding school and was tired of their attitudes. They were spoiled brats and never thought of anyone but themselves. They all just wanted to get married.

I laughed and told him not all girls just want to get married.

He answered, "Yes, all of them."

I told him I had been there and done that and wasn't in a hurry to do it again. We got into a heated discussion, and I ended up not talking to him until I got to the arena. I introduced him to Janet and Henry and that kind of broke the ice. It ended up being a fun evening.

It was time to start my hill training on cross-country skis. One Friday I was doing the Avon run for Ram Messenger. While I was loading up the boxes, I asked Gord what streets I had to go on to get to the hill at Lindenwoods. He had bought a condo in Lindenwoods, so he knew the area well. He asked me why, and I told him. He stated that was far too healthy for him and directed me how to get to the hill. When my deliveries were done, I got changed into my ski tights in the van and went to the hill.

It was a brutal workout. However, the area was beautiful, and I felt safe even though it was dark. The park was very well lit and was on a man-made lake. The lake was frozen and there was a bridge to the hill. I must have gone up and down the hill forty times before I decided I was starving and needed food.

I got into the van and started to drive away. When I got to a stop sign and stopped, a truck pulled up beside me. It was odd since I was on a two way street. I couldn't see the guy in the truck; it was too dark. He was motioning for me to pull over. I did and locked my doors in the process. I looked in my mirror and was surprised when the guy got out. It was Gord. He was heading to the hill to see if I was still there when he passed me. He just finished work and was hungry and wanted to know if I wanted to go to Swiss Chalet with him for a bite to eat. It was almost eight o'clock and I was really hungry but I told him no because I was in my ski tights and in need of a shower. He didn't care. I agreed and stopped on the way to phone Gwen. She offered to stay as long as I wanted.

Gord and I sat and as usual talked and ate. We drank several coffees before the waiter finally came up and said they were closed, out of coffee, and he wanted to go home. We couldn't believe it was already twelve-thirty. We had talked all that time.

One night I was doing the Avon Deliveries and had boxes left over. I took them back to the shop. Gord was dispatch for the deliveries and always stayed till all the trucks were finished. When I gave him the boxes he asked if I wanted to stick around. I guess it got pretty lonely there by himself. I did sit and talk for an hour, and then I had to go. As I was leaving, he asked what I was doing the next day. I had an aerobics class in the morning but that was all until evening. He asked me if I wanted to go for lunch. Something was different. We ate together lots of times, but it was always spur of the moment. Never planned like this. I agreed and would meet him at the Restaurant on Henderson at noon.

It was a real rush to do my class the next morning, get showered and changed and to the restaurant by noon. Gord was waiting when I got there. I just ordered a salad. I was tired from the class and wasn't hungry. We talked for a few minutes then I asked him how come he asked me out for lunch on a weekend. That was not normal for him and me. He said he hadn't talked to me much lately because we were both busy, and he just wanted to catch up on what was happening. I was hoping there was more to it than that. I told him I had a phone call that morning from a country and western band that was playing in the city for the next week. I didn't know where they got my name, but they were doing an album and needed some different extravagant clothes to wear for the cover. Glitter and shine. I was supposed to go to watch them play then come up with some different ideas to run by them. They were playing downtown. I wasn't thrilled with the idea of going, but business was business. Gord asked me when I was going. I told him more than likely early in the week. He suggested I go on Wednesday evening after work and he would come with me. He said it wasn't a good place for me to go on my own. I took him up on his offer.

I could have spent the whole afternoon talking to him, but I was lined up for a blind date. He asked who lined me up and who the guy was. Sharron had lined me up. It was someone she knew through her cousin in Lorette. Lorette was a small town about twenty minutes outside of Winnipeg. His name was Eric and he was an engineer. That was all I knew for now. I wasn't too thrilled with going, but he called and wanted me to go for supper with him. I accepted. He was supposed to pick me up. Gord laughed and told me to make sure I had cab fare with me.

I started to tell Gord about a friend of mine that I met through Community Respite Services at SMD. One afternoon, I was at the office making arrangements for respite when Shelly started talking about cross-country skiing. I started to ski some trails with her and her fiancé, John, and it didn't take long before we became good friends. When John asked Shelly to marry him, she came to me to make the wedding dress and all the bridesmaids' dresses. Their wedding party was putting on a social night in their honour in the next month or so. Gord asked me to let him know when I found out the date of the social evening. He would be interested in going.

We kept talking and drinking coffee, and I finally told him I had to go to get ready. He said I looked fine just like I was. It was a strange lunch. I really liked Gord and would definitely want more than a friendship with him, but he was younger than me and was never married and didn't have any kids. He walked me to my van and made a comment that there was something special about me and don't put up with any blind date being a jerk. I just smiled and drove away. It felt really good that Gord cared.

Eric picked me up right on time. He had a big smile on his face, so I take it he approved and didn't want to run. We went out in his half-ton truck. I knew nothing would come of this because he had rifles hanging on a rack in the rear window. I figured all that was missing was the cowboy hat. He had the boots. We talked during supper about his wife and how she walked out on him. I didn't say too much about myself. He was all right but like a farmer–not a farmer, but a country boy. He was a bit older than me and had been married for ten years. They had no kids. One thing for sure was he was very tall, dark hair, and good looking. The evening was short. I made it known that I had to be home early because I had church the next morning.

When Eric dropped me off, he said he had a curling banquet the next Friday night and wanted to know if I would go with him. I had nothing better to do so I said why not. He phoned me every day during that week. I thought that was a little too much. I didn't answer the phone to him; I just let him leave a message on the answering service.

Gord and I went to see the country and western band that Wednesday. He had asked me how my blind date went. I told him he was a real cowboy. He asked why I agreed to go out with Eric again. I told him I was tired of the same old grind. I hadn't dated in so long; now I may as well take advantage of it. We sat and talked for a couple of hours then I realized I was supposed to be there to decide what these guys should wear.

I introduced myself to the band during their break and the lead guy came and sat with us and told us what he had in mind. It was a lot of work in such a short time. He left me with his hotel phone number, and I said I would get back to him the next day. He asked if we could meet for lunch and talk about it. I told him I had a lunch appointment but would call him. We left.

Gord was talking to me through the window of the van. When we were saying goodnight he went to open my door. For a second I remembered the kiss at Tiffany's and wouldn't you know it, the door wouldn't open. He went around to the sliding door and sat in the bench seat and we talked for a while longer. He suggested I bring the van into the back of the building the next day and he would fix the door on his lunch hour.

The next morning, one of the girls from the company that rented the front office came in and asked me if I was busy the following weekend.

I told her, "No." Gord was sitting in the lunchroom at the time and could hear this.

She started to tell me about a friend of hers who was an airline pilot and that she had been telling him about me. She asked if he could call me to go out for supper.

I was so tired of people trying to set me up. I hated blind dates. I got the rundown on this guy. Finally I said, "Fine. Give him my phone number." Gord just shook his head.

The kids pretty well got into doing their own thing. P.J. didn't really settle down. He was still going to school but his grades showed he had no interest, and I had no answers, and the system had no help. Tammy was in school all day. She loved being with Patti, so it worked out well. J.J. was integrated in high school. It never took much to make him happy. He loved life. The only question he ever had was when could he drive. The answer was not good, so I just avoided it, which was probably wrong. P.J. still had hockey in the evenings. His friends ended up at a different level of hockey than he did. It was a money thing. When they would go to try out, they would just ask the parents to produce their bankbook and the decision was made from there. It really wasn't that bad, but the politics were cruel. He quit going to the Boys Club at the Church. He did come to church with us on Sundays as we were now going to Grant Memorial Baptist Church. It was quite a drive on Sunday mornings, but they had a great youth group and all three kids were involved.

P.J. didn't like me dating, but I made it clear he didn't have to like the guys I went out with. I told him someday he would have a woman of his own, and I really didn't want to spend my life alone. I thought then there would only be a few more years and the kids would move out whether it would be to group homes or just get married. They didn't have to approve of anyone I was with, just respect them. I would feel like P.J. would put me on a guilt trip about it. He still wanted me with Rudi and would find a way to rub in the fact that he was with Helena. I would make it clear to him that I was in the better position. I wasn't the one who cheated and revenge wasn't mine. God would handle Rudi and Helena in whatever way He saw fit for what they did. They were not my problem.

One day he made a comment about how God let this happen to J.J. and Tammy. I tried to tell him it wasn't God who did it. He said God allowed it. I knew that line. I had used it myself, but it wasn't true. What God allowed was the freedom of choice and because of that, this is what happened. I didn't have the right answers for him but at that time, I don't know if anyone did. He really hated the world around him and was running away.

I did get a phone call from the airline pilot. He asked me if I would go out with him for supper on the Friday night. I agreed but told him I would meet him at the restaurant. He was determined he would pick me up, so I finally agreed that he could get me from work. It was too cold to leave my van out so long without being plugged in and I made sure I had enough cash with me to take a cab if I had to. It was sad to go out with excuses to leave in case it didn't go well, but I just didn't know anything about this guy and didn't want to be stuck.

I called Janet and asked her what I should wear. She said to wear a dress and make it some kind of flight attendant style but with fancier material. The next day I rummaged through the leftover fabric with the girls to see what I could find. By the end of the day, we had made a cream coloured brocade dress, very fitted and above the knee. I felt good in it and that was enough for me.

Friday came too fast and I stayed after work. The kids were at respite so there was no reason to go home. I killed time until an hour before Chuck was to pick me up, and then I started to get ready. Mr. Sobey came in to say to have a good time. Sharron kept him filled in on my dating schedule. He said Gord was in the back and he would let him know I was still there, so he wouldn't lock me in. I was just about to go out front to meet Charles as we agreed, when Gord came in.

He expressed, "Wow, what's the occasion?"

I told him I had a date, a blind date. Gord had grease all over his hands and up to his elbows, and I asked him what he was doing.

He explained, "The forklift broke." He then said a guy came in the back looking for me. He didn't want to send a strange guy to see me when I was alone, so offered to come and get me. He didn't realize this was my blind date.

I asked him what he looked like.

Gord laughed and looked upward as if he was trying to remember, "Short, bald and is wearing a funny uniform."

I knew he was lying.

He said he would walk me back. As I was going out the door he commented he would guide me there and jokingly went to put his greasy hands on the back of my dress.

Charles wasn't tall, but he was taller than me. He wasn't bald, but his hairline was thinning. He was older than me, but I never was good at judging the age of people. I suggested I take my van so he didn't have to bring me back after. He wouldn't hear of it, he didn't mind at all. He was driving a 4x4, and as we were driving he asked if I had ever been at The Brothers Restaurant on Portage Avenue. I told him many times and that was great.

We sat in the Restaurant, and for the first fifteen minutes, he talked about himself. I just listened, and then he suggested we share a Caesar Salad. He said he didn't want to have garlic on his breath if I didn't.

I wanted to say to him, "Oh don't worry, you won't be kissing me anyway, so go for it." I didn't, I said, "I would love to."

He ordered wine, and for the next half hour we ate the salad and drank the wine and listened to Charles tell me all about himself. I didn't talk, I just listened until he started to tell me about when he was younger, and he had to learn how to land a plane on the Bonn Adventure.

I finally had something to say. I told him I was born in Dartmouth and lived there in my early teens. The Bonn Adventure was an aircraft carrier that was usually parked under the Agnes L. MacDonald Bridge on the Halifax side. When the bridge was built, there was a prediction. It would fall down on this certain date and land on the aircraft carrier. It just happened that on the certain date predicted, I was going to junior high in Dartmouth. It was such an event that we were let out of school early to watch the bridge fall–maritime entertainment. It was supposed to fall at noon. It didn't and still hasn't fallen to this day. When I finished the story, Charles just looked at me as if to say, "So." I didn't say too much after that. I felt intimidated.

The conversation didn't stop there. Charles had a lot to say, and I just kept smiling and sipped my wine. I didn't sip it slow enough I guess because I excused myself to go to the ladies washroom and felt pretty dazed on the way. When I came back, I switched to coffee. The meal was good and I was ready for him to take me back. It was close to eleven and he had to fly at seven in the morning, so I was sure he would drive me back to the van.

He had other intentions. He took me to his place that was just down the street from the restaurant. He asked me if I wanted a drink.

I said, "No, but I wouldn't mind a cup of coffee."

The living room was set up almost like a designer had been there–like a bachelor pad–leather chesterfield and chair and huge glass tables with a centrepiece that looked like a pod thing. His kitchen had a nook and the fancy high stools. There was a bar set up. He had all the appliances in his kitchen that I only dreamed of having some day. He did make me coffee and poured me a liquor to go with it. We sat in the living room and he sat uncomfortably close to me.

I prayed in my head, please Lord; get me out of this situation. Then I just kept thanking Him. Thank you for getting me out of this. I thought maybe I should start to preach to him. Maybe if I told him about my closeness to God he would suddenly realize how late it was and take me to my van. God had another idea. Charles put his arm around me and started to kiss me. In my head I was screaming, "God, I don't want to be in this situation."

I got an idea and asked him how he could ever fly such a big plane. I knew that he would love to answer that, and I was right. He explained in great detail how it was a computer that flew the plane. He only had to punch in the code number. He even went and got his black bag to show me what Pilots carry in their black bags. He showed me the book they follow to get the codes. I had asked all the questions I could and knew time was running out. Charles had just thrown the book in the bag and didn't hesitate to pick up where he left off.

He just planted a big kiss on me when the front door opened and in walked this young man. Charles quickly straightened out when the guy said hello. He introduced him as his son then asked him what he was doing home. He never gave the boy a chance to answer before he stated, "I thought you were staying at your mom's tonight."

His son answered, "No," and went to bed. Charles apologized for the interruption.

I told him not to worry, I had to go anyway. I offered to take a cab. It was late. He insisted on driving me.

Before he left, he said, "Hey, I have an idea." I was afraid to hear it. He then went on to say that I should just stay overnight and drive him to the plane in the morning. He was flying back at seven in the evening and I could pick him up and we would go out again. He said I could just keep the 4x4 for the day and leave the van at the shop. I was quick to say I had other plans for the next evening as if I had another date. He then asked if he could take me out again and I told him to call me.

He did call Monday, Tuesday and finally, on Wednesday, I returned his call. We just talked. He asked if I would have any interest in flying with him. I didn't know what he meant by that. He started to explain that he was thinking what would be fun for me to do with him since I was such a woman of adventure.

I interpreted that as, "What would I have to do with this woman to get her into bed?"

He went on to say I could fly to Toronto with him on his morning flight on a Friday. We could have breakfast together when I got there. He would then have to fly out again before lunch. He would arrange for me to have a room in the hotel. I could shop or go see one of the shows in town then he would fly back on Saturday morning. We could go to Niagara Falls for the day and come back on the noon flight on Sunday.

Ahhhhh, I thought, I knew it. What would happen on Saturday night? I asked him if I could think about it for a couple of days then get back to him. I said it sounded interesting as I have never seen Niagara Falls, but it would take some arranging on my part to take a long weekend without the kids. He suggested he pick me up for a late lunch on Friday and we would discuss it then. I agreed. He said he would pick me up right after he landed. It would be about two o'clock.

I told him that was fine but I wouldn't have much time because Fridays were always the busiest day.

He said we could go somewhere fast and close by. I could decide where and let him know when he got there.

We went to the restaurant across the street for a quick soup and sandwich when Charles came. I decided to be totally honest with him. I would lay it on the line. I pretty well stated in not so many words that I was really interested in going and getting to know him better, but I was a Christian and had no intention of sleeping with any man until I was married and I didn't have any plans to do that too soon in the future. He agreed quite quickly. I told him I could go, and had a sister going to University there. I would get in touch with her and stay with her on the Friday, and overnight, and then I would meet him when he came in on Saturday. He agreed. Then I would accept the hotel room for Saturday night, but my own room. He smiled and thought that would be great. He was really looking forward to it.

Charles then suggested I pick the weekend I wanted and all the arrangements would be made. I looked at my schedule and the following weekend was set-aside for Shelly and John's social. The weekend after that was a respite weekend so that would be perfect. He wrote it down and walked me back to work. He asked if we could go out the following week and I told him if I was planning to take a long weekend at the busy time of year, I would have to work overtime to be able to take it. I really didn't but I didn't want to go out again until we were leaving. Besides, the social was the following weekend.

Gord was standing in the lunchroom when I came back and asked, "Second date? I take it, it's is going well?"

I told him about the first date and about the plans to go to Toronto. He just laughed and asked when I was going. I told him Shelly and John's social was the following weekend so I was thinking about the week after that. He wanted to go to Shelly and John's social, so offered to be my escort. I told him it would be great, but only if he let me buy him supper before the social. He said he was looking after his stepsister Marcia's horses while they were away that weekend. He could be back in the city to pick me up by six to go for supper. He was driving her Bonneville for the weekend so he insisted on picking me up.

I again made a new dress. I was thinking, dress for success and since I was making all the dresses including the wedding dress for Shelly, I should dress the part for the social. I made a dress that was tailored and above the knee. It would have been overdressing normally, but I made it out of denim so it made it more fun.

Chapter 24

FALLING IN LOVE

*"There is no fear in love; but perfect love casts out fear
. . ." I John 4:18 (New King James Version)*

Gord arrived at ten to six, and I suggested we go to Brannigan's. He liked their food and there was a good selection. We ate and talked and caught up on each other's news. He then asked me about dating Eric and Chuck at the same time.

I wanted to have fun after not dating for so long, but I told him, "I hate going out with a guy and thinking if he pays for my meal, then I owe."

He was quick to say not to fall for that.

I told him, "I haven't slept with a guy for three years, and that wasn't about to change with any Eric or Charles." Gord referred to Charles as Captain Chuckles.

I went to take the bill when it came, as I did offer to take Gord out. He was insisting on paying it.

He offered once, twice and on the third time laughed and promised if I let him pay for the meal, he wouldn't expect anything from me in return.

I laughed and paid it myself.

His answer to that was I didn't trust him.

We went to the social and when he parked the car, Gord didn't get out. He had something to say. He said to never let any guy convince me I owed, and if it ever comes down to that then pay the bill myself. To make sure I always have the money with me to do that and the money for cab fare. He was very serious and said that I was far too good of a person for any guy to play that game with. Now coming from Gord, that was a compliment.

The social was really crowded. Gord asked me to dance.

I knew he hated dancing, so I said, "No."

Then a slow song came on and he grabbed my hand and pulled me up. We danced so close, it reminded me of Tiffany's Restaurant. I thought again about the kiss. That kiss had lingered for a couple of years. We danced until my head was spinning. There was no doubt in my mind that Gord was my best friend but was really more to me than that. My insides were floating like when I was in love when I was a teenager. When the dance was finished, Gord gave me a look that I would never forget. I didn't know what to think. I was confused.

I went into the washroom, and Shelly asked me if Gord and I had become more than "Just friends."

I replied no but why did she ask?

She smiled and answered it looked to her like it was taking a step further. So it wasn't my imagination!

Shelly and John invited us–after the social along with the wedding party–over to their new apartment. It was on the side of the city close to where Gord was looking after the horses. He asked me if I wanted to drive out with him to tend to the horses then we could go back to Shelly and John's apartment. It was late, but I was game. I loved horses and these were supposed to be very impressive horses, not what I was used to. They were "very expensive horses."

Gord was telling me about Marcia's husband Hermann. He was originally from Germany, and Gord went there for a visit. He was telling me about how they treated him so well when he was there and about driving a Mercedes on the Audubon and how he was speeding but everyone was still passing him. It's a guy thing. I thought how much fun it would be to go on a trip like that with Gord. We would have a lot of fun traveling together.

When we got to Shelly and John's there were a lot of people there. There was one space left to sit on the end of the couch and Gord sat down. I found that strange. He was always such a gentleman and normally would give me the seat with no question. After he sat down, he took my arm and whispered, "There is room for you," and sat me down on his lap. I was melting. The whole time he was talking to people, he was lightly touching my hand. I was surprised and I was confused. Shelly looked at me and winked. I think I turned red. We didn't stay too long. It was already two o'clock in the morning. We had a quick drink and left.

It was a quiet ride back to my place. It was about a half hour drive from Shelly's and I felt bad that Gord had to go all the way back to look after the horses.

When he pulled up in front of my apartment, I offered to make him a coffee for the road. I made a big pot of coffee and poured us each a cup then put the rest in a traveling mug for him to take. I sat beside him on the couch, and we were drinking the coffee. He said he wanted to talk to me about something. There was a fine line here that he wanted to step over, but he didn't want to ruin our friendship.

I couldn't believe my ears and I couldn't believe my answer. Without even thinking about it I answered don't step, jump. He smiled as if knowing I felt the same way was such a relief. I was in a state of shock and melted away when he took me in his arms and kissed me. There was that kiss! The one I never forgot about for the past couple of years. We sat quietly with his arm around me and my head on his shoulders while he finished his coffee. Then he left and promised he would call me as soon as he got up.

I was so tired when he left that I fell asleep right away. I woke up a couple of hours later and had to pinch myself to know I didn't just dream the whole thing. I was really going out with Gord. I kept it quiet though I felt like when I was a teenager and wanted to phone everyone I knew and tell them. I didn't.

Shelly was quick to phone and ask me what was going on. She wanted to get tickets to the playoff games for the Winnipeg Jets hockey playoffs. I just told her to get four tickets and form her own opinion. I did call Janet and told her because I told Janet everything. She asked me what I was going to do about the trip with Charles. I didn't know.

I had written a letter to my sister Estella saying I was coming for the weekend and asking if she had room for me. She really wasn't in Toronto, but I said if it was a problem that Charles was getting me a room in a hotel and she could just come in and stay there. I hadn't heard from her yet, but was sure I would. I included in the letter that I wanted her to pick out all the really expensive shops, and we could shop all day Friday. Neither of us could afford to buy, but the stores didn't have to know that. I hadn't seen Estella for a long time and really didn't know her that well, so I thought it would be good for us to spend time together. I told Janet on that note, I would still like to go. I was baffled and new at this. I would talk to Gord and see what he thought.

Gord called when he woke up and sounded as tired as I was. I thought maybe he would regret what he said and made sure there was an opening for him to say in case that was true. It wasn't. He made it very clear he was happy with the situation. For a long time already, if we were in a restaurant talking and the time was going by, I would say to Gord, "Have you had enough of me yet?"

He would always say "not near enough." That was when we were only friends.

I repeated that question to him on the phone and he laughed and answered, "Not even remotely close to near enough." He always had the right answers and if he didn't at first he just wouldn't answer until he did. I told him Shelly got tickets to the Jets game for that night and she got one for him.

He asked if he had to wait 'til then to see me.

I replied no, but the kids were home, so if he was coming over then be prepared for a lot of questions. I wasn't worried about Gord not being able to handle the fact that both J.J. and Tammy had disabilities.

Gord's mom left when he was a year old, and his dad raised him with a nanny until he was five. The nanny was Margaret, and she drove a little Volkswagen. Gord said that he drove her up the wall constantly in that car. When Gord was five, his dad, John, married Carol. Carol had a daughter, Marcia. She was two years older than Gord. Carol had polio and eventually had to walk with the help of a cane, then with crutches, so Gord was quite used to that kind of life.

Gord did come over in the afternoon, and yes Tammy and J.J. questioned him. I was sure he felt like he was getting the third degree. I invited him for supper and we went to the game. I felt so good. I had been out with Gord so many times in the past couple of years, but this time it was so different. He was still the gentleman he always was, but now he could take that a step further. We could hold hands and that alone to me was such a thrill. I knew everything there was to know about Gord, and he knew most things about me. I knew I would have to let him know my beliefs about God in more detail but could talk to him so freely, it didn't matter. I didn't have to be phony in any way with Gord. I could just be myself.

At half-time at the game, I had to go to the washroom. We were way up in the nosebleed section of the arena. That is where Shelly, John and I always got the tickets for, or we couldn't afford to go to all the games. I knew that Sharron and Rick were in the front section. They had season tickets. I thought there were so many people; we would never run into them. Wrong! Gord and I were walking back from the washrooms and ran into Sharron face to face. Gord stood and talked with his hand lying on my shoulder. I have to say the look on Sharron's face was priceless. I could tell she wanted to pull me aside and say, "What is going on?" And for me to tell her every detail.

Shelly, John, Gord, and I went to every playoff game that week. It was great. I didn't talk to Gord about going the following weekend. He knew I was scheduled to go but neither of us brought it up.

I didn't hear from my sister. I tried to call her, but she never answered.

I thought maybe she just thought she was meeting me at the airport when I flew in. I gave her all the details in the letter. How could I not go now? I prayed that if I wasn't suppose to go that I would get a hold of Estella so I could tell her, and she wouldn't travel to Toronto for nothing.

Charles phoned me and told me he would send a car for me at five-thirty in the morning. He called me back the next day and said to make it between six and six-thirty. I told him fine. He was looking forward to the weekend. I didn't tell him I wasn't. I was thinking to myself while I was talking to him one evening, I should ask him if there is an extra seat on the plane for Gord. I would love to go to Niagara Falls with Gord. Of course, I would have gone anywhere with Gord and loved it.

Thursday night came, and Gord and I had to talk about it. I told him I was going.

He wasn't surprised, he expected that. If he were too upset, I wouldn't have gone. He told me he would pick me up at the airport on Sunday. He would be the one with rings on his fingers and bells on his toes.

I laughed and told him he can't do that. I would be getting off the plane with Charles. I would find the right time to tell Charles but it would be really tacky saying, "Thanks for the trip, Charles. Oh, there is my boyfriend now to pick me up."

Gord just laughed and said, "Hey, I like that idea."

When he left, I told him at noon the next day that he would know that I was thinking of him.

He asked how.

I told him to wait and see. He gave me one of those long lingering kisses to make sure I wouldn't forget what that was like over the next three days. Little did he know at the time, I had no idea what I was going to do to let him know I was thinking of him at noon the next day.

I was packed and ready to go. The car came late. I was so unsure of what I was doing right up to the plane taking off and it coming over the announcement. "This is your Captain speaking." I knew at that point, there was no turning back. The driver took me to the plane. I didn't have to wait for the people to board. Charles met me at he door of the plane and told me he saved the best seat in the house. I was put in first class and had a window seat. I didn't feel very comfortable and didn't hesitate to let him know that flying wasn't my favorite thing in life. He assured me I had nothing to worry about; this plane had the best pilots. The attendants knew I was with Charles and I got the royal treatment.

I was feeling guilty in two directions and thought to myself this is really stupid. Not only is this not fair to Gord, but it was really unfair to Charles. I was living a lie here with him and not feeling very good about myself. I thought I would deal with it when we landed because I was not very comfortable with the flight though it was quite smooth. I was served champagne and orange juice with my breakfast, and sipped it very slowly as I knew what happened to me when I drank and flew at the same time.

Estella wasn't there when I got there. I figured I would try to phone her. I got really uncomfortable with the whole situation and thought I had better think about doing the right thing. Charles had a few things to do so arranged to meet me in the restaurant in half an hour. I was really glad because it gave me time to make a plan. I tried to call Estella first, praying God if you want me to stay then have her answer the phone. There was no answer.

I called my neighbour at home. She owed me a couple of favours because I looked after her daughter for her on a couple of occasions. She always wanted to find a way to repay me because I wouldn't accept any money from her. I called her and told her I had a way she could repay me, and she was game for anything.

She was to go across the street to the florist shop and find an arrangement with the most masculine flower. I was really hoping they had a Bird of Paradise because I always thought that was masculine. I told her to get a card and to write in it, "Have you had enough of me yet?" I wanted Gord to know it was really from me and I knew that line would do it. Then I told her to write, "If not, meet me at Yamato's Restaurant at seven." She had to deliver it to Gord through the back door of Ram Messenger at exactly noon. Then she had to phone Yamato's Restaurant and make a reservation for two for seven o'clock. I would explain it all and pay her back when I got home. She said to consider it done.

Now was the hard part. Telling Charles the truth and that I wanted to fly back with him. He was so disappointed, and I said I was so sorry and meant it. He didn't really want to talk about it anymore and arranged to meet me at the plane. I had an hour to kill until we flew, but I didn't do anything but sit there because I didn't want to miss the plane.

It was finally time to go. I wasn't the first on the plane and when I gave my name at the desk I could see my name was changed to mud. I was put in the last seat in the very back of the plane and didn't get a window seat. I guess that said it all. It was a rough flight and I am sure that was planned. The attendants didn't pay any attention to me.

I got back into Winnipeg at one, and the first thing I did was phone my neighbour. I asked her how it went and she said she got the Bird of Paradise and delivered it precisely at noon to Gord with the card. So now I had six hours to kill 'til then. I wasn't going to call him.

I called Janet and she laughed when I said I came back. She told me to pick up the key and go to her house for the afternoon. I had my hair, nails and make-up done. After that I did go to Janet's to get changed. She and Henry laughed when they got home from work and said they would love to be a fly on the wall at Yamato's.

Yamato's was a Japanese Restaurant and you sit on the floor. You don't actually sit on the floor, there is a square opening under the tables and the floor is raised so you look and feel like you are sitting on the floor. It was Janet's and my favourite place to meet for lunch, and I always thought a supper there in the evening would be so romantic.

I got to the restaurant early because I wanted to be seated with Gord's favourite bottle of wine already opened and poured in two glasses when he came in. It went perfectly. He came into the restaurant. I could hear him give my name. He was brought through these curtains and was standing a distance away looking at me.

The restaurant was full and he said out loud, "It is you! You are really here!" It was great. He sat down on the floor.

I picked up my wine glass and stated, "I couldn't stay away for three days." I told him the whole story and he was thrilled. I asked him what he thought when he got the card and flowers.

He said he couldn't believe it and called Yamato's and asked if they had a reservation for two for seven for a Gord Kell. They said "No." He said he had spent the afternoon being angry and not understanding why I would do that, and then about three-thirty called them back and asked, "Do you have a reservation for two for seven for a Tricia Hardt?" She said, "Yes." That put him in panic. His suit had to be steamed and he needed to clean his condo just in case we went back there–being it was so close to the restaurant. He left work early and cleaned his apartment then found a place he could get his suit steamed. I just kept laughing. It was all so great. He just kept telling me he was so glad I was there. He couldn't imagine thinking about me with Captain Chuckles all weekend.

He asked if I was going home and I told him I couldn't. They thought I was gone for the weekend and I was going to leave it at that. Janet and Henry offered me their guest room for the weekend. He offered for me to stay at his place. I gave him a look and he just smiled and said you can have the bed and I will take the couch.

His condo was nice. Good for him. It was a one bedroom with a sunken living room. In the corner of the living room was a wood-burning fireplace. The dining room overlooked the living room. The kitchen was small but big enough to hold a table with two chairs. He had all the necessities, fridge, stove, dishwasher, toaster oven and percolator. It was down a hall to a large bathroom and off the bathroom was a door that led to a washer and dryer.

An independent bachelor. Wow, I never knew what that was like before. He actually cooked, (only because he had to). He never liked cooking and had a very selected few things he could pull off. He did his own laundry. (He said he had thirty shirts in his closet and would only wash and iron them once a month because he had to).

I felt very guilty when I saw I would be sleeping in the middle of a King Size Waterbed and Gord would be sleeping on a couch.

Janet and Henry didn't live too far away. I could stay there for the night and he could come to get me in the morning.

He said "No way." He then promised he wouldn't come into the bedroom. I made it clear that wasn't my problem. I knew he was a true gentleman and never had any doubt that he would respect my beliefs. I did stay at his house.

I didn't sleep too much that night thinking I needed to get up extra early to shower and get dressed. Going out with Gord would normally mean a good hour in the bathroom for make-up and hair. Now that I was at his condo, I would want to do it without disturbing his routine.

I was ready with all necessities by eight o'clock. I went into the kitchen to make coffee and Gord rolled over on the couch and said he was taking me to meet his family at a restaurant in Headingly. I was glad I was in the kitchen and he couldn't see the look on my face. Meet his family? That would take a week to mentally and physically prepare for; then I still wouldn't be ready and he wanted to go when?

He just looked at his watch when I asked him, meaning real soon. "Like we have to be at the restaurant in one hour."

Gord came out of the shower and was ready. How can one man just have to shower and run a comb through his hair and look so good? Some things in life are just not fair. We sat and had a quick cup of coffee before we left, and Gord filled me in on what to expect from the family. Saturday morning breakfast was a ritual. His step-mother, Marcia and Herman and sometimes some of the neighbours from the farm would meet in a restaurant just out of the city, have breakfast and leave.

We pulled up the restaurant. It was really cold and snowy. We sat in the car and waited for the rest to pull in before we got out. A champagne coloured car pulled into the Handicap Parking Stall. The door opened and an older lady got out with two crutches. The kind of metal crutches that wrap around your arms. I thought for a moment as we headed for the door, that she and I would get along great.

That was wishful thinking. She looked at me as I stood back and let her go through the door first. *THAT LOOK!* One of those that threw a thousand darts and after I fell over, she beat me with her crutches. I could say it wasn't that bad, but that is how it made me feel. When we got through the door, I offered to hang up her coat when she took it off but she just gave me another one of those *LOOKS!* And asked me if I thought she was crippled or something.

Gord introduced her to me as Carolyn, and then introduced me as his girlfriend, Tricia. I said hello and went to sit down with Gord. He gave me a smile that was so warm and told me not to think twice about it. That was the benefit of our relationship. The fact that we had been friends for so long and had already developed a sixth sense of knowing what the other person is thinking by the look on our faces. I decided after we were sitting (even after I ended up face to face across from Carolyn), that it really didn't matter what they thought. Gord and I were strong together. That was all that mattered. I knew he wouldn't let Carolyn push this too far.

Marcia was full of questions but pleasant, and her husband, Herman, was a real comedian. By the time the breakfast was over, they knew I had three children and what had happened to them. What I didn't know was they had formed an opinion that I was a welfare case, out looking for a man and managed to latch on to Gord. It was too bad they didn't really get to know me. Herman had asked Gord to help them move a piano from their old house to the new one. He already had planned for it and was meeting someone from Ram Messenger that had a truck that could handle it. He told them WE would be there around one o'clock.

As we were pulling out, Gord told me he never liked to take his girlfriends to meet Carolyn. Apparently the last time was quite a long time ago and was so bad that he told Carolyn he wasn't going to bring the girls to meet her. The next time she would meet a girlfriend it would be the one he was going to marry. I looked at him in shock. No, I knew that wasn't in any way talking about marriage, but the fact that she thought this welfare case with her stepson was going to be married into her high fallutin' family was more than she could stand. No wonder she gave me the look. She wanted Gord to marry one of the equestrian horse jumping girls–one with a rich daddy. Like Gord said, he had been there and dated them, and had no interest in any of these girls. He was just tired of these girls taking and taking, and still he could never please them.

I thought how I would feel, given the situation with P.J., when he grew up and kind of understood a little bit (even though I knew it was wrong) why Carolyn was so bitter. Gord asked me why I was so quiet all the way back in the city and I told him I was praying for his family. He laughed, but I am sure he didn't know I was serious.

We did move the piano and had a coffee at Marcia and Herman's, then left.

I was glad to spend time alone with Gord again. He took me out to the Crystal Bay Restaurant across from the condo for supper, and again we sat and talked over coffee until the restaurant was closing. We had a lot of new things to talk about. He told me about his dad marrying Carolyn and when Marcia started with the horses. His dad bought her the first horse, and it took up so much time. He told me how they owned two golden retrievers, Rover and Gypsy when he was growing up. Rover was owned by a relative of Carolyn's but didn't like the way they treated him so kept going to Gord's house. Gord's dad kept taking him back home, but Rover was persistent until Gord's dad finally gave up and let the dog adopt them. He started to show Rover in shows and a year later bought another purebred golden retriever and called her Gypsy. Gord was only seven when Rover came, so he grew up with the two dogs. In Gord's mind, the only real dog was a golden retriever; anything else was just an imitation.

He told me Carolyn and his dad split up a couple of years after Gord had been put in boarding school. Since he could only come home for a few hours on Sunday, he lost track of any details of what was happening with the family, and therefore never really knew what led them to splitting up. It was something neither of them seemed to want to share with him at first and he respected that. He said afterwards, he did hear stories. Carolyn and Marcia were very emotionally open about the situation. Gord could tell it had been magnified several times over so just chose to distance himself from the problem and not choose sides.

His dad was on his own and worked for years for Investors Group, but

Gord never really knew the details of his job. He just knew he was one of the chief stock traders. They didn't see much of each other simply because Gord was always so busy. They lived about ten minutes from each other, so I couldn't really understand that. I never could comprehend why people in the same city as their family didn't spend time together because of my situation with my family living so far away. Gord said Carolyn and his granny (Carolyn's mother) would call for him to help them on several occasions and because of the Saturday morning breakfast standard, he saw more of them.

The next day, Gord and I both went to church. Shelly and John met us there. The church was across the street from Gord's condo. We pretty well spent the rest of the afternoon discussing my Christian beliefs.

When I got home, the first thing the kids asked me was what I brought them from Toronto. Of course I did think of that, and gave them each T-shirts that I quickly grabbed from one of the airport souvenir shops before I left. They didn't realize I was in Winnipeg for the weekend.

Gord and I saw each other every day at work, and we decided to not tell anyone at Ram Messenger that we were "an item." We didn't want anyone saying conflict in the company. It didn't take long though for everyone to figure it out.

Gord decided to come with me to do the Pumpkin Creek Mystery Tour. We drove out in the morning with Shelly and John and had to ski a brutal run of twenty kilometers all up and down hill. It was really a tough run. I kept running out of energy. It was the first time I saw Gord really frustrated. He had done so much of this kind of thing at school; he just didn't want to be doing it anymore. He did it for me. We went to all the Jets Games together and on weekends when it warmed up enough, we went cycling together.

One Friday, I cycled to Gord's house and when I walked in the condo, he was on the phone. He put his finger up for just a minute and kept talking. I went in the fridge and got a drink and sat down. The conversation on the phone was really odd. He was talking to a woman and said, "It will be great to see you again; it has been so long."

I asked him who he was talking to and he wrote on a piece of paper, Jennifer. I just sat quietly and was wondering who is Jennifer and why would it be great to see her after so long? I was really uncomfortable hearing this conversation and felt I shouldn't be there listening in.

He then went on to tell her he was now six feet tall and had blonde curly hair. He laughed and was just so pleasant. He then said, "Absolutely, call me when you get here and I will take you out for supper."

That was it; I couldn't stand it any more. I quickly wrote a note to him in the kitchen that he could call me after he finished his conversation; I was going to cycle back home. I laid it beside him on the table and walked toward the door.

He quickly said on the phone. "Jennifer something has come up and I have to go right away. Call me."

I tried to get out the door because I could feel the waterworks starting. Gord stopped me and asked me what was wrong. I told him I just was really uncomfortable listening to the conversation and I wanted to leave. I would talk to him later.

He gave me a hug and started to laugh and explained, "Trish, Jennifer is my long lost mother that left when I was just a baby."

I couldn't look at him. I was so crushed. I felt so stupid and said I was sorry. I started to laugh through my tears and that was the end of it. He just told me that she called to say she was coming to the city and wanted to see him. I was so embarrassed. He ordered in some supper for us and afterward we were sitting on the love seat. He came and gave me a kiss and I knew if we didn't stop (I didn't want to) where it would be headed. We had to come up with a plan. After batting around a few crazy ideas, we decided whenever we were going to sit together like this or start a necking session, we would first put the timer on the stove for fifteen minutes. It was a little bit too long and put it back to ten minutes. We finally decided it would be better if we just stayed active and I don't mean on the coach.

I was going to a Bible study group with about eight couples that met in a house once a week. Gord didn't take long to ask if he could come with me. One day at lunch at work, he asked me how much I loved him.

I answered with "I love you as far as the north is from the south and as far as the east is from the west."

He was so impressed with my answer and asked me where I got it. I told him that is just how much I love him. God gave it away. That night we went to Bible study and Gord almost fell over when we were reading scriptures and the one they gave him to read was Psalm 103:12–*"How far has the Lord taken our sins from us? Farther than the distance from east to west!"* He read it and just looked at me. I slouched down on the couch and started to laugh.

Gord said, "Just made it up, eh."

I told him, "God has a sense of humor." It was really the first time

Gord realized what I meant when I said things that happen aren't coincidence. We told the rest of the group what was going on.

For the next few days, most of Gord's discussions and mine were about God. Being raised in a private boy's school like he was, the Bible and religious studies were very important. He seemed to develop a hunger to know more. We talked about what becoming a Christian meant and went through the questions one at a time.

I explained that God would meet him where he was. It didn't mean he had to not drink or swear. God would guide us one step at a time to what His will is for us.

One afternoon Gord came into the shop and whispered to me, "If I become a Christian, does it mean I can't dance anymore."

I looked at him and said, "You hate dancing."

He smiled and said, "I know."

I said, "No, that is not what it means."

He said, "Oh that is too bad," smiling back at me as he walked back out the door.

The following week, Gord did accept Christ at our Bible study. Now he completed the list of what I was looking for in a man. I was so thrilled I could talk so openly with him and not be so careful in what I said.

Chapter 25

THE PERFECT HOUSE

"Every good and perfect gift comes down from the Father
who created all the lights in the heavens." James 1:17

The business was doing well, and I knew it was time to move out of the low rental and buy a house. I managed to put away some money earmarked for the down payment. I was looking in the "under $100,000 range."

J.J. was turning eighteen and because of his disability was able to attend school till he was twenty-one. P.J. was sixteen and was angry. He didn't want to be in school anymore. I was still going to Tough Love and was still very confused by the difference of Tough Love and God's Love. I think I was a mother that didn't want to see my son make mistakes, and if he did make mistakes, I didn't want to see him suffer the consequences for those mistakes. A teenage boy living with his mother with an attitude hanging over his shoulder tends to make him not want to grow up but to run away instead. Tammy was fifteen, still in junior high, still with Patti and loved it. She had started to talk much better, but sometimes she would babble on and forget she had to watch how she was talking if she wanted people to understand. We finally let the therapists know she could talk. They were really surprised because they were sure her vocal cords had been damaged past the point of functioning again.

Because the kids were raised in the same area of the city most of their lives, I was planning on looking in that neighborhood to buy a house. Gord was trying to convince me to move closer to his condo. Janet and Henry were helping him convince me because they lived out there too.

I usually saw Staci during the week because she was doing a lot of singing with the orchestra, so I made most of her stage clothes. Pastor Ron gave me a name of a Real Estate agent he thought would be very patient and show me all that was available in my price range. She was really good.

Gord and I looked at so many houses in my area, but none of them seemed to be worth the money. I was getting discouraged and told Gord I was praying so much to find a good deal. Gord said he had been praying I would move into his area. I decided then if that is what God wanted, then who am I to argue.

I finally gave God the whole situation and asked Him to show me where the house is He wanted me to buy. For a week we looked at houses in Gord's area. There was one right down the street from Janet and Henry's that finally seemed like a good deal. It was smaller than I really wanted, and it was a bi-level. I was hoping for the potential of a four bedroom, but this one didn't. It had a small living room and no family room but had a rec room. There was a small computer room that could be used as a really small bedroom. They were asking for $95,000, and I put an offer in at $90,000. I again gave it to God and said if He didn't want me to have it, they wouldn't even counter offer. Another offer had beaten me at $92,500 and I knew it wasn't the house I was supposed to have. I told Gord I was tired of looking at houses and was going to take a break from it.

November came and there was already so much snow. The kids were at respite one weekend, and on Sunday morning Gord and I were coming out of church when he said there was an open house on Peacock Place. He asked if I wanted to go to look. I laughed and asked him where Peacock Place was. He said in Waverly Heights. I told him I didn't like Waverly Heights. It was ten minutes from his condo in a nice area. The street was like a large cul-de-sac with fifteen houses, and this house was at the end on the bend. That gave it a large pie-shaped lot. We pulled up in front and there was a gravel driveway that went into a double attached garage but the house wasn't much bigger than the garage. It looked like a little bungalow. I stated, "This place is way too small." Gord agreed but wanted to go in and look anyway since we were there. The agent was sitting on a chair in the sunken living room. The living room was large and had a Tyndalstone fireplace covering one wall. There was a cathedral ceiling that went up to the next level. From the front door entrance I could see into the next level. There was a dining room and kitchen. The place was huge. The guy asked if were interested in seeing everything, and I replied yes. About seven stairs went up to the next level from the living room and another seven beside it going down to another level. He took us upstairs first. The dining room was divided off from the kitchen with dark wood cabinets with fancy window doors opening to the dining room like a china cabinet. To the left was another room open to the dining room with a large opening overlooking the living room. We headed for the kitchen and to the left was a full bathroom and next to that was a really big, and I mean really big, master bedroom with wall-to-wall closets and two windows looking out on the back yard. I went into the kitchen and there were so many cabinets and running along one wall was a nook. At the end of the kitchen were patio doors that went out to a large screened in deck. The agent then asked if we wanted to see the pool. He told us it was covered for the winter, but we could see the size of it. Pool? Did this man say pool? I looked at Gord and whispered, how much is this house? He didn't know. Here I was drooling over the house, and we didn't know how much. We stepped out on to the deck that overlooked the pool.

The pool was sooo big. Gord asked the guy what size the pool was, and he said it was the biggest pool made for residential homes. It was sixteen by thirty-six feet and had a diving board and slide. The deep end was nine feet. The pool was set off to just less than half of the yard, and as we looked out at the rest of the yard, I was definitely falling in love.

The agent just laughed and said the first owner took pride in doing the landscaping. He showed us all the trees and explained what kind they were. The yard was so big. Gord and I just looked at each other and I said out loud, "This is way over my budget." The agent didn't say how much at that point. He asked if we wanted to see the rest of the house. At that point I thought why not; torture me a bit more. We went back to the living room and down the small staircase to another level. There was a long hallway with a lot of doors. He opened the first door on one side and it was a laundry room–A real laundry room, not in the basement. The room was big enough for a washer and dryer and a table or shelves to put the clothes on. There was even room for an ironing board if I wanted. We continued on down the hall to the second bathroom–two bathrooms, two bathrooms with full shower and bath.

I turned to Gord and whispered, "This is the house I asked Pastor Ron to pray for," and he laughed.

Across the hall was a bedroom the agent referred to as a small bedroom, but was bigger than the kids' rooms they had now. At the end of the hall was another huge bedroom with two big windows. We were walking back down the hall to go back to the living room when the guy opened a door I thought was a closet. My eyes popped open when it led down another small staircase to the bottom level. This was the basement, but had the definite potential for a rec room. We went down and around the corner was a huge bedroom framed out but not finished–the potential fourth bedroom. We went back upstairs and the agent handed us a piece of paper with all the information on. The asking price was $129,900.

I was so disappointed though I knew the house was well worth it. I went home and didn't say too much on the way. The phone was ringing when I walked in the door. It was Pastor Ron. He asked me how we made out. I told him it was the house I asked him to pray for. He explained the house was eleven years old and he checked it out.

He said to offer $100,000. I told him that was ridiculous and he replied, "No, the guy who owns the house has two daughters and his wife left him. The house is going to go into receivership if it doesn't sell in the next week. The guy only owes $89,000 so if you offer $100,000 he still gets something out of it. If he loses it, he gets nothing."

I told Gord. He figured out that I would need about $18,000 down payment if I got it for $100,000 and took over the mortgage.

He suggested, "Go for it."

We called our agent and she wrote up the papers. I offered $100,000 with the possession date in three months, so I could figure out how to get the down payment together.

The conditions were that all the appliances stay because I didn't have any appliances. Our agent left, and we prayed. I think Gord was praying harder because he really liked the idea of having me ten minutes away from his condo.

The guy counter offered. He came back with $119,000 and no appliances. I was really not surprised but disappointed. I called Pastor Ron, and he said don't give up and reminded me of the scripture in Galatians 6:9 *"Let us not become weary in doing good, for at the proper time we will reap a harvest if we do not give up." (NIV)*

He suggested to counter offer $101,000. I told him I couldn't get the money together for the down payment.

He asked how long would it take to save another $1000.

I replied, "If I work my butt off and do nothing else, then one month."

He then suggested I counter offer and put the possession one month longer. I did.

The guy counter offered $112,000 and no appliances. I was getting frustrated and a little crazy, so I countered again, $102,000 and five months until possession date. He came back with $105,000 and no appliances.

I accepted the offer but with six months possession. We closed the deal. It only took five minutes after signing the papers for me to start to panic. How was I going to come up with $23,000 in six months for the down payment? Only one way–give it to God.

Gord and I discussed going to Calgary after Christmas so he could meet the family. I cringed at the expense but he offered to pay the bill. I couldn't let him do that but knew it was only fair that we go. God would somehow provide, so I agreed. He also wanted me to meet his dad; he called him and asked him to come over for supper. I was a little nervous but really wanted to meet him. Gord was doing the cooking. His specialty was cooking steak. He baked potatoes, and I made a salad and dessert. We were totally organized and had the table set quite nicely when the buzzer went. Gord rang him in, and isn't it funny when you are meeting someone like that for the first time, you don't know what to do with yourself. I thought should I stand in the dining room by the table and close to the front door. Maybe I would sit in the living room with a glass of wine–no not good. Maybe I would keep my apron on and be busy in the kitchen. Did I really want someone's first impression of me to be in the kitchen with my apron on? Never!

I just went to the door with Gord and when he opened the door there stood a very tall, distinguished gentleman with curly gray hair and such a nice smile, though it was a nervous smile. He was dressed in slacks, shirt and a casual blazer and there was no mistake this was Gord's dad. He was so pleasant, and when we sat down to eat, it was quite obvious he had been raised in life with etiquette. He knew exactly what utensils to use in what order and was so fine tuned to conversation. If I were going to a really classy dinner where so many courses were to be served, this is who I wanted to sit next to, so I could follow his lead.

He had just gotten back from a cruise off the coast of Florida and was telling us he met a lady friend on the ship. Her name was Sonya, and he called her Sonny. She lived in Miami. He said she was coming for a visit, and he wanted us to meet her. We sat and talked over coffee for hours, and by the time he was leaving; I felt that I had known him a long time. It was such a comfortable evening and very enjoyable.

Quite literally, I had to give the purchase of the house situation to God. There was no possible way in my life I could come up with that money. Sure Gord offered to help me pay for the house, but I wouldn't hear of it. He understood that I had to do this myself. There were too many years I had nothing, and I had to prove that with God helping, I could have this house. I didn't want to lean on anyone. This was a real test of faith.

We started having an unwelcome guest come to our door a couple of times a day. It was a kitten. P.J. really wanted to keep it, but what was I going to do with a kitten? It looked to be a little over six months old. P.J. called her

Samantha. Every time we would come home, this cat would be meowing at the door as if she lived at our house. P.J. kept telling me the cat wanted to adopt us. It was obviously looked after, and I couldn't understand why she was so determined to come to live with us.

I said, "No, no, no. I had a cat when I was a little girl and lived in North Bay, Ontario. Her name was Precious, and she was. She had kittens, and one day when the kittens were out on the doorstep with Precious, a very nasty neighbour came out and threw Javex water on them. I think it really did some damage to my insides because after that time I had no desire to ever own a cat again."

I didn't think P.J. would make me cave in. If anything, it would be the cat being so determined and Gord. He was the type of person that would bring home every stray animal around.

I slowly started to pack my good dishes and anything that we wouldn't need for the next few months. I also started doing as much aerobics as possible and all the extra Avon runs. Gord hated to see me do the Avon runs. I would pull in the back of Ram Messenger in thirty below with my ski-do suit on and have fifty heavy boxes to deliver. He always said I was too much of a lady to be lifting those boxes. I told him it was because of those boxes we had met each other. He helped me as much as he could, but was still running the dispatch during the delivery. Deposits were coming in for weddings being ordered. I just kept banking as much as I possibly could. By Christmas, there was $13,000 in the account. I had a long way to go. I budgeted everything I could, and every penny that wasn't being used to live went into the account.

Gord came over at Christmas with a pile of gifts. I had most of the packing done, so he started to load up the van with suitcases while we waited for the kids to get up. They finally had to get up at seven because I woke up J.J. to get his pills. (We did see some more seizures after the big one he had at Patti and Warren's, but they were few and far between. The neurologist was finally coming up with a pill plan that was working.)

The gifts were opened fast as the kids just wanted to get to Calgary. I saved the best gift till last. The kids were each given one gift at the end and had to open it together. In J.J.'s parcel was a cat dish and a bag of cat food. In P.J.'s gift there was a litter box with a big bag of litter. In Tammy's box there were kitty toys. They got the message real fast that they could keep the cat and as long as she didn't go home and no one claimed her by the time we moved, she would be moving with us. Sam was on trial for adoption.

Gord had given me all kinds of things for the new house and a gorgeous pair of gold earrings. It was strange when I pulled a gift out from under the tree that was from Gord's dad. He had sent a bottle of French perfume so nicely wrapped with a card. He knew all about the kids and the situation and still gave me the bottle of perfume. It was like an acceptance in a way, so considerate.

Marcia, Hermann and Carolyn never managed to send a card. It was being made very clear to me that I wasn't welcome in their lives. That was all right. Gord stood by me, and I stood by him. I was looking forward to meeting Sonny when she came.

We left for Calgary. We were going for ten days. The shop was closed and the kids were off school. We had left the tree up with some unwrapped gifts under it and the neighbour offered to check on the apartment for us while we were gone.

It was so good to see Mom. We never saw enough of her. I had always prayed she would move to Winnipeg, but God only answers prayers to the good. So I just always chalked it up to the fact that mom must be better off in Calgary. We talked on the phone sometimes–long distance but not often enough because neither she nor I were in the financial position to pay for it.

The entire trip was great for the first part. I can't imagine having that many people stay with you for so many days. Tammy was in my mom's room one evening while we were there and noticed my dad's urn with ashes on the dresser. She asked my mom what that was, and my mom told her Grampa's ashes. Tammy went in to a screaming fit that none of us could control. She was so angry that Grampa was in that box. When we were talking about it over her screaming, we realized that Tammy had her accident the week after Grampa's funeral, and she never had the time to deal with it and didn't know that he was cremated or even what that was. It got so bad we almost had to sit on her. She was so out of control. She hadn't regained the ability to cry after the accident. So I guess this was her way of letting loose. It went on for hours. No one was getting any sleep, and everyone was getting more irritable. I thought maybe we should just leave and go home. Tammy was too out of control to drive with. P.J. was really getting angry and went out the door for a walk. Estella was there, and the comment that came out of her was that Tammy was just a spoiled brat. I had to agree that was what she was acting like, but I guess if any of us had our life kicked out from under us going into our teen years like she did and remembers fully what her life was like before the accident, we could have the out of control fits too. I don't think I was so much angry for what was said about Tammy, but I was more hurt for Tammy's sake. My kids thought the world of their Aunt Thelma and Aunt Estella, and I would have hoped for more understanding. I blamed it on everyone being tired and saying things without thinking.

We did pack up and go home the next day. It was a hard trip. For some strange reason, the out of control behaviour kept up with Tammy. All I wanted was to get home. The roads weren't the greatest. For a couple of long stretches, it had snowed so hard we almost had to pull off the highway. Things finally did settle down with all the kids, and they fell asleep.

It was nice and quiet after Regina, and Gord did all the driving, so I decided to make a plan for the house and catch up on my schedule. I had gotten a new schedule book from my mother for Christmas, so I was filling in what was already scheduled for the next day. J.J. had more surgery on his arm, and I knew the specialist appointment was coming up soon to get the results checked. (His fingers were clenched fairly tightly on his one hand, caused from little use of it, and the tendons were clipped to loosen it.) It seemed to work quite well. When I looked up the appointment, I mentioned to Gord it was a good thing we were heading back because J.J.'s appointment was scheduled for the next morning. I kind of forgot about it over the holidays.

I finished filling in the schedule book and just sat looking out the window. There was a sign that said Virden, five miles. I hated the stretch we were on. It always dragged. For all the times I traveled home from Calgary, Virden to Brandon, and then to Winnipeg, was always such a long stretch. In about three more hours, we would be home.

There was a noise, and then Gord had to pull the van over to the side of the highway. Virden was right in front of us. It was already later in the evening and dark. The noise didn't stop. He thought it was a tire, but it sounded like something was dragging. Gord managed to get the van pulled into a gas station. The guy pulled it into a bay to check it out. It was far worse than any tire. It was the rear end. It was not only going to be very expensive to repair, but it would take time to get the parts brought in. The guy told us to get ourselves a hotel room and he would have an answer for us the next morning as to the damages and how long it would take.

There was a hotel just a two-minute walk from the gas station so we went and booked one double room just so we could all get comfortable while we waited. Tammy refused to come into the hotel. She recalled a movie she had watched years ago before her accident and said she would not come into the hotel with us. We had to force her, and if we thought we had seen her out of control the night before, we found out we hadn't seen anything yet.

She just kept screaming and yelling. She was fighting to leave the room. She was very small but was very solid and hard to hang on to. I started to cry. We had to bodily force her to stay. The Trans Canada Highway was right outside the door, and we couldn't let her get out the door. She finally did settle down enough to tell us about the movie that had her so out of control, about a young boy who went into a hotel room with his dad. His dad was taking him to Disneyland or something like that. After the boy went to sleep, the dad poured gas around his bed and lit it on fire to kill the boy. He lived and was severely burned. I asked her why she was so afraid of that movie. She told us she was afraid because her dad didn't like her anymore because she was handicapped. It was sick to think of how much she had bottled up inside of her. I thought I would get her some help when we got home. We tried to ease her mind about the whole situation, but she was too wound up. It was to the point of us having to sit on her to hold her down. We knew what it meant to restrain someone but didn't know the proper way of doing it.

She finally did fall asleep for a short time. Gord dozed off, and I stayed up and got the Bible out. I brought my Bible on the trip with me, but it is very hard to get up in the morning and do your devotions when you are on a trip. It definitely showed on Gord and me.

At about ten I was reading and made the decision I was going to give God all this mess: the van, the money to fix it, the down payment on the house, with the kids, the bitterness that I saw growing in P.J., and the out of control behaviour with Tammy, mine and Gord's relationship and where it was going. I gave it all to God and asked Him to handle it all for me and guide me to wherever He wanted. I recommitted my life to Jesus and decided to run this race to win. I was going to look up and not allow fear to drag me down. I made a promise to spend at least an hour a day with the Lord. (I thought I should be able to give Him one out of the twenty-four hours he gives me.) I really needed to be strong in Spirit to get through because when a person does this, they can be sure that the enemy gets out the big guns. There was one thing I did know for sure and that was the time I spent with God in private was no one's business, and I could share everything with Him, knowing He would never tell my secrets. What did Jesus do all the years He travelled the earth? He learned and prayed and was tempted just like we all are. Why didn't He fall for the temptations? Because He was strong in spirit, and anyone who doesn't believe that should read Hebrews 5.

There wasn't anything wrong with Gord's and my relationship. We stood strong together in all the mess, and that said a lot for Gord. I didn't want to lean on him. I didn't want a relationship because I needed financial help or because I was now sure I was becoming a virgin again. I didn't want someone to put a big diamond on my finger. I wanted the friendship and someone to share with open and honestly. Neither of us had talked about marriage. I still wanted God to show me how to make it on my own financially and show me how to buy the house of my dreams. I knew God would provide whatever I needed if it were good for me. I felt good when I put the Bible back in my bag. I felt sure and confident that all would be well. What better person to handle all of this but God.

I called my neighbour. It was late already. I had tried several times to call her, and she wasn't answering. She did answer this time, and I told her where we were and what happened. I asked if she could do me a big favour and call the doctor's office in the morning and explain why we won't make it in for the appointment, apologize for me and rebook. She said it wasn't a problem but didn't seem to want to talk. I asked her if there was a problem, and she didn't answer me. She said she would talk to me when I got back. I told her she couldn't leave it at that, I had enough on my mind and that could open a whole can of worms. Finally she agreed and thought I may as well know now what has happened. By the sound of her voice, I closed my eyes and braced myself, knowing whatever I was about to hear was not going to be good.

She said she was walking in the hallway close to my apartment a couple of days after I left and heard a noise from inside the apartment. She thought I left the TV on and went back to her apartment to get the key to check things out. When she got back in her apartment, the phone rang. It was bad news and they had to go out of town for a few days. She didn't check the apartment. She explained that she came back after four days and heard a loud noise coming from my apartment like there was a party going on. She checked to see if my van was back, and it wasn't so she called the police. Two police officers came and first talked to her about us. She told them we were gone for a few more days. There was such a loud party going on and obviously a lot of people in the apartment that the officers called for backup before they knocked on the door. There were six officers standing in the hallway when they finally knocked. A girl answered the door and stepped back quite quickly when she saw the police officers.

There were six other people in the apartment, and the place was a mess. The officers had spent quite a while inside talking to them, and when they came out, they had all the people with them. The officer said they had permission to be there by the owner. She told them this wasn't true and explained she was asked to look after the suite while I was in Calgary. The officers believed the people inside and asked them to leave and even gave them all a ride home because they had been drinking and it was cold outside.

I asked her who they were.

She said they were teenagers, and she had never seen any of them before.

I asked her if the place was a mess, and she said it was a crying shame. I was supposed to phone the police as soon as I came back. They wanted the whole story and wanted to give me an incident number in case there were any problems. She wouldn't give me any more details.

I woke Gord up and told him. He said there was nothing we could do about it until we got back and see for ourselves, so just try to put it out of my mind until we got home. Then we would deal with whatever we were faced with.

The van was fixed in the morning. We were home by noon. All the way back, I was thinking about who it could have been. I asked P.J. if he gave anyone permission to use the apartment while we were gone, and he was angry with me for even thinking it. I thought of the kids gifts we left under the tree when we left so fast.

We pulled into my parking space and didn't even take anything out of the van. Gord got Tammy out, and P.J. helped J.J. out, and I went straight to the apartment to unlock the door. It was bitterly cold outside. So cold, skin could freeze in one minute. For a second, I thought to myself, why do we live in this deep freeze when there are so many warmer places to live. I was really tired and don't think I was even remotely prepared for what I was about to see.

The whole place was trashed. The neighbour came right over when she heard us, and I asked her if the police officers thought this was normal. She had asked them the same thing. Their answer was they have seen people living in far worse situations, so they didn't question it. Every room we walked into was torn apart. The living room couch and chair were filthy. It was black velvet with gold trim and small gold spots. At least that was how it started out. There were disgusting white spots in places, and I thought I would be sick. There were dishes and bottles all over the table. When I got closer, there were cigarette burns everywhere. The couch was burned, the chair was burned and there were cigarette butts put out on the floor as if it were a road. Broken glass was everywhere. In the kitchen, there was ketchup all over the counter and broken glass everywhere. I looked up in the cupboard and there were no dishes left. No glasses, no plates. It stunk so badly. I went into the next room, and P.J. just said, "Mom, look at this." Tammy's computer was finished. It looked like someone poured a glass of coke into the keyboard. It was all unbelievable. Tammy's bedroom was the worst. Her waterbed had been cut, but all the water stayed in the bladder. There were no clothes left in the closet or in her dresser. The same in the boys' room–their beds were trashed and even the curtains were torn down off the windows. I didn't bother going into my bedroom.

I went right to the phone and phoned the police number on the card my neighbour gave me. I couldn't hold back the tears when I started to talk. I told him no one had permission to be here and asked how they got in.

The officer told me they used a crow bar to pry the bedroom window open.

I was angry and asked him how they could believe these people had permission to use the apartment if they had to use a crow bar to get in.

He never answered.

I asked who these people were.

He read off a list of names that I never even heard of. I wrote them down.

He told me they would come by and talk to me and make out a more detailed report.

I asked P.J. and Gord if they knew any of the people on the list, and neither of them did. Gord started to sweep up, but I told him to just go home and I would handle it. (He had to go back to work the next day, and I knew he was really tired.)

He said he would wait till the police came to see what would happen. He didn't think we could stay in the apartment. He invited us to stay at his place–a one-bedroom condo with my crew.

I just laughed and reminded him what it was like staying in the hotel room. I said to Gord, "Look at all of my belongings, and we were moving into this house." How was I ever going to do it?

Gord said, "Hey, one thing at a time, don't get ahead of yourself."

The police officers came in and started to ask me questions. I told them we had been eight hundred miles away since Christmas Day, visiting my brother who is a cop. We come back to this. I asked them how they thought these kids had permission to be here after they trashed the place like this.

They told me the same as they told the neighbour. They had seen lots of people live worse than this.

I started to cry as I showed them Tammy's computer. Tammy started to tell them she needed it for her homework. That was when the officers found compassion. I guess when they met Tammy and J.J.; they realized this situation wasn't what they thought. J.J. was really upset because the Christmas presents left under the tree were gone. I asked if they knew of any place that would help us, Salvation Army? Anyone? We couldn't sleep in our beds. Who knew what was going on in them for the past week? I showed him the couch and asked if he would like to sit on it.

The officer asked me if I had insurance.

I said, "No, when I moved into the suite, I couldn't afford luxuries like insurance." That was something beyond me. I knew nothing about insurances, only that I couldn't drive my vehicle without it. I told them when I moved in the Low Income Housing, they told me I had to get some kind of special insurance to cover us in case the water beds broke in the apartment. Then I ran across the street and told the insurance company what I needed. Now I pay about $80 to that every year. They send me a bill, but other than that, I have nothing.

The officer asked me if I had a copy of that paper they send.

I looked in the desk where I kept it, but the drawer was empty. All around my feet were papers, but I didn't know where to start to look.

We went into Tammy's room next. The officers just looked at Tammy and the room and shook their heads. They realized this wasn't at all a good situation. They suggested I borrow sleeping bags for the night and clean out one room that we can all sleep in. They suggested the living room. It would be the least work. They told me to go to the social worker the next day, tell her what happened, and see what kind of help I could get. They agreed it wasn't fair for the kids to have to live in this mess. They also suggested I phone the insurance company the next day and see if I am insured for anything else other than a waterbed break. They gave me my incident number and told me good luck.

Gord helped me clean the living room. I told the kids not to sit on the couch until I covered it up with something. We phoned around to Gail and Bill and Sharron and Rick and scrounged up enough sleeping bags and pillows to borrow. Gord cleaned all the glass up and we washed the living room. By that time it was quite late. He went out and grabbed some supper for us and left. He apologized so many times for having to go, but I knew he was really tired and had to get his life back in order to go to work.

I got all three kids settled in sleeping bags and we decided to turn on the TV to watch a movie till they fell asleep. The TV didn't work. It looked like milk was poured down the inside. I called all the girls and told them to take an extra day off and explained why. Then I sat and prayed while the kids were sleeping. I asked God to show me the good in all of this.

The next morning, I cleaned the kitchen and sent P.J. to the grocery store to pick up paper plates, cups, plastic utensils, and a few groceries. I borrowed some pots from my neighbour and cooked the kids a half-butt breakfast. I phoned over to the insurance company and told them what happened, and that the police told me to check. To my surprise, my insurance covered the damage. They told me come over and talk to them after the kids went to school, and they would tell me what I had to do.

The insurance guys were so nice about the whole thing. Apparently, I had gotten an insurance that covered me for vandalism, and I had replacement value on all of my belongings. How wise of me. Like I said, I had no idea about insurance, so I knew it was God who arranged for me to have that without my even knowing what I was covered for. He knew this was all going to happen. They said an adjuster would contact me some time that day. I went back to the apartment and had started again to put all the broken dishes in a box. The torn and dirty clothing went in another box. By the time the adjuster called two hours later, I had put a pretty good dent in what was laying around on the floor.

The adjuster was at the house within two hours. He brought some other guy with him. He was introduced as Ken Klassen from a company that looks after all the damage. We walked through each room while the adjuster took notes. He wrote down all the damage to the furniture and told Ken that the most important thing was to get the bedrooms replaced for the kids.

Tammy's recliner was going to be recovered. The living room furniture would all be replaced along with the beds, dining room furniture televisions, stereo, computer, all the dishes, towels, dish clothes–etc.

I couldn't believe what I was hearing. I had told the guy I was praying to see the good in this and I had just bought a house. The good he was telling me was that I could go and buy all new furniture for the house. He said it was $500 deductible and that meant I would have to pay the first $500 of the damage.

I was thinking, oh no, I have to dip into the down payment account to get it out.

Suddenly the adjuster said, "You know you cleaned so much already and packed up so much of the mess. Normally, we would pay someone to do this for you, so let's just write off the deductible and say it was already paid in your labour.

I was so thrilled. This guy was so understanding towards the whole thing. Within an hour after he left, there were cleaning crews, guys packing boxes and moving out furniture. All the clothes were taken to the dry cleaners. I was really surprised how they did it all, and I couldn't keep up with what was going out the door. I was left with bare necessities to make do. They even offered to have the new furniture held to be delivered to the new house when I moved in, so it wouldn't be moved around so much.

By time the kids came home from school, the apartment was almost empty and totally cleaned up. P.J. came in the kitchen while I was making supper and asked me if I knew where his hockey equipment went.

I told him it was probably in his closet.

He told me I had better come and look. The closet was totally empty; my closet was totally empty and dito with Tammy's. The insurance company was supposed to take all the clothes to be cleaned then they would see if there was any damage to them after they were cleaned. I thought they were just taking the clothes that were thrown around. I had already done the laundry after I unpacked from Calgary and put the clothes away. There was absolutely nothing wrong with them. Most of them were new Christmas presents and weren't even in the house at the time of the vandalism. All we were left with was the clothes on our backs. We couldn't even change our underwear in the morning. P.J.s hockey equipment was taken to be cleaned too. He couldn't even play hockey.

It was too late to call the adjuster; they were closed. So Gord brought me a jacket to wear, and I had to run out after supper and buy us all underwear and socks at least for the next day. It was a good thing the kids were at school when they did this. At least they were left with their coats and mitts and toques. They never even left me with a jacket.

The next morning I sent the kids to school, and then went to work. I got the girls started working, then phoned the adjuster and told him what happened. He was so apologetic and said not to worry. He said the clothing would take at least two weeks to get back. It had to be put in a chamber for that long to air out before they even cleaned it. He said to buy all the clothes the kids and I would need for the next two weeks and they would cover the bill.

I had replaced all my dishes, pots and pans, silverware, and all the other small kitchen appliances that had been damaged in the break in. All the furniture was being held until I moved into the house. I was working every chance I got, and by the time we had two weeks left to move into the house, I had banked just over $20,000 for the down payment. I didn't think it was possible to make it but kept trying to shake that notion out of my head and thanked God for the money I needed. He had gotten me this far; I wasn't about to give up now.

The kids were being charged with break and enter and vandalism. I would have to appear in court with them and I had no problem with that. They had no right to do what they did.

Gord's dad called to say Sonny was in town and invited us over to his house for a casual evening and dessert. I was really looking forward to it. I think Gord was more nervous than I was as we pulled up in front of his dad's house. I was wondering if Sonny felt the way I did when I knew Gord's dad was coming to the door at the condo. I chuckled to myself as I thought of her quickly pulling an apron off not wanting first impressions to be someone seeing her like that in a kitchen. She wasn't. She knew where to be.

Gord's dad welcomed us in the house. A very smartly dressed lady came from the living room. She looked to me to be the type of person that could look dressed up in any style of clothing. She was shorter than I was and very petite. Her hair was black, and when she spoke, she had that hint of the down South American accent. We talked the night away. There was so much to talk about. Sonny had been married for many years to a military man. He passed away, and she went on the cruise with a friend to get a bit of rest and put her life back together. That was when she met John (Gord's dad). She was staying in Winnipeg for a while and offered to help with setting up the house when I moved.

It had become the week to meet the in-laws. Gord got a call during the week from his mother. He called her Jennifer. She was in the city and wanted to get together for supper. We didn't have much time but decided to do a supper again at Gord's condo. I threw together a chicken dish during the week and a salad, and we only had to heat the chicken before she got there. For some reason it didn't bother me where I was standing when she came in. Gord had seen her through the years at horse shows a couple of times, but there was no close contact. I was totally amazed when she came in; Gord was the spitting image of her. They had the same shaped face with the high cheekbones that made Gord so good-looking. She was tall and slim and had really curly hair. She walked like him and talked like him. She had the same gestures when she spoke. I had a hard time understanding how a mother could not have anything to do with the upbringing of her son and really not have any close contact for almost thirty years, but still he could be so much like her. Well at least in looks. She was really very different from Sonny. Sonny was such a lady, and Jennifer was very rough and tough in the way she spoke and her body language.

I could see Gord was really happy to finally spend time with her. There were no grudges held for not being in his life till now and no sign of bitterness of any kind. That was Gord though. Forgive and forget, put whatever it is behind you, go forward, and look for the good. Jennifer was going back to California the next day and said she would keep in touch.

The week before I was to move into the house, I was really tired and had no patience for anyone. Gord was such help. Not only was he over helping me get everything ready to move, but also he just kept me going. If I fell emotionally or mentally, he had a way of picking me back up and putting me right again. Possession date was April 1st, April Fools Day. It was also Easter Sunday. It was a respite weekend. We had set it up that way so we could get everything moved in before the kids came home at suppertime. We told them their Easter treats were being dropped off at the new house by the Easter Bunny.

All the new furniture was delivered and put in the garage of the house on the Friday before. The guy didn't mind. I requested everything be covered in heavy plastic, so it wouldn't get dirty.

I had to bring the cheque for $23,000 to the lawyer at noon on Friday, so I could pick up the key and sign the last of the papers. On Thursday, I had only $21,000. Gord offered to pay the rest. I wouldn't accept.

He asked, "Did you ever think maybe God wanted it that way?"

I said, "No." I believed it would come.

Gord talked to his dad, and his dad wrote a cheque. I still wouldn't accept it. I did, in the back of my head though, know that money was there if I needed it, but I believed I would get it somehow. I just kept thanking God.

On Thursday evening about five, I got a phone call from a bride. She wanted to come over to order her wedding dress. It was her birthday, and she had gotten a large cheque from her grandmother to order the dress. She came right away and showed me the picture. I charged $2,000 for the dress. She wrote me out a cheque for the 50% deposit. There was another $1,000.

I recalculated all the money I had saved in accounts and J.J.'s portion. I had miscounted by $500. I couldn't see how. I had counted all the money so many times a day for so long to see how much more I needed. I had $500 more than I thought. I now had $22,500, and it was seven in the evening.

The phone rang at five past nine. I thought it was Gord. When I answered, it was another bride who had already come and ordered her dress. Her dress was $1,000, and she had already paid the 50% deposit. For a moment I thought this isn't my answer. She told me she had gotten paid and had the rest of the money for her dress. She wanted to know if could she come the next day to pay in advance because the wedding was so expensive and she would just feel better if she knew her dress was paid for. I stayed very calm and told her she could if she wanted to. She asked if it was too late, or could she come right now. I told her I was just packing, so she could come if she wanted to. She did and right after she left, I called Gord and told him I had the $23,000. He laughed and couldn't believe it. I told him neither could I but it was true. He said, "So, you were right."

The next day I went to my lawyer's office by eleven forty-five. My appointment was at noon with George Ullyot. He came out of the office smiling and dangling the house keys in front of me. He put his hand out and I handed him the cheque for $23,000. It felt so good. He put his hand out again as if he was waiting for me to hand him something else. I just looked at him.

He said, "Do you have another one for the legal fees?" And there was some kind of tax deal I had to pay on the house.

I just stared at him. I said, "How much?"

He said, "I believe it was around $1,800."

I could have thrown up on his foot. I didn't pray for that. I didn't know about that. I thought the $23,000 covered everything. Not. I just sat back in the chair and fighting back tears asked him, "Now what?"

He told me to wait a minute and he would be back.

I waited for twenty minutes and fretted. I tried to get my peace back. I silently prayed to God that I knew He wouldn't take me this far into the house then drop me on my head now. He even made sure I had brand new furniture.

Finally, he came out and handed me a cheque for $1,800 written out to me and said, "Sign this." I did and he handed me the keys and said, "Paid in full, but somewhere down the road, you owe me the $1,800."

I told him I would do it as soon as I possibly could, took the keys and left.

Gord couldn't believe it when I told him what happened. I did it. That was all I could think. By the grace of God, I did it. It was so exciting.

My faith paid off, and it was a good lesson learned. On the Sunday, Janet, Henry and Gord showed up really early in the morning to start the move. It was snowing quite hard. By noon there was nothing left in the apartment and it was all clean. I picked up Samantha and put her in the cat cage that Gord brought. I bid farewell to my three year Low Rental apartment, and closed the door without looking back. I danced my way to the truck. Gord and I drove in one truck and Janet and Henry in the other. The snow had turned into a storm, and we could hardly see out the windshield. It was hard to believe there was weather like that on Easter Sunday.

I did accept the appliances as a gift. I got a fridge, stove, and heavy-duty washer and dryer. In our house, laundry was an everyday thing, and heavy duty was the only thing that would survive.

It didn't take very long to get established in the area. Between Gord and Janet and Henry, they knew where to shop, what drug store to use, and Janet took me to her hairdresser and introduced me. (The shop was called New Attitudes and the hairdresser's name was Gary. He was great. I never had a hairdresser in the past that I could say take off an inch and they took off only an inch.)

I went back to work and appreciated how smooth the girls had things running while I was taking the time with the house.

I was back one day when Maria, who was one of the better workers, had decided she had learned so much working with me that it was time she moved on and worked for herself. I had asked her to at least stay until the end of the rush, which would be a couple of more weeks of work. She didn't and I couldn't understand why she was in such a hurry to leave. It was like she talked to me about it at eleven in the morning and was gone by noon. She wanted me to pay her out right away before she left. I told her I would drop off her paycheque on my way home on Friday, which was payday. She was really angry with me for not paying her out, and I was really surprised because we had worked so long together. One of the other ladies that didn't speak very much English said something to her in Portuguese as she was walking out the door. Maria yelled something back at her, but I didn't understand what was being said. I told everyone to stop and have lunch and asked if something happened while I was off that would cause this? One of the girls said she is jealous of your new house. She said we were here doing your work and paying for your new house. I felt bad for what I was hearing. Maria was paid very well for what she did at the shop. Then came the crunch. I went to find my book, so I could cut out some dresses—my book that had every customer and phone number and measurements. It was nowhere to be found. One of the girls said Maria took it with her to call my customers and tell them she was going into business for herself. I couldn't believe it. I wasn't worried about losing customers, but I was more concerned with the fact that Maria would even consider this after we worked together for so long.

I called and left a message on her answering service that her cheque would be held until I got my book back. She showed up with her brother on Friday morning and threw my book on the cutting table. I quickly glanced through it to make sure it was all there then I handed her the cheque. I made it clear how I felt about her doing this.

I didn't realize just how much work a house would be. I was really lucky that Gord gave a hand every chance he got. Some evenings he didn't go home till really late because he was fixing something or putting shelves in the garage to hang things on. He bought a book on "HOW TO" for pools and started to figure out what chemicals had to be used and how to use them.

May came really fast, and our goal was to open the swimming pool for the May long weekend. The day came when we could take the cover off. We got a few tips from the next-door neighbour. He had a pool. He was a great help and a really good neighbour. We got the cover off, and Gord and I both stood in awe. It was hard to believe that this huge in ground swimming pool was in my backyard. Life is good. It didn't take very long before Gord had the water to the level it was supposed to be, and the water was crystal clear. The kids were bugging to jump in right away, but the temperature of the water was in the low sixties. It took three days after Gord turned on the gas heater for it to get to a perfect temperature. It was great. The kids spent so much time in the pool.

We ate lunch and supper on the deck. The trees in the back got their leaves, and three apple trees were filled with beautiful blossoms. I got up every morning and sat on the deck with my coffee to do my devotions. It was like being at a lake. Sometimes I would go and swim at five in the morning when I got up. At night I loved to sit on the deck and look at the pool. There was a huge round light set into the wall in the deep end under the diving board, and it would light up the whole pool. So many times I thought, Lord, what did I ever do to deserve all of this in my life? I meant Gord, the pool and the yard and the house.

Chapter 26

FALSELY ACCUSED

"But I tell you to love your enemies and pray for anyone
who mistreats you. Then you will be acting like your father
in heaven." Matthew 5:44

Gord ended his job in the Ram Messenger Building, and after a supper with Mr. Sobey to discuss it, they agreed Gord would go back on the road
to drive for the messenger part of the company. After so many years, he was
good at the job because he was already well established with the companies
he was couriering for.

P.J. was going to high school in the area, Fort Richmond Collegiate.
J.J. and Tammy were still going to the same schools they were going to before
we moved. Because they were in a specialized education program and it was
almost the end of the school year, the school board provided transportation for
them to stay in their school. They would have to change to schools in our new
area in September.

We were nicely settled into the new house, so I asked my mother to
come for a visit to see it. She called me while I was at work one morning. She
said the police were at the door looking for me. I asked her why. She said for
the insurance fraud. I couldn't believe what I was hearing.

I asked my mom, "What kind of insurance fraud?"

She said, "I don't know, but that isn't all of it." She went on to say
they were were on their way to the shop to pick me up.

It was the day before a lot of the high school graduations, and I had
ten girls booked to come to the shop that afternoon to pick up their dresses. I
started to cry and told the girls I had to clear out that something was happening and I would have to leave them to handle the shop. I knew they could, so
I quickly left them with a schedule and ran out the door.

I drove around trying to make sense of this and finally stopped at a
pay phone and called Janet at work. She told me to calm down and she would
get a hold of Gord and get him to meet me somewhere.

I called John Scurfield, the lawyer, and he said he would get one of his lawyers to contact the police and find out what it was all about. I was to get myself down to his office as soon as possible. I didn't want to drive my van. I felt like I was a criminal on the run and didn't even know what I had done wrong. Janet did get a hold of Gord and told him she would leave work early and drive down to pick me up. My mom had everything under control at home. I parked my van on a side street and went in Janet's car to the lawyer's office.

When I got there, Mr. Scurfield told me he had found out why this was happening. I was being charged with insurance fraud for the time the teenagers had broken into my apartment when we were in Calgary.

"I was eight hundred miles away when it happened. I didn't know any of them and they broke in with a crow bar!" I told him.

He suggested I talk to Tim Killeen who was their criminal lawyer and he would advise me on what to do.

Janet and I went into Tim Killeen's office and sat down to discuss what happened with the break in. I didn't understand why this was happening. The police knew the kids broke in, and they caught them red handed. What did I have to do with it? I was in Calgary when this happened and didn't even find out about it until I got back.

Mr. Killeen told me the most important thing now was to get the warrant straightened out so they didn't come and pick me up.

I asked if I had to go to jail.

He just said, "No, but you will have to go to the police station and turn yourself in. You will be released." He asked Janet if she could drive me to the police station and he would meet us there. He told me not to say anything to anyone without him there.

Janet did drive me to the police station. I cried all the way. I wasn't some kind of criminal. How can these teenagers break into my home, destroy the kids' belongings and mine and I get in trouble for it? It made no sense to me. The police were the ones that suggested I go and see if I was insured. The insurance company is the one that came into my home and told me what to replace and sent people to clean, etc. Where did I come in the picture of doing something wrong?

Janet pulled into the parking lot at the Transcona Police Station, and we went inside to wait for my lawyer. We were sitting in the reception area when one of the officers at the reception desk looked at us and said, "Hey, what are you two doing here." It was a guy we knew from the speedway. I got up and told him what happened and he just said "shhhhhh," like he couldn't listen to what I was saying or someone might figure out he knows us.

Then the door beside him opened, and two detectives came up to me and introduced themselves and told me to come with them.

I said, "No, I am waiting for my lawyer."

They hauled me out of the chair and started to read me my rights.

I just looked at Janet and she said, "Don't say anything until the lawyer gets there." I couldn't speak, she didn't have to worry.

They took me into an interrogation room and started to both talk so fast.

I ignored them and just kept crying out of control. I refused to open my mouth. I got so fed up with hearing lies from them, I just told them, "I will say nothing till my lawyer comes."

They didn't give up, they tried harder. It was worse than what I had seen on television. I was no criminal and was really angry that they would treat me the way they were. They had said I should just plead guilty, and I just gave them a clear look that asked WHY?

They threatened they had all the teenagers as witnesses.

I didn't say anything, but I just thought, they broke into my home and they are witnesses. Whatever!

They told me I could go to jail for up to ten years, and they could make it much easier on me if I just pleaded guilty.

I honestly was so angry by that point, I wanted to spit in his face. This was all so stupid, and I couldn't figure out how they couldn't see that this was so stupid.

They accused me that I arranged for these teenagers to wreck my belongings. I never even knew who they were. I just sat back in my chair and cried. I was so bewildered and angry.

The one detective then sat down and asked me what I was thinking, and for the first time I spoke.

I said, "I am just putting you two in God's hands and letting Him handle you."

At that moment my lawyer was standing in the door. He asked if anything was said.

I told him, "Not a word," but I could have thrown up with the performance. These detectives turned into the nicest, most considerate men with the lawyer standing there. I was released right away after I signed a paper that I would appear in court.

Janet took me to my van and I went to the shop and checked to make sure everything ran smoothly. I touched lightly on what happened, and the girls told me that Maria had called Crime Stoppers and told them I had ripped off the insurance company and arranged for my apartment to be broken into while I went away to Calgary. I couldn't believe Maria could do that.

I called and told my lawyer right away. My lawyer asked me if I would go and talk to a private investigator. I knew at that point it was going to be an expensive time again. I did go the following week. He asked that I take a lie detector test.

I told him, "At any time and any place." I had nothing to hide. Even though I knew I had nothing to worry about and that in the end they would all see this was totally stupid, I did feel like a criminal.

Chapter 27

Saying "Yes" Was So Right

"Well, having your own husband or wife should keep you
from doing something immoral." I Corinthians 7:2

It was Janet's parent's fortieth anniversary, and they had most of the family in the city to celebrate. The Sunday was a very hot day, so we invited them all to come to our house to spend the day by the pool. All afternoon they seemed to take turns asking Gord and I when we were going to get married. I was a little embarrassed for Gord. He didn't seem to mind. He just went along with it all.

In the evening after it got dark, it was really humid and seemed like it was going to rain. We all went into the screened-in deck. I was just going to cut the cake when Janet's brother Jimmy said to Gord, "Go and ask her now."

Gord just laughed. Janet went to the kitchen and got the tin foil out and made a ring, I can't remember who took the yellow rose off the top of the cake, but it ended up on the tin foil ring. They handed it to Gord and with a smile on his face he bent down on one knee (someone got him a cushion), and asked me to marry him. I was really laughing thinking this isn't good. I don't know if it is a joke or for real.

Just in case it was for real, I said, "Yes." As soon as I said it, the sky opened up and there was a lightning show like none of us had ever seen before in our lives. There were just flashes and flashes one right after the other. It went on for a long time.

After everyone had already left, Gord, Janet, and Henry and I sat out on the deck watching the lightning. Gord said, "I guess God really did approve of me asking and this is the fireworks show He set out for us." He then said we should feel very honored. That was when I realized, he was serious.

I always said I wouldn't get married until I had the house of my dreams. Just so I could say I did it and could be married knowing I didn't marry him because I needed him, I married him because I wanted him. Gord and Janet and Henry went home, and I stayed up and dug out my list of what

I was looking for in a man. Gord fit the T perfectly. I knew that was from God. (The only thing we never agreed on was that someday he wanted a Golden Retriever BUT someday I wanted an English Sheep dog.)

The following Sunday, we were sitting at the dining table finishing up breakfast after church. I started to clear off the table, and Gord told me to sit down for a minute and finish my coffee. There was something he wanted to show me. I sat back down and Gord went to the closet. He came out with a huge stuffed English Sheep Dog and laid it in my lap. I was just laughing and thought, "Alright now that he did this, I guess he figures someday he will get his Golden Retriever." He told me the dog had something for me, and around the neck under all the long hair was a red ribbon. At the end of the ribbon was a gift-wrapped box. It looked like a perfume size box. When I opened the wrapper, inside was a velvet case. It was rectangular and fairly wide. I didn't see Gord come around the table until he was on one knee in front of me. I was so shocked.

He just said, "This time it is the real thing and the way it should have been done. Will you marry me?"

I said, "Yes," and when I opened the box, he took out the most gorgeous engagement ring and put it on my finger. Then he turned the box around to show me that also inside was the wedding ring that went with it. This was for real. This is the way every girl wants it to be done. It was so perfect.

I called Pastor Ron and Donna to tell them my good news but the conversation was bittersweet. They were thrilled that we were getting married but then told me they were thinking about moving. Not just moving but all the way back to Oklahoma. They were glad to be going home and I had to be happy for them but I would really miss them as they were such an important part of my life.

I called my mom, and she was really happy for us. She really liked Gord, and I asked her if I could borrow her set of pearls to wear for the wedding. She asked me what I was going to wear. At that point I never even put much thought into it, but that was like me. I would know I was wearing my mom's pearls and make a wedding dress to match them.

Gord didn't want a wedding where we had to be concerned what colour the napkins were or what was going to be in the center of the tables. He just wanted to get married. We decided the wedding was going to be in Banff. We both loved the mountains, and a lot of the people we wanted to come to the wedding lived closer to Banff. Gord's dad and Sonny would have to travel out there, but they loved to travel so we were sure they wouldn't mind. Of course, we asked Janet and Henry to be our maid of honour and our best man, and they accepted. We asked Janet's mom, Jean, to play the organ at the church and her dad, Jim, to do the Bible reading. We knew it was a lot to ask because they would all have to fly out there and stay in hotels, but they didn't hesitate to say yes. We figured out that the best time to do it was right after Christmas when everyone was still on holidays. We chose the next Saturday, which was December 29, 1991, and started to make the plans. First, we found out that was high season in Banff, and the prices of hotel rooms were totally ridiculous.

The next step was to tell Gord's dad and Sonny. We took them out for lunch that following week. They didn't notice the ring on my finger at first. Before we ordered our lunch, Gord said to his dad, "We have come today bearing good news." Sonny then got a glimpse of my ring. There were hugs and congratulations. While we were eating, we told them what the plan was so far.

Sonny didn't think they could be there. John was still working and didn't know if he could get the time off. I could see Gord's heart drop to his feet. I think they had caught that too because John said, "Of course we would be there; we will figure out a way."

There was so much to do and such a little bit of time to do it in. By the time we made the decision to get married in Banff, we only had four months to find a chapel and where would the reception be? I had to figure out what would I wear as well as what Janet would wear? Would we get the tuxedos there or take them with us? What were the kids going to wear?

All Gord really wanted to know was, "Where did I want to go for the honeymoon?" (Not really, but that was very important.)

We had to make a list of who to invite and get it out right away, so anyone who did want to travel out there had the time to plan it. Within a week we had most of the answers.

We talked to our pastor and started to take marriage classes once a week. It was fun. But there were four other couples, and they were a lot younger than we were. Through the church, we found a Baptist Minister to marry us. He lived in Canmore, only a half hour drive from Banff. He told us about a small chapel right in Banff that sounded perfect. We inquired and rented it right away.

My sister Thelma's father-in-law lived in Banff and was a big help. He ran a restaurant in a hotel on the Main Street and said we could have our reception there and have a smorg for the meal.

We started to do all the invitations and ended up with far more than we thought, but we were pretty sure a lot of the people wouldn't be able to make it. We sent them out right away, so we could have some idea of how many meals we would have to order.

Gord invited his friend Chris from High School. It ended up he was married and lived in Lethbridge. He replied that his wife and he were coming. He owned a Sooter Studio in Lethbridge and offered to be the photographer as our wedding present.

I decided Janet and I would both wear the same colour, cream. I wanted lots of sequins and pearls on mine, and I wanted a full gown with a small train. I was going to make both Janet and I capes with fox fur around the hood. This was a mountain wedding, and I wanted us to dress the part. Janet decided on a two-piece suit with antique lace covered in pearls and sequins around the neck and across the bottom of the jacket and a full length fitted skirt.

We went downtown to try on dresses, so I could try on wedding dresses to see what kind I would make. The first one I tried felt so good. It was a mermaid style dress very fitted in the body and off the shoulder with the full skirt starting just above the knee. Janet and I stood looking at it in the mirror when I put my hand up to my chest and pretended to start hyperventilating. (That was the start of the joke. Janet and I never did anything more for the wedding without her making sure she had the paper bag in her purse.) I decided that would be the style I would wear.

We went right from there to my favorite fabric store, Fabric Centre, and started to look at fabric. Mr. and Mrs. Waxman, the storeowners, and their daughter Sheera, were all there and were excited to help me find my own wedding material. I had bought my supplies from them since I had started the business, and they always treated me so fairly. Mrs. Waxman came up with a cream antique lace that was so perfect. It had a snowflake design in the lace, and I could pearl and sequin every snowflake. We picked out a satin underlining and wool for the cape with the same lining as the dress. I was so excited. Janet picked out cream shantung and the most gorgeous antique lace for the trim. When I went to pay for the fabric, Mrs. Waxman bundled up my material separate from Janet's. She charged me for Janet's then I told her to put them both together. She handed me my bundle and said this is our wedding present to you. I walked out in tears. This was so exciting. Janet and I decided we would make my wedding dress at her house on the weekend.

Gord booked the hotel rooms for Janet and Henry and us, for the night before the wedding. He booked a room at the Chateau Lake Louise for the wedding night, then three nights at Emerald Lake Lodge. Patti offered to drive along with us in the van to watch the kids. She could take the kids to the wedding and my mom would take them back to her house while we were on our honeymoon. Patti had a sister in Canmore that she could visit till we got back.

Gord found a tuxedo shop in Winnipeg that was willing to give him a good deal for a one-week rental. Janet and I went with them to see them try the different tuxedos on. There was no question about it. They got black tuxedos with tails. They both looked really good in them. Gord was horsing around and wanted a cape with a top hat and cane. I nixed that idea and don't think he ever forgave me for it. He was right, and I was wrong. (That didn't come easy to say for a long time.) It would have been really appropriate, especially for pictures.

I went to Gary (my hairdresser) that Friday and begged him to come to the wedding. I told him he would love a holiday in Banff. He just laughed. I said there was no way I could go to another hairdresser there, and I really needed to have my hair straightened for the wedding. I was leaving on Boxing Day. The shop would have been closed already for the Christmas holiday, so I couldn't get my hair done by him any later than the week before the wedding. This was not acceptable. He just laughed and told me not to worry. He would train me over the next few weeks to do my own hair and Janet could come and watch and help. He said he would give me everything I needed to do it myself the same way he did it.

The replies started to come back right away. We were really surprised at just how many people were planning to come. It was great, but the time pressure was starting to get to us.

I knew I had to really lean on God. One morning I got up to do my devotions and was thanking God for all the blessings for this wedding, the blessings of material and the tuxes and everything else that was falling into place. I realized all of a sudden just what was happening. I thought about the first time I had gone out with Gord three years before and went home and prayed for positive people to be put across Gord's path with God's word in their mouths to share his good news. I realized God answered that prayer and used me to do it. I then thought of how I prayed for God to find Gord a good Christian wife that he would be drawn close to and thought wow, what a compliment. God thought of me as a good Christian wife. That blew me away. How could I have forgotten? I dug out my journal from three years before and showed Gord.

He just smiled and said, "Thanks."

When we went to our marriage class that week, I shared it with them, but the other couples were so young, I don't think they really appreciated what it meant. I shared with our Bible study group, and they thought that was pretty awesome.

Everything was falling into place and time was flying by. We planned on leaving Boxing Day with the kids. We would get to my mom's on the night of December 26th. Janet and Henry would fly in on the 28th, rent a van, and pick us up. Sonny and John were flying in on Friday afternoon and were leaving on Sunday. We heard from Jennifer, Gord's mom. It was very disappointing, but she couldn't make it. We were thrilled when we heard from the Stanwicks that the whole family was coming. It just kept getting more and more exciting–then the blow. We got a reply from Carolyn, Marcia and Hermann, and Granny. If Gord was marrying me, they wanted no part of it and would NOT be attending. Gord said not to worry about it, it was their loss in life and not ours. They had to live with it, and he had no intentions of trying to change it. Putting conditions on their love for Gord pretty well said it all, and that was fine with the two of us.

For my birthday, my mom sent me the pearls and said to do whatever I wanted with them; they were mine. She said I could have them made into a choker to go with my dress if I wanted to. They were so stunning. I took them to the jeweler and asked him what it would cost to have them made into a three-strand choker. He looked at them, then went and got the little magnifying glass and examined them closer. He looked at me very surprised and said, "Are you crazy? Why would you ever want to do that? Do you know what these are worth?"

I said, "No."

He said I am not going to count them now but this necklace is worth about $6,500.

I took them back and stood in shock. I carefully put them back in the case my mom sent them in. I said, "I had no idea."

He asked me where I got them.

I told him," They were a gift from my mother."

He asked me if she wanted to adopt a son.

I phoned Gord and told him what the guy had said.

Gord said, "You have to give them back. Your mom needs to know what they are worth. She probably has no idea."

I told him I would wrap them up and give them back to her for Christmas with a card explaining why I was giving them back.

Gord came over that night with an early wedding present for me. It was a pearl necklace set with rhinestones. It was perfect.

Tammy had a real problem with wearing dresses because she couldn't wear appropriate shoes for a dress. She was always bugging me to make her a pair of leather pants, so I made her a pair of really soft Burgundy leather pants to wear to the wedding with a sweater that had a design in beads and sequins.

Gord took J.J. and bought him a pair of dress pants and a new shirt and tie. They tried blazers, but they were too long and made his legs look short.

P.J. got a new black suit. It was the first suit he owned, and he looked really sharp in it.

Gord and I had to go Christmas shopping yet. It was so busy. We just went into the stores for two days in a row and shopped till we almost dropped. Finally we were ready. We went to the last Bible study before the wedding and got a real surprise. There were so many people, and it was a surprise wedding shower for both Gord and me. It was such a nice idea. It was a food shower. Everyone brought groceries. We had enough tin foil and saran wrap to last a couple of years. A lot of the groceries were geared around the Christmas season. One couple even gave us a big box of Christmas baking. It was a lot of fun. It was so thoughtful.

We decided to keep the condo and rent it out. Gord was going to move his things in slowly before Christmas and just keep what he needed to get through. It was funny watching him move in his belongings. Every day he would bring over a few things in the van after work. He brought in some clothes closer to Christmas and asked if he could have an advance on half of the closet. I gasped. I told him I didn't know getting married meant I had to give up half of my closet. I let him, but it did hurt. Then it was half of the medicine cabinet. Then we realized we had two microwaves, two toasters, and two sets of pots, dishes, and silverware. What to keep and what to get rid of, this was a test, and we knew it. We decided just to pile his boxes and furniture in the basement and go through it all after we were married. He did well. Before we left for the wedding, he had emptied the whole apartment–even the bed–and just kept the couch to sleep on and the television.

The condo was rented out to a single mother with one little baby and she was moving in on January 15th, so we had time to get it all clean after we got back.

We got through Christmas. Sonny and John came over for Christmas Dinner. With all the chaos, I still managed to do the traditional turkey, stuffing, cabbage rolls and meatballs. There were too many leftovers for a family that was leaving the next day. I sent some home with Sonny and John and kept enough to make sandwiches and goodies enough for the whole seventeen-hour drive to Calgary.

All was well, and we were on the road. It was a rowdy trip. It was fun. Patti had good control over the situation in the back of the van and I just napped. Gord and I would look at each other once in a while and just smile. I was thinking how wonderful he was with all that was happening and all the commotion in my life; he still wanted to marry me. He really did love me, and I had no doubt that I loved him. It was so different to be able to be myself with no inhibitions. He loved me for me and all that came with me. Wow. I am sure his smile wasn't for the same reason, but we never discussed it. There were kids around.

We got to Calgary pretty late and opened gifts with Mom. When she opened her pearls, she had a funny look on her face until she read the note and was quite surprised. She had no idea that they were worth so much money. I told her she should either have the right to sell them, wear them, or to do whatever she wanted with them. Every woman should have the luxury of wearing such elegance, and especially my mother. I said if she decided not to sell them then maybe one day they could be mine, but not now.

I had to laugh when the kids opened their gifts from my mother. It was all to entertain them while she was looking after them. Tammy got a crystal necklace and earrings from my mother (the ones Tammy always commented on when my mother wore them). I remember her wearing them when I was young.

Gord and I had to go to downtown Calgary to get our marriage license. We ran into a problem. Gord had all the identification he needed, but I didn't. My name was different than what was on my birth certificate, and I needed two pieces of identification with the same name. I just didn't have it. I begged. I was confused. I always prayed if God didn't want me to marry Gord, to stop me, and I didn't believe that we got this far for Him to stop us now. I told the people at the desk that my brother was a cop in Calgary and could vouch for me. They finally broke and gave us our marriage license. Gord was such an organized person when it came to things like that. I wasn't.

There was no time in my life to be that organized. Gord and I talked about it on the way back to my mom's. He said he would organize me after we were married. I thought, uh oh. He said God gave him what I didn't have and He gave me what Gord didn't have. That is why we blended together so well.

The next day we were all ready to leave. I must have gone over the list with my mother at least ten times. I felt bad leaving her with so much responsibility of getting the kids to Banff and keeping them. That wasn't easy for anyone. P.J. was already seventeen and could help her with everything. He knew all there was to know about looking after J.J. and Tammy. He could handle seizures and any other problem that arose, and so could my mom. My only concern was that Tammy wanted constant attention and could burn people out pretty fast.

Janet and Henry pulled up in a little mini van at one o'clock on the nose, just as planned. When we got to Banff, we went to the Banff Springs Hotel and had lunch, then went to the Hotel and put our bags in the rooms. The wedding dress and capes were already in Janet's and my room.

Henry suggested what better thing to do the day before our wedding but climb a mountain. I was definitely game. We were to be at the chapel for a short rehearsal at seven. We had a lot of time before that to walk up the path of Mount Norquay. That would be tame enough. Janet was the photographer. She was on the ground taking pictures of us going up until she couldn't see us. Then she would go up the Gondola and would take pictures of us coming up the mountain. When we got there, Gord got out of the van and started to tear apart everything in the van. Henry asked him what he lost. Gord came back with this put on English accent that he was really good at.

He said to Henry, "I lost me dickey. I can't climb a mountain without me dickey. I can't get married without me dickey."

We all just laughed and Gord didn't find his dickey.

We started up the mountain. After about an hour, the trail got very narrow and dropped off the edge quite deep. I noticed the air had changed, and I felt like I was a little drunk. Henry was leading and I was in the middle. Gord was behind me. I started to get hungry and a little giddy. I was giggling and at one point my foot slipped off the edge of the path and I almost toppled down the mountain. Gord had his jeans on under the tracksuit and told Henry to wait a minute. He said he didn't want to read the morning paper "Bride Falls Off Mountain," especially when it was his bride. He took his belt off and put it around my waist like a leash and hung on to the end. He said at least he could hang on to me if I went over. I laughed and said, "Not even married yet and already you have me on a short leash."

It was getting pretty late, and I slowed down. We were supposed to meet Janet on the top at four-thirty, but we weren't going to make it. Henry still had lots of power, so Gord told him to go ahead and he would stay at my pace. It wasn't too long after that, we looked up at the Gondola and saw Henry waving to us. We couldn't see that it was Henry, but the person waving to us had glasses shining from the sunlight. So we figured it was Henry. That meant that Henry and Janet were on their way down. I decided I wanted to slide back down under the Gondola. Gord just smiled and said, "Yes Dear," and before we knew it we were both on our butts sliding like little kids down this mountain. It was a long way. We had to go in short runs, or we would have gotten up too much speed and gone out of control.

It was getting dark by the time we got to the bottom. We saw Janet with the camera taking pictures. She looked at us surprised and asked where Henry was. We thought she was joking and told her he was being bad on the Mountain so we left him there for the night. The look on her face told us she wasn't joking. The person waving in the Gondola whose glasses caught the sunlight was Janet, and Henry wasn't with her. That meant that he wasn't at the top yet, and it was the last gondola coming down the mountain till the next day. So Janet had to take it. It was dark already and the three of us stood looking up at the top of the mountain thinking uh oh.

Gord said, "My best man is stuck at the top of a mountain." It was too dark for Henry to come down the trail. We all ran over to the guy closing up the Gondola for the night. We told him he had to do a run back up. We told him there was a guy stuck up there and would freeze over night. The guy didn't seem to care and said there was nothing he could do about it. Janet lost it and the guy changed his tone. He said he would call his boss. We all just stood there looking up at the dark mountain. I don't know what we expected to see, we just stared. All of a sudden there was a shadow of a large man coming from a distance.

I said, "If that isn't Henry, then it is Sasquatch." Janet called out Henry's name and he answered. He had already realized when he got to the top that there were no more Gondolas, so he just headed down. If Gord and I didn't take the shortcut and stayed with the trail, Henry would have probably caught up to us.

The chapel was very small and quaint and was perfect, just like you would picture a mountain chapel. When we got inside, the pastor was waiting. He was quite young and entertaining.

The front of the church still had the manger scene with sheep, wise men, angels, Mary, Joseph and baby Jesus. Everyone that was supposed to be there was there. They were all made out of wood and were held up in the back with a small stand just like I stood up my pop out dolls when I was younger. Janet and I politely asked if they were sticking around for the wedding ceremony. The pastor just laughed and said he thought in case not too many people showed up for the ceremony, he would fill up the first three rows. He said Mary, Joseph and baby Jesus in the front row, the three kings in the second row. I just whispered to Gord that we really wanted Jesus to be at our wedding.

We ran through the rehearsal a couple of times, and all was well. We said we would be there at four o'clock sharp the next afternoon.

Gord smiled and said, "Count down." We agreed to not see each other after midnight. We weren't superstitious, but just thought it would be nice. It was only eight so we still had four hours to be together.

When we got back to our room, there was a delivery of flowers from Sharron and Rick congratulating us and apologizing for not being able to come.

The next morning, I woke up just before seven and felt terrible. I got up to go to the washroom and stopped in front of the mirror. I had gone to sleep with wet hair, and Banff was so humid, it was standing on end and a big ball of fuzz. I let out a scream and Janet jumped up. She asked what was wrong. I turned on the light and asked, "How many hour do we have to make me into a bride?" We were both rolling on the bed laughing. She and Henry had made a schedule as to what time we were going for breakfast and what time we could go out, so we didn't run into them during the day. They were going to get their hair cut and Janet and I were giving ourselves the manicure/pedicure thing. We had ordered the flowers from a local florist the day before, and they were being delivered to the church. Janet stuck a hat on my head and told me to wash my face; we were going to walk to breakfast. While we were eating, we made a plan and wrote it down. We figured we had it all under control and when I realized how much we had to do, I asked Janet if she was ready. She pulled the paper bag out of her purse and said, "Ready."

I told her the least we could have done was find a bit fancier paper bag for my special day. That got us going again. We were laughing all the way back to the hotel.

By one o'clock in the afternoon, we had finished putting the faux fur on the capes, had our manicures and pedicures done and I had already showered and was ready to do my hair. I was standing in the room with my housecoat on when I all of a sudden realized I didn't have any earrings to go with the necklace Gord bought me. I was upset. How could I totally forget to get earrings? Janet told me not to panic. She said to have faith. Staci surprised us and strolled in during the afternoon. She was singing at the wedding and brought most of the clothes I had made her in the past, so she would make sure she was appropriately dressed. I had made her a cream satin suit with sequins and pearls and asked her if she brought it. She was under control. She asked me if I had everything I needed and was holding a box.

I said, "No, I didn't have earrings."

She smiled and said she had brought these earrings with her for something borrowed. When she opened the box, they were perfect. They matched the necklace as if they were made together. I knew at that point, God had control over this.

It was time to put my dress on. My hair was done and was very straight and sleek. Janet helped me get into the dress, and when she went to zip it up, she said, "Suck in."

I told her I was sucking in. The zipper wouldn't go up. I hadn't put on the dress for two weeks. I had two Christmas dinners, dainties at the shower, and just the usual Christmas goodies. She looked at me with that look. Janet never got that baffled look. She always knew what to do in a crisis. This was a crisis. I told her a customer of mine gave me her bustier that she wore to her wedding thirty years ago, and I brought it with me. We dug it out of the suitcase and just roared. It was a full-length bustier in the right colour but the cup part looked like something Madonna would wear with the flying saucers in the front–space age design. There must have been forty hooks to do up in the back. Janet said, "Let's try." It was like something out of the movies–her trying to do up all of the hooks. She really had to pull to get it to closed. That was how they got their twenty-three inch waists thirty years ago. I told her there was no way Gord could take my wedding dress off of me after waiting for so long and find this underneath. She promised we would deal with it later. I put the dress back on and Janet zipped up the zipper with no effort. It worked. The only thing was that there was so much push up in the bra and with the dress being off the shoulder; cleavage in the dress became CLEAVAGE. She said, "Never mind, Gord will love it."

Grant came in and said we were ready. It was three forty-five and the church was five minutes away. He helped me with my cape. Janet looked great. We gave each other the once over and walked out the door.

In the car Janet leaned forward and asked me if I needed this, showing me the paper bag.

I told her, "No." What I needed was to see Gord–to be married to Gord. I wasn't used to not seeing him or at least talking to him. It was ten above outside and really damp. I gave myself one last look in the car mirror to check my makeup and saw that the dampness got me. My hair was going frizzy. I just said, "So be it," and went into the church.

There was a guy snapping pictures as soon as the car door opened. I just smiled and said, "Hi, I am Gord's fiancé, Tricia." I asked if he was Chris.

He replied, "Yes," and shook my hand, then went on to take more pictures.

We got inside and I was more than ready. We had arranged that Gord's dad and my mom would go up and light the candles. Apparently it was great. My mom and Gord's dad had never met before. Gord's dad, being the gentleman he is, went over to my mom, introduced himself then lit her candle and his candle, and they went up together. I found that to be very touching. The door opened. Janet started in. Her mom started to play the organ, and Staci started to sing. I started in with Grant and was really surprised at how full the church was and glad to see that the three kings and the chickens and all their friends decided not to stay for the ceremony. Gord stood at the front in his tuxedo next to Henry in his. Gord looked really nervous. Whenever he got nervous his cheekbones would tense up. I really was hoping to get a reaction from him that he liked what he saw. He pretty well let that be known with his eyes when I got to the front.

We had planned a Christian Service and it was great. Janet's dad, Jim got up and read a scripture from the Bible, 1 Corinthians 13. All was said that had to be said about God being first in our lives and putting each other first after that. The best part was when he introduced us as Mr. and Mrs. Kell. Yes! Without a shadow of a doubt.

We went out the back of the church, and Gord helped me put on my cape. He announced that the bar was open at the reception, and we were going to Banff Springs Hotel for pictures and would join them soon.

We went into the Banff Springs Hotel. People were looking and asking who we were, as if we were of some importance. I think it was the tuxedos and the capes that were causing the attention.

The hotel had a thirty-foot Christmas tree decorated. That is where

Chris decided he would take most of the pictures. It was a perfect room done in Victorian, and that suited the dresses and tuxedos. We spent over an hour taking pictures and felt bad that everyone was waiting for us at the reception.

When we got back to the hotel for the reception, we realized there was nothing to feel bad about. Everyone was quite happy and entertained.

Everyone ate; there was a good selection of food in the smorg. I took a plate but just picked at it. I thought better I don't eat too much with this space age, antique chastity belt on.

My mom made the wedding cake and it was beautiful. So many pictures were taken. Staci sang. She changed into the gown she wore for the Miss Canada Pageant to sing at the reception. Gord and I got up to dance a waltz, and Staci sang the Bryan Adams song, "Everything I Do I Do It for You" Tammy was ecstatic. Bryan Adams was her favorite.

Henry did a great job of being the emcee for the night. He first got on the kick of Gord and Tricia, Patti, Pat, Patricia, all the names he had heard coming from different family members and friends as that day went on. Then he mentioned I would always be Pat to Janet and him. He told us how he was so glad we were finally married. I laughed and knew he was just glad to have another man on his side of the friendship. P.J. got up and did the toast to the bride and only managed to get through the first two minutes before he couldn't say any more without tears. So he just held his glass up to everyone, and they got the message.

It was time to leave, and we were so excited. Janet said she loaded up the back of the van with the gifts that people brought. I jumped in the van and told Gord he had to stop at the hotel room; I forgot something.

He told me I didn't need anything, but alright.

I did stop and changed with no trouble. The zipper did go up. I grabbed my overnight bag with the clothes for the next day and my make-up, and we left. The plan was we were spending the night in Chateau Lake Louise then driving another half hour to Emerald Lake Lodge for the next two days. Janet and Henry were driving to Kelowna to see Henry's mom and sister and were going to meet us at the lodge at noon the next day for lunch.

It was really dark when we got onto the highway going to Lake Louise. Gord was a little frustrated because he was having problems with the van. The transmission was making noise. He started to laugh and stated, "Can you see it? Van breaks down in mountains with you in your wedding gown and me in my tuxedo on our way to our honeymoon."

I smiled and told him, "God has a sense of humor, but doesn't give you more than you can handle. I definitely have faith that we will make it to the hotel without any problems." We drove up the hills and down the hills, and we listened to the noise coming from the transmission.

We finally made it to the hotel. A gentleman met us at the door of the hotel and took our entire luggage. Our room was gorgeous. On the nightstand were flowers and a bottle of champagne in a bucket with ice. Two champagne glasses were lying beside it. Gord tipped the gentleman very well.

Emerald Lake Lodge was at the top of a mountain where the snowflakes were so huge. It was breathtaking there. The restaurant was in the central lodge, and all around it were separate cabins. We were shown to our cabin. It was small but really cozy. In the corner there was a wood-burning fireplace, but no television. There was a radio and a phone and a bed and a bathroom. Everything we could possibly need.

The phone rang. It was Janet letting us know they were at the lodge and ready for lunch. How time flew by when you were having fun. Gord had grabbed his dickey as we were walking out the door of the cabin. He found it under the seat of the van. When we walked into the Lodge, Henry and Janet were sitting on a chesterfield down at the end of the room facing another couch. What a quaint place to have lunch. The fireplace was roaring. The room was full. As soon as we saw them, Gord threw his hand up in the air with the dickey and yelled with his English Accent to Henry. "All is well 'enry, I found me dickey." Everyone clapped and laughed and Henry was beet red. That was the start of it. Gord found his dickey and the honeymoon was grand. During all of lunch all that kept coming up was how you can't have a good honeymoon if you loose your dickey. Henry finally asked him where he found it, and Gord got started again in the accent that he left the darn thing under the seat of the van, what a stupid thing to do, it could have frozen.

Emerald Lake Lodge has a wonderful horse drawn sleigh that takes their guests down the mountain roads. On the front of the sleigh is a very small bell that rings the whole time it is moving. After lunch we went for a ride on the sleigh and all I kept thinking of was the saying, "When you hear a bell ring, you know an angel is getting his wings." After listening to the bells for a good five minutes, I thought maybe someday to write a book and start it with: "When I prayed for God to send his angels around Gord to find him a good Christian wife, God had sent all those angels, and now that Gord and I were finally married, all those angels were being given their wings." The bells rang the whole time we were out in the sleigh. I had to chuckle at the thought it took so many.

Chapter 28

LIFE IS GOOD

"Yes, the gladness you have given me is far greater than
their joys at harvest time as they gaze at their bountiful
crops." Psalm 4:7 (The Living Bible)

Gord and I rolled right into married life quite comfortably without too many problems. For the first year though, I don't think we were much different than anyone else getting married and adjusting. It was really me that was having the hardest time trying to conform. I was so used to being independent that I just wasn't too willing to let go of some of it.

We went to a seminar on Christian relationships and it was loud and clear that I submit to my husband. I had no problem at all giving Gord the final say if there were any differences in opinions. He was very good at putting God first in his life and me next on the list. Sometimes it seemed he was afraid to have the final say in case he ended up wrong–a man thing. It was really hard for us to say to each other the first year, "I am wrong and you are right." We barreled through every bump and mountain that was trying to prevent us from getting closer together, and for every battle we won, it was that much better. We had no problem being best of friends but to learn to live together after both of us were so independent after so many years was not an easy task. P.J. had left and went back out west for a while. His love for the mountains never changed.

Gord wanted me to bring the business home. A couple of the girls in the shop wanted to be home sewers, and it was stupid to keep paying the bills when I could run it from the house. I told him I would think about it, but it would take some time. It would be a lot of work running it from here, but it sure is easier than going back and forth to the shop. We were more established in this area and I was seeing the customers from this area at home anyway.

I did eventually run the business out of the house. Judy had moved back to Portugal, so I tried to work on my own at first and farmed out sewing to the girls at their homes. It was getting to be too much, so I prayed for God to send someone across my path to help me one or two days a week. One afternoon I was going to the fabric store and Betty Baergen, a lady in our Bible study group, was coming out. I asked Betty if she was still sewing.

She replied, "Yes."

I asked her if she would be interested in doing some sewing with me.

She started the following week and was such a blessing in my life. I definitely knew she was Heaven sent. She was so full of knowledge and wisdom and would spend her time working, and sharing it with me.

We were still going to Grant Memorial Church every Sunday. The kids loved to go to their summer camp with the teen group. They were almost too old to go anymore. We knew they would get lost in the shuffle once they got to the age they couldn't be in the youth group anymore. I started to pray for knowledge on what to do. The church was so large; it had attendance of two thousand. My company was involved in the Fashion Show in the church for a couple of years with Staci. She would organize the whole show, which seemed to be second nature for her. I brought a lot of customers back to do the modeling for the show. It did help me to get to know some of the people from the church. Gord and I attended a small Bible study group once a week. Still, it bothered me when people would come up to us on Sunday and say, "Are you new here?"

It was embarrassing to come back with, "No, we have been coming here for six years."

We prayed for a new church. Someone in our small group suggested we go and try Bethesda Church, which was a non-denominational church around the corner from Grant Memorial. I had never heard of it and prayed that if that is where God wants us, then could He give us some confirmation.

I was also praying those days for a female doctor. I was still seeing my doctor on the other side of the city. Tammy needed one too because she was becoming an adult and couldn't go to Dr. Weidman anymore. Every time I called another doctor in the area, they weren't taking any more patients. So I just gave it to God and asked Him to handle it.

I got a phone call from a new customer who had gotten my name from someone I knew. She was a receptionist in a doctor's office and was going to the Christmas dinner and needed a suit to wear. I was heading downtown, and said I would stop at her house to see her because it was on the way. Her name was Clara Browning. She was a very pleasant lady and made me a cup of coffee while we talked about what she wanted to wear.

I was not in the habit of telling new customers about my

beliefs, but there was something about Clara that caused me to pour my heart out to her about our situation of looking for a new church. She smiled after I finished telling her and picked up a brochure she had laying on the buffet and handed it to me.

She said, "Maybe you want to try coming to my church."

I asked her what church she went to.

She said, "Bethesda."

That definitely was confirmation from God. That is where He wanted us to go. We were there on the following Sunday and were so impressed with the warm welcome we had gotten. The church was very small and held about two hundred people. We knew it was going to be our church for a long time.

When I went back to do the fitting on Clara's outfit, we were talking about her job. She was telling me she was a receptionist for a female doctor, and the office was around the corner from our house. She said she would ask if the doctor would be willing to take on Tammy and me. The answer was "Yes." That doctor stopped working not long after we started to see her. Clara got a job with Dr. Evans, and her husband Dr. Sharkey. Tammy and I went along with her. Two more prayers answered.

Mother's Day weekend came, and I always hated Mother's Day weekends. It was a reminder of past years when the kids had their accidents. Gord decided that was going to stop, and he was going to give me something to celebrate on Mother's Day weekend. The kids were at respite, and he arranged when they came home on Sunday, we would have supper brought in and celebrate.

On Saturday morning, he told me to hurry and get ready; we were going to pick up a Golden Retriever puppy. I couldn't believe it. I just thought he had put up with so much from me and my trouble; we could go and get his retriever. He had found a place that had seven pups ready to go, but it was first come, first served. He knew they would go fast. On the way there, I asked him how we would know which one to take? He said it has to be a female and we would know.

We pulled up in front of this house with a huge yard. The guy was outside, and we told him we were interested in one of the pups. There was a big doghouse in the yard. He called, "Come on pups," and out of the doghouse came six of the most adorable little eight-week-old Golden Retriever pups. We just laughed as they all came running, and I thought we are just going to take them all and make it easy. Then I looked back at the doghouse, and from behind the back of it peaked a little gold head. I told Gord to look. I asked the guy if it was a female peaking out from behind the house.

He said, "Yes."

I told Gord that if we were really going to do this, it had to be her. We took her and her papers and paid the man and left.

We named her Cherubim, and called her Cherry for short. She was an American Golden Retriever and was much redder in colour than you usually see. She was adorable.

We went right to the pet store and bought her everything she needed. Then I got a receiving blanket hoping she would settle down if I wrapped her up and held her like a baby. It worked. Up to that point she was quite upset we were taking her away from all her brothers and sisters and her mother. We even got her a huge green soother as a joke, but she really did keep it in her mouth. Just like a baby.

We had her wrapped up and went over to Gord's dad's house. When we stood on the doorstep ringing the bell, I put the corner of the receiving blanket over her head, and I was holding the soother so it was in the open. Gord's dad answered the door and we said we had a surprise to show him. He looked at the bundle and his eyes were popping. Then I took down the corner of the blanket and out came this red head. He and Sonny spent the next hour snapping pictures.

Cherry cried all night. We had her bed in the kitchen in a traveling dog cage. We even tried to put a clock under her blanket, but she just kept crying. The rule was she could not sleep in our bed. That lasted till three o'clock in the morning. She finally fell asleep at the foot of our bed.

We started to have problems with Tammy. She wanted to call Rudi. Her speech was getting really good, and we decided to give her the phone number and let her call. There was no reason for her not to talk to her dad. It had already been about five years since he talked to her. She called, but he just never answered the phone. It was always Helena or her daughters Petra and Sandra that answered the phone. Tammy would be very polite and ask if she could talk to her dad. They would either make like they couldn't understand her or imitate her speech problem. After talking to a psychologist about this, it was suggested we stop allowing her to call because it was too hard on her. She would always come off the phone really upset and tell us her dad didn't like her anymore because she was handicapped. We couldn't understand how anyone could be so cruel. Our hearts broke for her. We tried to explain that Rudi did love her, but the girls had a problem with him having anything to do with her. We spent many days praying that God would give Tammy peace in this situation.

Chapter 29

A Fair Trial?

"May integrity and uprightness preserve me, for I wait for thee." Psalm 25:21 (Revised Standard Version)

The investigator was finally finished with his investigation, and I was going to court for the fraud charge. Five days we spent in court. The judge was an elderly gentleman with a very kind face. I heard this was the last trial he was doing before retirement. He had one more to sum up in Brandon. For five days we sat and listened to each of the kids tell their stories.

One girl heard from friends that I was gone for ten days. She was the one who broke into my bedroom window with the crowbar. After she had done that, she went downtown to a bar and met a guy. She asked the guy if he wanted to come back to her place. HER PLACE! He said he was with some friends so she invited them too. When they got back to MY PLACE!, she had to go in through the bedroom window.

The lawyer asked each of them individually if they thought it was funny that she went into the apartment through her bedroom window.

They all had the same answer. She forgot her key.

They had a party that got really carried away. It was very straightforward that she was guilty of break and enter and vandalism. I was called up on the stand and was just asked some simple questions like did I know any of these people before?

"No."

Did I give anyone permission to stay at my apartment while I was gone?

"No."

Did I do any damage to my apartment?

"No."

After hearing all there was to hear, the judge said he was going to Brandon to finish a different trial, and then would be back and give his verdict. We were to be back in court the following week. It was pretty straightforward.

I couldn't see why he couldn't tell us his verdict for my trial before he left. We met with the lawyer, Tim Killeen, before court and he said I had nothing to worry about. It was really straightforward and the kids all admitted to breaking in and doing the damage.

Betty and another friend from church came along to court to be prayer warriors. Betty was working with me for a while already. They sat behind Gord and me in the courtroom.

The court came to order and the judge took his seat and pretty well just came out with: "I find Mrs. Kell guilty."

No one could believe what they were hearing. It almost seemed to me that the judge forgot what the case was. It didn't take long before I was in tears. Betty put her hand on my shoulder, and I turned and said to pray harder. She just squeezed my shoulder, and I knew it meant she was already.

The judge said to take a ten minute break to let me pull myself together then he would hear the closing arguments and sentence me. I was in shock. After all these teenagers admitted to breaking in and partying for days, how he did he ever come to the conclusion that I was guilty? I was eight hundred miles away when all of this was going on.

I told the lawyer I wanted to go into the washroom, and a guy stood up with sheriff written on his shirt and said he would have to take me.

I looked at Tim, and he said he would straighten it out, just co-operate. I asked him what happened and he said he didn't know.

I asked him, "What is the usual punishment?"

He said, "Two to ten years."

I looked at Gord, and he turned a terrible shade of white. I started to cry again and told Gord, "They want to put me in jail. Who would look after the kids?"

He said not to worry, I wasn't going to jail.

I told him, "Right answer." I went into the washroom and prayed. I told satan to get away from me, I wanted to see Jesus. *" . . . Get behind me satan, you are a stumbling block . . ."* Matthew 16:23 (New American Standard) I prayed if God before me, who could be against me? *" . . . If God is on our side, can anyone be against us?"* Romans 8:31

The crown's lawyer got up and said some terrible things about me being guilty of fraud. He thought I should be incarcerated and I should pay back all the money I defrauded the insurance company for and I should pay all court costs.

My lawyer got up and told the judge, "It is ridiculous to think of having her incarcerated. The kids that broke into her apartment admitted to breaking in her home she was eight hundred miles away." He then went on telling the judge: I had never before been found guilty of any charge, and I had two handicapped kids and a husband at home.

The judge was listening to every word my lawyer said. Suddenly it was like a light went on above the judge. He said to the crown, "This lady isn't capable of doing the things you are talking about. She is not going to jail."

It looked to me like, all of a sudden, the judge remembered what this case was about.

He then stated, "One-year probation and you are free to leave."

I was out of there, fast and fuming.

Tim walked partway back with us and said he was definitely going to appeal. He agreed with what I had thought. It was ridiculous.

Gord took a while to calm me down. I felt like a criminal. I had legal fees to pay, and it seemed so unfair. I felt bad that this was the first year we were married and Gord had to put up with all of this.

It didn't take long for Tim Killeen to get an appeal date. We had to go before three judges. They were to read the transcripts on the whole trial, then tell their opinion.

Gord and I were changing the title on the house and the condo to have each of our names included. We were told by the title office we had to have a copy of our actual marriage certificate with the registration number to be able to do it. Of course we had to go through Alberta's Vital Statistics offices to get it because we were married in Banff. That would take a lot of hassle and time so I called my brother Grant, who was still in the Calgary Police Force and asked him to put on his uniform and go down to get it for me. He promised he would see what he could do.

The day finally came for the appeal. Gord went to work and we agreed to meet fifteen minutes before court by the elevators in the courthouse. Mr. Killeen would meet us there too. I was just getting ready to go when the phone rang a long distance ring and with P.J. on the west coast, I didn't want to not answer it. I grabbed the phone and it was Grant.

He asked, "How do I tell my sister she is not legally married?"

I answered, "Very funny, I am on my way to the appeal. I have to run; did you get the marriage license?"

He let me know that he wished he was joking then went on to say, "The pastor who married you seems to have forgotten to register your marriage. Sooooo it makes it not legal, and no one seems to know where that pastor is."

I told him I would call him for the details when I got home. I went flying down to the court. Gord and Mr. Killeen were waiting for me in front of the elevator. I said to Gord "What better way to break this to you, but with my lawyer present as a witness." He looked at me as if I was strange and I continued on with, "You have always told me if you had to do it again, you would marry me all over again. Would you still?"

He laughed, "Of course I would."

I said, "Good, you might have to. Grant phoned and said we are not legally married." By then we were at the courtroom door so I just said I would fill him in later. Boy was that cruel.

There were three judges sitting at the front. From what I remember, the first judge said, "I read over the trial and I would have to say, I would not have found you guilty of what you were charged with." I thought good, that is one.

The second judge said, "I have to agree, I wouldn't have found you guilty of insurance fraud either." That was two. I didn't know if best two out of three counted or not.

The third judge (he was the one in the middle, and I think he had the final say.) said, "Well Mrs. Kell, I wouldn't have found you guilty of this charge at all but I don't understand what you want us to do about it. There hasn't been a technical or legal error made. It was an opinion of another judge and for whatever reason he chose to say you were guilty, we can't change an opinion of another judge." He then said, "I don't know what the problem is. He let you off. You don't have to pay any restitution and you don't have to serve any time. He just let you go."

I answered, "He let me go with a guilty charge, and I am not guilty. I haven't had a record up till now, and I don't want one for something I didn't do. I went on holidays and came back to my house broken into and destroyed, and I was found guilty. That isn't right." He shrugged his shoulders and that was the end of it.

I talked to Mr. Scurfield about it a few days later and will never forget what he said. His words were words that my dad always told me when he was alive, and I have thought of many times when I got into different situations.

He said, "Sometimes it is just time to drop your shoulders and let it roll off. It isn't worth the time or the money to fight. It just ends up costing more in the end."

I took his advice and dropped my shoulders. It took time, but eventually did roll off.

Gord went back to work and I came home. Janet and Henry came over for a coffee after work, and we were talking about not being legally married.

When Gord walked in he said, "Hi, what a pleasant surprise. I didn't know you guys were coming over."

Janet jokingly answered, "We were just discussing how to change the rooms around, so you could have your own room since you aren't legally married."

Gord came back quite quickly with, "I have been there and done that and don't even dream it. God knows we were married that day. That is all that counts, so don't go moving any beds."

We just laughed. The bottom line of the problem was the pastor didn't register our marriage, so we had to do it all over again. We had to apply for a license then do all the steps. We didn't have to do the actual ceremony because Grant went to the chapel we got married in, and because we had signed the register in the chapel, that part we could skip over.

A few days later we did receive our legal marriage certificate at the door by Purolator with the new date on it. We have never acknowledged that date; we were married on December 29, 1991. God knows, and that is all that matters.

Chapter 30

P.J.

"The Lord's kindness never fails! If he had not been mer-ciful, we would have been destroyed. The Lord can always be trusted to show mercy each morning. Deep in my heart I say, ' The Lord is all I need; I can depend on him!'"
Lamentations 3:22–24

P.J. came back to Winnipeg for a visit but decided to stick around for a while. He got a job with a restoration company helping do clean ups. He planned to do that for a few months, and then he would go back out west.

One day, I was cleaning the house at lunchtime when a cab pulled in the driveway and P.J. got out. I asked him what he was doing home at lunchtime.

He answered, "Never mind that. Did you see who drove me home?"

I replied, "No."

He said, "Mom that was Grampa."

I just looked at him and never said another word. I called Gord on the cell phone and told him what happened. He stated that P.J. was out late last night so maybe he got into something he shouldn't have. He suggested letting him sleep it off.

The next morning P.J. got up and went to work without any problems. At lunchtime a cab pulled up and out came P.J. I was really bugged and questioned him. He just kept laughing and went to bed.

I called Gord and said, "Either he is on some kind of drugs or is having some kind of breakdown which wouldn't surprise me after everything he had been through."

He came to the table at suppertime, and we couldn't make heads or tails what he was talking about. It was like there was a bunch of his friends at the table and he was carrying on a conversation that we knew nothing about. The next morning he didn't get up to go to work.

I called the police and explained the situation and asked if there was something I could do. They suggested they send a couple of officers to talk to him to see if they could figure out what the problem was. Two officers came to the door about fifteen minutes later. It ended up one was a girl and the other a guy. The girl knew P.J. from a teen dance club. I let them talk to him on their own in the living room.

Afterward they said he had been at a party a couple of nights ago and someone gave him some kind of pill to try. It was obviously a bad drug. P.J. had told them it would wear off.

I wasn't putting up with any drug problems in the house. If he were going to live here, he would have to get help.

It was thirty below outside, and when Gord came home, I said, "We will have to do the Tough Love routine."

We put phone numbers in P.J.'s pockets to the Salvation Army, Union Gospel and the Addictions Foundations and dropped him off at the Addictions Foundations Building downtown. Then I did one of the hardest things I have ever had to do with him. I told him he couldn't come home unless he got help, and we drove away leaving him standing there in thirty below.

I didn't sleep that whole night. I just kept praying that God would keep him from freezing and find him a warm place to stay and guide him to one of the numbers for help.

At seven in the morning, P.J. walked in the door. I reminded him he couldn't come home until he got some help. He didn't remember. I called the police officer that had been here and told him what happened.

He said he would normally suggest I put him back out.

I said, "He doesn't remember when I tell him, and I can't put him out in thirty below anymore." He was still my son and I still loved him, but I knew he couldn't stay at home as long as that drug was still in his system.

The officer made a suggestion. He said he had a charge from when P.J. was younger that he could pick him up on and take him to the Remand Center. While he was staying at the Remand Center, we could request a bed at PX3, which was a rehabilitation center. He could get help there. I talked to Gord and we all agreed it was far better than having him outside in thirty below. The officers came and picked him up.

The next morning he had to appear before a judge. I went down to the court. The judge tried to talk to P.J. but he was making no sense. P.J. was still too drugged. The judge said to put him on a waiting list for PX3.

He was there for two weeks and was still on the waiting list. He would phone in the evenings and was really angry. The drug had worn off and all he kept saying was how could I ever have him locked up. He said it was a stupid mistake at a stupid party and he took a bad drug. He said he learned his lesson and wanted to get out. I just stood my ground. I thought that even if he did just make a stupid mistake and even if he did learn a lesson, it wouldn't hurt for him to do the program at PX3 to deal with some of the issues. He had been through so much since he was young, and it would only help, not hurt, I thought.

Two more weeks went by, and he was still on a waiting list. P.J. said a psychiatrist to determine whether he still needed to go to PX3 was interviewing him. After assessing him several times, he came to the conclusion that this was a one-time thing and he didn't need PX3. P.J. was fuming mad at me.

He had to go to court again. The judge knew what the plan was. P.J. was very much back to normal and was dressed very decent and looked very decent. The judge said to him, "You look like an intelligent, clean cut young man. I could give you a slap on your hand and send you on your way, but what is that telling the world? I sentence you to another twelve weeks in lock up."

I felt really bad but believed he needed to have some kind of counseling. That evening he phoned home and told us there was a real problem.

I asked him what it was.

He said, "They need the bed in the Remand Centre and are sending me to Headingly Prison."

I called the officers that had taken him there and they suggested to me that this was not a good move in any way and we should try to get him out of there. It was a Friday and nothing could be done until Monday. We went to visit P.J. on the weekend, and told him we were going to see a lawyer the following week.

He said he was running out of tobacco. Romona from our church was going out to see him on the Tuesday if he was still in and I promised I would send some with her. He said he would run out before that but would borrow some from the inmates.

On Monday we phoned around and got absolutely nowhere. P.J. had borrowed some tobacco from one of the guys and had to give his gold ring as collateral. When Romona gave him the tobacco, he went to give it back to the guy. He asked for his ring back and the guy just laughed. P.J. was talking to the guard after and told the guard he wanted his ring back. The guard went to the guy and P.J. was then labeled "the informant." There was lots of trouble after that. P.J. was being beaten up.

We went to the lawyer. He said it would take about a week to get this mess sorted out, but in the meantime he would have P.J. put into protective custody. At least we felt better about that. The lawyer told us to give him till Friday to see what he could do.

On Friday morning, I had told Gord I would phone the lawyer then call him to let him know what we could do. Gord went to work. I turned the TV on in the bedroom to hear the weather. There was a special news bulletin on. I was watching and sat down on the bed not believing what I was hearing. They were showing Headingley Prison. There was smoke pouring out of it. The announcer was saying there was a riot, and the prisoners had taken over the prison. I was sick. I went to run to phone Gord when he ran in the door. He had heard it on the radio, and by the look on my face, he knew I had already heard. He said to get my coat on. We drove out of the city to the prison.

The road was already blocked off, and we could see smoke coming out of the prison from the road. The guard stated we were to go home and use this phone number for information. We couldn't go home. We drove into Headingly and stopped at a restaurant and got a coffee. There was a television with the station on the riot. We were watching. This had been going on since the night before. One of the gangs in the prison had taken over the prison. There was a bus outside and prisoners were starting to surrender. They were putting them on the bus as they came out.

I said to Gord, "Oh P.J. would be the first one to come out. He wouldn't stay in there and go along with that." He agreed. We went home and phoned the number. We asked if they had a list of the prisoners that surrendered. They said yes there was over a hundred names already but P.J. wasn't on it. Why wouldn't he surrender? We turned the news on and they were saying the prisoners that were surrendering were telling them the gang was cutting off fingers, brutalizing other prisoners, castrating them and some were being hung, especially the ones in protective custody. I started to scream, this couldn't be happening. P.J. was in protective custody. He would have been the first one to surrender. What did they do to him?

Gord phoned Betty to come and help him. He couldn't settle me down. Betty came and just sat and prayed. She suggested I not to listen to the television anymore but to just pray and believe that God would keep him safe.

I called Romona and she said the prayer circle at the church would be praying right away. Betty phoned her church and started prayers there.

Gord was on the phone to the people from the prison again. They told him to turn off the television and radio and don't listen anymore. He said to remember those horrible stories are coming from prisoners surrendering.

I didn't remember ever feeling as sick to my stomach over a disgusting situation as this was. We stayed in constant touch with the people. By the time the kids came home, they said there were almost three hundred surrendered but no sign of P.J. yet.

We talked to our social worker and she suggested we not let J.J. and Tammy know about any of this. There was a social that night that they could go to. Gord phoned Janet and she said she would come and stay with me while he drove the kids to the social and when he went back to pick them up. She did come right after supper.

J.J. and Tammy wanted to know why I was so upset and why Gord took them to MacDonald's for supper. He told them I was just angry about something that happened at work. They believed him. When Gord left, I was laying on the floor with my Bible in my hands begging God. I really lost it. I needed some kind of hope. Janet was telling me it was going to be all right. She said I always told her God would not give me more than I could handle *"No temptation has overtaken you that is not common to man. God is faithful, and will not let you be tempted beyond your strength, but with the temptation also provide the escape, that you may be able to endure it."* I Corinthians 10:13 (Revised Standard Version)–so she knew without a doubt P.J. would be all right.

The phone rang and I grabbed it. It was the same officer I had spent the day talking to. He wanted to know when I went to see P.J., if I remembered what part of the prison he was in. I asked why. He explained everyone had surrendered and there were ten missing. The riot squad was inside the prison looking for them, and they couldn't find them. They needed an idea of where to look.

My heart dropped–only ten missing. Were they dead? Was he laying somewhere hurt or dead? I couldn't stand it anymore and said to the man, "Is there any hope?"

He was very quick to say, "Don't you dare give up. There is always hope and we will find him."

I hung up and just sat against the desk holding the Bible. Janet was asking me what they said and I could just sit and say to God, "This is in your hands." I think Janet's head must have been spinning listening to me quote scriptures. She was so sure he was all right.

Gord had come in the door from picking up the kids when the phone rang. It was after ten o'clock, and I was scared to answer it. I did and it was the same guy. He spoke very quiet and to the point. He said, "We found your son, and he is in rough shape, but he is alive. He is in the ambulance and on the way to the Grace Hospital."

I told him, "Thank you," and he added he would be praying for us.

Gord grabbed my coat and was running me out the door. Janet offered to stay with the kids. We had just gotten into the van when Janet came back out and yelled, "They just called and said they were taking him to the Health Sciences Centre." We drove there right away.

Gord was trying to prepare me for whatever we were about to walk into. He was good for that. He said we would go and talk to the nurse or doctor first so we would know what he had gone through. We walked through the doors of the Emergency and told the nurse who we were. There were police officers and prison guards all over.

The nurse came to talk to us and said P.J. had a guard with him.

I told her it wasn't necessary. Where was he going to go?

She said she wanted us to know the guard was to protect P.J. The guys in the jail that caused all of the problems were part of a gang, and there was more of that gang out on the street. She said we could go in and see him but she wanted us to be prepared for what has happened. She said he was quite beaten up and cut up, but he also had his pointer finger cut off.

At that point I was just so glad he was still alive. We were taken in to see him. He was sitting up in the bed and when he saw me, he said, "That was a real close one Mom." I couldn't speak.

I knew the comment was sarcastic and I had no answer. I couldn't deal with anything else but just knowing he was going to be all right. He was really beaten up. His face was so swollen and he had so many cuts on his head that I thought I wouldn't recognize him if he came by me without me knowing it was him.

He told me, "I am not going back there."

Gord answered, "That is for sure." He asked if he could come home. We promised we would work something out. His hand was all bandaged and the doctor said he would have to have it operated on, it was really a mess. He said he was starving and hadn't eaten for a couple of days.

Gord asked him what he felt hungry for. We offered to get him whatever he wanted.

The doctor was still examining him and said, "Nothing too heavy because we don't know what time he will be operated on." He then said it would probably be good to have something before midnight though.

P.J. told Gord to just bring him something from the hospital.

We went to the cafeteria and started to look through the food. Gord hadn't eaten all day either and was getting hungry. He just loaded up the tray with a bunch of choices: Jell-O, soup, sandwiches, coke, fruit, chocolate milk, and cinnamon buns. The tray was full of enough food for four people. The doctor was just finishing up with P.J. He had stitched up all the cuts and did a complete examination.

Gord put the tray of food in front of him and said, "Choose what you want, and I will take what you don't want."

P.J. just kept eating and eating as if he had been starving for days. Gord and I laughed when he was just finishing up the last of the fruit and looked at Gord almost guilty and said, "Oh, I was supposed to save you some."

Gord told him it didn't matter, just eat.

He was really tired after that and said he wanted to sleep and we should go home with the kids; he would be all right. He asked if we could come in the morning when they were doing his surgery and if we could bring him some clothes and shoes. The ones he was wearing were full of blood. We told him we would be there first thing in the morning.

We stayed and talked to the police and the guards for a bit to make sure we could leave with piece of mind that he would be looked after while we were gone. He was being well guarded around the clock, so we did go home. I didn't sleep much. Every time I closed my eyes I would see this guy cutting off fingers, so I got up and got together some clothes, and shoes and a coat.

About six thirty in the morning, the phone rang and it was Henry. He asked when we were going to the hospital. We told him in about an hour. He was bringing his camera to take pictures of P.J. We stopped at the police station on the way down to let them know P.J. was in the hospital and was going to be all right. They had phoned during the day of the riot to find out how he was. The officers were very concerned that trying to help him turned out the way it did.

When we got to the hospital, P.J. was already out of surgery and back to his room. There was a guard on the door and in the room with him were two other guys that had their baby fingers cut off. Even on morphine P.J. was wide awake and wanted us to take him out of there right away. We started to take pictures of his injuries when the guard came in to try to stop us. Gord kept the guard talking and just told him P.J. had a lawyer and would we have to get him to come to take the pictures. The guard just backed off and took time to talk to Gord almost as if it was on purpose to let us get the pictures finished. I couldn't believe when he undid his Johnny shirt, all the bruises. It was probably easier to pick out what skin wasn't bruised rather than what was.

P.J. asked me again to take him home, and the guard said, "No." He said it wasn't safe.

We laughed and asked how safe it was for him under their care.

I gave P.J. the clothes, and he tried to get dressed but was having a real hard time. Gord asked Henry to get the van and bring it to the front doors so we could get him out. The guard was very insistent.

I just went to him and said, "Go to hell." I knew I was losing it, and I had a lot of asking God to forgive me, but this was all too much already.

Finally the other guard came and said, "Let him go home." He had made a phone call, and P.J. wasn't really held in custody for any reason that he couldn't go home. He said he was waiting for counseling, and it could be done from home."

The doctor came as we were taking him out and gave us a prescription for antibiotics and painkillers. He told us to bring him back in a couple of days to get the bandage changed on is finger. We were to just let him rest for the next couple of days. He also suggested we call his lawyer.

When we got home, we called the police station to say he was at home. That afternoon the pastor from the police station came to see him and told us if there was any kind of problem or trouble to not hesitate to call the station right away. P.J. pretty well slept for the next two days. The two dogs lay beside him almost the whole time except to go out to the washroom once in a while. It is funny how they sense something going on.

On Monday morning, the phone rang early; it was the prison officials asking if we could bring him in for questioning. I told them it would be up to his lawyer and him, and it wouldn't be for a few days. P.J. started to get up and walk around a bit, but he was in such pain that he couldn't stay up long. He slept a lot, and I didn't know if it was the painkillers or just an escape.

We talked to our lawyer, and he assigned P.J. a lawyer from his office. He told us to cooperate with the RCMP. He said they would be calling to question him on the whole thing. They did. We booked an appointment with them for the end of the week. I took P.J. in. He was so emotional. It was really hard.

The newspapers were full of the story every day and his name was in the story. I didn't hear all the details from P.J. It was hard for him to tell the story and hard for me to listen. It was so brutal. He did say he was picked to be beaten up because he was considered an informant. He told the guards the guy stole his ring. They kept showing the pictures on the television and in the paper of the cell that all of them were thrown into after they were beaten. P.J. said he just curled up in the corner. I asked him if the other guys in the cell bothered him.

He was very quick to say, "Mom, those guys were just as scared as I was." He told me at one point he knew I was praying, he could see it.

I asked him what he meant.

He explained, "I was already beaten up, and the guy already cut off my finger. He came back and said he was going to kill me. I thought that was it. It was already in the afternoon. I thought that was the end. He was yelling to get the guy that had the key to the cell. When he locked the cell door, he gave another guy the key. He was screaming then to get the key. One of the other inmates came back and said the guy that had the key had turned himself in and left already. He took the key with him." He said, "It was so dark and there was so much water." He knew it was really late, but it had gotten so quiet. Then he heard dogs barking and knew they were looking for them. The guys started to yell. Then P.J. said he could hear the dogs yelping and there was so much glass around, he was yelling to take the dogs out it wasn't safe. (I thought, "Yeah that was P.J.") Finally they saw some lights coming and it was the riot squad. They opened the cell door and let them out. One of the guys from the riot squad was a guard from the remand Centre that P.J. played chess with every night when he was there. P.J. was the last to come out of the cell and told the guy, "Yeah, I am always last the last one now to be rescued."

The guy told every one to stop, and when they did, he walked P.J. to the front of the line and led him out of the prison first and into the first ambulance. He knew that P.J. should never have been in there. I had a hard time listening to P.J. tell the stories but just thought listening to it was nothing; he lived it. Surely he knew I never put him in there to get hurt but to get him help. It was weird the way it turned out, but we had a lot more to deal with than anything I was thinking at that time.

I took him to see the RCMP. It was a female officer that questioned him. They had to keep taking breaks because P.J. was very emotional. That eventually turned to anger. The crisis people came to see us and brought us papers with lists of the process it would take to get P.J. through the trauma. It had another list on the bottom of what to watch for. He was hurt and he was angry. He had every reason to be. What right did anyone have to do what they did to him? His finger healed. Gord did the bandage changes for the first while. I couldn't. We could see his finger healed fairly fast and all the bruises and cuts, but inside was going to take longer.

Every week got better, but it seemed so slow. He would never go downtown at first unless we took him. He said he was marked out. We drove him to his doctor appointments, to his lawyer appointments and lots of appointments with the prison people to ask him questions. They knew P.J. shouldn't have been in there but wouldn't admit any guilt. That was politics.

The first few months were rough but then he started to come around. He found jokes to make about his finger. He really didn't like the fact it showed so much. He kept going to the specialist because the stump was almost up to his first knuckle and was in the way. He asked if they could take off the stump. It was finally suggested they take off the stump and the hand knuckle. That would give him a grip. He had started working on construction. He really wanted to build houses, but it was hard to use the hammer with it the way it was. He agreed to the operation. It took two surgeries the following year to finally achieve what they were trying to do, but in the end P.J. was quite comfortable with the outcome. The legal part of it all went on. They said no one could really sue. P.J. did have a leg to stand on, though. The lawyer said he would be looked after, and finally, he was. From that point, it only got better.

Henry called one morning; he was working for Ken Klassen Construction, the company that did restorations for insurance claims and new construction. He knew I had lots of experience doing wallpaper and painting when I was with Rudi, and he asked if I could help him out. The company had a claim just outside of Winnipeg. The ceiling in the house had leaked, and they ended up having to replace the whole ceiling. That in turn wrecked the wallpaper on the walls in the living room and dining room. When the wallpaper started to come down, they found out there were more than five layers on the walls, and all five were damaged. That meant they would have to either take off all five layers or do repairs and hang new wallpaper. I did the job to help Henry out but realized I really enjoyed it. For some time later, I was used as the troubleshooter for the company. Every time they had a problem with painting or wallpapering, I would get called for the job.

A year later we had a horrendous storm in Winnipeg. It was like a tornado swept through part of the city leaving chaos behind. Our property was part of that. Our house had to have the roof replaced. It left a hole in the swimming pool, all nine windows in the back of the house were smashed and both of our vehicles were borderline to being written off. Because of so much damage, insurance companies in the city had to bring other adjusters in from other parts of Canada to keep up. Roofers, painters and other trades were working day and night to keep up. Because of this, my little Troubleshooting paint business I did on the side became a full-blown paint company. There was so much work. There were so many houses that had to be completely repainted outside. I had to hire people to help. I would get up in the morning and cut out whatever needed to be sewn for the day then go and make sure the painters were still doing what they were supposed to be doing. I would work with the workers for a while then go back and help with the dresses. Gord was still so busy with the courier business and could only help during the evenings.

Chapter 31

TRIUMPH OVER TRAGEDY

"But we live by faith, not by what we see."
II Corinthians 5:7

One thing that never changed over the years was my love of racecar driving. From day one of Gord and I dating, we went to the speedway. After we were married, we started to volunteer for the track every summer.

It was the summer of 1997, the year that Winnipeg went through "The Flood of The Century." The speedway did run that year, but it was really late starting due to the fact it had been almost totally submerged in water. By the time the water had finally disappeared, and the track was put back to race ready and the buildings were put back to where they started; it had already cut well into racing season.

The track had been sold to one of the racecar drivers, Larry Neibel, a couple of years before this. The Vernaus family who had originally built the track on some land they had outside the city (and put so many years into it) had just had enough. Pete Vernaus (the flying Dutchman), and his wife, Tiny, were getting on in their years. Their children were all married, and it just got to be too much work. Gord and I weren't planning to go back after it was sold, but Larry didn't have too much knowledge on all the positions that had to be filled to run the track. So he asked that we come back at least one more season, and we did.

This was now his third year with the track, and we were still there. I was the head lap counter in the tower, and Gord was down on the track looking after number 1 turn. We talked Janet into sticking around for another year with us. She was running the show. She worked up in the tower with me. Pat Mooney was still the announcer in the tower and was partnered up with Norm King (another old timer with the track), who did his share of the announcing from the pits. Sometimes Norm would interview the drivers in the pits during the intermission or after their race. The Stanwick family was still selling the programs and doing the 50/50 draw every week. I think we only stuck around because of those people. Everyone else was new. The track just wasn't the same as it used to be. The agreement with Larry was we would go to the track but were volunteers. We would get free supper from the concession and drinks, as we wanted them. If the kids came with workers, they would get in free and get their snacks. We got to park inside the gate, and if the kids were with us, we got to park right behind the hill.

My mom was still living in Calgary and called one day to ask what we were up to. I told her the usual. I was working on my niece Shanna's wedding dress. The wedding was in August, and the wedding gown and accessories was her present from us. We were planning to drive to Calgary in a motor home for the wedding. The dress was already finished, but I still had to put all the appliqués. My mom said it was wedding extravaganza there and asked if she could come for a visit. She knew she could come for a visit at any time and never had to ask. She wanted to come right away. I told her I would get her ticket, and I booked her to come on August 6th.

It was August 6th and Gord went to work that morning. It was a really nice day, so we weren't questioning if the race would be rained out or not. I got a call from Janet. She asked us if we would pick her up for the races. She lived on the way out to the track. I went to the airport to pick up my mother. She was really looking tired. Normally she would come to the speedway with us and sit with the kids. That night she was too tired, so she said she would just stay home and watch a movie with the kids. P.J. was home, so I knew he could help out if she needed it.

We picked Janet up at six, and from her house it was only a fifteen-minute drive to the track. With Gord driving it was only about ten minutes. It seemed to be a normal race day though really busy. There was a sprint special running that night and there were so many Americans in. We did the norm. We came in through the front gate. I went into the tower, and it was like an oven in there. Gord went down to the track. We both had headsets on so we could chat back and forth if they weren't racing. During the race we had to keep our conversations more to business. We had intermission at a good time, which meant the races were running smooth. After intermission, the Stanwicks were up counting the money on the other side of the tower for the 50/50 draw. Their son Chris was working down in the pits. He was raised coming to the track and now that he was older, he had enough knowledge to run the races himself. Janet, Pat and I were sitting and chatting. Pat was grumbling that the intermission was running too long. We were teasing him that it was past his bedtime and he was getting grouchy. Janet was getting everything ready for the features and I was finishing up my lap counting sheets and putting the finishing order of the heats on the sheet.

The Sprint feature was running and with so many cars running so fast, it was everything to keep up with the lap counting. There were a lot of yellow flags pulled in that race. We thought they might run out of gas before the end so a red flag was pulled to give the guys a chance to gas up. That was an ordeal because Sprint cars didn't have starters and had to be push started to get going again. Most of them just stopped on the track. I saw Gord pull out the red flag after the flagman did. That was to show the guys that already passed the front straightaway that they were now on a red. After everyone stopped, I looked down at the track a couple of times to see what Gord was up to. From where I was, I could see him no matter where he was on the front side of the track as long as there were not any huge haulers in the way.

All the vehicles stopped, and he was headed to the front of the flag tower to talk to the official, Dave Brown to see if there was anything they wanted him to do while they were waiting. I could see he was checking the track on the way. That got to be a habit with him. As he walked he looked for any debris on the track and would pick it up if there were. It was surprising what he would find sometimes–what would fall off the cars when they were racing.

I looked down at the track again and Gord was standing back on the track in front of the weigh scales still holding the red flag in his hand. He had just turned around and looked like he was going to head back to number 1 turn. I knew that meant we were going to think about push starting all the cars again so I went back to my sheets. Janet looked out the back window of the tower and said it looked like there were rain clouds coming in. That meant we had to get the show on the road and done before the rain hit the track. Pat was cracking jokes and keeping the crowd entertained until we started again and Norm was helping him from the pits with his microphone. All was normal and all was well.

All of a sudden it was all thirty-five hundred people in the stands gasping at the same time. I looked up to see what was going on and over my headset I could hear a strange scream. When I looked down at the track, something took over me. Here was a tow truck with two long legs in white pants and a red flag coming out from under the trucks dual tires in the back. The rest of the body of the person was under the truck. The truck was still driving and I guess in the split second of this happening, I knew it was Gord under the tires and I knew it was him screaming on my head set. I got up so fast and threw off my headset. I think it either hit Janet or Pat. I remember saying something like, "Oh my God!" Then, I turned and ran to the back of the tower to the window. I looked out the window and said out loud. "God, you promised not to give me more than I can handle, and I can't handle Gord dying." I remember yelling at Janet "Is it Gord? Tell me it isn't Gord." I knew it was Gord. I knew Gord was the only one holding the red flag.

Janet was trying to listen to what was going on over the headset. All of a sudden she looked me and said, "It is Gord."

I told her to tell me he was alive. I thought for a second, "How can anyone be alive after a big tow truck like that runs over his stomach with dual tires?" Then I quickly put that out of my head, knelt down and yelled "God!"

Pat then said, "Gord is talking."

I told Pat not to lie to me. Norm had run over to the tow truck and was telling Pat what was going on.

Janet then turned to me and said, "He is talking, and he is alive." I went for the door to go down to see Gord, but someone stopped me and stood in front of the door so I couldn't get out. Janet then said, "Wait till they get him out from under the truck and we will take you down." They couldn't see what was happening from the tower because the track ambulance had pulled up in front of the tow truck.

Pat told me that Norm said they were trying to get him out from under the truck. He was still talking.

I remember sliding down on the floor in the corner of the door and the wall and praying and crying and praying and crying. I couldn't think. I was probably in shock. Someone came through the door. I think it was Chris Stanwick and said some people had passed out in the stands and there were some throwing up. Chris was an ambulance attendant so was going to help.

He told Janet to keep me in the tower till they could get Gord in the ambulance. I knew it was really bad and they didn't want me to see.

I kept asking Pat if he is still talking.

He was relaying "Yes" from Norm. He said Gord was talking about how bad he felt that you had to see this.

I knew that is something Gord would say and knew they were telling me the truth. It seemed like forever before they got him out. There was some kind of dispute going on as to whether Gord could be transported by the track ambulance or if they had to call in the city ambulance.

Finally, Janet and Chris were standing there telling me they were taking me down to meet Gord in the ambulance.

I asked again if he was alive.

Pat said there was a message from Gord to tell me, "He was alright but don't expect any romancing tonight."

When I went out the door with Janet and Chris, one on each side, Jamie Vernaus and his wife Nicole were standing there saying they would follow the ambulance to the hospital. They told me they would bring my purse with them and pick up my cell phone off of the counter, they would put it in my purse. Janet had phoned Henry at home and told him to meet me and the ambulance at the hospital.

While Janet and Chris walked me down the staircase in the middle of the crowd, I recall thinking this was very strange. There were so many people, but it was so quiet, you could almost hear a pin drop. When I got to the ambulance, Chris and Janet helped me get in the passenger seat. I turned and looked at Gord lying on the stretcher in the back. He was moaning and that was music to my ears. Where there is breath, there is hope.

They told him I was in the ambulance and he called "Trish."

I answered, "Yes, I am here."

He said he was sorry. Then he asked me the strangest question. He asked me "how many people were in the stands?"

I told him around thirty-five hundred.

He replied, "Thirty-five hundred people just seen me in my underwear."

We told him that we didn't think anyone would have noticed. I looked back again and saw him lying in his underwear. They had to cut his clothes off him.

I felt a hand on my arm at the window and it was Janet. She said Henry was going to meet me at the hospital and she was coming right away.

Then the driver of the ambulance helped me do up my seatbelt. I was fighting back tears because I didn't want to upset Gord. The driver must have seen that and told me, "It helps to take a deep breath."

I turned and Norm was standing at the window. He squeezed my arm but didn't say anything. His look said it all without words.

Then the tears did fall. They were all good friends for so long. The ambulance started to drive but so slowly. They knew it was going to be painful for Gord, trying to get him out of the pits in the ambulance and across the track when it was all clay and so many ruts. Every bump they hit, Gord yelled. I looked at number 4 turn and saw a line of sprint cars sitting. All the drivers

433

were standing watching the ambulance leave. I didn't realize then just what effect this had on everyone.

We got out of the pits and were driving down pit road. The attendant asked Gord if he knew what day it was? I think he was just trying to keep Gord talking.

He said, "Race day, Wednesday"

He then asked Gord if he knew where he was? Gord said, "Wait a minute, I know this."

I thought, "Oh no, is he drifting out of consciousness? Of course he knew he was at the speedway."

It was quiet and the ambulance went to turn the corner on pit road, then Gord answered, "Yes, we are on pit road and just turning the bend." Then he said, "That means we are about to go over the train tracks, and that one is going to hurt" (meaning the bump).

The attendant told him they would hold him as steady as they could. It wasn't steady enough. Gord was yelling with pain as we went over the tracks. Then we turned onto the highway, and we all knew including Gord that the ride would be smooth all the way to the hospital.

When we pulled into the emergency ramp at Victoria Hospital, Jamie and Nicole were standing there and handed me my purse. Henry was standing waiting by the ambulance. He just looked at me and said, "Just looking at you, I know it is bad."

I answered, "It is real bad." While they were unloading Gord out of the ambulance, Jamie and Nicole told me my cell phone was ringing on the way to the hospital. They didn't know what to do, so they answered it. It was P.J.

I panicked, "Oh no, what did you tell him?" They said nothing. They told him I was lap counting and couldn't take the phone and they would tell me he called.

He said, "He just wanted to know if it was almost over."

I couldn't even begin to think of telling the kids that Gord was run over. I didn't want to think of that until they could tell me he was going to be all right. Of course he was going to be all right. God wouldn't give me more than I could handle.

They wheeled Gord into the emergency department, and a doctor took me into a family quiet room and told me to wait until they finished examining him, and then they would come back and talk to me.

Henry, Jamie and Nicole came in with me. We were sitting for about five minutes talking, and Jamie was telling Henry how it happened. Then Jamie and Nicole were gone. I don't remember when they left or where they went. Henry was trying to lighten up the conversation but he was never very good at that (at least not with me). I think when something bad happened, Henry was afraid of me. He was afraid of saying the wrong thing. He always let Janet handle me.

The doctor came into the room and told me to get back in the ambulance. He said they were loading up Gord to take him to Health Sciences Centre.

I asked, "What happened? What was going on?"

He said, "They think the tires ran over part of Gord's heart." He was going along, with a nurse. He literally ran me out to the ambulance and I knew it was going badly. I told Henry to come. He said, as I was running, he had to wait there for Janet to come and she would come right away.

I got in the front of the ambulance and the driver asked the doctor, "What pace do you want this?"

The doctor answered, "Put it to the floor!"

Gord was moaning in such pain and the siren was so loud. I just kept thanking God for healing Gord and not letting him die. The ambulance was driving so fast but I really didn't notice. It was the matter of minutes and we were at the emergency entrance of the Health Sciences Centre. Both the doctor and the nurse went running with the stretcher through the doors and I followed. Another nurse in the lobby of the emergency stopped me and the doctor and nurse just kept running through other doors with Gord's stretcher. The doors closed, and I stood there in the middle of the lobby. I felt so alone. I wanted to go with Gord, but they wouldn't let me.

The nurse asked me if I attended church. I answered, "Yes."

She quietly stated, "Maybe I should phone your pastor."

I screamed at her, "We don't need a pastor, Gord is not going to die!"

She suggested we just call him for prayers.

I told her "No, we don't need the pastor!"

She then said she would call the hospital pastor.

I stood there till she showed me to a quiet room. My head started to spin. I had to tell my mother what was going on. She was probably worried because we weren't home yet. I had to call Gord's dad. How could I ever tell him what happened? I had to make arrangements for the kids to be looked after. I knew my mother was there, but there were pill routines and things she didn't know. The kids were a full time job, and even though my mother was really good at handling them, it was a lot for anyone.

The nurse came in the room and told me the hospital pastor was outside in the lobby. I went out to see her, and Janet was just coming in the door.

The pastor asked if I wanted to talk.

I totally exploded in tears and said, "Right now, I am a good Christian, but I need a cigarette." I had quit, but I needed a cigarette. Janet said she would go and buy some. Normally she would have fought me tooth and nail, but under the circumstances she just went and got some. I sat on the ground in the parking lot and had a cigarette. Janet and the pastor just stood by me. I took the cell phone and called Gord's dad, but the answering service came on. I left a message that I was going to keep trying and to turn off the answering service and answer the phone. Sonny was in Florida. Then I called Betty. Her husband Bob answered and he said it was so late. It was really late but I told him I had to talk to Betty. When she came to the phone I told her what happened and told her I needed her to start a prayer circle. She said to consider it already done.

Janet said she stopped at my house to tell my mother. The kids were all sleeping, and my mom had fallen asleep on the couch in the living room. That was my mother, still trying to wait up for us. She said she tapped my mother to wake her up and it scared her. She wasn't sure if she understood what she was trying to tell her. She just told her there was an accident at the track and Gord had to be taken to the hospital. She assured her I was all right and she would get back to her with the details. She said she didn't know if maybe my mom didn't have her hearing aid on or if she just wasn't awake all the way, but she wasn't sure she caught what Janet was saying. Janet said she was telling her so quietly because she didn't want the kids to wake up.

The pastor was just a young girl and was trying to convince me to call my pastor. Janet finally gave her the number. She came back after calling and said, "The pastor is on holidays."

I said "See, that is God telling us we won't need him, Gord is not going to die."

I called Family Services Emergency, and told them we needed help right away with the kids. She asked me who the social worker was and I told her Jim Sanders. She asked what time their meds had to be given and I told her at eight in the morning. She asked me what pills they had to take and I couldn't remember. I always knew it off by heart, but I couldn't remember. She asked if my mom could handle getting the kids off in the morning and that would give them time to set up a crisis plan. I told her if J.J. didn't get his pills on time he would have a seizure. She promised she would work on it.

I called Gord's dad again and the answering service came on again. The doctor finally came out and told me that the tire just missed the heart. He said they were going to finish off a couple of more tests then send Gord upstairs to intensive care. He told me that Gord's pelvis was crushed and he had broken ribs. He said his urethra was severed. I asked if he was going to be all right and he said he was stable, but it didn't look good.

I told him, "You can't go by how it looks!" Gord was not going to die.

He said they thought Gord's neck was broken too, but it would take a couple of days till the swelling went down to be able to x-ray properly. We were supposed to go upstairs and wait for them to bring him up. Janet and I were taken upstairs by the pastor and told to sit in a waiting room. From the waiting room we could see them bring Gord off the elevator.

I tried to call Gord's dad again, and the answering service answered. It was four o'clock in the morning, and I tried again. If I didn't get a hold of Gord's dad this time, we were going to call Henry and tell him he had to go to the house to get him. Gord's dad answered. I cried, "John I don't even know how to tell you this but something terrible happened at the Speedway last night. I am at the hospital with Gord, they are still doing tests on him, and he was run over by the tow truck."

There was such a silence then he asked, "How bad is it?"

I told him, "It is bad."

He said he was coming. I told him to take a cab and not to drive, but he assured me he would be fine. I told him where to meet us.

Janet started to tell me she had talked to the guys after the race. They couldn't find the tow truck driver for an hour. They found him crying in the farmer's field next to the track. He was the son of the tow truck company's owner. He was only sixteen years old and didn't have a license. He backed up, which isn't a normal routine for the speedway. Tow trucks always have to go forward. When he backed up, Gord had his back to the truck. Gord turned around and the back boom of the truck hit him in the head. (I thought, "That is what must have damaged his neck. I didn't know any of this.") Gord then made a grab for the back of the truck because it was still coming at him, and he was falling. He ended up grabbing the dolly wheels on the back, and it spun him under the truck. The dual wheels went over his pelvis. The driver thought it was a bump and kept on going. Everyone was screaming at him to stop at this point but he couldn't hear. He kept on going and the front tire got up to

Gord. The driver again thought it was a bump in the track and started to rev to get over him. They finally stopped him before the front tire could get over Gord.

John got there before Gord was brought back upstairs. Janet was filling him in on what happened when the elevator door finally opened and they brought Gord out. I ran up to him and he smiled and said, "Oh there you are, I was wondering where you went." He asked if I was all right, and I started to laugh and asked him how he was.

He said, "I think they broke me." They took him to his room. There was a nurse in there all the time. It was so painful to move him off the stretcher and into the bed. He was still on the same fracture board as they brought him from the speedway on. They couldn't move him until they could find out if his neck was broken. I sat with him for a while then he said, "The kids have to have their pills." I told him we were trying to get a respite set up to help my mom with the kids till we got him fixed up. He told me to go home and help my mom with the morning routine.

He asked me to call Rick Sobey and tell him he wouldn't be at work today.

I just smiled at him and said "I think I will tell him you won't be there tomorrow either."

He asked Janet to take me home. I told him I wasn't leaving, and his dad said he would stay till I got back. I finally had to give in, we didn't have a choice.

I got home just when the kids were getting up. I gave them their pills and sat them down and told them that there was an accident at the speedway and Gord was in the hospital. They looked scared, and I calmly said there was nothing to worry about, he would be all right. Janet took my mom to another room and gave her all the details. My mom came out and told me to go back and she could handle the situation. Betty came before I left and I gave her the orders of the day for the sewing. There were weddings coming, and the work still had to be done. My mom could help her. I told my mom what the pill routine was for the evening and she could take it from there. P.J. knew how the house was run and he could help.

I called Rick, Gord's boss, but he wasn't at work yet. So I called him at home. He said he heard it on the news. He asked me to keep them informed of how he was doing. I quickly grabbed a change of clothes and we left.

I was so glad to see Gord when I got back. He was glad to see me. His dad left to go home for a bit. He had called Sonny and told her what happened and she was making arrangements to fly in. He had to call her back again to find out what her agenda was, so he could pick her up from the airport.

Janet left to go home. She had to go to work. She had her new office in the Health Sciences Centre so she was right there all day and I could just go to her office anytime I wanted. Her phone number was the checkpoint. She had so many calls from people at the speedway but also in case my mom or Betty had any questions about the kids or work they could call Janet and leave a message with her. Family Services used her number to keep in touch with me. Jim Sanders, the social worker, called and told Janet he would meet me at her office at noon to make a plan.

All of a sudden it hit the news. It was in both newspapers and on the radio and television. I had to get Janet to help me make calls to the kid's programs, so they could tell the workers and the people they worked with to not discuss it in front of the kids. Tammy was working five days a week portioning food for a city restaurant, and J.J. was working in the maintenance department of the Holiday Inn. Mr. Scurfield's secretary had left a message with Janet. She said he was on holidays but was coming back the next day. When they heard it on the news they called him and he asked them to get in touch with me to tell me to meet him at his office eight o'clock Monday morning.

They turned Gord on a bit of an angle every twenty minutes to take some of the pressure off his back. He was in a neck brace and was complaining of being really uncomfortable. He was put on morphine for the pain, but it was self-administered and he wouldn't push the button because he was afraid if he did it too much he would become addicted. Because he didn't use it as much as he should, he was having a real problem with his breathing.

At noon, I met with Jim Sanders. Family Services had set up around the clock care but was not sure if he could get enough workers to come during the night. (I called my mother, and she said she didn't need any help during the night.) He said he would arrange workers from seven in the morning till ten at night. The pill routine was written down and all was set. He said I could stay at the hospital with Gord and not worry about what was happening at home. At least I didn't feel that I was being pulled in two directions any more.

I called home and talked to Mom. She said a lady from the church brought supper and said supper would be brought every day by different people in the church until Gord was better. I couldn't believe it but knew it was God telling me He had it all under control.

Gord was so uncomfortable, and it got to be trying to get him through every minute. There was nothing they could do to help him until they knew what condition his neck was in. I fell asleep for a couple of hours that night with my head on the edge of his bed. He kept asking me for ice chips. That was all he was allowed to have. The whites of his eyes were pure red like blood because the pressure of the truck on his abdomen caused all the vessels to break. He could only see directly in front of him, so whenever I talked to him, I had to put my face right in front of him. He had a big cut on his forehead from the truck's boom hitting him and his nose was so bad it looked like raw meat. That was from the bottom of the truck scraping him as it went over him. His arms were really bruised and cut up, but we never really figured out how that came about. He was hooked up to oxygen and hated it in his nose, and all the monitors constantly keeping tabs on him. There was an IV in one arm, and he was just a really sad sight. I just kept thanking God for his healing.

The next morning was considered day three and Gord was taken for the x-rays on his neck. When he was brought back to the room, there was a team of doctors that came in behind him. In that team was Dr. Fewer the neurologist that J.J. and Tammy had. He just said, "Oh no, don't tell me this is your husband." I nodded my head yes. He was sent to tell me that Gord's neck wasn't only broken, but he had broken C3 and C4. He said the fact that Gord could still wiggle his toes and move his hands was a really a good sign. Gord had two choices. They could operate and repair his neck or he could go into a halo. The decision was Gord's. The nurse had started to push the button on Gord's morphine for him when he moaned, so he was in fairly good spirits but wasn't remembering too much. We would discuss it later.

One of the other doctors there was the specialist for his pelvis. Dr. Irving. There were two ways to fix Gord's pelvis. He could be put in a sling from the ceiling for three months and have it heal like that, or he could have it all bolted together with a fixator apparatus set in. They said the problem was they didn't know who would do what first. It may be dangerous to operate on his pelvis while his neck is broken and no one really could decide who should fix what first. His urethra would heal itself with time.

It was the fifth day and I was sitting by Gord after supper. Gord had decided to go the halo route and have his neck fixed like that rather than the surgery. He said at least then there was no risk of infection. They decided to operate on his pelvis and that was enough surgery.

That night he was really having problems breathing. His dad came. It was getting really bad, and I went out to get the nurse. When I told her, the answer to me was, "Yes we know, and you knew it could make a turn for the worse, he was very badly injured."

I was too tired to fight anymore. I had obviously lost my focus on God. I didn't know what to do. I ran out of the hospital, got into the van and started to drive. I knew I shouldn't have been driving in that state. I called Janet on the cell phone and told her what they said. She told me to drive to her house. I did. She poured me a coffee in a traveling mug and was putting her shoes on to drive me back to the hospital. It hit me. I said to her and Henry in the middle of my tears that he is suppose to get his halo in the morning, then I said, "What halo is God going to give him?" I don't think I will ever forget the look on Henry's face when I said that.

Janet was driving me back to the hospital and I was quoting scriptures to her all the way back. It was giving me my strength back. By the time we got to the hospital, I was feeling very positive and was mad at myself for having fallen so hard and leaving the hospital. I said to Janet as we were getting out of the van that death was knocking on Gord's door, but broken bones and crushed bones were only names for his injuries. Jesus was a name, and it was above all other names and nothing was impossible with God. She just smiled and said, "She is back."

Janet was the best of friends. I could say anything to her with no fear that she would consider me a whacko or something. She had told me that I was the strongest person she knew, and I told her it was only because my strength all came from God. Any time anything like this happened, she would always say, "It is just another chapter in the book." It was always meant to be a joke.

When we got back upstairs, they were taking Gord out of the room and moving him to the top floor, the main intensive care unit where he would have a nurse with him twenty-four hours a day, monitoring his every move. As they were wheeling him, he was quite alert and seemed angry and scared. He asked me what was going on. I told him it was going to be all right.

He said, "I want to talk to you!" I was stopped at the door of the intensive care unit and told they had a lot of setting up to do with Gord and we should wait in the waiting room till someone came to tell me I could go in to see him. Gord really wanted to talk to me, and I just looked at the nurse.

She told Gord, "You can talk to her when we are done."

I just said to Gord, "Boss's orders."

Janet and I were in the waiting room, and it was about four o'clock in the morning. A man walked in and told me he was the hospital pastor and was asked to come and talk to me. I jumped up and asked if Gord was all right. He said not to panic, there was no change, but it really wasn't looking good. He told me he was from a Christian church in Steinbach, a small town outside of Winnipeg. I told him God was not going to give me more than I could handle and Gord wasn't going to die from these injuries. He was very insistent that maybe his injuries were just too much for him to handle. I fought his every word. I pulled scriptures from the Bible. *"I am the Lord your God. I am holding your hand, so don't be afraid. I am here to help you."* Isaiah 41:13

"But when you ask for something, you must have faith and not doubt. Anyone who doubts is like an ocean wave tossed around in a storm. If you are that kind of person, you can't make up your mind, and you surely can't be trusted. So don't expect the Lord to give you anything at all. James 1:6–8

This went on for two hours, and after the two hours I felt that I was so full of the Spirit of God. I knew the enemy would flee from that hospital room because he hated hearing scripture, and there was a lot said. I was so peaceful, and the pastor said to that he was convinced that Gord would live. God used me and gave me the strength and the knowledge I needed to convince him.

I was finally told I could go in and see Gord. The pastor asked me if he could come in with me and pray. I told him sure. Janet came in with us. Gord smiled when I woke him up. I introduced him to the pastor and said he just asked if he could pray with us.

Gord said, "The more the merrier." He took my hand and looked me straight in the eye and asked, "Am I going to die?"

I looked right at him and said, "Of course not, how could you even think that?" I then said, "Are you doubting?"

He just smiled and said, "Not any more."

I was told I could only see Gord for ten minutes every twenty minutes. I had to call to arrange to come into the intensive care.

The waiting room had a lot of comfortable couches and pillows and blankets. For the first time in five days, I actually was peaceful enough to lie down and sleep for three hours without waking up every fifteen minutes. The next few days were rocky. Gord was having real problems breathing. It was because of pain. They couldn't put the halo on or operate on the pelvis till they got him more stable. The therapists kept coming in to make sure he was using his Morphine button. I think they had finally convinced him he wasn't going to become addicted. He didn't have much choice. Janet and Henry were coming in every day. They couldn't see him while he was in intensive care. Only his dad and I could go in.

I did run out for a short time to meet with Mr. Scurfield in his office. He found it very hard to believe we had another terrible accident happen in our family. I asked him if he would take the case. I didn't have a clue what to do about insurance or answering questions the RCMP were coming to the hospital asking me. I didn't want to deal with any of those issues. I just wanted to be with Gord. He eased my mind when he said he would look after it, but would really hope this is the last time his lawyers would have to help me with this sort of case. He said he would hope the next time they would deal with me would be because I wrote a book and needed legal advice. I had gained lots of respect for that law firm over the years after dealing with so many of their lawyers.

I was tired and wearing down after three days of Gord being in intensive care. The truth was I really missed him. I wasn't used to doing things without him. He was there, but on the morphine. He wasn't able to talk to me from the heart because he was too drugged. I just prayed a lot, but I was losing power. I would go home every morning long enough to see the kids out the door to their programs, then shower, change and go back to the hospital.

One morning, I just got back and walked into the lobby when I got a real surprise. Jennifer, Gord's mother was standing there. She said she was in Winnipeg for a horse show and read about it in the papers. She was quite angry that no one had called her. She walked by me and picked up the phone. It was the phone we used to call into the intensive care area to get permission to come in. She was obviously getting hassled by them because her name wasn't on the list to see Gord. Who knew she would ever show up? I heard her say that she had a right to see him, she was his mother. I got her to sit down and relax for a minute and called Gord's dad to come to the hospital to handle it because I couldn't handle this right now. He said he was on his way. I went in to see Gord and told him Jennifer was here and wanted to see him.

"No." He said, "Not today."

I told his nurse the situation, and she said it was so important to keep Gord stable and it wasn't a good idea. She would not be put on the list.

I went back out but I didn't feel that I should be the one to tell her. I thought I would just bide my time until Gord's dad got there. I told Jennifer to come with me and I would buy her breakfast in the cafeteria, and I left a message for Gord's dad that he should meet us there.

I kept her talking in the cafeteria, and she said she wanted to go to see Gord. I just kept talking. An hour went by and I couldn't stop her anymore. I was frustrated.

When we got outside the cafeteria, I said I had to make a phone call. She was standing close to me, so I couldn't talk very loud. I didn't want her to know that I was calling Gord's dad. Sonny answered the phone and I asked her if he left yet.

She said, "Yes, about fifteen minutes ago."

I said good-bye and we went to the elevator. When we got upstairs, I told her I would go into the room with Gord for ten minutes to tell him she was there. She said she would wait. Gord's dad was in with him. I told him he had to go and deal with Jennifer. I didn't see her after that. I fell apart at that point and had to get out of the room. The nurse came out to talk to me to ask if there was anything they could do for me to help. I told her what had happened with Gord's mom. She told me to only focus on Gord. He needed all the strength I had. She said my kids were looked after and anyone else or anything else didn't matter. It could handle itself. She said Gord needed me to be strong, and it wouldn't help him if I fell apart. She explained I had to learn to stand my ground with everything else because this was going to be a long haul no matter what the outcome was. I knew what she meant by that and I thanked her for her advice and made it clear that Gord was not going to die. It was the kick I needed. From that point on, I never let anything or anyone bother me. Gord was my main focus and I started to pray for God to put positive people across our path. I prayed for strength and wisdom and knowledge on how to help Gord.

Betty and my mom were doing the work at home, and I told them if any new customers called, we wouldn't be accepting any more orders till further notice. I had to get things off my mind. There was still a rotation of Family Service Workers, and I didn't have any worries at home. Janet was stopping into the house every day on her way home to see if they needed anything. I wasn't worrying about the finances because with Gord off work and me not taking any more orders, there were no finances to worry about. God would provide. I knew He wouldn't let us fall.

Gord was doing much better by the end of the day and the next morning he was taken to surgery. I just read and prayed while I waited for them to bring him back. I was called in to sit with him after the surgery. I was really surprised how wide-awake he was. He took down his blanket to show me what he called "his crash place." There were two steel rods coming out of each side of the pelvis. The rods were about five inches long. They were held stable to each other with long bars on top. It was quite the thing. Gord said it was his barbecue grill. It was so good to have him back. That night they took him back down to the 5th floor.

The next morning Dr. Fewer was coming to put the halo on him. We were slowly coming out of the danger zone. That is what the nurse said to me when she saw me. Gord asked me to be there with him when they put the halo on. He stated that I could make sure they used the right sized bit in the drill they were using.

I really didn't want to watch, but I thought if Gord had to put up with a doctor drilling holes in his head, then the least I could do is be with him when it was done. I told him I would promise to be there if I didn't have to watch.

Gord was having concerns about the finances, so I told him he didn't have to worry; somehow God would provide what we needed.

Janet came in later that day. She was at the speedway the night before. She was very emotional when she was explaining that they decided to have a 50/50 night. They would ask the drivers if anyone was interested on giving 50% of their winnings that night to a trust fund opened for our family. It was totally voluntary. She started to cry when she told Gord every single driver volunteered. She handed him a bankbook and in the account was $4,000. She then dragged in a huge card that was bigger than she was. The front of it had the Tasmanian Devil drawn very professionally, and inside were signatures from all the drivers and staff and lots of the fans. Tears were falling from Gord's eyes. He was so surprised they would do that for him. I was so thankful because I could see it gave Gord the peace of mind he needed to not worry. Gord sent me to pick up his cheque from work. It wasn't far from the hospital.

I called the bank to see if we were insured in any way for what happened. They said no we weren't covered.

Ron and Carol had come in. They said they came back from holidays and heard someone got run over at the speedway. Ron said to Carol, "No, it couldn't be." He phoned our place and couldn't believe it when my mom told them it was Gord. They were so much fun when they came to the hospital to visit. They always had a way of lightening up the conversation and turning it into a laughing session.

Dr. Fewer came bright and early to put the halo on. Like a good wife, I stood at the end of the bed to watch. Gord wasn't too impressed when the doctor took out the drill. He marked four spots. Two were on the front sides of Gord's forehead and two on the back of his head. Then he froze the marks and started to drill. He actually drilled right into the head with a normal drill.

I managed to get through the first one only because I was so impressed that Doctor Fewer did all of this himself without a nurse to help. He actually looked like he was enjoying his work. I made a comment that even a doctor felt the same way about his drill as any other man. He started to drill the second hole and I knew I wasn't going to make it through this time. My stomach started to turn and I was feeling pretty light-headed. I think Gord caught this because he suggested I go to the cafeteria and get him a container of chocolate milk. He was just giving me an out.

When I got back, the holes were all drilled and the doctor was screwing in the screws for the halo. It didn't take very long and it was done. He put a sheepskin on his back and front before he strapped on the brace. This was to keep it from rubbing. He said the sheepskin could come out and be washed and it would have to come out for baths. Baths? Gord had so many bars and rods coming out of his body, how was he ever going to bathe? The doctor said it would have to be sponge baths for the next few months. After that the nurses had to come in three times a day with sterilized materials and clean all the points of entry of all the rods, so Gord wouldn't get an infection.

Gord just kept getting better but it was so hard for him to move. He was pretty well bed ridden until they finally got him a reclining wheelchair that I could take him for walks in. It had to recline because he couldn't sit up with the bars coming out of his pelvis. It was really hard to get him out of the bed and in the chair. It took a lot of people to do it so he didn't want to get up very much. He had to use the bedpan and wasn't very impressed. At least he was eating. They started him on light food. He had been on ice chips for over a week. He lost lots of weight already and couldn't really afford to. Gord asked the doctor when he could go home, and the doctor said if all keeps going well, in three months.

My mom had to go back to Calgary for Shannon's wedding. She was taking the wedding dress back with her. The workers were set to come to the house at seven in the morning and be here when the kids got home from the program. They would stay until ten-thirty. Gord was doing much better so I told him I was going home every evening at ten and would come back in at seven-thirty in the morning. He was fine with that. Janet and Henry took my mom to the airport. They stopped to see Gord on the way. My mom hadn't seen him since the day of the accident. Gord told her we would see her at Shannon's wedding. She knew he was joking of course.

Betty had caught up on most of the work by the time my mom left. After that I would cut everything out early in the morning and drop it off for

446

her to work on the way to the hospital in the mornings. On weekends, workers were sent for the whole day and usually would take the kids out to do something.

P.J. was trying to keep the outside of the house intact. He mowed the lawn and cleaned the pool but didn't know what chemicals to use. It didn't take very long before the pool turned green. He called Henry and asked what he should do. Henry got the details from Gord when he came in to see him and wrote down what to do to get it back clear. No one was in the mood for swimming anyway.

The ladies from the church were still bringing hot suppers every day. J.J. was taking reading lessons from a really nice lady that wrote a book on problem readers. She even stopped by with some meals and some baking. She understood that J.J. would be taking a break from his lessons. There was no one to take him.

The first night I was home to sleep was really terrible. I think I spent the night in tears. I just wasn't used to sleeping in such a big bed without Gord. I told him the next morning, I hated it and couldn't sleep. He told me not to get used to sleeping without him. He really wanted to come home and was getting pretty frustrated. I rented him a television but he wasn't really that interested.

After almost two weeks, Gord was told he was being moved to the Rehabilitation Hospital. There he would have therapy.

The first day at Rehab, I asked the nurse if Gord could have his hair washed. It hadn't been washed since the accident and he still had the same mud stuck in the back from the track.

She told me, "Sure, go ahead."

I just looked at her and asked, "How?" I didn't know if it was possible with the halo on. She came to show me how to do it. We wheeled the chair into the shower stall and totally covered the halo and the rest of him with plastic bags. I stood in the shower and shampooed his hair then rinsed. I was soaked from head toe.

Lots of friends came to visit. The pastor came in several times and people from the church. It really helped to pass the time. One evening, Carol and Jim Neufeld, friends of ours from the next street over, whose daughter Jacquie was one of Tammy's workers, came in to see Gord. Gord wanted to get in the wheelchair and go down to the lounge to visit. The nurses helped me get him in the chair, but he was very uncomfortable and was becoming very aggravated. We had a visit for about fifteen minutes, then Gord couldn't sit any more. Jim and Carol left, and I took Gord back to his room. He was really upset and was in tears. I kept asking him what was wrong but he was too upset to speak. Finally he told me, "I just want to go home." I thought to myself, we had two and a half months to go. How was he ever going to make it? He finally settled down and I told him I would be in the next morning and we would talk to the therapist when she did his therapy. He couldn't walk at all and couldn't stand up. We had a four level house and front stairs to get in the house. I racked my brains that night to see if I could figure out a way of convincing them to let him come home. It really seemed hopeless, so I gave it to God. I knew everything was possible with God. *"Why do you say 'if you can'? Anything is possible for someone who has faith!"* Mark 9:23

The next day I talked to the therapist and asked her if there was any possible way Gord could get home sooner than the three months. She said the bottom line was we had to be able to do everything at home on our own and she couldn't see how that was possible. He also had to be at the hospital five days a week for therapy. I made a list of everything that would have to change in order for Gord to come home. It was a really lengthy and expensive list.

One of the guys at the speedway offered to come and build a wheelchair ramp coming in the front door. Norm King from the speedway worked at Curtis Carpet. He came to the house and suggested we build an extension to the front entrance to make the floor level with the first step coming up to the upper level of the house. The floor was part of a sunken living room and would have to come up about eight inches. Henry said it wouldn't be hard to do.

Henry then got a friend of his that handled elevators and stair lifts to call me. He came in and told us we could have a chair lift attached to the railing that would bring Gord up to the upper level. The upper level had the dining room, kitchen, bathroom, deck and our bedroom. That was all he needed. He was bed ridden and would need the bathroom. The bathtub wouldn't matter because I would only be able to give him sponge baths for the next couple of months anyway. The stair lift was very expensive but there was enough money in the account from the drivers to handle that with a bit left over. The guy told us he could rent it to us for as long as we needed it.

I told the therapists all of this, and then asked her, "Now what do you need from me?"

She said I had to learn to get Gord out of the chair on a sliding board. I would have to slide him from the wheelchair to the chairlift and when the chairlift got to the top of the stairs, I would have to transfer him from the chairlift to the chair. That meant I would have to fold up the chair and get it past the chairlift while Gord was in it. From there I had to be able to transfer him into the bed. He would have to be turned fairly often in the bed to save him from bedsores. I knew I could learn all of this. I had to learn how to clean all the points where the bars went into the skin, three times a day. I had to bathe Gord and help him get dressed. I had to help him with his food. He would have to be transported every day of the week for therapy.

I made a big list and went through it over and over again eliminating it slowly. Every once in a while I would hit a wall with something and would have to ask God for more strength and wisdom and especially knowledge to show me what to do to fix it. Money was a big part of the problem. I took the van to Gary Paul's at Vital Transit, and he installed a ramp and belts for me to transport Gord for therapy. I had tried to get Handi transit to transport him, but it was really expensive. The stair lift was installed and the floor in the living room was raised. The ramp was finished in the front of the house and P.J. stained it and put down slip proof vinyl to help me get him up the ramp and it was the grip under my feet if it rained. Norm gave us a roll of the proper grip vinyl. Everything was moved out of the bedroom that was in the way of the wheelchair coming in.

At therapy, they taught me how to transfer him from the chair on the sliding board. I went to social workers in the hospital and asked if there was anywhere I could go for financial assistance. The answer was always no. There was no welfare, no unemployment insurance, nothing to help in our situation because of the fact we were both self employed. I just kept giving it to God, knowing He would provide.

I paid the bills with Gord's paycheque and started to budget. We had a cleaning lady that came in once a week, and she was the first to go. I axed the budget as much as possible and still was $1,000 short at the end of every month. We had enough money saved in the bank to get us through another month. I went to the store at the hospital and bought wedges to prop him over in the bed, new pillows that would sit him partially up in the bed, and a bed tray to help him eat. The list was going down.

Gord couldn't wear normal clothes because of the apparatus, so Janet went to the sport shop and bought two pairs of pants that snapped up the sides. It worked. I cut up his underwear and found a way to sew them so he could still wear them with the bars coming out of him. I took a couple of his shirts to try to sew them to work but they weren't big enough. Janet went back to the sports store and got him extra large pullover shirts and I cut the neck hole bigger and sliced four lines to go around the bars of the halo, then I put Velcro on the tops to close them back up.

The nurses taught me, and then watched me clean the points three times a day and rebandage them. I was told a VON nurse would come once a day to clean the points and check to make sure I was alright with everything. They would help me change the sheepskin on the halo because it took two people to do that. They gave me an extra set of sheepskin, so I could wash one set and have it ready to change. I would be supplied with all the sterilized kits to clean the points. I was told about all the medications that were given in a day. Finally, the list was totally finished–now the big test.

I cleaned the house spotless and the plan was to bring Gord home in a stretcher van. The therapists were coming with us. They would take him out of the stretcher van, and I would have to get him up the ramp, in the house, up the stair lift, and into the bedroom. I had brought home a commode wheelchair for Gord to use as his bathroom. He could wheel himself into the bathroom and use it there. After the therapists watched all of this happening at home the first visit, they would take Gord back to the hospital, and we would have a meeting to discuss what I did wrong and what else I would need help with. I asked God to let the therapists only see good and to not see anything wrong unless it were something that would harm Gord while he was home.

It was morning, August 29th. I got the kids out the door and gave the house a once over. Then I washed the sheets on the bed, and remade the bed with white cotton sheets. They were supposed to help fight the bedsores. I went over my list once more to make sure I didn't forget anything. Janet was going to come to the house. When she saw us pull up; she was going to put the dogs outside so they wouldn't go nuts on Gord. They really missed him. I got Gord washed and dressed and cleaned the points in time for the medivan to pick him up. The therapists watched me do it all. Then they watched while I got Gord up and transferred him from the bed to the wheelchair. I just kept thanking God for the strength I needed. Finally, we went to the van and the driver loaded him in the van. He had a hard time coming home because any bump in the road was really bothering him.

We got to the house, and I stood back while they unloaded him. I took the back of the chair, aimed it toward the ramp, and told Gord to hold tight. I started off running up the ramp or I knew I wouldn't make it. Janet opened the door and I carried on right into the house. I got Gord's coat off and transferred him from the wheelchair to the chairlift then folded up his chair and squeezed by him carrying it up the stairs. He went up the lift, and I told him to go slow.

I didn't tell him I wanted him to go slow because I needed a few minutes to catch my breath. When he got to the top, I transferred him to the wheelchair, and we went into the bedroom. The final point was getting him in the bed, and it ran really smooth. The therapist checked out the wedges I was using to prop Gord up, and made sure the commode would fit in the bathroom.

Gord told Janet he needed some excitement and she should let the dogs in. Both Cherry and Peyote were up on the bed whining and going on like two babies. Gord was thrilled to be home.

I looked at the therapist and she just said, "Good job, you both worked very hard to make this work. No one goes home with injuries like yours Gord, but you deserve this. I am not taking you back at all and I will see you at therapy Monday afternoon."

I just stood in shock and wanted someone to pinch me. We did it and Gord was home. I knew who to thank. It was so good.

The days were really busy. I had let the pastor know we were home and how much we had appreciated all the suppers while Gord was in the hospital. Pastor Bill and his wife Betty from our church stopped by the house to visit. It became a joke that everyone who came to visit had to come into Gord's and my bedroom to see him. Our bedroom became an open house. They had said the church was going to keep the meals coming for at least another month to help out with the homecoming. We had really appreciated that, but Gord and I had a hard time accepting all the help we were getting.

Mornings were pretty tough. I had to get the kids ready to go to their program and give them their medications. Then it was Gord's turn, get him up to go to the bathroom, then breakfast and medications. After the kids left, I did the morning cleaning of all the points then gave him a bath. Until it was Gord's turn, I would hand him the newspaper and a cup of coffee. Usually around ten o'clock, a nurse would come in to help me change the sheep skin in the halo vest and check his points to make sure I was cleaning them good and there was no infection.

We got a call from Mr. Scurfield saying the insurance company would be coming to talk to Gord. They came that afternoon and just asked a few questions. They were very nice people and left telling us they didn't know what they would decide but would be in touch with Mr. Scurfield to let him know. It wasn't long after they left that one his other lawyers came to see Gord and let us know that the insurance for the tow truck company wouldn't cover Gord, but would allow him to sue the Speedway.

After lunch on Tuesdays and Thursdays, Gord's dad and Sonny would come over to sit with Gord while I finished off a paint job. On Mondays, Wednesdays and Fridays, I took Gord back to the hospital for his therapy. They would show me what to do, and on the days he didn't go, I would do the exercises with him. I was painting a house from an insurance claim at the time of the accident and it was worth a couple of thousand dollars. I didn't have too much left to do, so P.J. and I would go for a couple of hours in the afternoon to finish. I was always back for supper and the evening routine.

When we went to the hospital or anywhere else, I would pull the van up in front of the driveway and pull down the ramp that Vital Transit installed in the side door. That would give me a running start to get Gord in. He was much too tall for the side door of the van so his seat of the wheelchair had to be reclined the right amount when I went or it would clip his halo bars. (That would definitely not be good.) He hated it and would close his eyes every time I would load him. I am sure he was praying. He couldn't travel very long, it was too painful. We mastered the trip to the hospital and back, but any longer was a real problem to him.

One morning, the nurse came to check on Gord. He had been home for about a week. I showed him one of the points in the pelvis looked really red and I was afraid of infection. The nurse agreed and told me to make an appointment with Gord's own doctor who was around the corner. Gord had gotten Dr. Scott Young as his, J.J., and P.J.'s doctor but had never seen him yet. Gord wasn't the type like most men who run for yearly checkups. I called and explained the situation to the receptionist, and she said Dr. Young said to bring him in right away. He was on the same floor as mine and Tammy's doctor. It was pouring rain that day and I just couldn't see me trying to get Gord in the van at home and out of the van at the doctor who was only five minutes away. Then get him up the elevator to see the doctor and back out and do it all in reverse. I didn't think I had enough power left, and in the pouring rain I was afraid of slipping. I called Vital Transit, and they sent me a van right away.

When we arrived at the doctor's office, Dr. Young took us right away. He was telling us when he heard about the accident on the news, he was telling his friend, "The guy doesn't have much hope," not realizing at the time that it was one of his own patients. He checked the point and agreed that it was getting infected and put him on antibiotics. He then offered to come to the house to keep tabs on it to make sure it would heal. A doctor doing house calls, that was unheard of but much appreciated. He did come and check it the following week and it was healed.

Gord was in desperate need of a haircut and a good wash. Gary offered to come over to the house on his day off. The hairdresser was closed on Sunday, and Monday, so he offered to come on Monday. We managed to wash his hair really good while he was reclined back in the wheelchair in the kitchen. Then Gary sat him up as much as he could and started to cut. I could see him wince as he cut around the halo posts screwed into Gord's head. Gord told Gary that when his hair got too long, he always wore a hat until he could find the time to get it cut. He said he couldn't wait this time because he couldn't find a hat big enough to fit over his halo. We offered Gary money for coming, we really appreciated him going beyond the call, but he said he wouldn't hear of it.

Janet, Henry, and Pat Mooney had planned a benefit social for Gord. We were embarrassed and had to decide if I was going to bring Gord for a short amount of time just to make an appearance. The original plan was we would, but that changed as time went on. It was a huge social and they all put so much time into it. There were so many companies in the city that contributed towards it. We just kept hearing about how well it was going and didn't know what to say. There were eight hundred tickets, and people had bought that didn't even know us or that I hadn't seen for so many years. Everyone involved had worked so hard, and it was all for Gord. We just didn't know what to say. As the date of the social got closer, we were deciding against going. It was hard to get Gord loaded into the van as it was, and we would only be able to stay for about fifteen minutes then it would be too much for him. We would have to leave with so many people to thank, so many companies to thank. Gord was just too emotional about the whole thing and I knew it was better if he didn't go.

Instead, that night I made a nice supper and we sat in bed and watched a movie. We never spoke a word all night.

The next day, Janet came over and told us the money from the social was put in the trust account. We could use it, as we needed it. She handed Gord the book and there was now $10,000 in the account. We were totally speechless and didn't know what to say. What do people say when things like this happen? Thank you just doesn't cut it. We definitely thanked God.

October came and Gord was to go to have the pelvis fixator (barbecue) taken out. It was scary. We went to the Health Sciences Centre and met with Dr. Irving. They wheeled Gord behind a curtain, and I could see the tools going in to unscrew all the screws that went through the skin and into the bones in his pelvis. I had to plug my ears to block his yelling. He was white when they brought him back out. He was sitting in the wheelchair, and Dr.

Irving asked him if he thought maybe he could try to stand for a minute. Keep in mind he still had the halo on. No one knew at that point how long it would take for Gord to be able to walk again. He had lost twenty pounds and all of his muscle mass in his legs. His legs were very thin and frail looking. He was handed a cane to help him get up. He got up with hardly any struggle and looked at me with that look. I knew he was up to something. He started to walk very slowly away. Even Dr. Irving looked very surprised.

I said to the nurse, "Some days are easy, some days are tougher, some days I find totally ridiculous, but then there are the days I experience the miracles . . . !

I wheeled Gord out to the van and helped him get in the front seat. That was really exciting. I folded up the wheelchair and put it in the back. Gord was laughing and insisting all the way back, that he could drive. He couldn't turn his head in the halo but he could still drive and I could look back for him. I told him "I would be very happy if he could drive." It was something I never did before when Gord was in the vehicle. He always did the driving.

On the way home, we stopped at Gord's dad's house and Gord got out and took a couple of steps up to his dad when he came out. His dad shook his hand, then he ran into the house and got Gord a really fancy cane he had. He gave it to him, and we just said at least now he was a very distinguished crash victim. That was the joke. He referred to himself as a crash victim and his pelvis and neck were his crash sites. He had been referred to by friends joking as the crash test dummy, Superman, and speed bump. Gord milked all of these names to the max.

We passed our turnoff and kept going to Janet and Henry's house. I called on the cell phone to tell Henry to come outside; we had something to show him. As Henry was coming out the front door, Gord opened his door and started to get out. Henry just stood back and watched as Gord took two steps toward him. I don't think he had too many more steps in him at that point. Henry shook his hand and told Gord he was thrilled. He said he was having a really lousy day up till then and now it has turned around. That was the start of the real healing.

We kept going to therapy and Gord was getting stronger with his walking. He had gained the weight back that he lost and a bit more. Every week, he was able to take a few more steps and was able to sit up in the wheelchair for longer periods of time.

It was Halloween day that we were to meet Dr. Fewer at his office to take off the halo. After the suffering of the pelvic fixator coming out, Gord was really anticipating what would happen when the halo was taken off. It wasn't near as bad as he thought and we only had to sit for ten minutes for the colour to come back into his face. He had no neck movement when it came off, but Dr. Fewer said they would work on it at therapy while we were there and see how much movement he could get back.

With every little step, life just kept getting a bit easier. We were invited to come to the Speedway Banquet. I told them I would bring Gord for the supper, but we would have to leave right after. That was already pushing it time-wise. Gord insisted he wanted to walk into the banquet. I told him we would have to leave an hour early if he was walking because he was so slow and had to sit down to take breaks if it was too many steps at once.

That evening, he got dressed in his suit and it was so nice to have my husband back with no steel bars blocking his face and body. He could actually wear normal clothes again. I wore a jumpsuit I had because I knew getting Gord in and out of the banquet hall wouldn't be very ladylike, so I couldn't wear a dress. I found a handicap parking space right by the door, so that helped. We wandered in very slowly. Gord had his cane. We only had to sit down once on the way to take a break. When we got in the hall, everyone was so glad we made it and that Gord was walking. They aimed us for the front table right by the stage. The table was already full and there were two seats left for us. I was glad Gord didn't say he had to go to the washroom at any time. It was way on the other side of the hall.

Pat Mooney was the emcee for the evening. When he picked up the microphone, he expressed, "Every year I start off telling you about my favorite incident at the track This year it will be a little different because the best was when Gord Kell *walked* into the room tonight." Every one stood and applauded.

CONCLUSION

"Brothers, I do not consider myself yet to have taken hold of it. But one thing I do: Forgetting what is behind and straining toward what is ahead, I press on toward the goal to win the prize for which God has called me heavenward in Christ Jesus." Philippians 3:13–14 (NIV)

Sharing my "secret to success" and how I made it through the tough times gives me a great sense of freedom and joy in knowing my life has purpose. I went to hear a speaker, Angeline Schellenberg, give a sermon and part of her message resonated in me, especially when she said, *"I may not have been addicted to drugs or crime but I was addicted to fear and criticism. That was before I realized how much God had done for me and what a difference surrendering my life to Jesus had actually made. I was holding a cheque from God for eternal joy, peace and forgiveness, and I finally cashed it in! Now I have a story to tell and I don't feel silly sharing it with anyone, inside or outside the church, because I am really living and I know for a fact it's only because of Jesus."*

My faith today is stronger than ever and I know, without a doubt, that God truly does love and care for me as one of His children. God has a specific destiny and plan for my life. Some people seem to "tiptoe through the tulips" and go through life with nothing really challenging ever happening. That could be their destiny and God's plan for them. Other people, like me, seemed to have gotten beat up, bruised and battered. The beautiful part for me was when I asked God to help me, I immediately experienced the love, grace, mercy and forgiveness God has made available to every human being. To think of all the years I lived doing my own thing, while all the time God's remarkable provision, guidance and blessings were available to me–all I had to do was to commit and submit to His plan for my life.

The title of this book, "Chain of Miracles" was chosen for a specific reason. My "chain of miracles" were the many friends, relatives, support teams, ministers and other "earth angels" that carried me through each challenging event in my life. No one can be a whole chain. Each one is a link. God gave me many "miracle links" to help me through the tough times. I believe the destiny intended for each of us is to link together to help each other through life's ups and downs.

This is the end of this book but it isn't the end of my life's journey . . . it continues on. My many years in the school of tough times and the lessons I learned there have qualified me to help other people in their life journeys. I know that the comfort and assistance given to me along the way is what God wants me to share with other people also. My prayer for you is that no matter where you are and what the circumstances of your life may be, that you may come to know Jesus Christ as your personal Saviour, invite Him into your heart today, give Him your past and all it includes (good and bad), and then be encouraged to press on, and determined to trust in God's unconditional love and plan for your life. God is Good!

Contact Tricia Kell at
www.chainofmiracles.com
or order more copies of this book at

Word Alive Inc.
131 Cordite Rd.
Winnipeg, Man
R3W 1S1

1-800-665-1468
www.wordalive.ca